LENGTHEN
YOUR STRIDE

LENGTHEN YOUR STRIDE

THE PRESIDENCY OF
SPENCER W. KIMBALL

EDWARD L. KIMBALL

DESERET
BOOK

SALT LAKE CITY, UTAH

Library of Congress Cataloging-in-Publication Data

Kimball, Edward L., 1930–
  Lengthen your stride : the presidency of Spencer W. Kimball / Edward L. Kimball.
    p. cm.
  Includes bibliographical references and index.
  ISBN 1-59038-457-1 (hardcover : alk. paper)
  1. Kimball, Spencer W., 1895– 2. Church of Jesus Christ of Latter-day
Saints—Presidents—Biography. 3. Mormon Church—Presidents—Biography.
4. Church of Jesus Christ of Latter-day Saints—Doctrines. 5. Mormon
Church—Doctrines.
  BX8695.K53A35 2005
  289.3'092—dc22   2005013298

Printed in the United States of America   18961
R. R. Donnelley and Sons, Crawfordsville, IN

10   9   8   7   6   5   4   3   2   1

LENGTHEN YOUR STRIDE

"MY BRETHREN, I WONDER IF WE ARE DOING all we can. Are we complacent in our approach to teaching all the world? We have been proselyting now 144 years. Are we prepared to lengthen our stride? To enlarge our vision? . . . Somehow I feel that when we have done all in our power that the Lord will find a way to open doors. That is my faith. Is anything too hard for the Lord?" (address to General Authorities and Regional Representatives, April 4, 1974).

"So much depends upon our willingness to make up our minds, collectively and individually, that present levels of performance are not acceptable, either to ourselves or to the Lord. In saying that I am not calling for flashy, temporary differences to our performance levels, but a quiet resolve . . . to do a better job, to lengthen our stride" (David Croft, "Pres. Kimball: Convert World," *Church News,* March 22, 1975, 5).

"The lengthening of our stride suggests urgency instead of hesitancy, now instead of tomorrow. It suggests not only an acceleration, but more efficiency. It suggests, too, that the whole body of the Church move forward in unison with a quickened pace and pulse, doing our duty with all our heart, instead of half-heartedly. . . . We are not suggesting in the lengthening of our stride that we try to move faster than we are able or than would be wise, but rather a mobilization of our potential in order to move the kingdom forward for the more rapid and deeper benefit of our fellow men everywhere" ("Historic Conferences End," *Church News,* July 5, 1975, 3).

"Let us therefore press forward, lengthening our stride and rejoicing in our blessings and opportunities. I suppose if I have learned anything in life it is to keep moving, keep going" (in Conference Report, April 1981, 105).

Contents

Publisher's Preface ix
Preface xi

New Challenges: The First Year

  1 Spencer W. Kimball: Called and Chosen 3
  2 New Responsibilities, New Stresses 7
  3 The New Prophet's Counsel: Lengthen Your Stride 18

A Personal Style

  4 Ministering More Than Administering 27
  5 Shaking Hands and Warming Hearts 42
  6 Private Life 50
  7 Camilla: Equal Partner 68

Teachings of a Prophet

  8 Boldly Proclaimed: A Prophet's Mission 79
  9 Persuasion to Chastity 83
10 Of Gardens and Journals: General Conference Themes . . . 88
11 Concern for Doctrine 95
12 Teaching Moments, One-on-One 104

Witnessing to the World: Missionary Work

13 A Vision of Worldwide Missionary Work 113
14 Opening the Doors of Nations 129
15 The President As Public Representative 141

Controversial Issues

16 Public Relations, Public Issues 153

17 Issues of Concern to Women 162
18 The Equal Rights Amendment 176
19 Personal and Institutional History 184

The Revelation on Priesthood

20 The Question of Priesthood Denial 195
21 The Questioner 209
22 Decision and Confirmation 215
23 Announcement and Reactions 225
24 Aftermath and Africa 236

Innovation for a Growing Church

25 Revising Priesthood Organization 249
26 Changes in Auxiliary Organizations 260
27 Accommodating Growth 265
28 Management of Resources 274
29 Policy and Practice 282
30 Children of Lehi 288
31 The Church Welfare Program 296

On God's Errand: Traveling the Globe

32 Area Conferences, 1974–1976 311
33 Area Conferences, 1977–1980 328
34 Solemn Assemblies and Other Travels 344

Redeeming the Dead

35 A Burst of New Temples 357
36 Temple Practices and Family History 373

Completing a Lifetime of Service

37 The Struggle for Health 383
38 Decline and Death, 1981–1985 397
39 Farewell 415

Appendix I: Personal Encounters with Spencer Kimball ... 421
Appendix II: The Presidency Years, 1974–1985:
             An Overview 448
Photo and Other Credits 459
Index 461

PUBLISHER'S PREFACE

IN 1977, BOOKCRAFT PUBLISHED *Spencer W. Kimball,* the biography of a beloved Church leader written by Edward L. Kimball and Andrew E. Kimball Jr. This best-selling biography received wide praise for the depth of its research and the quality of its writing. Many reviewers have also commented favorably on the candid nature of the biography.

Lengthen Your Stride, written by Edward L. Kimball, is a sequel to *Spencer W. Kimball.* This new volume focuses almost exclusively on the years Spencer W. Kimball was President of The Church of Jesus Christ of Latter-day Saints. The author has spent many years researching and writing this book. However, because the book describes events, meetings, and conversations at which the author was not present, he must of necessity rely on the reports of others.

In actuality there is no such thing as an objective biography. In every case the life and events and experiences of the person being profiled are funneled through the eyes of the biographer, who by the very nature of what he chooses to include creates a slant to the biography. This is to be expected both by a publisher and a reader. In this case, the publisher and the biographer do not agree on the interpretations or weight of importance given to a number of events, or the choices of characterization of some of the people. The author and the publisher have had open and energetic discussions on these issues, and there has been some give and take in the editorial process. The resulting book reflects a compromise between the two points of view. Some readers may wish that the result sometimes was different, but even they can greatly benefit from the deeper understanding this book will give them of the ministry of Spencer W. Kimball as president of the Church.

President Spencer W. Kimball was a remarkable person, a devoted disciple of Christ, and a dynamic leader. *Lengthen Your Stride* offers the reader many interesting insights into his personality and character and into important events and developments during his presidency. We believe the reader will come away from this book with an increased appreciation for the life and ministry of Spencer W. Kimball.

The publisher expresses appreciation to the staff of BYU Studies for organizing, formatting, and editing the material that is included on the CD inserted inside the back of this book.

PREFACE

THIS VOLUME RECOUNTS THE LIFE OF Spencer W. Kimball during the twelve years he presided over The Church of Jesus Christ of Latter-day Saints, from December 1973 to November 1985. A biography covering his life from childhood through his three-decades-long apostleship and the first years of his presidency appeared in 1977, but President Kimball lived until 1985, and many events in those eight years proved important for him personally and for the church he led. This book also undertakes to describe the history of the institutional Church during that same period. The two stories naturally overlap.

Some people distinguish between bio-history and biography, in that history tells of the events in which a person participated, while biography also looks inside and seeks to define character, motivation, and intent. This book generally calls on readers to draw their own conclusions about the meaning and importance of events and the motivations of the characters who were players in them.

In his first press conference, President Kimball said that he expected to introduce no dramatic changes, because he had had a hand in formulating Church policy for the previous thirty years. But in that prediction he proved too conservative, for great changes occurred during the twelve years of his presidency. However, his statement does remind us that the basic agenda for a President is set by factors outside himself— Church history, doctrine, political conditions, existing policies, and divine inspiration. He is the most important leader, but he still works within a well-established structure. The Church follows its own institutional dynamic, so that its history during those twelve years would in many respects have been the same no matter who served as President. However, the personal traits and commitments of this particular leader undoubtedly had some significant influence on direction and pace. The rapid worldwide growth, administrative innovations, changes in programs, and the announcement of a major new revelation mark the period as perhaps the most significant of the twentieth century, partly at least because Spencer Kimball led the Church.

Many developments in the Church have a long gestation. For example, work on the first temple President Kimball dedicated, in Washington, D.C., had begun during the administration of David O. McKay, three Presidents earlier. Discussions of a temple in South America and of the Orson Hyde Memorial Garden in Jerusalem had begun in 1972, under President Harold B. Lee, but came to fruition in the Kimball administration.

Innovations typically undergo a time of discussion, study, and even of testing in pilot programs. Many organizational matters and programs under consideration during the Kimball administration came to a conclusion during the Benson years or even later. On the other hand, some proposals seriously discussed among Church leaders never became visible at all, because they were not adopted.

The Church is a large, complex organization, supported by a growing bureaucracy. Even during the years when President Kimball was vigorous, there is usually no public record to show how deeply he was involved in detailed consideration of policies and programs. Many items required his approval, but sometimes this approval became largely a formality. For example, missionary call letters had, since the nineteenth century, traditionally carried the President's personal signature, but decisions about individual missionary calls and assignments had long been made by a committee of General Authorities. During the Kimball administration, the number of missionaries became so large that even these letters of call were signed by a machine.

However, one indication that this President was extensively involved in details is a journal entry early in his presidency that lists the wide variety of matters dealt with that day by the First Presidency. This and the stream of administrators whose consultations with him are logged in his journal suggest his real awareness of every significant decision, at least while he was well. For example, although applications for restoration of temple blessings went through the hands of a General Authority who summarized each file, President Kimball acted on these applications personally.

This first book on the administration of President Kimball will undoubtedly not be the last. More information will yet come to light. Other perspectives will be offered. Distance from events will make us better able to assess their significance. Still, the effort can begin here of describing and assessing the place in Church history of this man, so unexpectedly thrust into a position of the greatest responsibility, affecting the lives of many millions, present and future, through his leadership and ministry.

As a son of Spencer and Camilla Kimball, I acknowledge that I probably cannot write this biography completely free from bias, but my training in history and my fifty years as a student and teacher of law have impressed me with a determination to tell the story as fairly as I can.

That the anecdotes almost all illustrate good character comes not by conscious selection but because Spencer was, on all the evidence, a truly good man, with unusual measures of intelligence, kindliness, integrity, commitment, patience, and unaffected love. I did not exclude any evidence to the contrary, but nearly all of the anecdotes came from people who admired him, people who predictably remembered and interpreted events favorably. But the huge number of his admirers and the existence of so many similar anecdotes offer assurance that the general picture is correct.

When people reported to me conversations as they remembered them, I have frequently used the dialogue for its dramatic value, although I recognize that, unless the informant recorded the event promptly, the language imputed to Spencer is at best approximate. The most accurate picture comes from the sum of the recollections, and no one anecdote should be relied on too heavily.

In this study, the personal journals of Spencer and Camilla Kimball constituted important sources. As an apostle, despite other demands on his energies and time, Spencer kept an extensive, sometimes introspective journal almost daily, understanding it to be part of his apostolic responsibility. Spencer taught Church members the importance of keeping a personal journal and followed his own admonition. However, his

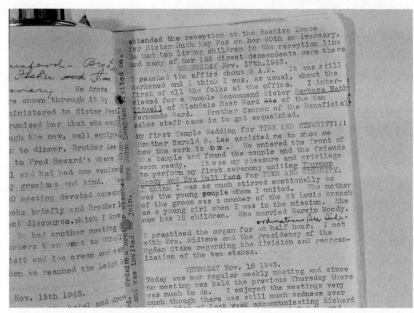

Spencer W. Kimball journal recording his first temple sealing, November 1943.

journals rarely mentioned world events unless they impinged rather directly on his work—for example, on expanding missionary work into new countries, or on building a temple in Communist East Germany, or on responding to the U.S. Department of Defense proposal to situate nuclear missiles in Utah's desert.

Spencer once showed Church historian Leonard J. Arrington his journals, particularly those recording his life since his calling as an apostle in 1943. Arrington reported to his colleagues in the history division:

"Three great diaries have chronicled the history of the Church. The first is the diary of President Wilford Woodruff, which provides a day-by-day record of the Church from 1834 until his death in 1898. The second is the diary of President Heber J. Grant, which supplies a daily history of the Church from 1882 until 1944. The third is the diary of Elder Spencer W. Kimball, which carries the history of the Church, in painstaking detail, from 1942 [1943]."[1]

1. Citation to sources and additional comments are available on the accompanying compact disc. One must bear in mind that Arrington was not acquainted with the journals of all the Church leaders and that the quality of the Kimball record declined markedly after he became President. See, for example, Gregory A. Prince and William Robert Wright, *David O. McKay and the Rise of*

During Spencer's years as President, he generally dictated the daily entries, resulting in less disclosure of his personal views than when he typed entries himself. Beginning in 1974 his personal secretary, D. Arthur Haycock, made some of the entries.[2] A tip to actual authorship is the inclusion of minutiae that Arthur, but not Spencer, would include: for example, "I gave the concluding remarks, speaking about 29 minutes" or "taking Eastern Airlines flight #210 for Chicago, arriving at 1:24 Central Time."

The later journal gives us disappointingly little detail, merely alluding to a subject of discussion without its gist, and often not even that. Spencer personally made entries, at least some of the time, through 1980.[3] As he aged and his energy declined, the journal became ever less complete and less useful, so that by 1980 it constituted little more than a list of appointments and visitors. No personal journal exists for the final years, 1982 to 1985.

Camilla kept a sporadic journal, most often when traveling. Her observations and reactions serve to add detail and color.

I had access to correspondence files in my parents' home office, but not to the correspondence kept at my father's Church office. To broaden and deepen my understanding of the historical context, I skimmed every item in the *Church News, Ensign,* Conference Reports, and *Deseret News Church Almanacs* for 1974–85, and *Sunstone* and *Dialogue* to the present. Many books by and about other Church leaders provided useful information about President Kimball and about the Church during his presidency.[4]

Another source was my own recollections. During the presidential

---

Modern Mormonism (Salt Lake City: University of Utah Press, 2005), 405–11, for the remarkable record of David O. McKay from 1935 to 1970.

2. Spencer W. Kimball, memo to D. Arthur Haycock, April 10, 1974, gave instructions on helping Spencer maintain his journal. Arthur also kept scrapbooks including news clippings, programs, and copies of talks given.

3. The Spencer W. Kimball journals cease at the end of 1981, at which point he was almost completely inactive from age and ill health. There are also large, unexplained gaps in the journals before that, about twenty-three months during the eight active years, 1974–1981. The gaps are April 5–May 31, 1974; July 1–October 31, 1974; January 1–April 30, 1975; June 20–December 31, 1975; and January 22–August 31, 1976. The fact that these journals are missing, without plausible explanation, is frustrating, but I still see nothing sinister in it.

4. See particularly Francis M. Gibbons, *Spencer W. Kimball: Resolute Disciple, Prophet of God* (Salt Lake City: Deseret Book, 1995).

years, I lived in Provo, an hour's drive from my parents' home, and we visited frequently. Early in his administration, when his schedule was tight, such visits occurred perhaps only once every three or four weeks. After his travel slowed in 1979 and then stopped in September 1981, my wife, Bee, and I saw them two or three evenings a week.

My memory of these visits is augmented by my personal journal. Because people received the 1977 biography so warmly, I intended from that time to one day publish a revised and enlarged edition. Consequently, I included in my journal details about my parents that I might not otherwise have thought to record. Ultimately, two-thirds of my father's presidency occurred after the biography appeared and my aim shifted from a revised edition to a sequel that would focus on the man and the Church during his presidency. He was aware of my intention to write more, and he had no objection. Indeed, on one occasion he gave me a specific charge, saying, "I want you to tell about bringing the blacks in . . . to the priesthood."

Beginning in September 1981, my father became relatively uncommunicative. We often just sat together in his Church-owned apartment in the Hotel Utah. I might play the piano and sing for him. Sometimes he answered questions, but not always and never at length. It was not always clear whether he could not or simply would not respond. During most of President Kimball's inactive years, his counselor Gordon B. Hinckley was the member of the First Presidency who carried the load and visited my father often to discuss Church business. I was never present, but it is my opinion that in general, even during his last years, President Kimball could understand what was said to him and approve or disapprove proposals. Responsibility for initiating action rested at the end completely with President Hinckley, although he cleared all decisions of consequence with President Kimball and with the Twelve.

Despite my personal access to President Kimball, I was never an insider in Church affairs. After my father became President, my interaction with him rarely related to Church administration or doctrine. He never discussed confidential matters with me or with any other family member. One of my mother's long-standing complaints was that "he never tells me anything." I did not deal with my parents extensively as information sources. I did not think it my place to ask questions or give advice on Church administration (although of course on occasion I did both). My father was never as comfortable debating doctrine or policy as I was, and his sensibilities influenced our choice of conversational subjects. My mother had fewer topics that she felt were beyond discussion, so in my younger years she was the one with whom I argued to shape my understanding. Despite her occasional exasperation at my challenges, she allowed me to test my views with her. Psychologically I am more like my mother than my father.

In my biographical writing I have tried to always deal with sensitive issues cautiously but candidly. I want the reader to receive a fair telling of the full story, rather than a sanitized version from which the humanness has been leached. My father and I occasionally talked about that question, and he agreed that the story of a life should be told candidly, "warts and all." His concern was that there should not be unfair emphasis on the warts. He knew that people's mistakes often result from misunderstanding or from simple differences of perception and not from evil intent.

I am grateful for the kindness of many people who provided me anecdotes or answered my questions by letter, telephone, or in person. And I express thanks to friends who reviewed parts of the book in draft form and made valuable suggestions: Barbara B. Smith, Cheryl Preston, and Mary Dollahite (women's issues), Kahlile Mehr (genealogy and missionary work in Eastern Europe), Thomas Sawyer (Lamanites), James B. Allen (becoming President), Barbara B. Smith (Relief Society and the ERA), Darius Gray (revelation on priesthood), Bruce L. Christensen (communications network), and Ronald W. Walker, Andrew E. Kimball Jr., Evelyn M. Kimball, Spencer L. Kimball, Cory Maxwell, and John W. Welch (the full manuscript, at various stages). William Slaughter helped with procuring illustrations. Lavina Fielding Anderson, Sue Bergin, and Doris Dant acted as editors at successive steps in the manuscript's development. I am grateful for the care given in preparation of the manuscript for publication by the staff of *BYU Studies,* particularly Rebecca Boyce, Bonnie Landry, Kelli Skinner, and Anastasia Sutherland Tyler, and Deseret Book, particularly Lisa Mangum (editorial assistance), Richard Erickson (art direction), and Laurie Cook (typography).

With respect to citation form in the notes, I have made no distinction between e-mail and letters delivered by the postal service and none between formal interviews and simple conversations, whether in person or by telephone (all are "interviews"). Often I simply entered information learned by oral communication directly into the computer database without intermediate notes. I observed some of the incidents personally and rely on both my journal and my memory in reporting them.

Nearly all of the documents cited that are not in the public arena, including letters and interviews for which there are transcripts or notes, are part of the Kimball Papers, to be given by the Kimball family to the Church and located in the Church Archives. The journals of Spencer and Camilla Kimball are among those papers.

I am acutely aware how much this book has relied on secondary sources and on people's memories, with the inevitable distortions and errors that result. Most incidents are also reported from only one point of view and there may be differing perceptions. I would be most grateful for corrections and clarifications, so that subsequent printings might be more nearly accurate. The publisher's e-mail address is dbol@deseretbook.com. Messages relating to the book will be forwarded to me.

COMPACT DISC

This book, as first written, was much too long for publication at reasonable cost and sometimes too detailed to hold the interest of most readers. Nearly every author has gone through the painful process of relinquishing text over which he labored long and lovingly, but modern technology has provided a new solution to the problem. This printed book, of reasonable size and with skeletal notes, is accompanied by a compact disc that provides supplementary materials for readers who wish more detail, including this same text with 1,600 footnote citations to the sources relied upon. Another feature of the CD is the full text of the much longer book manuscript, with its more extensive footnotes. In this longer version the material on the CD that is essentially duplicative of the book is identified by being underlined. Because the CD also includes a copy of this book, when the index proves inadequate the book can be searched electronically for a particular word or phrase.

Material Included on the CD

the text of this book, with additional footnotes and sources
an earlier, longer draft of this book

additional photographs

audio illustrating the voice of Spencer Kimball before and after
throat surgery

Books

Spencer W. Kimball (Bookcraft, 1977) (with Andrew E. Kimball Jr.);
also in Spanish translation: *Spencer W. Kimball: Historia del
Profeta* (APAK, 1979)

The Story of Spencer W. Kimball: A Short Man, a Long Stride (Bookcraft, 1985) (with Andrew E. Kimball Jr.)

Spencer W. Kimball, *One Silent, Sleepless Night* (Bookcraft, 1975)

Camilla (Deseret Book, 1980) (with Caroline E. Miner)

The Writings of Camilla Eyring Kimball (Deseret Book, 1988)

Articles

"The Mission Experience of Spencer W. Kimball," *BYU Studies* 25,
no. 4 (fall 1985): 109–40.

"Spencer W. Kimball," *Church News,* December 11, 1993, 8–10.

"Spencer W. Kimball as Extemporaneous Speaker," *BYU Studies* 25,
no. 4 (fall 1985): 147–59.

"Spencer W. Kimball and the Lamanite Cause," *BYU Studies* 25, no.
4 (fall 1985): 73–75.

"Spencer W. Kimball and Poetry," *BYU Studies* 25, no. 4 (fall 1985):
161–66.

James B. Allen, Ronald W. Walker, and David J. Whittaker, *Studies
in Mormon History 1830–1997: An Indexed Bibliography* (Urbana
and Chicago: University of Illinois Press, 2000), 724, entries
relating to Spencer W. Kimball.

Eugene England, "A Small and Piercing Voice: the Sermons of
Spencer W. Kimball," *BYU Studies* 25, no. 4 (fall 1985): 77–90.

Edward L. Kimball, "The Administration of Spencer W. Kimball,"
from *Sunstone* 11, no. 2 (issue 58, March 1987): 8–14.

Edward L. Kimball, "In Recognition of a Remarkable Life: Camilla
Kimball," *This People* 2, no. 5 (fall 1981): 10–15.

Edward L. Kimball, "I Sustain Him As a Prophet, I Love Him As an
Affectionate Father," *Dialogue* 11, no. 4 (winter 1978): 48–62.

Edward L. Kimball, "Remembering Mother," *This People* 6, no. 3 (May 1985): 40–41.

Edward L. Kimball, "Spencer W. Kimball," in *Encyclopedia of Mormonism* (New York: Macmillan, 1992), 785–89.

Edward L. Kimball, "Spencer W. Kimball," in Leonard J. Arrington, ed., *The Presidents of the Church* (Deseret Book, 1986): 373–418, included as chapter 1A of the longer manuscript.

Edward L. Kimball, "Spencer W. Kimball: A Man of Good Humor," *BYU Studies* 25, no. 4 (fall 1985): 59–71.

Edward L. Kimball, "Spencer W. Kimball: A Man for His Times," *Dialogue* 18, no. 4 (winter 1985): 19–22.

Edward L. Kimball, "Spencer W. Kimball: Stories about the 12th President Reflect His Love for Others, Concern," *Church News,* December 11, 1993, 8–10.

Edward L. Kimball, "Spencer W. Kimball at College," *BYU Studies* 25, no. 4 (fall 1985): 141–45.

Edward L. Kimball and Andrew E. Kimball Jr., "Spencer W. Kimball, the Athlete," *Mormon Sport* (January 1980): 12–14.

Edward L. Kimball and Marshall E. Smith, "I Fell among Cutthroats: Spencer W. Kimball and Cancer of the Larynx," *Journal of Collegium Aesculapium* (1990): 15–25.

Stanley B. Kimball, "'Uncle Spencer': 1944–1945," *BYU Studies* 25, no. 4 (fall 1985): 43–47.

Dennis Lythgoe, "Lengthening Our Stride: the Remarkable Administration of Spencer W. Kimball," *BYU Studies* 25, no. 4 (fall 1985): 5–17.

Dell Van Orden and J Malan Heslop, "A Prophet for All the World: Glimpses into the Life of President Spencer W. Kimball," *BYU Studies* 25, no. 4 (fall 1985): 49–57.

Ronald W. Walker, "Mesquite and Sage: Spencer W. Kimball's Early Years," *BYU Studies* 25, no. 4 (fall 1985): 19–41.

John Whiting, "Spencer Kimball and the Service Station Guy," from *Sunstone* 13, no. 3 (issue 71, June 1989): 10–15, excerpt published as "Spencer Kimball and Charging the Battery," *Ensign* 23 (December 1993): 22.

I am grateful for the help of Eden Rasmussen and Heather Seferovich in preparing the CD.

NEW CHALLENGES

THE FIRST YEAR

1

SPENCER W. KIMBALL:
CALLED AND CHOSEN

"Spencer, you are not to die!"

IN MARCH 1972, SEVENTY-SEVEN-YEAR-OLD Spencer W. Kimball felt his heart failing rapidly. He suffered breathlessness and bone-weary fatigue; he sensed his body might give out at any time. As an apostle he felt it his duty to inform the First Presidency of his condition. To that end, he arranged a meeting with them and his doctors, cardiologist Ernest L. Wilkinson Jr. and heart surgeon Russell M. Nelson. Spencer described his condition: "I am a dying man. I can feel my life slipping. At the present rate of deterioration I believe that I can live only about two more months." Dr. Wilkinson agreed.

Dr. Nelson then explained that he could surgically replace Spencer's aortic valve and bypass a blocked artery, but he had no experience doing both procedures on a patient so old. The risk would be very high. Not fearing death, only disability, Spencer wearily added, "I am an old man and ready to die. It is well for a younger man to come to the Quorum and do the work I can no longer do." Harold B. Lee, counselor to the aged President, Joseph Fielding Smith, rose to his feet and pounded his fist on the desk: "Spencer, you have been called! You are not to die! You are to do everything you need to do in order to care for yourself and continue to live!"

"Then I'll have the operation performed," Spencer responded.

Surgery was set for a few days later, after the conclusion of April general conference. Because of his weakness, Spencer could attend only one session of the conference. Understanding that his chances of

Greeting Harold B. Lee, October 1973.

surviving the surgery were no better than fifty-fifty, he put his financial affairs in order.

Dr. Nelson performed the surgery. Afterward, he marveled that from the first incision to final closing the procedure went perfectly—not one broken stitch, not one instrument dropped, not one technical flaw among a thousand intricate manipulations.

"I shall never forget the feeling I had as his heart resumed beating, leaping with power and vigor," Dr. Nelson later recalled. "At that very moment, the Spirit made known to me that this special patient would live to become the prophet of God on earth."

No stranger to pain, Spencer experienced such agony during the first days in the hospital that he wished he had died. But the pain gradually receded, and he resumed his work, thinking he might serve a few more years in his apostolic calling.

Just ten weeks later, President Joseph Fielding Smith passed away, and Harold B. Lee, at age seventy-three the youngest Church President in more than forty years, assumed the position. President Lee's forceful personality and administrative skills, in addition to a general expectation that he would one day become President, had made him highly influential long before that event. He had championed such innovations as area conferences, regional representatives, and the correlation program. His secretary, D. Arthur Haycock, described him as of a practical bent, but complex, thoughtful, and deeply spiritual.

President Lee was a robust, active man in apparent good health, four years to the day younger than Elder Kimball. Everyone expected his administration would be long and vigorous, but it was not to be.

Eighteen months later, on December 18, 1973, he arrived late to the Beneficial Life Insurance Company's Christmas party, showing deep fatigue, his face pale and puffy. On Christmas Eve, he asked Arthur Haycock to deliver his Christmas remembrances to friends and neighbors, something he had always done himself. The day after Christmas, President Lee awoke from a long sleep, still exhausted. At his doctor's recommendation, he checked into the hospital for tests but without any sense of urgency. After dinner he dozed off. About eight o'clock he sat up, spoke a few words to Arthur, and tried to get out of his hospital bed. When Arthur spoke to him, President Lee did not respond; perspiration beaded the President's ashen face. Arthur called for help. A doctor saw immediately that the patient was in cardiac arrest. He shouted for more help and began CPR.

As the resuscitation efforts continued, Arthur telephoned President Lee's counselors, Marion G. Romney, at home, and N. Eldon Tanner, in Arizona. He also called Spencer W. Kimball, who would as president of the Quorum of Twelve lead the Church should President Lee die. Within minutes, Spencer and President Romney joined Lee family members at the hospital.

Spencer asked, "President Romney, what would you like me to do?"

"All we can do is pray and wait."

About nine o'clock, after an hour of desperate effort, a doctor came into the waiting room, shaking his head: "The Lord has spoken. We've done all we can. President Lee is gone." Elder Romney, acknowledging the dissolution of the First Presidency, turned to Spencer and asked the same question Spencer had posed a little earlier: "President Kimball, what would you like me to do?"

As soon as he could, Spencer called Camilla: "Pray for me. President Lee is dead."

Camilla could hardly believe it. Since Spencer had rushed off, she had spent the time in fervent prayer for President Lee. She and Spencer had always realized that only one life stood between them and the awesome burden of the presidency, for which neither had any aspirations. But when Harold B. Lee died suddenly, Spencer had no doubt that God intended him to become President. He believed and had preached repeatedly that the senior apostle in years of service was the Lord's choice for the next President. It was simply so, despite all the misgivings he had in this case about the wisdom of the choice. Spencer might have asked himself, "What business has an Arizona farm boy here?" but in faith he bowed his head and said, as he had said before, "Lord, I shall do my best.

At President Lee's graveside, December 1973. At left is L. Brent Goates, President Lee's son-in-law and biographer.

2

NEW RESPONSIBILITIES, NEW STRESSES

"There is in very deed a prophet in Israel."

PRESIDENT HAROLD B. LEE's sudden death shocked the Church. He was relatively young, and members had expected he would serve long and masterfully. He was, as Spencer said at his funeral, "a giant of a man." Spencer seemed rather another sort of person. Small of stature and self-effacing, he seemed frail. But members did love and respect him. During thirty years as an apostle, he had demonstrated humility, natural leadership, a capacity to work at a level of intensity and endurance few others could match, unaffected geniality, spirituality without excessive piety, empathy with others' sufferings because of his own, and warmly demonstrative love. Still, he was now nearly seventy-nine and had a laundry list of health problems. No one had expected him to become President of the Church, and when he did, most thought his tenure would be short and uneventful.

The day after President Lee's funeral, the Quorum of the Twelve met and decided to reorganize the First Presidency immediately, with Spencer W. Kimball, the senior apostle in years of service, as President of the Church, prophet, seer, revelator, and trustee-in-trust. He chose to retain N. Eldon Tanner and Marion G. Romney as his counselors.

On Monday Spencer met with the press to announce the new First Presidency. To questions about new directions or emphasis, he answered that he had no plans to deviate from the past, though he would follow whatever direction the Lord might point. When a reporter asked specifically about the Church's racial restriction on priesthood ordination, he said, "I am not sure that there will be a change, although there could

Speaking at President Lee's funeral in the Salt Lake Tabernacle, December 1973.

be. . . . We are subject to revelations of the Lord in case he should ever wish to make a change."

William Smart, editor of the *Deseret News,* attended the press conference and later reflected that he had difficulty imagining this quiet man as the prophet of God. The Church knew him as an earnest, humble, loving, and lovable apostle. "But a forceful leader? A man deeply involved and schooled in the complexities of church administration? It did not seem likely. Moreover, he was physically frail. . . . His presidency seemed likely to be pretty much a caretaker administration."

Elder W. Grant Bangerter of the First Quorum of Seventy also recalled the low expectations: "We had never expected Spencer W. Kimball to become the President, and we had not looked to him for the same leadership evident in the life of Harold B. Lee. . . . 'O Lord,' we prayed, 'please bless President Kimball. He needs all the help you can give him.'"

Soon after Spencer moved into the corner office traditionally occupied by the Church President, Elder Boyd K. Packer found Spencer weeping at his desk. Concerned, he asked, "President Kimball, what is the matter?"

The quiet response: "I am such a little man for such a big responsibility!"

Elder Packer assumed that the era of innovation instituted by President Lee had ended and that a new era of consolidation and refinement had arrived. He later admitted wryly, "I've never been so wrong."

The new level of stress surprised Spencer. His work as President did not occupy more time than before; that would have been impossible.

First press conference with new leaders: Presidents Tanner, Kimball, Romney, and Benson, January 1974.

But the weight of ultimate decision making proved greater than he had ever imagined. One day, dragging with fatigue, he joked with his family, "If I had known it was going to be like this, I would never have run for the office."

For thirty years Spencer had taken his major problems to the First Presidency for their counsel or decision. He had asked their advice in life-and-death matters, such as whether to undergo surgery for cancer or to have a failing heart repaired. Now there was no one on earth to whom he could turn with his problems. Yet he did not feel alone. He dreamed one night that he and President Lee were looking at real estate together. The dream left him with a warm feeling of assurance.[1]

Camilla tried to ease the crushing burden. She could do nothing about the pace and stress of his work, but she promised herself that when he was home he would find a haven. They switched to an unlisted telephone number to screen out crank and intrusive calls. Camilla continued handling the business of house and yard, seeing to repairs,

---

1. A loose sheet among President Kimball's papers identifies the place as a Tallahassee hotel. Spencer had a sense that President Lee continued to have an active interest in the work of the Church.

arranging for the lawn to be mowed, cultivating the flowers and vegetables in their garden, and juggling mealtimes to fit his fragmented schedule. Spencer insisted that keeping their financial records was still his responsibility, although she offered to take over that chore, too. She accompanied him on all trips that involved public meetings, both to look after him and to model a supportive marriage relationship.

Some Church members expected Spencer's every word to be inspired and even gave Camilla unwanted status. She complained, "This responsibility . . . puts us on a pedestal neither Spencer nor I would ever have chosen."

When not traveling, President Kimball's work had a rhythm. On most weekdays, he and his counselors met in the morning to review a wide range of matters. For example, in their 8:00 A.M. meeting on Friday, February 1, 1974, they heard a report on an antiabortion rally in which a stake president had participated, decided on a nominee to the National Council on the Humanities, authorized a General Authority to accept an appointment to a state advisory committee, sent a letter of condolence to the family of a deceased relative of another General Authority, designated a Church representative to attend an antiabortion program in California, discussed and referred to the Missionary Executive Committee a request by a mission president that his assistant be allowed to conduct interviews for temple recommends, and clarified an existing policy so that an unendowed divorced person could enter the temple to be sealed to her living parents if she was worthy of a temple recommend. They also referred to the Department of Public Communications an inquiry about the Church's possible participation in a forthcoming film on Joseph Smith, reviewed a report of the Investment Advisory Committee, discussed employment of a fund-raiser for the Church Education Department, reviewed and denied an appeal from a doctor who had been excommunicated for performing nontherapeutic abortions, and discussed the proper relationship between the Nauvoo Mission and Nauvoo Restoration, Inc. The counselors urged the President to rest a few days in Laguna Beach, California, while he was there on Church business, and he agreed.

After an hour of dealing briskly with these issues, the First Presidency had the Presiding Bishopric and the presidency of the Aaronic Priesthood–MIA join them. They discussed the transition of the

MIA from an auxiliary to a priesthood-correlated program. The AP–MIA leaders excused themselves, and the Presiding Bishopric remained. The Presidency and the Bishopric discussed raising funds to expand Utah Valley LDS Hospital, decided to instruct the Missionary Committee to ensure Church courts follow proper procedures in cases of missionaries excommunicated for misconduct, discussed sending a letter to bishops warning about moral risks in certain popular courses on human sexuality, approved the wearing of pantsuits as part of nurses' uniforms in Church hospitals, concluded that publicly announcing that a disfellowshipped member had been received back into full fellowship unnecessarily publicized the original transgression, discussed the failure of some units to submit timely reports, and considered a management consultant's study of the Presiding Bishop's Office.[2]

When the Presiding Bishopric left, the First Presidency returned to half a dozen items they had not completed in the first hour. Spencer observed, "It seems as though we can never get caught up"—not surprising considering the level of detail they attended to. They adjourned at 11:10.

President Kimball managed to nap at noon, then signed letters extending formal missionary calls[3] and made other calls to Church service. Miscellaneous appointments filled the remainder of the day.

Weekly on Thursday mornings, the First Presidency met at 10:00 A.M.

---

2. N. Eldon Tanner listed as issues considered by the Presidency "almost everything from questions about pierced ears to appeals from decisions of excommunication by the stake presidency and high council. There are questions about dress and grooming standards, hypnotism, Sabbath observance, scripture interpretation, sensitivity training, sealings, complaints against the local officers, reincarnation, donation of body parts to science or to others, cremation, transplants, legal matters, ad infinitum.

"Their decisions also involve the selection of new temple presidencies, when and where new temples should be built, and other matters to be discussed when meeting with the Council of the Twelve Apostles and with the Presiding Bishopric. They also plan solemn assemblies and area conferences held throughout the world."

President Tanner noted as a typical presidency schedule that on Tuesday at ten they met with the Expenditures Committee, on Wednesday they heard reports from departments over which they had direct supervision, one Wednesday a month they met with the Church Board of Education and Board of Trustees of Church educational institutions, one Wednesday a month they met with the Coordinating Council and with the Welfare Services Committee, on Thursday at 10 A.M. they met with the Council of the Twelve, on Friday they met with the Presiding Bishopric.

3. There were more than 160 letters in his first batch. Missionary calls each week ranged between 100 and 300.

The new First Presidency: Spencer W. Kimball, N. Eldon Tanner, and Marion G. Romney, January 1974.

with the Twelve to consider another range of issues.[4] These meetings took place in the upper room of the Salt Lake Temple, where they sang, partook of the sacrament, participated in a prayer circle in their temple robes, and then changed into street clothes to discuss Church business. After the meeting the men ate a buffet lunch together in the temple. Spencer then routinely conferred with Elder Ezra Taft Benson, President of the Twelve, to coordinate the activities of the two bodies. Elder Benson, an experienced administrator, proved an excellent quorum leader. He demonstrated loyalty, efficiency, and ability to delegate well.

Once each month on Thursday morning, the Presidency and the Twelve were joined by the other General Authorities for a sacrament and testimony meeting and a prayer circle. Their stake conference visits usually kept them from their own ward sacrament and testimony meetings, and this monthly meeting provided those opportunities.

Much more than before, Spencer had administrative responsibilities. Although for a time he tried to respond personally to mail addressed to him from all over world, it quickly became clear that he had no choice but to pass much of the correspondence on to others, at least for initial screening. He once pointed out to a visitor three piles of paper on his desk and commented wryly, "I am like a mailman; I sort the mail and send it on to others." He continued to act personally on many things—for example, applications for cancellations of temple sealings, the restoration of blessings for people who had been excommunicated, and clearance to receive a temple recommend for people divorced after being sealed.

---

4. The Twelve considered their Thursday morning meetings so important that the meetings generally began fifteen minutes early, as soon as all had gathered.

His counselors were indispensable. He told one interviewer, "It's my counselors that carry me." He allocated responsibility the same way Harold B. Lee had: President Tanner dealt with Church finances and organizational issues, President Romney with welfare, and President Kimball with temple and missionary matters.[5]

Nathan Eldon Tanner, previously a Canadian oil executive and government minister, served as counselor to four Presidents of the Church. In 1963, at age sixty-five, he became David O. McKay's counselor after only three years as a General Authority. President Tanner found that deficit spending from an aggressive building program had created a financial crisis, but his financial acumen and organizational skills allowed him to bring the Church back to a firm financial footing.[6] Spencer once said of President Tanner, "My first counselor is a man of few words. But when he speaks, one had better listen."[7] Impassive of demeanor, President Tanner earned deep respect for his loyalty, fairness, consideration of both sides of issues, and good judgment. Spencer called him Mr. Integrity.

Marion George Romney, an attorney, was called in 1941 as an Assistant to the Twelve and promptly assigned to be assistant manager of the Church Welfare Plan. In 1951, David O. McKay ordained him an apostle, and in 1972, President Lee chose him as a counselor. When a Church employee asked to speak to President Romney in confidence, President Romney, the soul of loyalty, replied, "What you tell me, you tell the prophet. I cannot bind myself to keep anything from him."

When Spencer urged members of the Church to plant gardens, Marion Romney was the first on his block to comply. He dug up part of his back lawn and, down on his hands and knees, planted vegetables.

---

5. First Presidency duties included area conferences; auditing; budgeting; cancellation of sealings, divorce clearances, and restoration of blessings; the Coordinating Council; the Council of the First Presidency and Quorum of Twelve; education; general conferences; historical department; legal matters; personnel; the public communications department; solemn assemblies; Mormon Tabernacle Choir; and temples. Neal A. Maxwell praised the First Presidency's complementary strengths in vision, organizational skill, and closeness to the Spirit.

6. "President Tanner has done superb work and is dependable as the 'rock.' . . . Not so eloquent in speech, but strong, good judgment, friendly manner. . . . He has the ability to isolate the central problem."—Spencer W. Kimball.

7. Neal A. Maxwell spoke of President Tanner's "quiet competence" and "remarkable ability in organizational, financial, and spiritual matters." He felt that "when the history of the Church is written, it will be very kind to President Tanner."

With D. Arthur Haycock, President Kimball's personal aide and secretary.

Francis M. Gibbons served the First Presidency as its secretary, and D. Arthur Haycock served as Spencer's personal secretary. Arthur had also been personal secretary to Presidents George Albert Smith, Joseph Fielding Smith, and Harold B. Lee. Ever faithful, he carried out his duties with deep commitment. Much more than a secretary, Arthur was a constant aide and friend, at Spencer's elbow whenever the President traveled.

Spencer recognized the importance of making friends for the Church and welcomed the many public figures who called on him at his office. A few days after he became President, he greeted Utah's Democratic governor, Calvin Rampton, and Rampton's wife, Lucybeth. A week later Spencer offered a prayer at the opening session of the Utah State Senate. In March, Governor John Connally of Texas visited, as part of positioning himself for a run at the presidency. In June, Vice President Gerald Ford and his wife, Betty, paid a call on the First Presidency. As the fall election neared, Spencer was visited by presidential candidates Gerald Ford (Republican) and Jimmy Carter (Democrat), as well as Tom Anderson, national chairman of the American Independent Party. In each instance, the talk was about religion, not politics.

SECURITY ISSUES

During his previous years as a General Authority, Spencer experienced only a few minor security incidents. But now that he was President, security concerns loomed much larger. The first crisis occurred just a few months into his term when police learned that Ervil LeBaron, leader of a violent polygamous group, might be planning to kill him. Ervil had already engineered the murder in Mexico of his brother Joel in a dispute over leadership of the group. The evening after April 1974 general conference, a police escort accompanied Spencer and Camilla to their home.

That evening the Kimballs held an open house for about 150 relatives and friends. An officer stationed himself in a patrol car in front of the house. After the guests left, Spencer returned to his office to discuss the security situation. At about ten o'clock he telephoned Camilla that Church security officials wanted them to spend the night at the Hotel Utah. She packed fresh clothes for both of them, and a Church security man took her to the hotel through a service door and up the freight elevator. Throughout the night, a guard sat outside their door. He instructed them to open the door only upon hearing four knocks and the password "Cumorah." It was "a very disconcerting experience," wrote Camilla.

For a week security remained tight. On Monday a guard drove Camilla home so she could do her washing. On Tuesday a guard took her home to clean the house. When Spencer arrived home that evening with his own guard-driver, all four sat down to a supper of hot stew. Camilla wrote in her journal, "Who would have thought that we who love our independence and our privacy so much would be surrounded by guards?"

As soon as security devices were installed, the Kimballs returned to their home to stay. Spencer instructed his counselors that if he were ever kidnapped no ransom should be paid. Paying ransom, he said, would only expose all Church representatives to increased risk.

In 1974, Ervil LeBaron tried to kill his brother Verlan by sending an armed squad to attack a Mexican village where Verlan was believed to be. The attackers killed two young men and wounded thirteen people, but Verlan was not there. In 1975, Ervil's followers murdered two more men whom their leader thought disloyal.

Church security suggested that the Kimballs move permanently to an apartment in the Hotel Utah, where it would be easier to protect them. Spencer was willing. He did not much care where he lived, and the apartment was just a short walk from his office. But for Camilla, moving would mean giving up any semblance of independence and privacy. Her flowers and garden, life on a quiet residential street among neighbors of thirty years—all would be forfeited. After considerable discussion, they decided to remain in their home.

The LeBaron threat was real. In 1977, Ervil's stepdaughter and one of his wives murdered rival polygamous leader Dr. Rulon Allred in Salt Lake City. At Ervil's 1980 trial for ordering the murder, a witness testified that LeBaron had talked of sending assassins with automatic weapons to attack Church headquarters and kill President Kimball and as many General Authorities as possible.[8] LeBaron was convicted of complicity in the Allred murder and of conspiring to murder Verlan. Ervil was then sentenced to life in the Utah state prison, where he died in 1981 of a heart attack.[9]

While the LeBaron threat was the most worrisome because of the number of followers Ervil commanded and their proven willingness to commit murder, other threats proved genuine as well. In November 1975, when Spencer went to St. George, Utah, to rededicate the remodeled temple there, a young man who had been sent home early from a mission and hospitalized for mental problems was arrested in the parking lot near the temple with a rifle and scope. He had felt humiliated by the release from his mission. After spending more time in the state hospital, he was discharged, and when Spencer returned to St. George for a youth conference, the man was again discovered, lying down in the back seat of a car in the parking lot with a shotgun.

In November 1977 a mentally disturbed returned missionary came to the Church Administration Building and demanded to see President Kimball. Security personnel believed that the man had a gun and

---

8. An alternate plan was to ambush Spencer at his home. This plan was postponed because of the intense official investigation after the Allred murder. Dick Forbes, prosecutor's investigator who followed the LeBaron family saga from 1975 to 1997, believed the family responsible for twenty-eight murders. He counted sixteen family members in prison for "conspiracy, murder, theft, and racketeering."

9. Coincidentally, Verlan was killed two days later in an automobile accident near Mexico City.

persuaded him to leave the building by showing him that President Kimball was not in his office. But after the man left, he went to the adjacent Hotel Utah and at gunpoint took two hostages, demanding again to see the President. The .22 pistol discharged twice without hurting anyone, and the hostages were able to grab the young man. Salt Lake police quickly took him into custody.

During the area conference in Santiago in 1977, Church security learned from police that a left-wing terrorist group intended to kill President Kimball. They planned to set off explosives that would topple the wall of a vacant bottling plant onto President Kimball's motorcade as it passed, with police escort, through an alley on its way from the hotel to the airport. Chilean authorities raided the site during the night and killed three of the ambushers. Part of the explosives went off and caved in some walls. Some of the LDS party heard a noise but they did not know the cause. The plan presumably was designed to embarrass the Pinochet government by killing distinguished American visitors to the country.

3

THE NEW PROPHET'S COUNSEL:
LENGTHEN YOUR STRIDE

"Spiritually speaking, our hair began to stand on end."

AS THE APRIL 1974 GENERAL CONFERENCE approached, President Kimball spoke to the Regional Representatives and General Authorities for the first time in his new calling. He delivered an electrifying landmark address focused on missionary work. He envisioned a time when nations now dependent on missionaries from the United States would not only develop enough missionaries to serve their own peoples but would provide a surplus to help reach the billions of people in India, China, and the Soviet Union, sweeping over the entire world. This unfolding, he said, would fulfill the Savior's instruction to preach the gospel to "every people." Though many countries' doors were then closed to missionaries, the Lord would open them when Church members had done all they could. It was, he said, time for all the Church to "lengthen our stride," an expression that would become the catchphrase of his administration.

W. Grant Bangerter, then a regional representative, recalled:

"As he proceeded with his address, . . . he had not spoken very long when a new awareness seemed suddenly to fall on the congregation. We became alert to an astonishing spiritual presence, and we realized that we were listening to something unusual, powerful, different from any of our previous meetings. It was as if, spiritually speaking, our hair began to stand on end. Our minds were suddenly vibrant and marveling at the transcendent message that was coming to our ears. With a new perceptiveness we realized that President Kimball was opening spiritual windows and beckoning to us to come and gaze with him on the plans

With Ezra Taft Benson, president of the Quorum of the Twelve.

of eternity. It was as if he were drawing back the curtains which covered the purpose of the Almighty and inviting us to view with him the destiny of the gospel and the vision of its ministry.

"I doubt that any person present that day will ever forget the occasion. . . .

"President Kimball spoke under this special influence for an hour and ten minutes. It was a message totally unlike any other in my experience."

After the address, Elder Benson, who was conducting the meeting, told the gathering, "No greater address has been given before any seminar. . . . There is in very deed a prophet in Israel."

Gordon B. Hinckley handed President Kimball a note that said, "That was the greatest talk ever given in these seminars. You thrilled us. You challenged us. None of us can ever be quite the same after that."[1]

Duane Cardall, religion reporter for KSL, said of the presentation, "I was astounded at what was coming out of his mouth." And Jerry

---

1. Robert E. Wells had the sense that a few of the hearers were uncomfortable and resisted the hard push. "President Kimball leaned very heavy on the Twelve for more results and some were a bit offended as I remember." But "the rest of us felt like cheering. It was the greatest leadership talk I have ever heard." His perception of others' reactions may, of course, have been in error.

Sustaining by new First Presidency, solemn assembly, April 1974.

Cahill observed, "I came out of there knowing who was in charge and knowing we had as dynamic a person as we've ever had. He had strong and forceful ideas. This was not a caretaker administration. He was in charge."

It was not just the words President Kimball spoke. He had given essentially the same message to the same gathering the previous year as President of the Quorum of Twelve. But this time there was a palpable difference. He spoke with a power that came with his prophetic calling, and people heard with ears differently attuned. The message was no longer a mere suggestion of something good to do. This message was to them the word of the Lord through his prophet.

In this first general conference under his direction, President Kimball established a pattern that characterized his administration—a focus more on the specific than on the general. The gospel to him was not so much a matter of theory or theology as a guide for action. He began each conference with a listing of items he wished to comment on, either to praise or to prod. On this first occasion, he remarked on President Lee's passing, the challenge of Church growth, Church neutrality in politics, avoidance of worldliness, the importance of the family, motherhood as a sacred calling, and the evils of drugs, abortion, and avoidable divorce.

In the opening session of the next general conference, in October 1974, President Kimball gave a detailed report on the progress of the Church and again called the Saints' attention to a long list of specific issues: cleaning up farms and homes, being alert to fundamentalist recruitment of members into polygamy, teaching honesty, living the Word of Wisdom, obeying the Sabbath, storing food for use in emergencies, working hard, exercising thrift, rigorously observing sexual fidelity in marriage, and avoiding divorce. He also decried profanity, pornography, crime, elective abortion, and homosexual activity—all that in a few minutes. His other addresses in these first two conferences each focused on a single subject: the centrality of Christ's mission as taught by prophets through the ages, the responsibility of parents to teach their children righteousness, and individual responsibility to succeed—with God's help—against all challenges.

One session of the first conference constituted a solemn assembly in which each priesthood group (First Presidency, Quorum of the Twelve, Quorums of the Seventies, patriarchs, high priests, elders, and Aaronic Priesthood holders) and then all Church members together stood in turn. They sustained separately each member of the new First Presidency, the President of the Twelve, and the Quorum of the Twelve (as a group), and the Patriarch, and all the foregoing as prophets, seers, and revelators. Other groups of General Authorities and President Kimball as trustee-in-trust for the Church were then sustained by vote of the whole congregation.[2]

---

2. Voting was done in succession by the following groups, who sat separately in the Tabernacle—the First Presidency, the Twelve, Melchizedek Priesthood holders, Aaronic Priesthood holders—then by all Church members together. Voting was done separately on the President, his first counselor, his second counselor, the President of the Twelve, the Twelve, and the Patriarch, then on all the foregoing as prophets, seers, and revelators. Thereafter, the whole congregation voted to sustain successively the Assistants to the Twelve, Spencer W. Kimball as Trustee-in-Trust, the First Council of the Seventy, the Presiding Bishopric, the Regional Representatives of the Twelve and Mission Representatives of the Seventy, and one hundred named others as heads of departments and auxiliaries and committees as well as unnamed members of boards "as presently constituted." Later Presidents adopted a less complex procedure. When Ezra Taft Benson was sustained as President in April 1986, the priesthood groups did not sit together, and the ceremony was substantially shortened, requiring only ten votes. When Howard W. Hunter was sustained in 1994, eleven votes were called for. When Gordon B. Hinckley was sustained in April 1995, for the first time in Church history the Relief Society (consisting of all women over age eighteen) voted after the Aaronic Priesthood holders, followed by the Young Women (girls ages twelve to eighteen), and then by the total membership, including children of both sexes under twelve.

This pattern involved sixty-four separate votes and occupied most of an hour. Spencer Kimball had for three months led the Church after being ordained and set apart by the Quorum of the Twelve; he now presided with the assent of the people.

It quickly became apparent that the demand for the President as a public speaker was insatiable. General and area conference addresses were just the tip of the iceberg. In nearly every meeting he attended, he was expected to speak. In an October 1974 letter, he noted that he had spoken in Arizona the previous week, in Provo the day before, and he had about twenty more speaking engagements before the end of the year. As a result, he was often "frantically wrestling and studying, trying to get something appropriate." He knew that each occasion was, for most of his listeners, an unusual occasion. They expected a great deal from him, and he tried to respond.

In July 1974 Spencer flew to Spokane to speak at the World's Fair, "Expo '74." At a banquet sponsored by the Spokane Stake, the young women of one ward served as waitresses. Instructed to act professionally, they lined up along a far wall to wait until the guests were all seated. A receiving line of dignitaries had formed to meet President Kimball when he arrived. As he entered, the room quieted. He was ushered toward the receiving line but veered away toward the young women. A hand at his elbow redirected him until he said in his hoarse voice, "Excuse me, I have some important people I need to greet first." He walked across the stake center floor to the young women waitresses and spoke to each one as the people in the receiving line waited, surprised.

In August, President Kimball accepted an invitation to speak at a youth conference and stake meeting in Alamosa, Colorado. When the stake president, Robert W. Garris, called Arthur Haycock to ask whether the President could be a guest in his home, Arthur said, "President Kimball is sitting at my desk. Let me put him on the phone." Spencer asked to speak to the stake president's wife. "Sister Garris," he reportedly asked, "do you have an extra blanket and a pillow that you can put on the floor? I would like to sleep at your home, if I may."

President Kimball spoke to six hundred at the youth conference and to five thousand at the stake meeting. President Garris had asked whether the sacrament might be administered at the stake meeting, and President Kimball agreed, if it would take not more than thirty minutes.

At the stake meeting, learning that about five hundred of those present were not members, President Kimball announced, "I am highly honored to know that there are nearly five hundred of you who are not members of the Church. We are honored by your presence. The fact that you are here is an indication that you have great love for the Savior. So I would like to invite each of you to partake of the sacrament with us." Forty priests and one hundred deacons efficiently distributed the emblems to the large congregation. In his address, President Kimball talked for an hour on the Savior, bearing a strong personal testimony.

There was never a time when a row of speaking appointments did not stretch out before him. As December 1974 ended, Camilla wrote reflectively in her journal, "This marks the first year of Spencer's Presidency. It has been an extremely busy, eventful year. I feel he has been greatly blessed with health and strength and the inspiration which we have both prayed so earnestly he might have."

A Personal Style

4

MINISTERING MORE THAN
ADMINISTERING

"He's so kind and gentle, but he's as dogged as an English bulldog."

EVERY PRESIDENT OF THE CHURCH automatically receives the devotion that
flows from members' belief in his divine call as a spokesman for God.
At an area conference in South America, where "masses of people surged
forward to personally greet President Kimball, Gordon B. Hinckley
remarked, 'There's the Prophet. He is the only one they have come to
see and hear. The rest of us are just window dressing.'" Spencer inspired
extraordinary loyalty, resulting in his people's willing response, commitment to high expectations, and confidence in the success of the
enterprise.[1]

But members' feelings for President Kimball grew far beyond respect
for his prophetic position to include a feeling of deep affection. He
became greatly loved, and his leadership must be described as in significant measure charismatic. He was articulate but spoke simply and
directly. His sense of his prophetic calling was enhanced by his humility
and openness. In 1977 his limitations and foibles were laid out for all
to see in a widely read biography of his life. The book helped members
see their prophet as a real person; hundreds of thousands came to feel
they knew him personally.

Some leaders have a strong need for power, but not President
Kimball. Sociologist Armand L. Mauss observed, "President Kimball

---

1. A Church leader must relate both to subordinate administrators and to the rank and file
membership. His administrative style has a number of elements, among them whether he is formal or informal, a delegator or a micro-manager, people-oriented or outcome-oriented, leading
with personal magnetism or reliant on position.

Mingling with the Saints, kissing a hand.

[had] an inclination toward pastoral and exemplary leadership, rather than the exercise of power and control."

Leadership operates more effectively in person than by written communication or messages relayed through others. President Kimball had relatively high visibility by virtue of his extensive travel, his personal appearances at numerous solemn assemblies, and the sixty area conferences he attended between 1974 and 1981. Beginning in 1975, satellite broadcasts of general conferences and firesides added to the numbers who saw and heard him. No President before him "had spoken so directly and personally to so many members" in so many places.[2]

Spiritual Character of Leadership

President Kimball infused even the secular aspects of his office with the spiritual. Elder Boyd K. Packer recalled that President Kimball gave instructions to include a spiritual message in every administrative

---

2. David O. McKay traveled extensively for his time, but slow transportation and the newness of television limited his ability to reach the people. Presidents Benson and Hunter both found themselves restricted by age and health. But, as of 2005, President Hinckley, despite his age, had the energy to travel and speak widely, exceeding any President before him. Utah industrialist and philanthropist Jon Huntsman made an executive jet available, thus freeing President Hinckley from the schedules of commercial carriers.

meeting. Likewise Elder Thomas S. Monson observed, "In all of our mechanical aspects of administration, Spencer W. Kimball has been the leading advocate of introducing the spiritual as well." President Kimball felt the Spirit should never become subordinate to the program.

To focus more sharply on spiritual matters, in June 1975 President Kimball resigned all corporate directorships except two: Deseret Management Corporation, which exercises control over most Church business properties, and Bonneville International, which controls the Church's communication network. He considered these two corporations vital to the Church's economic and missionary activities. He also remained on the Church Board of Education, which oversees Church schools, institutes, and seminaries.[3]

He sought to keep in touch with the Spirit. Typically by the end of general conference on Sunday afternoon, Spencer felt deeply weary, especially since he often fasted. Nevertheless, after one conference, as Young Women general president Elaine Cannon walked through the tunnel that led from the Tabernacle to the Church Office Building, she saw President and Sister Kimball and Arthur Haycock pass her, riding on an electric cart. They stopped at a passageway that branched off to the temple. Arthur handed President Kimball a pair of white shoes and a white suit. Spencer then kissed Camilla and went through a private entrance directly into the temple. A distinct impression came to Elaine that the President, despite his tiredness, felt it his responsibility at the end of the conference to report to the Lord. The next day, she mentioned this impression to Arthur, and he said, "You're right."[4]

Because his personal warmth tended to create a relaxed atmosphere, Spencer sometimes felt the need to emphasize the seriousness of the enterprise: "We are not fooling; this is no game; this is *exceedingly* important."

Informality

President Lee, President Kimball's predecessor, cultivated a degree of formality that he felt proper for the dignity of the office. President

---

3. Brigham Young had similarly in his last years resigned from the presidency of some corporations. President Kimball's action helped modernize Church administration by divesting the leader of distractions. In January 1996, President Hinckley advised all General Authorities to resign from corporate boards, including Church-owned corporations.

4. President Harold B. Lee was known to make similar "reports."

Kimball's personal style was decidedly less formal. Although he felt the members of the First Presidency should be referred to by title as a gesture of respect for the office, his style seemed to reduce any distance between himself and his co-workers. He had a habit of going to others' offices, despite their willingness to drop everything to go to him. The people he worked with never knew when he would tap at the door, asking if they could spare him a moment. In the opinion of Duane Cardall, long-time religion reporter for KSL-TV, President Kimball's was the very antithesis of an "imperial presidency."

To call people to Church positions, he would often go to their homes. In October 1974, he called Barbara Bradshaw Smith to serve as general president of the Relief Society. She related how, instead of having his secretary ask her and her husband to come to his office, "he called me on the telephone and told me that he wanted to come to my home."

While general and area conferences were tightly scripted, Spencer was more relaxed in meetings with General Authorities. He did not normally make a "presentation," Paul H. Dunn, a Seventy, noted. "He would pull out a folder from his omnipresent briefcase, leaf through the papers, and comment as items caught his eye, willing to deal with matters informally."

The serious business of the weekly meetings of the First Presidency and the Twelve did not bar a spirit of camaraderie, a little gentle teasing. The group usually lunched together in the temple after the meeting, and for dessert they passed around a box of Cummings chocolates—beginning with the First Presidency. As one of these meetings ended, President Kimball asked, "Is there any further business?"

David B. Haight, then the junior apostle, queried, in fun, "Is there any chance to reverse the usual order of choosing chocolates? I don't care for dark chocolate, and by the time the box gets to me, that's all there is left."

Spencer joked, "If you live long enough, you'll move up into the light chocolates."

Traditionally General Authorities and their wives had dinner together after each general conference. Before President Kimball took office, those at the head table were served by waiters while the others served themselves buffet style. President Kimball eliminated the head table and asked for round tables, creating a more companionable environment. And rather than clustering only with members of the First Presidency, the Kimballs invited other leaders and their families to share their table.[5]

On one such occasion, when Paul and Jeanne Dunn shared a table with the Kimballs, Paul asked, "President Kimball, of all the beds you have ever slept in, which is most memorable?" Spencer told of visiting a stake where the well-to-do stake president showed him to a special suite decorated in French Provincial style, with its own bath and a high-standing canopied bed. Spencer found the bed so high that he couldn't climb into it easily, so he hopped up, landed on the edge, and, to his horror, felt the mattress and springs thump to the floor. The hostess, hearing a noise, called out, "Is everything all right?" He called back quickly, "Yes, everything is fine," then spent the next hour quietly fixing the bed.

Spencer had a light touch. In October 1975, he, Paul Dunn, and eleven others crowded into a Church Administration Building elevator. The elevator stalled, and a woman with claustrophobia started to panic. President Kimball said, "Paul, teach her."

Paul genially announced, "Folks, how many times have you had a chance like this to ask the President of the Church any question you want?" The ensuing discussion distracted the passengers from their discomfort.

After waiting a time, Spencer quipped to the much taller man, "Paul, I hope you're enjoying the air up there. It's terrible down here."

It took almost an hour for mechanics to get the elevator running again.

Presidents Kimball and Tanner once called Elders Maxwell and Faust in and asked them to take on a difficult assignment. President Tanner said reassuringly, "I can't think of two finer men for this job."

Elder Maxwell responded self-deprecatingly, "Surely you can find two better men than we are."

President Kimball replied quickly, "Well, while we're looking, would you mind going ahead with the assignment?"

Jeffrey R. Holland recalled a similar experience. In May 1980, as

---

5. As the number of General Authorities quickly grew with the addition of Seventies, the Kimballs had to stretch themselves to make sure they visited at least briefly with each person at the traditional social.

Church Commissioner of Education, he served on a search committee to find a replacement for Dallin H. Oaks as president of Brigham Young University. The committee had barely begun its search when the First Presidency requested that Holland come meet with them. Without his knowledge, the other committee members had nominated him for the position, and the First Presidency had concurred. Holland was so astonished when President Kimball asked him to take the job that he blurted out, "President, you must be kidding!"

Spencer smiled as he replied, "Brother Holland, in this room we don't kid a lot."

Openness to Change

David Kennedy said that President Kimball generally knew just what he wanted and directed his and others' efforts accordingly. He nonetheless remained remarkably open to change. His willingness to listen and to reconsider his own ideas was reflected in the innovations of his administration. Such innovations caught off-guard those who expected little change, given his generally conservative character, loyalty to the previous Presidents, respect for tradition, and advanced age. This openness to change seemed to be rooted in selflessness and humility. He focused on the task at hand with no investment in what he himself may once have thought or believed. As a result, he willingly considered proposals from any source.

As Church President, he eagerly used airplanes to take him swiftly to far parts of the earth, employed satellite transmissions to communicate with members, authorized substantial investment of Church funds in public relations and advertising, made major structural adjustments in priesthood organization, and overturned what many considered to be an unchangeable doctrine with his seeking revelation to extend priesthood to all worthy men.

Elaine A. Cannon recalled that as president of the Young Women she met in about 1981 with President Kimball to discuss the situation of unwed mothers. The general attitude in the Church at the time was to encourage marriage, regardless of age or maturity. In the meeting, she noted that marriage so young could be disastrous, pointed to the high rate of divorce resulting from teen marriages, and asserted that, from the baby's perspective, adoption often proved the better course. Arthur

Haycock, who was present, put his hand on Spencer's shoulder and reminded him, "President, you think that marriage is the wise action for a couple that has started a pregnancy. Right?" Sister Cannon countered that the welfare of the child should take precedence.

President Kimball paused to carefully reflect and then responded, "We can't be doing this. Two wrongs don't make a right." In time the policy was changed to prefer adoption if the parents seemed unlikely to make a good marriage and a good home for the child.[6] Single parenthood was apparently not then considered an alternative.

Building Consensus

During his years as a Church leader in Arizona and the thirty years he served as an apostle, President Kimball experienced how the Church government system of councils works. Elder M. Russell Ballard described decision-making:

"We bring to the Council of the Twelve Apostles a diverse

---

6. Compare *General Handbook of Instructions*, 1989: "Whenever possible, unwed parents should marry and establish a family. When this is not possible, adoption through LDS Social Services is preferred" with First Presidency letter, June 15, 1998: "When the possibility of a successful marriage is unlikely, unwed parents should be encouraged to place the child for adoption." During the past century a new *General Handbook of Instructions* has been issued every few years that supersedes all previous issues. The latest, published in 1998, effective 1999, is the current statement of Church policies.

assortment of experiences in the Church and in the world. In our meetings, we do not just sit around and wait for [the] President . . . to tell us
what to do. We counsel openly with each other, and we listen to each
other with profound respect for the abilities and experiences our
brethren bring to the council. We discuss a wide variety of issues, from
Church administration to world events, and we do so frankly and
openly. Sometimes we discuss issues for weeks before reaching a decision. We do not always agree during our discussions. But once a
decision is made, we are always both united and determined."

The First Presidency and Quorum of the Twelve place a high value
on unity. Matters on which unanimous agreement cannot be reached are
typically postponed for further discussion.[7]

President Kimball valued consensus and regularly sought compromise and concurrence. Neither forceful nor reticent, Spencer persuaded
people to his position with persistence. Arthur Haycock, from his perspective as personal secretary, noted, "Some people think that he's a soft
touch because he's so kind and gentle, but he's as dogged as an English
bulldog and anybody who thinks he's an easy mark is mistaken because
he . . . [has] great determination."

Sociologist Armand Mauss stated his belief that President Kimball
was politically astute. An example is the change in policy concerning
who could hold the priesthood. President Kimball was both patient and
persistent as he involved his counselors and all of the Twelve in considering the question over a long period of time. His approach assured him
that he had their support and avoided potential resistance.

For President Kimball to express an opinion baldly and expect compliance was rare, but years later Francis Gibbons remembered an incident because it was so unusual. In a joint meeting of the First
Presidency and the Twelve considering whether illegal aliens should be
baptized, some of the Brethren expressed the view that as law breakers
they should not be baptized. After hearing all the views, President
Kimball reportedly said, "I think they should be baptized." That ended
the discussion.[8]

---

7. Joseph F. Smith on one occasion announced finally "what the Lord wants," although it
conflicted with views of some apostles.

8. A close associate who asked not to be identified said, "President Kimball is inscrutable
sometimes. He takes in everything that is said, but he is not amenable to being manipulated. He is

Delegation

Spencer W. Kimball's personality and experience predisposed him to careful attention to detail. In his work as a bank teller, stake clerk, businessman, and apostle, he had always prepared and reviewed records meticulously. During his apostleship

One of Spencer's mottos.

years, he was legendary for scrutinizing stake statistics line by line.[9] As President, he delegated only because he had to. Neal A. Maxwell commented, "Frankly, President Kimball had not been especially known for his capacity to delegate prior to the assumption of the presidency. But, my, how he delegated once he was there! . . . His kind and personal way of checking up on how this or that project was coming was expressed without scolding but with an unmistakable expression of interest."

President Hinckley said that "President Kimball was a different kind of delegator" in that after President Kimball delegated he continued to work on the issue himself. Arthur Haycock corroborated that assessment. President Kimball, he said, focused heavily on detail and had difficulty letting go of things. He sometimes assigned tasks to Arthur but then did them himself. Or he might ask Arthur whether one of the secretaries could type something for him "whenever they can get to it" and return a few minutes later to ask gently whether his material was ready yet. Arthur learned to expedite such projects.

Francis M. Gibbons, secretary to the First Presidency, agreed that President Kimball "never really let go, but often asked for a report. He

---

one of the toughest men I have ever known. If any have the impression that he is a prisoner of the brethren, they are wrong."

9. Elder Dunn reported that ten or fifteen times he had followed Elder Kimball as a stake quarterly conference visitor. Over and over he heard stake officers say that Elder Kimball was the most demanding General Authority in reviewing stake statistics and programs, item by item. Only Theodore Burton compared with him. And usually Spencer would ask the stake president to continue reporting to him on improvements being made until the next General Authority visit.

considered himself equally responsible."[10] This attitude may account for the way Spencer included himself in the slogan he became known for: "When I think of the concept of 'lengthening our stride,' I, of course, apply it to myself as well as urging it upon the Church."[11]

Encouraging Excellence

At the conclusion of the October 1975 conference, President Kimball set an example of determination and humility when he said, "We hope you have made copious notes of the thoughts that have come to your mind as the Brethren have addressed you. . . .

"While sitting here, I have made up my mind that when I go home from this conference this night there are many, many areas in my life that I can perfect. I have made a mental list of them, and I expect to go to work as soon as we get through with conference."

Spencer used time to its limits. In November 1975, he and many General Authorities traveled by bus to a solemn assembly in the St. George Temple. As the bus moved into traffic, he took the microphone and announced, "It is more than five hours to St. George and we don't want to waste time. I'll call each of you in turn to sit by me and we can have a personal interview."

One evening Elder David B. Haight and President Kimball left the Church offices at the same time. Carrying his bulging briefcase, Spencer got on the elevator and eyed Elder Haight, who had only a slim leather folder tucked under his arm. Spencer looked at his friend, then at the folder, then back again. He asked teasingly, "Are we overworking you?"

Spencer asked no one to work harder than he did, driven sometimes mercilessly by his sense that there was "so much to do and so little time." As he left the office on the last workday of 1978, he wished the staff a Happy New Year, then promised, "Next year we will lengthen our stride," news perhaps not completely reassuring to employees.

He gave sincere appreciation to his colleagues for their achievements but was seldom fully satisfied. "You've done wonderfully," he would say, then add, "Can we do more?"

---

10. Francis M. Gibbons noted Benson's skill at delegation, in contrast with Spencer's inability to let go.

11. He occasionally said "lengthen *your* stride," but more often he phrased the motto to include himself.

According to Elder Thomas S. Monson, when President Kimball heard apostles report that a stake they had visited had a problem, he would say, "Did you correct it? Did you leave the stake in better condition than when you went?" He wanted to see improvement taking place—soon.

First Presidency at Mesa Arizona Temple rededication, April 1975.

Reproof

Any leader faces occasions when he must correct and reprove. President Kimball did not flinch when he felt action was needed, though he had a soft manner. President Kimball instructed David Kennedy, the Church's ambassador-at-large, to report directly to the First Presidency, but after Kennedy obtained permission for missionary work to commence in Portugal in August 1974, a senior apostle pressured him for a memorandum on the situation. Kennedy resisted, saying he had not yet reported to President Kimball. The apostle insisted, promising to keep the memo confidential, and Kennedy reluctantly complied.

When President Kimball met with the Twelve to relay the good news about developments in Portugal, he was chagrined to discover they already knew all about it. When asked by President Kimball for an explanation, Kennedy, with deep remorse, explained how he had responded to the apostle's request. Spencer accepted the explanation but repeated soberly that Kennedy should report only to the First Presidency. Then, to protect Kennedy from future pressure, President Kimball instructed the Twelve that Kennedy should not be distracted from his main task by any extraneous requests.

Entering Temple Square from the north one day, President Kimball and others encountered workmen finishing some cement. The foreman said, "You'll have to go around to the south side." After they had taken a few steps to go around, Spencer returned and said, "I wonder if it would be a little better to say, 'Would you mind going around to the south entrance?'"

In April 1975, President Kimball flew to Mesa for the rededication of the temple there. Oscar McConkie Jr., who had formerly served as mission president in Arizona, came with his wife, Judy. As they walked in the temple grounds, Judy saw a kumquat tree with ripe fruit, walked over, and picked one. A groundskeeper scolded her sharply. Chagrined at the harsh response, Spencer walked over to the tree, picked a number of kumquats into his hat, and offered them to Judy, both as an apology to her and perhaps as a silent rebuke to the overzealous groundskeeper.

Personal Kindness

Spencer never wavered in upholding Church standards and setting a personal example of total dedication to duty, but he was not harsh in his expectations of others. President Kimball once expressed concern about general Church leaders who used an authoritarian style; he instructed, "We've got to let local leaders know they can rule themselves without someone dictating what they must do."

A returned missionary who wrote President Kimball about a problem he observed in his mission received an invitation to come talk. After their conversation, Spencer referred him to two other General Authorities. The missionary later contrasted Spencer's loving concern with the coolness of the other men, who he thought regarded him as a critic of the Church when he meant only to point out a problem.

When Church discipline was necessary, Spencer accompanied it with great love. Elder Packer related an incident:

"A few years ago, it was my sad privilege to accompany President Kimball, then President of the Twelve, to a distant stake to replace a stake leader who had been excommunicated for a transgression. Our hearts went out to this good man who had done such an unworthy thing. His sorrow and anguish and suffering brought to my mind the phrase 'gall of bitterness.'

"Thereafter, on intermittent occasions, I would receive a call from President Kimball: 'Have you heard from this brother? How is he doing? Have you been in touch with him?' After Brother Kimball became President of the Church, the calls did not cease. They increased in frequency.

"One day I received a call from the President. 'I have been thinking of this brother. Do you think it is too soon to have him baptized?' (Always a question, never a command.) I responded with my feelings, and he said, 'Why don't you see if he could come here to see you? If you feel good about it after an interview, we could proceed.'

"A short time later, I arrived very early at the office. As I left my car I saw President Kimball enter his. He was going to the airport on his way to Europe. He rolled down the window to greet me, and I told him I had good news about our brother. 'He was baptized last night,' I said.

"He motioned for me to get into the car and sit beside him and asked me to tell him all about it. I told him of the interview and that I had concluded by telling our brother very plainly that his baptism must not be a signal that his priesthood blessings would be restored in the foreseeable future. I told him that it would be a long, long time before that would happen.

"President Kimball patted me on the knee in a gentle gesture of correction and said, 'Well, maybe not so long. . . .' Soon thereafter the intermittent phone calls began again."

Conferring with President Tanner, March 1975.

Spencer seemed acutely conscious of others' feelings. In May 1975 a young missionary assigned to offer the opening prayer before a crowd of many thousands in a San Diego football stadium felt paralyzed by overwhelming anxiety. During the last verse of the opening hymn, President Kimball leaned over and asked, "Are you as nervous as I am?" That moment of empathy restored the elder's calm, and he was able to give the prayer.

In another instance, in 1980 a new stake president from Sydney, Australia, arrived early for an appointment with one of the General Authorities. He entered the waiting room near the entrance of the Church Administration Building and noticed President Kimball visiting with a family. Not wanting to intrude, he moved to a far corner and looked out the window. Spencer, sensing the man's discomfort, left the family and greeted the stake president, kissing him on the cheek.

H. Burke Peterson, then a counselor in the Presiding Bishopric, passed President Kimball in the hall one day, each rushing to a meeting. Spencer stopped, took Bishop Peterson's hand, looked him in the eye, and said simply, "I'm sorry we're sometimes so busy. I guess I haven't told you lately how much I love you and appreciate you."

In June 1978, President Kimball rededicated the Hawaii Temple. During the several days of services, local drivers drove the General Authorities to and from their hotel. Ben Nihipali, driver of Spencer's limousine, asked President Kimball if he would be willing to meet Ben's mother. President Kimball readily agreed, so while he participated in a meeting, Ben contacted his mother and told her to come to the prophet's car immediately after the conference. She felt so nervous at the prospect of meeting him that when Spencer came out to the car she hid. Spencer refused to leave until they found her. Ben located her, but she held back fearfully until he said, "President Kimball is not leaving until he gets to see you." She finally came and received his embrace.

In traveling to a series of area conferences in Asia in spring 1980, Elaine Cannon, president of the Young Women, was the only unaccompanied woman. As a result, Spencer quietly added watching over her welfare to his other responsibilities. In Manila, she came out of her hotel room one morning to find Spencer in the corridor, dressed but unshaven, his hair tousled. He asked her if everything was all right. Later one of the security team who stood on duty around the clock told her that every night and morning in Manila Spencer had stopped by her hotel room to be sure nothing was amiss. Once he had called out to her through the door, "Is everything all right in there?"

5

SHAKING HANDS AND
WARMING HEARTS

"President Kimball is going to the prison tomorrow."

SPENCER KIMBALL HAD ALWAYS BEEN a people person. As a youth, he was the center of every group. To earn a living he chose service and sales occupations. As an apostle, he enjoyed staying in Church members' homes during stake conference visits. In 1952 he wrote in a stake president's guest book, in a space asking his hobby, "I love people." Five years later in the same book, he listed his hobby as "people."

His administration reflects that aspect of his personality. He made an effort to be among the people as much as possible. He had a phenomenal rapport with people, often remembering their names years after even minor interaction. He felt comfortable in hut, hogan, or bungalow, less so in mansion or palace.

He felt uncomfortable with special treatment. After Spencer assumed the presidency, the first time he and Camilla attended sacrament meeting in their home ward they quietly entered the back of the chapel and began conversing with ward members. The congregation, seeing them, rose. President Kimball waved for them to be seated. He remarked more than once that when Church members stood out of respect or swarmed to greet him, "they honor me because of the position I hold. It's not me."

For thirty years after becoming an apostle, Spencer had counseled a stream of troubled Latter-day Saints. That flow now diminished greatly in deference to the overriding importance of his new responsibilities, but on occasion he still dealt with some individual problems. For example, he advised a bishop's daughter pregnant out of wedlock to give

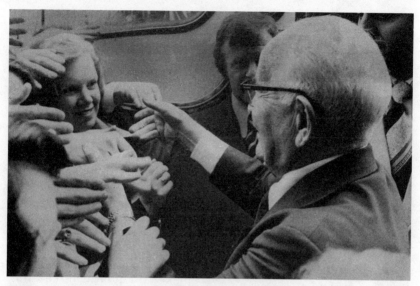

birth to her child and place it for adoption rather than undergo an abortion. He counseled with a young woman who wished to be married in the temple yet not offend her non-Mormon parents, whose only child she was. He encouraged a young man to stay close to his bishop while struggling to regain a testimony.

In 1975, the Reverend Norman Vincent Peale spoke in Salt Lake City and took the opportunity to meet the First Presidency. He was struggling with a personal challenge and asked President Kimball to bless him.

"You mean you want me to give you a blessing such as I give our people?" Spencer queried.

"Yes."

President Kimball and his counselors laid their hands on Dr. Peale's head and, as Dr. Peale related:

"President Kimball in his quiet, sincere, loving manner prayed for me by name. He asked the Lord to be near to me and love me and to take care of me and to guide me. As he prayed, I began to be very broken up and touched, and then all of a sudden I had a wondrous feeling of the Presence and I said to him, 'Sir, He is here; I feel His presence.'

"We said goodbye; I walked out into that crisp, sun-kissed morning and . . . as I walked along, I suddenly felt the burden lift, and I saw the answer to the difficulty and I felt the victory."

Piano duet with Carole Koizumi, Sapporo Mission home, August 1975.

There was a sense that he was accessible. A child wrote:

"Dear president Kimbal,

"I am 9 years old. My mother and father have some problms they ask me and ask me to pray fore them. I pray 3 and 4 times a day. My mom gets upset at my dad and they might half to live away from each other fore awile. I herd that prophets have special inning with the lord. If you can try and talk to the lord maby he will listen to you. If you can make an apiontment eny time will be good. Love, N——."

He received both the devout and the curious. One little boy, brought into his office to shake his hand, stated with refreshing candor, "I wanted to see you before you died." A great many others who did not say it came with the same thought in mind. President Kimball squeezed them into cracks of time between other appointments. He did not consider greeting them a chore, as some might, but a pleasure. An early visitor was March of Dimes poster boy Scott Hafen, age five, very small and wearing full-length braces on both legs. The visit reminded Spencer of his own son Ed, who since childhood had walked awkwardly from the effects of polio, and of the help the March of Dimes had given him with the expenses of that illness forty years earlier.[1]

His visitors could represent a wide range of people on a single day. On March 16, 1979, he received his brother-in-law Joseph Eyring, professional basketball player Greg Kite, the Native American family of Howard Rainer, John Balles of the Federal Reserve Bank of San Francisco, and African-American Latter-day Saint entertainer Alan Cherry.

---

1. Polio ceased to be a major problem in the mid-1950s with the widespread use of an effective vaccine. In 1958 the March of Dimes shifted its primary concern to birth defects.

Later Alan Cherry was again in the Church Office Building with friends when the elevator opened and President Kimball walked out. Instead of passing by with a brief greeting, Spencer walked up to the group, hugged Alan, kissed him on the cheek, and chatted a moment. As they parted, Spencer said, "Is there anything I can do for you?"

Knowing that Alan was a professional comedian, one of his friends grimaced, thinking, "He's going to tease the prophet!"

Alan, still single, said, "You can tell me where I'll find my future companion."

Taken aback momentarily, Spencer recovered and, with a smile, walked Alan toward the front door, saying, "She's out there. You go find her!"

Filmmaker Wetzel O. "Judge" Whitaker and three assistants came to Spencer's office from BYU to film some statements by President Kimball for stake conference training sessions. They finished their task about noon, and Spencer invited them to join him for lunch at the Lion House cafeteria next door. As they stood in line, a hostess said, "President Kimball, let me take you and your guests to a table and we'll serve you there."

He replied, "No, thank you. We'll take our turn." Then he asked his guests, "You don't mind, do you?" They didn't mind. At the stack of self-service trays, he got trays and utensils for his guests before he equipped himself.

In August 1976, among the 2,300 attending the Amsterdam area conference was Lou Martherus, a nonmember who came with his Latter-day Saint wife. He felt relieved when the two-hour meeting ended. He agreed to wait for his wife while she stood by President Kimball's bus, hoping to shake his hand.

As Lou waited perhaps one hundred feet from the auditorium, he saw a cluster of people leave the building and move toward the bus. He could not see Spencer, who was surrounded by taller people, but suddenly the group changed direction and came toward him. Before he knew it, the crowd engulfed him, and he saw the prophet standing in front of him, gazing at him with penetrating eyes. Spencer put out his hand and asked hoarsely, "How are you, Brother?" The encounter lasted only seconds, but in that instant, the skeptic became a believer. He felt

an overwhelming and unforgettable feeling of peace and love that changed his life.

Visitors came also to his home. For example, one Christmas a busload of seminary students stopped at the Kimball home while caroling in the neighborhood. Spencer invited them all inside and would not accept their refusals. "It's cold and snowy outside," he insisted. "And besides, you can't go without something to eat." He passed around Christmas cookies and candy.

A delivery man who brought packages to many homes during that holiday season reported that the President of the Church was the only person who invited him in.

On one occasion a woman brought her grandson, about ten years old, to the Kimball home. Spencer received them graciously, and they visited on and on, while he showed no visible sign of irritation or weariness. After half an hour or more, the visitors finally left. Son Ed, who was present, observed, "Perhaps Dad needs a lesson in how to bring an overlong conversation to polite termination."

In 1980, the Church made a large, unpublicized contribution toward construction of an interdenominational chapel at the Utah State Prison. Spencer asked Marvin J. Ashton about visiting the prison. Elder Ashton expressed concern: "President Kimball, I don't want you to go to the prison for a visit. I've had enough experience there to know that your life would be in danger, and some people would do anything to get attention, embarrass, or even harm you." Spencer accepted that advice without protest. But a few weeks later Arthur Haycock called Elder Ashton and said, "President Kimball is going to the prison tomorrow with Governor [Scott] Matheson and [Salt Lake City] Mayor [Ted] Wilson and would like you to go with them." Of course he agreed.

Two inmates were invited to meet with President Kimball in the warden's office. He did not ask about their crimes but about their families. At the chapel construction site, a number of the prisoners working there jumped down from the scaffolding to meet him. Spencer shook hands warmly and spoke briefly with each one. A photographer asked him to pose, and Spencer put his arms around two prisoners and drew them into the photograph.

On the way back to the city, Spencer repeatedly thanked Elder Ashton for taking him to the prison and remarked, "All men are basically good. Some just lose their way and need to be led back into proper paths and habits. Those people need our love and constant encouragement."[2]

Spencer identified himself with the troubles of others, even those far away. In June 1974, Dr. Russell M. Nelson, in his capacity as Sunday School general president, was preparing to board a plane for Argentina. A messenger ran up to him carrying an envelope with a handwritten note from President Kimball asking him to inquire about the welfare of an unemployed man the President had counseled with on his last visit to Argentina.

A few months later, Spencer felt sick and asked Dr. Nelson to check him over. The doctor found nothing physically wrong, yet Spencer was visibly distressed. Probing, Dr. Nelson learned that Spencer had received news that two missionaries in Texas had been murdered and dismembered by a mentally disturbed man. Spencer's concern for the families of the missionaries made him literally ill.[3]

---

2. Elder Ashton recounted the prison visit at April 1980 general conference to illustrate leadership principles. President Kimball (1) interviewed without criticism, (2) made others comfortable without condescension, (3) listened, (4) showed courtesy, (5) treated all as basically good, (6) expressed appreciation, (7) exhibited dignity and poise, (8) loved the sinner, (9) made himself available, without excuse of tiredness or busyness, and (10) took initiative in moving toward those inclined to hesitate.

3. The elders were Gary S. Darley and Mark F. Fischer. Spencer was able to meet with Elder Darley's parents.

Security man is included in Spencer's grandchild's birthday celebration.

Among the people who received Spencer's personal warmth and attention were the men employed by the Church to serve him as drivers and protectors. A security man was on duty in his car outside the Kimball home one evening in November 1977 when Spencer appeared at the door and beckoned him to come inside. Seeing it as just a polite gesture, the man waved but stayed in his car. Spencer signaled more insistently and called, "Come in, right now!" When the man entered, he saw President and Sister Kimball sitting intently before the television, watching Anwar Sadat, prime minister of Egypt, as he made his historic trip to Jerusalem to meet with Israeli prime minister Menachem Begin. Spencer wanted the security man to share in the excitement of this historic moment. As Sadat left his airplane and embraced Begin, the Kimballs applauded in pleasure at this step toward peace in the Middle East.

Spencer always personally saw that the security men who drove him to social occasions were fed. If it was not appropriate for them to join the group, he took a plate to them in the car. He also expressed concern about the length of time they might have to sit outside in the car waiting for him, even though that was their employment.

On one occasion, while a Church security staff member was driving President Kimball home, Spencer leaned back to rest. After a bit, he suddenly sat bolt upright, took off his glasses, and looked intently at the driver. "Is this your first family?" he asked.

Taken aback, the driver answered, "No, sir, I was married before. I tried all I could, but it did not work out."

President Kimball said, "I'm sorry if I have said something to cause you pain." He lay back again briefly, then sat up again, looked intently, and asked, "How is your son?"

The driver, who had only daughters by his second marriage, explained that he had not been allowed to see the son by his first marriage since the child was an infant, nearly twenty years earlier. They arrived at the Kimball home, and Spencer, embracing him, said, "You have good things to look forward to."

Puzzled, the driver asked Arthur Haycock why the President would be reading his personnel file. Arthur assured him that the President had not seen the file.

"How then," the driver asked, "did he know about my family situation?"

Arthur smiled, "That's why he's President of the Church."

About a week later the driver heard a knock at his door. A young man of about twenty introduced himself as his son. Now an adult, he had chosen to find his father and establish a relationship.

After Spencer's death, one security man sent a note to Camilla: "[I came as] a total stranger to you and soon I was invited to join in your meals, family gatherings and in family prayer. What a blessing for me."

6

PRIVATE LIFE

No grief or physical pain was more intense than his sorrow over this disagreement.

SPENCER'S HEAVY SCHEDULE OF MEETINGS, frequent travel, numerous speaking engagements, and a briefcase full of work always close at hand limited his personal time. But he still managed to visit the dentist and the doctor, have lunch with a friend, get his hair cut, work on his tax returns, visit the sick, attend wedding receptions, join in the monthly dinners of a Church history study group, and read the Book of Mormon with Camilla in their Monday family home evening.

For many, he was "the Prophet," and for them it was hard to see him as a man with a failing body, human emotions, a life history, family connections and complications, likes and dislikes, character traits both admirable and troublesome, confidence and insecurities, a sense of humor. Once when his son Spencer L. returned a rental car, the agent, who happened to be a Latter-day Saint, asked, "Are you related to *the* Spencer Kimball?"

Spence said, "I'm his son."

The man, taken aback, responded, "I never thought of him as having children." But Spencer was a real person, with pills to take, children to look after, taxes to pay, and trash to be emptied.

Spencer was not rule-bound, nor, despite his orthodoxy, did he have a highly legalistic understanding of the gospel. As an apostle, when he was free from conferences, he did not always attend the Sunday meetings in his ward. On occasion he had stayed home, studying or writing or tending to correspondence. He lived in sacred time seven days a week and was always "on duty."

When one General Authority went to dedicate a meetinghouse on Sunday, he arrived half an hour earlier than expected and found the men working feverishly, laying the last of the sod before the service. Concerned with this working on the Sabbath, he reported the incident at the next meeting with the Presidency and Twelve. President Kimball said gently, "Maybe next time you shouldn't go so early."

Spencer read the scriptures often. He said that sometimes when he felt depressed, immersing himself in the scriptures for a time helped dispel the darkness. He squeezed studying into free moments. As a party of General Authorities returned from an area conference in Europe, they found themselves with a layover at Kennedy Airport in New York City. Several leaned back and closed their eyes, but Spencer said, "Brethren, this is an excellent opportunity to study while we wait." He opened his scriptures, and others followed his example.

In May 1975, while the Kimballs were visiting the Dean Curtis family in Arizona, Dean got up about 6:00 A.M., thinking to be the first one stirring, only to find Spencer in a corner of the living room reading the scriptures.

EDUCATION AND THE ARTS

Spencer greatly valued education. It bothered him that he had only one semester of college because family and Church responsibilities had made more schooling unfeasible. He feared that if people knew how little schooling he had, they would think less of a church represented by someone so unlettered. The standard Church press release that went out when he was an apostle touring missions or visiting stake conferences indicated that he had graduated from Gila Academy, "now Eastern Arizona State College." The statement was literally true, but misleading, because when Spencer attended the academy it was a high school. He did not correct the impression that most people probably drew from this press release. When Spencer received honorary degrees from three Utah universities, he could not bring himself to think the honor was deserved except as a tribute to the Church in which he served.

Although his formal education was modest, Spencer educated himself by reading widely. His personal library included about 1,600 books, each numbered on the spine with a location code and listed in an inventory. His many file cabinets bulged with items gleaned from books and magazines. He screened materials primarily for information relevant to his gospel preaching, but in the process he became knowledgeable about many things.

When Florence Jacobsen, Church curator and director of historic sites, and Elder G. Homer Durham proposed a Church museum of art and history, they found ready approval. Construction was financed directly by the First Presidency.[1] The museum formalized the Church's commitment to the arts. Museum curators had the charge to conserve art or structures in danger of deterioration or loss,[2] collect new art relevant to the Church, commission art such as portraits of the apostles and depiction of historic events, create special exhibits, sponsor art competitions, and publicize the Church's art holdings.[3]

Spencer's interest in music and the visual arts was focused especially on their ability to foster the Church's message. In 1967 at BYU he issued a plea: "For years I have been waiting for someone to do justice in recording in song and story and painting and sculpture the story of the Restoration, the reestablishment of the kingdom of God on earth; the

---

1. The building was announced in 1980 along with the new genealogy library and was dedicated April 1984.

2. Murals in the Manti Temple by Minerva Teichert, Robert Shepherd, and C. C. A. Christensen and others in the Cardston, Mesa, and Logan Temples were restored. The refurbishing of Cove Fort; the Jacob Hamblin home in Santa Clara, Utah; and the Brigham Young winter residence in St. George was begun.

3. Elder Packer and Florence Jacobsen also played vital roles.

Spencer W. Kimball exhibit in Kimball Administration Building at BYU–Idaho.

struggles and frustrations; the apostasies and inner revolutions and counterrevolutions of those first decades; of the exodus; of the counter-reactions; of the transitions; of the persecution days; of plural marriage and the underground; of the miracle man, Joseph Smith, . . . and of the giant colonizer and builder, Brigham Young."[4]

He republished this appeal in a 1977 issue of the *Ensign* devoted to the arts.

Spencer loved music also for its own sake. He often listened to records in the evening as he worked in his study. Symphonies, Tabernacle Choir anthems, and Hawaiian music were among his favorites. He played the piano at home for his own pleasure until arthritis stiffened his fingers.

Once Spencer and Harvey Dahl[5] tried playing an organ duet. Harvey

---

4. Orson F. Whitney said, "We will yet have Miltons and Shakespeares of our own. God's ammunition is not exhausted. His brightest spirits are held in reserve for the latter times. In God's name and by His help we will build up a literature whose top shall touch heaven, though its foundations may now be low on earth." President Kimball's plea extended to scientists and statesmen as well as to writers, painters, and sculptors.

5. Spencer had known Harvey A. Dahl, a Nevada rancher, for many years, as stake president, Northern Indian Mission president, patriarch, and since about 1971 as manager of the Deseret Ranch.

complimented Spencer on his musical skill. Spencer responded that he hoped Harvey would soon be able to get some help with his hearing problems.

SIMPLE LIVING

Spencer paid little attention to his clothing, although Camilla and Arthur conspired to keep him looking presentable. Spencer hated to take the time to shop, so Camilla often brought clothes home for him to try on. Arthur sometimes did the same at the office. Camilla shopped for Spencer's suits at Mr. Mac's, a downtown Salt Lake City clothier, but owner Mac Christensen refused payment. In an effort to reciprocate, Spencer sent money to Brother Christensen's son while the young man was serving a mission in Australia.

On occasion, Spencer left home wearing pants and coat from similar but different suits. He seldom noticed. Sometimes Spencer returned home to change, and other times he simply carried on. One trip to Arizona included an appointment with the governor. Arthur discovered on the plane that again Spencer's pants and coat did not match. Between their arrival and the appointment, Arthur managed to come up with a borrowed suit for him.

Just before a trip to Lakeland, Florida, Arthur tried to persuade Spencer to buy a new pair of shoes. Spencer protested that he liked his old, comfortable shoes and that he had no time for shopping. Arthur went to the store and obtained on approval three pairs of shoes in the President's size. Spencer chose one pair under protest but grumbled on the trip to Florida that the new shoes felt stiff and too tight. In Lakeland the resourceful Arthur enlisted a security aide with feet the right size to put on Spencer's new shoes and walk up and down the hotel corridor to break them in.

But the old shoes resurfaced. In a temple meeting, Elder Monson noticed a hole in Spencer's shoe and mentioned it to Arthur, who groaned, "Has he got that pair on again? I've taken that pair away from him and hidden them a dozen times! He's got all kind[s] of new shoes, but he loves that old pair."

In 1980, shortly after a meeting in the Rose Bowl, a letter containing a check for $40 reached Spencer's office. A man who had viewed the proceedings through binoculars had observed that Spencer's shoes

showed signs of serious wear.
Spencer laughed and told
Arthur to put the money in the
missionary fund.

Tying neckties presented a
special challenge to Spencer.
One Christmas day neighbor
Sam Parker went to visit the
Kimballs, and Spencer showed
Sam his gifts. "Sam," he asked,
"do you know how to tie a tie?"

"You bet. Would you like
me to show you?"

"Yes, please, if you have
time."

Sam selected a new tie

At his desk at home.

and put it around President
Kimball's neck. They stood in front of a mirror, with Sam behind and
reaching over his shoulders to demonstrate how to tie a neat Windsor
knot.

"How does that look?" asked Sam.

"Fine." Spencer loosened the tie and very carefully lifted it over his
head, still knotted. With a smile he said, "Would you like to do
another?"

Sam laughed, then proceeded to knot all the new ties and slip them
off so that Spencer could simply lift one off the rack and pull it over his
head.[6]

Once a small professional committee on which Ed served met in
Salt Lake City. The members asked to see where his father, the President
of the Mormon Church, lived. On their way they passed the Kearns
Mansion on South Temple, the official residence of Utah's governor.
When the visitors saw the Kimball home, they expressed surprise at the
contrast. The modest home, built in 1947, had five rooms and a bath
on the main floor plus second and third bedrooms, a bath, and a play-
room and storage area in the basement. Camilla's deaf sister, Mary,

---

6. Other times Spencer's sons performed the ritual.

occupied one of these bedrooms for more than twenty years. Spencer's study, which was by the front door, had high bookcases on two walls, a desk, a bank of filing cabinets, a separate large table on and under which he piled papers and books, and a record player cabinet. Only a few square feet of open floor space—not even enough for a second chair—remained.

Spencer's taste in food was simple.[7] He ate very little meat and preferred soup or bread and milk, with a little cheese or perhaps some green onions, to a fancy meal. Camilla was an excellent cook and, until her later years, baked her own bread. Spencer liked Camilla's cooking and told her so regularly, but food was a matter of small importance to him.

Spencer was frugal. For example, he salvaged and used sheets of paper with a blank side. When the stack of scratch paper grew too high, Camilla would secretly dispose of some of the excess he would never use.

Despite his frugality, Spencer was generous. He gave to many organized charities and was not infrequently asked by individuals for help. In many cases he did give money, but it usually was in the form of a loan, for which he asked the recipient to sign a promissory note, even though he knew full well that few would actually repay. Many of the loans were to Native Americans who asked for money to return home. When they did not pay, as he believed they should, he would write a letter with a plea that they keep their word and return the money so that he would have it available to lend to others in similar straits.

Many years before, Linton Claridge had given Spencer $4,000 for his own use, but Spencer put it into a savings account out of which he gave help to people in distress. He asked each beneficiary to write a note of thanks to their anonymous benefactor and forwarded the notes to Linton.

His brother-in-law Henry Eyring once asked him how he dealt with the scripture in Mosiah about not denying the beggar. Acknowledging the difficulty in complying, Spencer smiled wryly as he said self-deprecatingly, "I always read fast when I get to those verses."

---

7. On trips, Spencer courteously would eat almost any food set before him. A rare exception was a trip to Japan in 1975 where he was offered a side dish of pungent fermented beans at the mission home. He declined.

One time Ed asked whether the covenant of consecration made in the temple meant that one should contribute all surplus to the Church or to charitable causes, rather than build up savings for security or as an inheritance. Spencer did not answer for others, but said, "I haven't the strength to be able to do that."

"Perhaps all that means is that you're not perfect."

"Oh, I thought I was," said Spencer dryly.

"If one were perfect," Ed pursued, "would he give all his surplus, or would he build up his capital, holding it in readiness for any use, when called on?"

Spencer agreed that for himself consecration meant at least the latter, but he did not undertake to answer the basic question for anyone else.

RECREATION

As an apostle, before his open-heart surgery, Spencer often swam at the Church-owned Deseret Gymnasium. He and Elder Mark Petersen had a standing appointment to visit "Uncle Gym" together when they were both in town. Spencer still went often, but now for a relaxing massage rather than for exercise. He began experiencing dizzy spells and high blood pressure (170/110), probably caused by anxiety. To regulate a premature heartbeat that was causing the dizziness, he started taking a new medication, but his first recourse for handling stress was to take a brief nap.

Camilla and Spencer both enjoyed traveling. Spencer told an interviewer in 1979, "I like to travel. . . . [I] always have. I extend my life from horse-and-buggy days up to supersonic plane. The other day we went to England from New York in 3 hours and 29 minutes." The annual conventions of Beneficial Life Insurance Company and Bonneville International Corporation provided some of the few occasions that seemed much like a vacation. In 1979, for example, attending the BIC convention gave the Kimballs a trip to Hawaii without formal Church responsibilities. They had several welcome days to walk the beach, watch whales swimming near the shore, and soak up the sun.

They were game for new experiences. In June 1977 friends took them to a Utah ranch with a lake stocked with fish. Spencer had been fishing a few times, but Camilla had not. Here they could hardly miss.

Camilla fishing in a stocked pond at Parnell Johnson ranch, June 1977.

Camilla screamed in excitement when she caught a six-pound trout, the biggest catch of the day. "This is the most fun I have ever had in my life," she exclaimed.

Spencer winked, "She'll remember this for the next eighty years."

That same month, after an appointment in Florida, they drove on Sunday to the 300,000-acre Church-owned Deseret Ranches of Florida. The ranch, fifty miles southeast of Orlando, included 60,000 head of cattle, 30,000 acres of citrus, and groves of cypress timber. More than eighty employees and their families lived there. The local ward chapel stood on ranch property as well. Because the Kimballs were there, visitors filled the chapel to overflowing.

Monday morning, hosted by ranch manager Harvey Dahl and his wife, Margaret, they toured the ranch, admiring the deer, wild hogs, alligators, and a bobcat. The next day they fished and went horseback riding and rode an airboat through canals, lakes, and a river. In the evening they enjoyed a cookout and an impromptu rodeo.

On another visit to the ranch, someone suggested that the Kimballs go horseback riding. This time Spencer said with a smile, "I don't know whether I want to do that or not." He explained that at a recent area conference a man had prayed for President Kimball to "die in the saddle."

On this visit they saw vultures circling over the road. When Camilla wondered aloud what the birds were looking for, Spencer shot back, "They're looking for me!"

Despite Spencer's heavy schedule, when he traveled local members sometimes arranged for Camilla and him to enjoy local attractions. He cooperated when side excursions did not conflict with meetings. Over the years the couple saw a variety of entertainments—Disney World and Cypress Gardens in Florida, professional baseball games in New York and Kansas City, a rodeo, an ice show.

Spencer and Camilla both had a very even temperament, slow to anger. Therefore the occasional lapse was memorable, inevitably retold at family gatherings. Once when Camilla was asked what Spencer said when she let out a rare "Damn," she replied, "He says I'll be sorry when someone overhears me."

"And what do you say when he swears?"

"I laugh myself sick!"

Spencer was so careful of his language that any kind of verbal outburst came from him awkwardly. Once he hit his head hard on the corner of a cupboard door and when he exclaimed, "Damn!" Camilla chuckled and said, "You may know the words, but you don't know the music."

Spencer often spoke as many as three times in a single day to different groups. His voice, faint and hoarse since surgery on his vocal cords, sometimes gave out. Beginning with the October 1975 general conference, Spencer used a tiny microphone attached to the frame of his eyeglasses. The device amplified his voice well and gave him freedom of movement at the lectern.

Spencer wished he were more dynamic as a speaker. He once told Paul Dunn wistfully but sincerely, "I wish I had your enthusiasm in my presentation." Even so, his thoughtful discourse and soft, husky voice caused people to "lean forward" mentally and stretch for what he said. Spencer was usually highly self-critical, so it is surprising to read in his journal after one regional representatives meeting, "I spoke well, I thought."

Spencer and Camilla Kimball with their four children, 60th wedding anniversary, January 1978. Sitting: Camilla, Spencer W., Olive Beth. Standing: Edward, Spencer L., Andrew.

FAMILY

Family was of great importance to Spencer. When he became President, his four children were well settled. Spence, fifty-five, held a chair in law at the University of Chicago.[8] He and Kathryn Murphy had six children. Olive Beth, fifty-one, taught elementary school in a Salt Lake City suburb. She and her husband, Grant Mack, an insurance agent who had lost his sight a few years earlier, had seven children. Andy, forty-six, worked as a manager in General Electric's new headquarters in Connecticut. He and Phyllis Jones had six living children; another daughter had died in childhood. Ed, forty-three, had recently moved from the University of Wisconsin to teach in Brigham Young University's newly established law school. He and his wife, Evelyn Bee Madsen, had seven children, six still at home. All together, Spencer and Camilla had twenty-seven grandchildren.

All the children were much loved by their parents. Son Andy, visiting at his parents' home at Christmas 1979, saw a new sweater that Spencer had received as a gift, still in its box. It had such a bold pattern that he thought Spencer would likely never wear it. Andy asked his mother, "Do you think Dad would give me that sweater?"

"I don't know," Camilla responded. "Ask him."

Andy went into the study and said: "Dad, would you be willing to give me that sweater . . ." Before Andy could finish his question about the gift sweater, Spencer began to take off the sweater he was wearing.

---

8. Spencer LeVan went by his middle name until he was a young adult. Thereafter he went by "Spence." His father never went by the shortened form.

With five grandchildren, Christmas 1974. Clockwise from left: Spencer, Miles, Camilla, Sarah, Mary, Jordan, and Joseph.

Although Spencer gave all his children ample evidence of his love, Spencer had a strained relationship with his eldest son and namesake. After his mission, Spence had become less involved in the Church because of doubts that grew until they overwhelmed his belief. By 1974 he and his family had been almost completely uninvolved with the Church for at least ten years.

Spencer's 1943 call to the Quorum of the Twelve had crystallized the problem. He wrote to his children about his feelings of inadequacy and told them that he could succeed in his new calling only with their support, including faithfulness in the Church to which he was committing his life. But support in that sense was something that Spence felt he could not give with integrity. Even though he had no interest in leaving the Church and was proud of his father's calling as an apostle, he simply did not believe Mormonism's truth claims. He considered them unfounded wishful thinking.

Over the years Spencer's repeated, anguished efforts to call his son to repentance only widened the gap between them. The son believed he should not be expected to profess faith and live his life in a way inconsistent with his convictions. The father kept hoping that perhaps one

Holding a great-grandchild.

more appeal would make the difference. Even if it did not, he felt it his responsibility as a parent to make the effort.[9]

Spence lived honorably, contributed significantly to his community, valued his pioneer Mormon heritage, excelled in his profession, and avoided causing any public embarrassment to his father. He felt hurt and resentful that his father would persist in trying to reclaim him when his father knew that such efforts further corroded their relationship. He felt devalued by his father's inability or unwillingness to accept him as he was; his father felt sure his beloved son simply did not understand what he was forfeiting.

This son's choice to follow a different path seemed to Spencer a mark of his own inadequacy. How could he preach effectively to others when he had failed in the circle closest to him? Spence's prominence in his profession only lent greater visibility to the father's failure. The intellectual achievement the son valued, his father disparaged as of limited value. Spencer once said, "[I] would rather have had [you] be a day

9. Spencer wrote many letters to his son, including letters dated July 31, 1944 (four single-spaced pages); February 13, 1945 (two single-spaced pages); October 27, 1945 (seven single-spaced pages, apparently sent two years later); September 5, 1965 (four single-spaced pages); October 27, 1971 (seven single-spaced pages; a P.S. indicates it was not sent until 1973 or later); January 16, 1972 (three single-spaced pages, probably not sent because the original as well as a carbon copy is still in Kimball Papers); October 4, 1976 (two pages); July 19, 1979 (longhand draft, approximate date from internal evidence). Spence's letters to his father were ever respectful but insistent that he was not capable of pretending belief to smooth their relationship.

In 1974 Spencer made oblique reference to his own situation in a talk called "Ocean Currents and Family Influences," an assertion that children who depart from their parents' path may be ultimately influenced by the parents' teachings more deeply than either can realize at the moment; for parents who have done their best there is no guilt and always hope.

The Kimballs were not alone among Church leaders in having children who were estranged from the Church. J. Golden Kimball, Spencer's uncle, was one. Fawn McKay Brodie, daughter of one General Authority, Thomas E. McKay, and niece of another, David O. McKay; and Frank J. Cannon, son of George Q. Cannon, stand out because of their strongly anti-Mormon writings. The biographies of other General Authorities tend to be silent on the issue.

laborer and President of an Elder's Quorum than be inactive in the Church and get all the recognition [you] had received in the secular world."

Shortly after he became President, Spencer, almost eighty and feeling that his life was racing to its close, tried desperately one more time. He sent Spence a letter of seven typewritten, single-spaced pages. Though it used language of affection, it was a strong call to repentance. Spence considered the letter insulting, treating him as a wayward child rather than as a thoughtful and responsible adult. Although Spence never doubted his father's good intentions, this insistent letter brought Spence to the verge of rejecting his father completely. He wrote a letter that would have severed all ties but he ultimately decided not to mail it, in large part because of the heartbreaking effect it would have on his mother. Camilla was also distressed by her son's disbelief, but she did not alienate him. Their warm relationship helped Spence maintain a courteous but distant connection with his father, and the difficult relationship limped painfully on. No grief or physical suffering was more excruciating to Spencer than his sorrow over this disagreement.

On one trip, Spencer and Camilla arranged to visit briefly with Spence in the Chicago airport between flights. Because of a last-minute gate change, their plane arrived at a different concourse than where Spence waited. Spencer was determined to cross the tarmac directly to the other concourse so that he would not miss his son. Arthur said, "You can't do that, President. It isn't safe."

Spencer replied, "I can and that is what we are going to do." He had his way. Although he was weary from meetings and travel, he and Arthur and an airline representative hurried across the tarmac. Camilla had to stay behind. Her knees would not tolerate the hike.

Olive Beth lived close by, but Spencer and Camilla kept up faithful correspondence with their sons. Over the years Camilla almost always wrote a Sunday afternoon letter to each of the families who lived away from Utah. Although Spencer did not write as routinely, he still wrote frequently. The children wrote back, though not as faithfully as their parents. Telephone calls were infrequent; long distance charges ran up too fast.

Spencer and Camilla sent their grandchildren birthday and Christmas checks every year and occasionally other gifts. They created

With a portrait of his grandfather Heber C. Kimball.

education and mission trust funds for the grandchildren, with the boys receiving more for missions than for education and the girls receiving more for education. Any trust funds not used went to support "Lamanite" missionaries.

When grandchildren married outside the Church, as several did,[10] Church policy precluded General Authorities from performing civil weddings. The first such occasion was the wedding of Spence and Kathryn's daughter Barbara, the oldest grandchild. Spencer and Camilla attended the wedding in Ann Arbor, Michigan, which was performed by the local bishop. Privately Spencer shed tears of disappointment that Barbara did not share his religious commitment.

Extended family felt Spencer's warmth, too. Spencer was loyal to the Kimballs, Woolleys, Eyrings, Romneys, and other, more remote family. He once told Lorenzo Hoopes, then a stake president in California, "You know, you're a relative of mine." The Hoopes and Woolley lines intersected five generations back.

---

10. Spencer wrote a letter of over nine pages to a granddaughter urging her not to marry a man unless he conscientiously joined the Church (undated; if Spencer did not send it at the time, he did so later along with a handwritten note, possibly 1979, that her husband might yet be converted with her help).

At the time Spencer became President, only three of his siblings were alive: Gordon, Dell, and Alice Nelson. Of these, Gordon died first, in 1975. In 1976 Spencer was delighted to ordain his brother Dell an elder at age eighty-five, nearly seventy years after Dell had left home as a teenager. During all those years, Dell had maintained contact with the family but had not been involved in the Church. Spencer had never ceased encouraging him. When Dell came from California for a visit in 1977, Spencer deferred appointments and stayed home from the office to spend time with his brother. Dell died a few months later.

Then in 1981, while in Florida, Spencer received word that his sister Alice Nelson had died of stomach cancer. The family scheduled a memorial service nine days later so that Spencer could attend.[11] Spencer flew to Phoenix; from there the Arizona governor's plane transported Spencer to Thatcher, his childhood home, where Alice would be buried near their parents. Spencer was then the last survivor of his parents' eleven children. By contrast, when Camilla, the eldest child in her family, died in 1987 at ninety-one, ten brothers and sisters survived her.

Spencer and Camilla always attended family reunions. When he and Camilla moved to Salt Lake City in 1943, Spencer revitalized the Heber C. Kimball family organization. In 1974, after he became President of the Church, hundreds more cousins came to the annual reunion to hear their prominent relative speak. The organizers prepared refreshments for 300, but 700 came. In 1978, although Spencer had just returned from an exhausting trip, he came to the reunion long enough to speak. Attendance peaked at 1,400 but declined again when Spencer could no longer participate.

Extended family felt Spencer's warmth. A young cousin reported visiting Spencer's office: "I stood up to leave, but the President grabbed my arm and asked me to stay. We talked about the Kimball family organization. He said he appreciated all that my father had done when he had served as president of it. He then showed me around his office, holding up one hand to ward off Brother Haycock. It was filled with an

---

11. One of his commitments was breaking ground for the Atlanta Temple in the presence of ten thousand people. As a result of the service and favorable publicity, missionary work in the area surged. The highway patrolman who provided transportation for President Kimball asked for baptism.

Spencer W. Kimball autographing a copy of his biography for his son Ed, January 1978.

incredible array of gifts given to him from the members of the Church all over the world."

When Spencer's niece Grace Howells lay dying of cancer, he went often to her home in Taylorsville, Utah, to offer comfort, even though he was still recovering from his own throat surgery.

He sent his nephew Spencer Brinkerhoff a penny postcard that had announced the nephew's birth. It was postmarked Los Angeles, California, August 16, 1913. "I have kept this card for over 60 years," wrote the elder Spencer. "Perhaps you would like to have it." When the Brinkerhoff children asked what they should call him, Spencer suggested "Uncle Uncle Spencer."

Camilla's brother Joseph Eyring said, "I thought Spencer belonged to us. It has seldom crossed my mind that Camilla was my blood sister and Spencer an in-law."

Stanley B. Kimball, Heber C. Kimball's biographer and Spencer's first cousin twice removed, grew up without a father. When Stan was just a youth, Spencer agreed to be his "Uncle." In 1979 Stan wrote, "As much as you mean to me as President and Prophet, I value far above that the role you have played as surrogate father to me since I was a most mixed-up seventeen-year-old. . . . Thanks for 35 years of love and concern." Whenever Stan came to Salt Lake City, he could get access no matter how busy Spencer was, and their visits were never rushed. Spencer gave him personal and professional counsel and listened nonjudgmentally when Stan freely gave advice on how the Church should be run. Spencer loaned Stan his car, took him to lunch, answered Stan's numerous letters, and provided access to documents for Stan's biography of Heber C. Kimball.

When Spencer's own biography appeared in 1977, Spencer was surprised and pleased by how quickly it found a large and eager readership. He allowed the authors, son Ed and grandson Andrew Kimball Jr., freedom to tell his story candidly, including reference to his human foibles. Spencer presented a copy to each General Authority individually. Reactions varied. One reportedly said to a friend, "I don't believe a book should portray an apostle as less perfect than the people expect him to be." But other General Authorities and Church members appreciated the frankness. One reader wrote, "As I read that biography I suddenly discovered a very important thing: the Prophet had once struggled with many of the same trials I was facing. He had triumphed—and so could I."

7

CAMILLA: EQUAL PARTNER

"It was up to me to . . . have the gift to be healed."

SPENCER KIMBALL DID NOT BECOME who he was alone. Since the time he was an unemployed college freshman waiting to go off to war, Camilla Eyring had not only stood by him and supported him but had also helped shape him. Spencer said more than once to missionaries that he had brought his wife to give the young men a mark to aim for: "Marry someone better than you are. I would never be in the Council of the Twelve today if I had married some of the girls I have known. Sister Kimball kept me growing and never let me be satisfied with mediocrity." With high enthusiasm he applauded the dedication of his biography to "Camilla Eyring Kimball, equal partner."

Spencer's calling as apostle and President had brought her unwillingly into a brighter spotlight, and she expressed the humble hope that she would be worthy to be at his side. She was a "kindly, unassuming, intelligent, independent, sensitive, honest, hard-working, tolerant, generous, spiritual woman, worthy of the high regard" in which Spencer and others held her. But she was her own person, intelligent, holding her own views and possessing great spiritual strengths.[1]

EDUCATION

Camilla's Eyring family placed high value on education. Despite the family's poverty after fleeing Mexico, all of the fifteen siblings who grew to maturity graduated from college except for Mary, who was deaf, and Camilla, who began working as soon as she earned a teaching certificate.

---

1. Based on her own experience as a wife of a Church President, Camilla expressed at length her empathy with Emma Hale Smith.

Like her siblings, Camilla valued the life of the mind. After moving to Salt Lake City, she took many classes at the University of Utah and at the associated Institute of Religion until Spencer's intensive travel schedule made such classes impractical. She taught Relief Society classes much of her life, read a great deal, and often gave book reviews to clubs she belonged to.

Spencer and Camilla, April 1974.

She felt a personal responsibility to understand issues. For example, she studied literature on both sides of the controversial proposal to adopt an Equal Rights Amendment (ERA) to the United States Constitution. In her last years, she studied the black experience in America.[2] She taught that women should pursue education and if possible a profession, both to open their minds and to prepare for the day when they might need to support themselves and a family.[3]

Camilla's candor, curiosity, and thirst for knowledge made her something of a model for women who struggled with identity and role. But she was not an unbridled feminist. When Geraldine Ferraro was nominated as U.S. vice presidential candidate on the Democratic ticket in 1984, Camilla commented to Ed, "What do you think about the election? Do you think a woman could be vice president? I don't think a woman is suited to that."

---

2. Sensing in herself some remnants of prejudice, Camilla read books to try to understand the slavery experience.

3. Ruth Funk said, "I feel we're beginning to [have a sense of our own identity]. . . . I date it back to Sister Kimball's talk where in a glorious statement she . . . counseled us to pursue an education, that every woman should have that as a relentless goal. Since that time women have talked more openly about the importance of education."

PUBLIC ROLE

As the Church President's wife, Camilla did a great deal of public speaking, especially at area conferences and local Relief Society and visiting teaching conferences. Personally diffident, she did not seek out speaking opportunities, but rarely a week went by without one or more speaking engagements. In January 1977, for example, she spoke at five visiting teaching conferences. In the first three months of 1979, she spoke fourteen times, often about her favorite themes of love, service, and the value of visiting teaching.

She addressed the annual Brigham Young University women's conference several times, beginning in 1977.[4] Organizers sought her involvement not only because of her husband's position but also because of her faithfulness, intellect, and thoughtfulness. In 1981 she said, "I make no pretensions at perfection. People sometimes assume that because I am the President's wife I must already have arrived at that state, but I struggle every day with the same kinds of imperfections you all do. There is no place so high that it is beyond difficulty or temptation." In 1985, Camilla, at ninety, still had enough vigor to speak at the conference.

---

4. She was the keynote speaker at women's conferences and awarded the first Exemplary Womanhood Award by BYU women students. She also read Spencer's address to the second general women's conference, held while he was hospitalized.

Even though she had no official position, Camilla Kimball still played a significant role as the most visible woman of the Kimball administration after Relief Society general president Barbara Bradshaw Smith. She was sometimes embarrassed by praise, feeling that the recognition was only because of her husband's position. She freely chose to accept the supportive role and lived without dissatisfaction in Spencer's shadow, but it pleased her when she was recognized for her own efforts. She loved Relief Society and knew that praise for her long and effective service in that organization was not dependent on her husband's position; therefore, such tributes had special meaning to her.[5]

She initially refused a request from Brigham Young University to use her name in raising money for a professorial chair, but eventually, with her reluctant consent, BYU raised a million dollars for a Camilla Eyring Kimball Chair in Home and Family Life.[6]

Among Camilla's outstanding traits were her kindliness and her unpretentiousness. In October 1980, during a luncheon at the dedication of the N. Eldon Tanner Building at BYU, William G. Dyer, dean of the BYU School of Management, confided to Camilla that he felt nervous sitting with such important people. She responded, "There is no need to be nervous sitting by me. I'm nobody."

Once in 1978 when Spencer and Camilla stood waiting in a tunnel under the arena at an area conference, a couple spotted them and came over to talk. While the man conversed with Spencer, the woman confessed to Camilla, "I wish I could be like you, always so poised." Camilla responded, "If that is true, you need to remember that I wasn't that way when I was your age."

PERSONAL LIFE

Spencer's health problems drew more attention than Camilla's because they affected his ability to fulfill his responsibilities as President.

---

5. She rarely let anything get in the way of visiting teaching on the first Tuesday of each month. In 1976, she was honored at a luncheon similar to the ones she had held for many years for those women in her ward who met her scripture reading challenge.

6. The General Relief Society contributed $300,000 to the chair in 1984 "in recognition of Sister Kimball's generous words and deeds in her Relief Society callings." The Crabtree trust provided another major portion, while gifts from admirers, friends, and family, including such contributions as Camilla herself could offer, completed funding of the chair. Later a Camilla Kimball scholarship for students emphasizing home economics education in international settings also honored her.

Camilla visiting teaching with Erma Francom.

But Camilla grew older and more fragile as well. As she aged, she experienced several painful falls, an emergency appendectomy, severe arthritis of back and knees, spinal degeneration, carpal tunnel syndrome,[7] extreme anemia, a bleeding stomach ulcer, and a broken hip. On Spencer's eightieth birthday, she quipped, "I am glad he isn't any younger. I just hope I can keep up with him now!" They sometimes joked about her having married a younger man—younger by almost four months.

Until her very last years, Camilla took great pleasure in preparing holiday meals for as many of her family as could gather. On November 16, 1977, she and Spencer celebrated sixty years of marriage with a small family gathering at their home. Two weeks later they hosted a more elaborate reunion for fifty, including nearly all of their descendants, at the Hotel Utah.

For New Year's Day in 1979, Camilla cooked a prize-winning twenty-nine-pound turkey that had been given them. Thirty family members gathered for the holiday, eating well, singing traditional family songs, and rehearsing the old family anecdotes.

Camilla had her sister Mary, who was born deaf, living with them for the last twenty-five years of her life. Mary largely cared for her own needs, and Spencer never expressed any reservation about Mary's living with them. Mary treated Spencer deferentially, but she was not above arguing with Camilla, who sometimes found Mary's constant presence difficult. Mary helped around the home and was no great burden, but Spencer and Camilla always had to include her needs in their planning.

In late April 1979, Camilla had a speaking appointment and took

---

7. She had done a great deal of handwork all her life, particularly needlepoint in her later years, probably causing the carpal tunnel syndrome.

Mary to their sister Caroline's home for the night. Early the next morning, Caroline called to say that Mary had died in the night, apparently of a heart attack. Camilla reacted almost hysterically. After all these years as Mary's closest sister and caregiver, Camilla felt guilty and in a way betrayed that she had not been allowed to complete her stewardship—Mary had died "away from home." After the shock wore off, she felt relieved that Mary had escaped a long period of suffering.

Camilla was notably thrifty. On one flight back to Salt Lake City, Spencer and Camilla had been fed before they boarded the plane, so Camilla put their dinner steaks in a bag; when they changed to another plane in Denver and received yet another meal, Camilla again thriftily salvaged the meat. "We had meat at home for most of a week," she wrote in her diary with obvious satisfaction. In March 1977, before general conference, she congratulated herself on cannily shopping the spring sales and finding a new dress for $23.

In Hawaii on one trip to area conferences, Camilla fussed about their elaborate hotel suite until she learned that, as part of a package arrangement for the group, the group leader received a lovely suite for only three dollars more than an ordinary room. When Camilla celebrated her eighty-fifth birthday, Olive Beth brought her a large supply of frozen orange juice as a gift. Camilla and Spencer liked orange juice, but Camilla had stopped buying it when the price rose. She could afford it, but would not.

Camilla persisted in a lifelong habit of canning. While living at Hotel Utah, friends would bring produce and what she and Spencer could not use she bottled—peaches, raspberries, grape juice, watermelon pickles, pickled beets, chili sauce, jam. It gave her great satisfaction to be doing something for herself. And when harvest season arrived, she went to her home, collected the apples from her tree (including windfalls), carted them to the Hotel Utah, and took them up in the elevator to the apartment where they were living so she could make applesauce as she always had.

SPIRITUALITY

Camilla was a person deeply invested in her religion, and her faith had roots. A particularly meaningful experience came to her when she

Spencer and Camilla at Ricks College (now BYU–Idaho). Behind them is college president Henry B. Eyring.

served as a volunteer guide on Temple Square some years before Spencer's presidency.

"One morning as I was dressing to go, I was struck by a shattering question: 'How do I know that Joseph Smith actually saw the Savior and the Father? How could I know such a thing?' I wondered how I had the temerity to say [as a guide] that this thing actually happened. I was terribly disturbed. I knelt and prayed about it, but left the house still troubled. I can still feel the sensation I had when I stood up to tell the Joseph Smith story that day, as I had told it so many times before. Suddenly I had a manifestation—a burning in my bosom—that was so assuring, so reassuring, that I had no question in myself that this was actually the testimony that is promised if we seek and really want to know. What is amazing to me is that I'd never thought of that question before. My testimony was just such a fact of my existence. And then the question and the answer came in the same day! I was not a youngster; I was a mature woman."

Another experience came in November 1972 after an operation for a perforated appendix. Camilla's incision became infected, and she felt greatly discouraged. Marion G. Romney gave her a blessing, leaving an indelible impression with one statement: "I bless you with the gift to be healed."

"[Then] it was as if those words were imprinted on a banner before me. . . . It was borne in upon me with greater and greater clarity that I had had a special blessing given at a time of greatest need and that it was up to me to claim that blessing. It was up to me to take courage, to determine to do everything in my power that I might have the gift to be healed."

A reviewer of the book *The Writings of Camilla Eyring Kimball*, assessed her role:

"For many women it was her unpretentious ordinariness that made Sister Kimball more influential than she might have been in her otherwise glamorous position as the prophet's companion: 'I know something of losing one's parents, of seeing one's spouse racked with stress and pain, of having one's savings of many years wiped out by theft or bank failure, of watching loved ones stray from the gospel, of having a child stricken with crippling illness, and of feeling disabling old age creeping on.' She boldly revealed her own [religious] doubts and independence from her husband: 'I am a bit more restless than my husband. He has always been solid and unquestioning in his faith, and he has never been able to understand why I have to question and delve.' Sister Kimball upheld the traditional values of family and Church with nontraditional style. She championed the challenging 'profession' of homemaking and warned that 'rather than directing both marriage partners away from the home, we need to encourage both to make strengthening the family their primary concern.' Her writing is always full of gently persuasive common sense rather than intimidating authority.

"Sister Kimball has been an influential, effective spokesperson for women. Her example was influential because of her position as 'first lady' to the Church. Her voice was and continues to be effective because it is one of the few official voices that is personal, reasonable, candid, direct yet nonjudgmental—and female."

Teachings of a Prophet

8

Boldly Proclaimed:
A Prophet's Mission

For many people the stiff medicine was rightly prescribed.

A PROPHET IS PREEMINENTLY AN INSPIRED teacher and, in that sense, Spencer W. Kimball was a prophet for thirty years before he became President. Perhaps most significantly, as an apostle he had written *The Miracle of Forgiveness* to underscore the costs of sin and the way to repentance. The book filled a need, as evidenced by the printing of half a million copies in English and sixteen other languages between its publication in 1969 and his death in 1985.[1]

The Miracle of Forgiveness

The Miracle of Forgiveness grew out of the apostle's many years counseling thousands of troubled people. He had earlier stated his intention not to write books—"there were books enough"—but he finally concluded that the Church needed "an extensive treatise on repentance" and that it was his responsibility to create one. He spent uncountable hours over ten years, including summer "vacations" from conference assignments, to produce the manuscript.

The book's tone, tougher than Spencer's in-person counseling, reflected his belief that people rationalize sin too quickly and consider repentance easy. Indeed, it was a book more on sin and repentance than on forgiveness. Spencer later seemed to wish he had adopted a gentler

---

1. Foreign publication rights were given to the Church, and by 1974 arrangements had been made for translation into sixteen languages. By 1998 the total in all languages was roughly estimated at 1.6 million copies.

tone. In 1977 he said to Lyle Ward, his neighbor, "Sometimes I think I might have been a little too strong about some of the things I wrote in this book."

But he meant to shake people, and the hundreds of letters of thanks let him know that at least for many people the stiff medicine was rightly prescribed. One wrote, "You called me a culprit and a sinner and transgressor and that brought me to my senses." But when he heard of others who read the book and became discouraged by a standard that seemed to them unattainable, he wished he had communicated more understanding and encouragement.[2]

At first he responded personally to the steady stream of letters the book motivated, often writing at length. He tried to respond to specific questions, but ultimately his advice almost always was for people to go to their bishops. When people came for counseling who had not read the book, he gave them a copy. He bought copies by the hundred for that purpose.[3]

---

2. Armand Mauss said, "I saw him as one who held out for strict definitions of right and wrong, as strict as anyone's among the General Authorities. Even his well-known *Miracle of Forgiveness* does not strike me as having as much to do with forgiveness as with judgment and repentance! He could be very hard. Yet, on the other hand, he seemed always to have his arms open to the repentant, no matter how serious their sins."

Gary Huxford said that the book "has probably done more to define the process of repentance than all the official directives and handbooks. Sometimes overlooked in the eloquence of a truly passionate piece of writing is the greatly enhanced role, portrayed in the book, of the institutional Church and its leadership in this process so vital to all who take the Christian injunction seriously. Has doctrine, as well as procedure and style, been shaped by the prophet in ways more obscure than by official pronouncement, but equally as effective? Indeed, it is increasingly difficult to distinguish between doctrine and style when the leadership opts for the prophetic mode."

3. A note that appears to be from 1974 indicates that by then he had given away 1,300 copies. Invoices show that he bought another 120 copies on March 7, 1975, and 100 more copies on May 14, 1975.

PUBLIC TEACHING

Aside from the book, his public teaching primarily took the form of speaking at stake and general conferences. In preparing to speak, Spencer prayed for divine inspiration, and he took seriously his duty to respond energetically to insights that flowed to him. He spoke with unmistakable moral authority, sometimes critical and demanding, but more often loving and encouraging.

Though modest about personal accomplishments, President Kimball did not hesitate to proclaim boldly his prophetic mission. He testified that "revelation continues and the vaults and files of the Church contain these revelations which come month to month and day to day. We testify also that there is, since 1830 when The Church of Jesus Christ of Latter-day Saints was organized, and will continue to be, so long as time shall last, a prophet, recognized of God and his people, who will continue to interpret the mind and will of the Lord. . . .

"In our day, as in times past, many people expect that if there be revelation it will come with awe-inspiring, earth-shaking display. For many it is hard to accept as revelation those numerous ones in Moses' time, in Joseph's time, and in our own year—those revelations which come to prophets as deep, unassailable impressions settling down on the prophet's mind and heart as dew from heaven or as the dawn dissipates the darkness of night.

"Expecting the spectacular, one may not be fully alerted to the constant flow of revealed communication. I say, in the deepest of humility, but also by the power and force of a burning testimony in my soul, that from the prophet of the Restoration to the prophet of our own year, the communication line is unbroken, the authority is continuous, light, brilliant and penetrating, continues to shine. The sound of the voice of the Lord is a continuous melody and a thunderous appeal. For nearly a century and a half there has been no interruption."

At the April 1978 priesthood session of general conference, he ended his talk saying:

"Elijah shall reveal the covenants to seal the hearts of the fathers to the children and the children to the fathers. The anointing and sealing is to be called, elected, and the election made sure.

"'I *know* that God lives; I *know* that Jesus Christ lives,' said John

Taylor, my predecessor, 'for I have seen him.' I bear *this* testimony to you brethren, in the name of Jesus Christ. Amen" (italics added).[4]

Some, hearing the talk, took it as a statement that President Kimball had seen Christ, although he never publicly said so unambiguously.

After more than forty years of public teaching, Spencer had essentially no public role for his last several years as President. One man referred to him as "the silent prophet," raising the question of what good such a prophet could be. But in this case the prophet's words from previous years still echoed. And even in his silence, he taught the Church commitment, love, humility, and enduring to the end.

---

4. Such a statement was made by John Taylor's counselor George Q. Cannon in general conference, October 6, 1896. Perhaps John Taylor did also. In a talk in the 1960s to seminary and institute teachers, Spencer reportedly said, "I know he lives because I have seen him," but the statement did not appear in the printed version of the talk.

9

PERSUASION TO CHASTITY

He had great empathy for those individuals who struggled.

PRESIDENT KIMBALL PERCEIVED a pronounced national decline in chastity, marriage, and family values. In response to this trend, he gave substantial emphasis to teachings about right standards of conduct with respect to sexual morality. Church members continued to be distinctive in their lesser incidence of premarital sex, higher rate of marriage, less frequent divorce (and more frequent remarriage after divorce), larger families, and use of contraception more to space children than to minimize their number, but they still followed the national trends.[1]

PHYSICAL, EMOTIONAL, AND SEXUAL ABUSE OF CHILDREN

The problem of physical and sexual abuse of children began only gradually to receive the substantial attention in the community and in the Church that it later drew. In the 1960s Elder Kimball had urged local leaders to be on the alert for child abuse and incest, but in *The Miracle of Forgiveness* (1969) he did not mention these problems explicitly; there was only the more general heading of sexual perversion. At April 1978 general conference he said, broadly, "We are much concerned that there would be a single parent that would inflict damages on a child." It was finally April 1985 when President Hinckley, speaking in the priesthood

---

1. Changes among Latter-day Saints tend to follow those of the larger community, but they lag behind. Although modern Mormons have fewer children than earlier, they still are more family-oriented than the general society. Despite the "sexual revolution," LDS college students had a higher level of chastity; little changed between 1958 and 1978. Although the rate of unchastity was low, it increased significantly in percentage terms.

Speaking at a press conference before the rededication of the Mesa Arizona Temple, April 1975.

session of general conference, condemned child abuse directly and in the strongest terms:

"There appears to be a plague of child abuse spreading across the world. Perhaps it has always been with us but has not received the attention it presently receives. I am glad there is a hue and cry going up against this terrible evil, too much of which is found among our own. Fathers, you cannot abuse your little ones without offending God. Any man involved in an incestuous relationship is unworthy to hold the priesthood. He is unworthy to hold membership in the Church and should be dealt with accordingly. Any man who beats or in other ways abuses his children will be held accountable before the great judge of us all."

Also in 1985, Church Welfare Services published a first pamphlet for bishops on handling child abuse cases. Attention finally was coming to be focused sharply on this evil.

PORNOGRAPHY

President Kimball abhorred pornography and mentioned it often in his conference addresses. In October conference 1977 he asked for studied resistance to pornography.

The Church cooperated with other churches and civic organizations in promoting media decency. In 1976 Church members in Salt Lake City joined a rally for decency and by assignment picketed X-rated movie theaters in Salt Lake City, which soon closed.

In 1978 the First Presidency asked Church members to join with a national organization in turning off all television for one day (May 23, 1978) in symbolic protest against the sexual immorality and excessive violence on television.[2]

SEX AND TECHNOLOGY

The Church faced questions raised by the increased skill of doctors. A 1950 *Church News* editorial had flatly rejected artificial insemination, but by 1974 artificial insemination with the husband's semen was acceptable. Insemination with donor semen, however, was "not approve[d]." In 1977 the language changed to "the Church *discourages*" artificial insemination by donor. Artificial insemination of unmarried women was grounds for Church discipline.

Developments in medical technology that made successful sex-change operations possible raised a quasi-doctrinal issue not fully addressed until 1980. That year local leaders received instructions that participation as either surgeon or patient in such operations called for mandatory excommunication and "no readmission to the Church is possible." The 1983 *Handbook* softened the language slightly to "ordinarily justifies excommunication . . . [and] no readmission to the Church is possible." The 1985 *Handbook* allowed for rebaptism but only with consent of the First Presidency. None of these restrictions applied to surgery on persons with ambiguous genitalia.

For a person whose sex change operation preceded conversion, the 1983 *Handbook* allowed for baptism but not priesthood ordination or admission to the temple.[3]

HOMOSEXUAL ACTIVITY

Early in their ministry, Spencer W. Kimball and Mark E. Petersen were given special responsibility for counseling homosexual Church

---

2. The problem of pornography on the Internet had not yet begun.

3. The rejection of sex change is connected with a view that sex is not simply a mortal characteristic. See "The Family: A Proclamation to the World" (1995): "Gender is an essential characteristic of individual premortal, mortal, and eternal identity and purpose."

members. Over a period of many years Spencer had more experience
on this subject than other Church leaders and thus more to say.[4] Like
other Americans at midcentury, President Kimball's attitude toward
homosexuality was strongly negative, shaped in large part by his fervent
belief in chastity before marriage and fidelity after marriage as the Lord's
standard for sexual activity, by his belief that a major purpose of life is
bearing and rearing children, and by an abhorrence for what he was
convinced was unnatural.

In speaking about matters of sexual morality Spencer was more
explicit, emphatic, and strict than others. *The Miracle of Forgiveness*
described homosexual acts as an ugly sin, a perversion, an abomination.
He believed homosexual orientation could be shifted by effort and faith
and that, even in a case where the inclination did not change, conduct
could and should be controlled. To those who said that "this practice
. . . is incurable," he responded that they had simply not tried hard
enough. His logic was simple: homosexual acts are sinful and, since sin
can be overcome with God's help and sufficient effort, failure to overcome is a moral shortcoming.

Even so, though his views seemed harsh to some, he had great
empathy for those individuals who struggled.[5] When those he had
counseled capitulated to temptation, as it appeared most did, he
mourned for them.

During 1974, the first year of Spencer's presidency, Church Welfare
Services published a booklet called "Homosexuality" as part of its series
to inform bishops about problems they might expect to encounter in
counseling. Homosexual conduct was considered "sin in the same
degree as adultery and fornication."

In June 1977, President Kimball learned that a gathering of homosexuals under the title "Human Rights Convention" had reserved meeting facilities at the Church-owned Hotel Utah. The hotel management

---

4. Spencer W. Kimball and Mark E. Petersen reported that between 1961 and 1968 they had
counseled almost one thousand individuals, nearly all in Salt Lake City, Ogden, and Provo. They
employed Harold I. Bowman to assist them. They asked for more help and suggested training for
bishops and stake and mission presidents, and establishment of policies for handling situations.
They expressed their "willingness" to relinquish the time-consuming work.

5. For example, in Kimball Papers there are copies of a letter of twenty-three single-spaced
pages and another of twenty-six pages, seeking to persuade and encourage.

had not been aware of the group's character and asked for advice. The First Presidency advised the hotel to cancel the reservation.[6]

At October conference 1977 President Kimball urged Church members as citizens to combat permissiveness. "There is today a strong clamor to make such [homosexual] practices legal by passing legislation. . . . We do not hesitate to tell the world that the cure for these evils is not in surrender."

In 1977, too, Mormon gays and lesbians began to publicize their views that homosexuality is not "curable" and that homosexual acts based on "mature loving intimacy" should be accepted as essential to the development of an unfractured personality. They organized Affirmation, a support group that soon had chapters in most of the nation's large cities.[7]

President Kimball asked Elder Packer to address the issue of homosexuality at a BYU fireside in March 1978. Feeling inadequate, Elder Packer at first resisted, saying, "President, I just couldn't do it." But after soul-searching he decided he could not refuse "an assignment from the prophet"[8] and gave a very direct talk.

At October conference 1981, a group of seventeen Mormons and ex-Mormons marched at Temple Square and chanted for equality for homosexuals in Utah:

"Two, four, six, eight,

"Gay is just as good as straight."

Some of their posters read: "We are your children," "Liberty and justice for all," "Keep your religion out of our laws."

As more and more gay men and lesbian women declared themselves, lobbied to legalize their conduct, and sought to legitimize their lifestyle as socially acceptable, the Church reacted against this political movement that sought to change the moral standards of the nation.

---

6. A suit to require the hotel to accommodate the group failed because they were able to find another site. The group was identified as the Salt Lake Coalition for Human Rights, which had many homosexual members.

7. Affirmation continues to the present, holding an annual conference, publishing a newsletter, and sponsoring social and spiritual events. A competing support group for those who would resist homosexual impulses, called Evergreen, originated in 1989. It reflects the contrary view that homosexual impulses can be controlled and changed.

8. Elder Packer acknowledged again that the answers are not simple and that perhaps "leaders in the Church do not really understand these problems," but they do understand temptation. He said, "What one is may deserve unlimited tolerance; what one does only a measured amount."

10

OF GARDENS AND JOURNALS:
GENERAL CONFERENCE THEMES

"We are a throw-away people."

AT ONE TIME SPENCER had commitments for twenty-three speaking engagements and was working on talks for them all at the same time. With such relentless speaking demands, he of necessity relied on many sources. He had file cabinets full of subject folders containing clippings and notes he called "sermon seeds." To one audience President Kimball began his speech by explaining that he had missed some of their earlier activities because he was preparing his remarks: "Wouldn't it be nice if you could wait until you stood before an audience and then had all of the inspiration flow through you to that audience? But that isn't the way it works. If you want the inspiration of the Lord to accompany you, then you must prepare."

He often invited General Authorities, Church department heads, and individuals he respected to make suggestions about what he might say to further the cause of the Church. Sometimes he expressed his thanks but ignored their suggestions. Other times he used the ideas as raw materials in his preparation. Sometimes the suggestions said just what he wanted and he adopted them with only minor changes. He always took full responsibility for what he said.

Spencer also asked for feedback about his talks, always wanting to improve. At Ricks College about 1976, though suffering physically, he addressed the students about repentance for nearly two hours. He was in such pain that he took some medicine as soon as he sat down, something he would normally never do in public. Later he asked college president Henry B. Eyring, "How do you think it went?"

With BYU president Dallin H. Oaks.

When Eyring offered praise, Spencer interrupted to clarify. "I mean, did they hear me? Was I too hard?" He was not concerned with whether he had spoken well, but whether the audience understood and would accept his message.

During the late 1970s, Spencer and Camilla went to a Young Women general board Christmas party in the Lion House, and before his turn to speak he asked Camilla, "What shall I tell them?"

"Tell them to be good," she said.

"They don't want to hear that."

When he was called on, he went to the piano and played "I Am a Child of God" and some Christmas carols. Then he talked warmly and informally about the importance of their work.

TALKS AT BRIGHAM YOUNG UNIVERSITY

Spencer was a dedicated supporter of Brigham Young University, the Church's flagship educational institution. He spoke there once or more nearly every year between 1944 and 1980, and he took very seriously his preparation to speak there. During students' critical college years, Spencer felt it was especially important that they learn to live the basic virtues. His most frequent subject was honesty and integrity. He also spoke many times about marriage and at least five times about the students' obligation to foster the interests of Lamanites.[1]

In 1975–76, the university celebrated its centennial. President Kimball dedicated a new carillon tower and spoke about the century ahead, describing the challenge BYU faced of integrating faith and scholarship:

"The faculty has a double heritage which they must pass along: the secular knowledge that history has washed to the feet of mankind . . . [and] the vital and revealed truths that have been sent to us from heaven. . . . Your double heritage and dual concerns with the secular and the spiritual require you to be 'bilingual.' As LDS scholars you must speak with authority and excellence to your professional colleagues in the language of scholarship, and you must also be literate in the language of spiritual things."

THEMES IN GENERAL CONFERENCE ADDRESSES

President Kimball considered his prime speaking responsibility his addresses at each general conference. He typically spoke five times: to regional representatives and in the welfare session, opening general session, priesthood session, and closing general session. Most of his topics fell into the realm of the familiar, but some had a highly personal cast. He wanted to teach that "all things are spiritual" (see D&C 29:34).

As Spencer traveled in Mormon country in 1974, he noted many farms and homes in dilapidated condition. He remarked to his nephew Harden Eyring, traveling with him, "They may be poor, but that is no excuse for not having things neat and tidy." In September the First

---

1. His topics were peace of Christ (1944), spiritual vision (1946), miracles (1947), modest style (1951), marriage (1952), Indians (1953), repentance (1954), death as tragedy or destiny (1955), revelation and righteousness (1957), honesty (1958), apostasy (1959), prayer (1961), humility (1963), integrity (1964), lust (1965), Indians (1965), meeting challenges (1966), God not dead (1966), Indians (1967), "Education for Eternity" (1967), righteousness (1968), Indians (1969), Peter (1971), gospel solves problems (1971), Indians (1972), marriage (1973), righteousness (1974), centennial (1975), marriage (1976), truth absolute (1977), honor (1978), integrity (1979), keeping commitments and marriage (1980).

Using a teleprompter and tiny microphone in conference.

Presidency issued a statement in the *Church News* encouraging members to beautify their surroundings and clean up their yards. Then in October general conference, President Kimball repeated and expanded that special theme:

"We are a throw-away people. Trash piles grow faster than population by far. . . .

"Broken fences should be mended or removed. Unused barns . . . sheds and corrals should be repaired and painted or removed. Weedy ditch banks should be cleared. Abandoned homes could probably be razed. We [should] . . . make our properties a thing of beauty to behold."

He reinforced his point with a story:

"When an administrator in Africa rode out to inspect land that had been devastated in a storm, he came to a place where giant cedars had been uprooted and destroyed. He said to his official in charge. 'You will have to plant some cedars here.' The official replied, 'It takes 2,000 years to grow cedars of the size these were. They don't even bear cones until they are 50 years old.'

"'Then,' said the administrator, 'we must plant them at once.' And this is the admonition to you.

"'Let everyone sweep in front of his own door,' said Goethe, 'and the whole world will be clean.'"

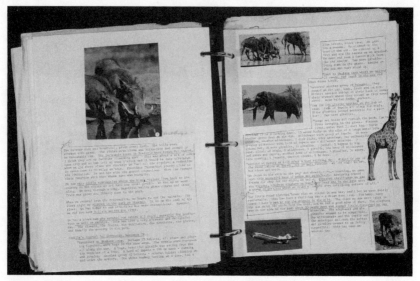

Journal of a trip to Kruger Park during an assignment to South Africa.

In ten of eleven successive general conferences, he mentioned the need for cleaning up.[2]

He also spoke repeatedly of making a record of one's life. Almost everyone who remembers President Kimball associates him with the keeping of journals. He stressed the sacred nature of journal writing and testified that journals and family histories strengthen family ties. People heeded his advice.[3]

He set the example. He once remarked: "There have been times when I have been so tired at the end of a day that the effort could hardly be managed, but I am so grateful that I have not let slip away from me and my posterity those things that needed to be recorded. People who care nothing for the past usually have no thought for the future and are selfish in the way they use the present."[4]

---

2. From October 1974 through October 1979, he missed mentioning the topic only once, in April 1977. These were not sermons but reminders.

3. In a sample of two hundred families identified by their stake presidents as among the "best" families, 25 percent of fathers, 45 percent of mothers, and 48 percent of children wrote in a journal "regularly."

4. Spencer said that he had "managed to fill seventy-eight large volumes which are my personal journal," but something less than half of this would consist of journal entries; the rest is sermons and notes for sermons, all in bulging two-inch loose-leaf binders. In Spencer's last years his secretary, Arthur Haycock, kept his journal. It thus became less a record of personal thoughts and actions and more a listing of meetings and appointments.

On several occasions President Kimball criticized cruelty to animals and hunting for sport. "I had a father who was infuriated if he saw a man beating a balky horse, or kicking his dog, or starving his other animals." He told of childhood friends who killed birds "with their flippers and their slings," while he was deterred by the Primary song that urged, "Don't kill the little birds/That sing on bush and tree." And he quoted Joseph F. Smith's statement: "I do not believe any man should kill animals or birds unless he needs them for food. . . . I think it is wicked for men to thirst in their souls to kill."[5] Those who were part of the hunting culture were offended, and the Church Public Communications Office issued a statement, approved by President Kimball, stating that the Church did not officially condemn all hunting.[6]

Spencer's repeated emphasis on gardens reflected not only the pleasure he took in Camilla's diligent gardening of vegetables and flowers in their small backyard, but also the social and spiritual dimensions of working the soil: "Even if the tomato you eat is a $2.00 tomato," he urged the Saints, "it will bring satisfaction anyway and remind us all of the law of the harvest, which is relentless in life. We do reap what we sow. Even if the plot of soil you cultivate, plant, and harvest is a small one, it brings [you] closer to nature."[7]

When a bishop in Tennessee asked Spencer, "President, tell me about your garden," Camilla spoke up: "That's *my* garden."

Arthur Haycock observed that the Kimball garden benefited from a fair division of labor. "She plants and tends it. He eats from it—and gives advice."

Spencer recorded with obvious pleasure in his 1977 journal:

---

5. A memorable Pat Bagley cartoon showed a smiling deer reading to a glum hunter from a book titled *Conference Report,* and saying, "And this is the part I like best."

6. The *Church News* reported: "The decision to hunt and fish . . . is left to the discretion of the individual. However, many clear guidelines . . . are designed to stop the unnecessary and wasteful slaughter of animals and birds, not to define public policy on predator control and game management." The language is clearly not Spencer's. Some listeners mailed President Kimball their hunting licenses. But it appears that his preaching had little general effect because deer hunting in Utah in the next three years actually increased substantially. The Deseret Land and Livestock Ranch in northern Utah, acquired by the Church in 1983, sold permits for hunting of trophy bull elk to the extent its elk herd had to be thinned. If President Kimball knew of the practice he did not act to stop it.

7. Spencer W. Kimball said, "We deal with many things which are thought to be not so spiritual; but all things are spiritual with the Lord."

Camilla in her rose garden.

"Nearly all of the dinner came from our garden—tomatoes, spinach, squash, string beans. Besides these we had our own potatoes, carrots, and . . . apricots in great quantity and apples. Camilla's garden has done very well, and we have followed our own advice."

11

CONCERN FOR DOCTRINE

"When we're able to understand it the Lord will tell us."

"DOCTRINE" IS NOT AN EASY TERM to define. As used here, it means official teaching drawn from the scriptures and from the teachings of modern prophets. A few doctrines are settled, such as the doctrine that Christ atoned for the sins of all mankind. But surrounding this doctrine are issues open to interpretation, such as exactly what the atonement means, how it operates, and how far it reaches.[1] The Bible is accepted as "the word of God as far as it is translated correctly" (Articles of Faith 1:8)—and also as far as it is interpreted correctly.

Church history shows that General Authorities frequently declare, clarify, refine, and qualify interpretations of doctrine, but these statements generally constitute only informed opinion. President Kimball spoke on a few issues that could properly be called doctrinal, sometimes expressing the view that a proposition urged by others is *not* doctrine.

ADAM-GOD THEORY

At October general conference in 1976, President Kimball stated formally:

---

1. Sociologist O. Kendall White identified the development of a neo-orthodoxy in Mormonism since World War I. This trend emphasizes Mormon doctrines—present since the earliest years of the Restoration—on the sovereignty of God (his omnipotence, omniscience, and omnipresence, and the concomitant contingency of humankind), on the natural depravity and carnality of human beings, and on salvation by grace. Joseph Smith's later theological developments, particularly in Nauvoo, stressed a more expansive definition of personhood, identified some limitations to which God is subject (for instance, he will not violate human agency), defined human nature as inherently good, and, while accepting that Christ's atonement affects universal salvation (meaning resurrection), explained that exaltation or glorification in an eternal status depends on merit. Both strands of doctrine have coexisted in LDS thought and authoritative teachings.

"We warn you against the dissemination of doctrines which are not according to the scriptures and which are alleged to have been taught by some of the General Authorities of past generations. Such, for instance, is the Adam-God theory. We denounce that theory and hope that everyone will be cautioned against this and other kinds of false doctrine."

Brigham Young had taught a confusing concept that involved Adam's status as a god, the father of men's spirits, and the literal father of Jesus. It is often asserted that Brigham Young was simply misunderstood by the conference reporter or made just a few references that have been taken out of context, but Elder McConkie acknowledged that Brigham Young did teach the Adam-God theory. He also noted that the theory was "out of harmony with the gospel."[2]

President Kimball sought by authoritative statement to put further speculation to rest.

Organic Evolution

A long-standing issue that has troubled most conservative religions since the mid-nineteenth century is whether God used the mechanism of organic evolution to create the species that populate the world. Despite much urging, the Church has never taken a definitive position on the matter.[3] In 1979 President Kimball met with the Presiding Bishopric (Victor L. Brown, H. Burke Peterson, and J. Richard Clarke) and Elder McConkie to discuss a proposal that on the Church's sesquicentennial the First Presidency publish an official statement on the creation and evolution.[4] But after extended discussion, they decided in 1980 not to issue any such official statement. According to Elder Ezra Taft Benson's grandson Stephen, Elder Benson had strong personal anti-evolution views but "acknowledged that 'the Lord may not have revealed enough to create unanimity among the Brethren.'" Elder Benson

---

2. Precisely what he believed is difficult to pin down.

3. In 1909 a formal First Presidency statement identified Adam as the "primal parent of the race." The statement did not address the uniformitarian hypothesis, the age of the earth, or the mutability of species. A First Presidency letter in 1931 said that on the existence of pre-Adamites the Church had no doctrine and the answer was not essential to salvation.

4. Counselors Peterson and Clarke have no recollection of the meeting or proposal.

reportedly said any statement would be "unwise" and serve only to "widen differences."

But in June 1980 Elder McConkie spoke to Brigham Young University and called it heresy to believe in organic evolution. In June 1982 he restated his position in the *Ensign,* and in the October 1984 general conference he criticized evolutionary theory.[5] In December 1984, Elder Benson spoke in a similar manner. These statements, without any public expression of a different view by other leaders, gave the mistaken impression that the Church had a position on the issue, despite the continuing hands-off position of the First Presidency and the Twelve.[6]

As President, Spencer said nothing directly about evolution or other science. He did say at the 1975 general women's meeting: "Man became a living soul—mankind, male and female. . . . We don't know exactly how their coming into this world happened, and when we're able to understand it the Lord will tell us." In family discussions he was noncommittal. He tended to leave such questions aside, considering them relatively unimportant and distracting from the task of building the kingdom.

ONE TRUE CHURCH

Church members sometimes use the scriptural phrase "the only true and living church" (D&C 1:30) to justify their disapproval of other religions. However, in February 1978 the First Presidency countered this inclination by issuing a broadly inclusive statement:

"The great religious leaders of the world such as Mohammed, Confucius, and the Reformers, as well as philosophers including Socrates, Plato, and others, received a portion of God's light. Moral

---

5. Bruce R. McConkie said, "There is no salvation in a system of religion . . . that assumes man is the end product of evolution and so was not subject to a fall. True believers know that this earth and man and all forms of life were created in an Edenic, or paradisiacal, state in which there was no mortality, no procreation, no death."

6. William E. Evenson, "Evolution," in *Encyclopedia of Mormonism,* cites principally the Heber J. Grant First Presidency's instructions to the General Authorities in 1931, "Leave geology, biology, archaeology, and anthropology, no one of which has to do with the salvation of the souls of mankind, to scientific research, while we magnify our calling in the realm of the Church. . . . Upon one thing we should all be able to agree, namely, that . . . 'Adam is the primal parent of our race.'" At BYU, students usually assumed that the Church rejects evolution as a means of creation. Since 1992, the university has made available to students at the Harold B. Lee Library a packet of information reflecting the varied views of past Church leaders and the absence of an official position on most aspects of the issue. The issue has raised less controversy since that time.

Joining in a Methodist Christmas celebration, 1975.

truths were given to them by God to enlighten whole nations and to bring a higher level of understanding to individuals."

Some had a significant portion of God's light and exemplify the promise that God will give to all peoples sufficient knowledge to help them on their way to eternal salvation, either in this life or in the life to come.

Although only pre-Restoration figures were named, there is no reason to think the statement would not apply to non-Christians and non-Mormons today. To receive "a portion of God's light" does not require that no greater truth was available—Mohammed knew Christianity yet did not embrace it. These words encourage tolerance for those who embrace such truth as is available to them and also for those who embrace as much of the available truth as they are able to understand. The formulation makes possible better relations with the good people of other religions. In 1978 President Kimball also urged local LDS leaders to work with other religious groups to achieve mutual goals.[7]

---

7. During the Kimball administration and since then Latter-day Saints have actively cooperated with other church groups in fighting pornography, abortion, and gambling. This trend has continued and even intensified in more recent times with interfaith teens working together and the

During President Kimball's administration, the Church sought to improve relations with other churches. For example, when Bishop Joseph Lennox Federal retired as bishop of the Roman Catholic diocese of Salt Lake City, President Kimball hosted a luncheon in his honor in the elegant banquet hall on the twenty-sixth floor of the Church Office Building. Attending were many LDS leaders as well as the newly appointed Catholic bishop, William Keith Weigand, and three other Catholic officials.

Relations between the LDS and RLDS churches improved as well. New bridges were being built by historians, especially genial Leonard J. Arrington, LDS Church Historian, and his RLDS counterpart, Richard P. Howard. The Mormon History Association created a meeting ground for many people with interest in the common origin of the two churches.

When President Kimball called Edward A. Johnson as president of the Missouri Independence Mission, he gave him a special charge to establish friendly relations with RLDS leaders. When Johnson learned that President Kimball planned to come to Independence in September 1978 to dedicate a stake center, he suggested to RLDS president Wallace B. Smith that the two presidents meet. The invitation was immediately extended and accepted. After a pleasant dinner, Spencer queried wistfully, "Arthur [Haycock], why has it taken us a hundred years to do that?"

BLOOD ATONEMENT

In 1977, after a hiatus of ten years without executions in the United States, the state of Utah executed convicted murderer Gary Gilmore by firing squad. Utah was nearly the only state in the union with the option for using this method of execution.[8] The Gilmore case renewed discussion about "blood atonement," the idea stated by Brigham Young

Church's formation of alliances with other churches to resist the approval of same-sex marriage legislation. The *Church Handbook of Instructions* says, "Much that is inspiring, noble, and worthy of the highest respect is found in many other faiths. . . . Be sensitive and respectful toward the beliefs of others and avoid giving offense."

8. Idaho Statutes §19–2716 provides for use of the firing squad if lethal injection is for some reason impractical. Oklahoma State Statutes §22–1014 allows the firing squad if both injection and electrocution are held unconstitutional.

and others that for serious crimes complete repentance included a willingness to have one's blood shed by constituted authority.[9]

The *Utah Law Review*, considering a manuscript tying capital punishment in Utah to LDS doctrine, asked the First Presidency for an authoritative explanation of blood atonement. The First Presidency asked Bruce R. McConkie to respond. He explained that references to blood atonement (leaving aside the atonement of Christ), if understood as applying to modern circumstances, "do *not* . . . represent the official stand of the Church." He said statements by Brigham Young and others to that effect referred to "*a theoretical principle* that operated in *ages past.* . . . [T]his doctrine can only operate in a day when there is no separation of Church and State and when the power to take life is vested in the ruling theocracy as was the case in the days of Moses." Capital punishment, he wrote, "executed by the lawfully appointed [state] officer," is not contrary to Church doctrine, and doctrine also "does not dictate any preferred method of execution." He expressed his own opinion that references to the "shedding of man's blood in legal executions [is] a figurative expression which means [only] the taking of life."[10]

---

9. Involuntary shedding of blood by vigilantes would be a distortion of the teaching.

10. In 1980 the Utah legislature abolished hanging as a means of execution and substituted lethal injection. The prisoner now has the option of injection or the firing squad. Although the Church has taken no position on the retention or abolition of capital punishment, the overwhelming majority of Utah citizens have favored its availability. The Utah legislature has prospectively banned the firing squad.

HERESY

President Kimball was not doctrinaire, and he felt a need to intervene in doctrinal matters only when he saw strong statements of personal opinion as being divisive. Elder McConkie's talk at BYU on "The Seven Deadly Heresies" implied he had authority to define heresy. Among other things, he denounced as heretical acceptance of organic evolution, a belief that God progresses in knowledge,[11] and the idea that progression from kingdom to kingdom in the afterlife is possible.[12] President Kimball responded to the uproar by calling Elder McConkie in to discuss the talk. As a consequence, Elder McConkie revised the talk for publication so as to clarify that he was stating personal views. As it appeared in *1980 BYU Speeches of the Year,* he had changed "we" to "I" and added "my reasoning causes me to conclude" and "every person must choose for himself what he will believe." But there was no corrective public criticism of the talk.

SCRIPTURES

Development of doctrinal understanding begins with the scriptures. In 1979, for the first time the Church published its own edition of the Bible. A new edition of the triple combination followed in 1981. This major project began during President Joseph Fielding Smith's tenure, but as acting president of the Council of the Twelve, Spencer appointed the committee and called specialists to assist them. The project moved forward rapidly, in part because of his personal interest.[13]

---

11. B. H. Roberts in 1911 wrote: "And is it too bold a thought that with this progress, even for the Mightiest, new thoughts, and new vistas may appear, inviting to new adventures and enterprises that will yield new experiences, advancement, and enlargement even for the Most High?" George Q. Cannon also said, "There is progress for our father and for our Lord Jesus. There is no such thing as standing still in the eternal work of our God. It is endless progress, progressing from one degree of knowledge to another degree. Thus the children of men will be continually exalted and drawn up toward God."

12. George Q. Cannon said, "There are different degrees of glory. Some attain to a more exalted glory. They must help those who are lower to rise up to their plane. Then there is another degree below them, and they must labor to lift those who are lower than they. Thus we can go on, every man in his sphere and in his glory endeavoring to lift up others to his height, until eternity will be filled with our labors in this direction, progressing from one degree of glory to another, without end, because there is no end to eternity."

13. The projected four to five years extended to ten years before the final product was in hand. Elder Thomas S. Monson oversaw the technical aspects, including the new footnote style, which began with new superscript letters in every verse. Elder McConkie oversaw the text and references, including new chapter headings; Elder Packer supervised the proofreading and helped

The Bible edition included a new footnoting system, a dictionary, and a 600-page topical guide that provided references to all of the standard works.[14] Alternative readings and short interpolations from the Joseph Smith Translation or inspired revision appeared in footnotes; lengthier passages appeared in an appendix. These additions elevated the Joseph Smith alternate text from something worth considering to a more nearly authoritative status.[15]

For more than a hundred years the Church had been wary of using the Inspired Version seriously because Joseph Smith never finished it and its exact status was somewhat uncertain. For instance, it was not clear whether scripture verses he did not change should be considered approved or as just not yet fully considered. Were changes he made final or only tentative?[16] The Bible Dictionary characterizes these changes as "interesting," a "fruitful source," and "an invaluable aid to biblical interpretation and understanding."[17] But, it says, the Joseph Smith Translation is "not the official Bible of the Church."

In October 1982 general conference, Elder Packer announced that the Church was adding to the Book of Mormon a subtitle—"Another Testament of Jesus Christ."[18] It was hoped the extended name would help counter accusations that Mormons are not Christians because they reject the traditional idea of the Trinity. Elder Packer expressed his view

---

generally. The Bible Aids Committee, appointed in 1970, consisted of three apostles and five others: Daniel H. Ludlow, William James Mortimer, Ellis G. Rasmussen, Robert J. Matthews, and Robert Patch. The committee's original charge soon expanded to republication of all the scriptures, as reflected by its name change to the Scriptures Publications Committee. The committee met monthly for ten years without fail. The apostles reported committee recommendations to the First Presidency, which was involved in all decisions. Elder McConkie proposed including in the Pearl of Great Price the *Lectures on Faith,* which had been printed in successive editions of the Doctrine and Covenants from 1835 to 1921, but that suggestion was not approved. Several studies had recently concluded that Sidney Rigdon was the principal author of the lectures.

14. The Topical Guide had been published separately in 1977. The indexes and other study aids took 852 pages, more than half as many pages as the Biblical text and footnotes.

15. While not strictly a matter of doctrine, the First Presidency stated on May 22, 1992, that the King James translation of the Bible is to be used as the standard Bible text in LDS meetings. In practice, therefore, the word choices made by the King James translators are semi-authoritative, even though other translations may at times be closer to the letter or spirit of the source documents.

16. Robert J. Matthews deserves special credit as the primary scholar of the Joseph Smith Translation.

17. The JST footnotes serve as frequent reminders that Mormons are wary of the biblical literalism that some other religious groups espouse.

18. Heber Wolsey's suggestion of this subtitle got approval in record time.

that "as the generations roll on, this [the publication of the new editions of the Book of Mormon and Bible] will be regarded, in the perspective of history, as the crowning achievement in the administration of President Spencer W. Kimball."

The new 1981 triple combination included three additions to the Doctrine and Covenants. Section 137 is Joseph Smith's 1836 vision that his brother Alvin, though not baptized a Latter-day Saint, would gain the celestial kingdom because if he had known of the restored gospel he would have accepted it.[19] Section 138 contains President Joseph F. Smith's vision shortly before his death in 1918 about the redemption of the dead by accepting the gospel in the spirit world.[20] These two revelations had been canonized by general conference vote in April 1976 and were included at that time in the Pearl of Great Price.

The third addition is "Official Declaration 2," the 1978 announcement of a revelation extending the priesthood to all worthy males. It too had first been added to the Pearl of Great Price but was moved to the new Doctrine and Covenants, where it joined Wilford Woodruff's 1890 Manifesto withdrawing Church support for new plural marriages, now renamed "Official Declaration 1."

---

19. This is not inconsistent with a requirement of vicarious baptism.

20. Although the Presidency and Twelve voted in 1918 to accept the revelation, they did not present it to the conference. In 1963 Spencer referred to the "remarkable revelation on the redemption of the dead."

12

TEACHING MOMENTS, ONE-ON-ONE

"You've never converted anybody in your life . . . and . . . you never will."

PRESIDENT KIMBALL'S TEACHING came not only by speaking to groups, but also through human interactions one person at a time, sometimes to members and sometimes to prospective members.

A relative once confided that when she and her husband were having a hard time paying tithing, Spencer helped simply by telling a story:

"A few years ago a man came into my office and said, 'Bro. Kimball I have just sold a grocery store that I have owned for a few years to a big chain grocery company. I have made quite a bit of money and I want you to know that if the Church wants it, it is all for the Church.'

"I said to him, 'We appreciate your wonderful attitude, but right now the law of the Church is tithing. If you pay this honestly, the Lord is satisfied.'

" . . . The good brother said, 'I think I have a talent for making money and if the Lord doesn't require it I know of some good subdivision land out in [Holladay], . . . and I feel that I'd like to invest the money there.' A few years later he came . . . again and said, 'Bro. Kimball, . . . I have sold the subdivision land and I have made a good profit. I want you to know that if the Church wants it, it is theirs.' Again I told him that the law of the Church is still tithing. . . . This is one man's attitude, . . . [but it] isn't an isolated case. As I travel over the Church the numbers of such men and women amaze me. They come into the Church office building often and make such offers."[1]

---

1. President Kimball's position gave him reason to know of the generosity of many people. He attended a banquet for Guy Anderson, an Arizona friend who had given BYU a multimillion dollar mining property. Others contributed cash to Church programs, especially the missionary

In 1978, J. Brent Haymond, a member of the Church and successful businessman, shook President Kimball's hand in San Diego. President Kimball looked intently into his eyes and said, "I know you are a great man. I feel your spirit." That one comment left Haymond with a feeling of serious responsibility to measure up to the capacity a prophet had seen in him.

Haymond was also present with President Kimball's party as they waited on the airport apron for the connecting flight to arrive. One of the first debarking passengers was a young woman, and when she saw a group of men in blue suits looking like bodyguards, she asked Haymond, "Is there someone important getting off the plane?"

"Not to my knowledge," he answered, "but there is a very important person who will be boarding the plane. His name is President Spencer W. Kimball, the President of The Church of Jesus Christ of Latter-day Saints."

"I used to be a member of that Church," she commented. "I married someone outside the Church, and eventually quit going."

Haymond asked her name and said, "Come with me. I want you to meet someone." He then took her to President Kimball and said, "President Kimball, I would like you to meet Shirley. She says she used to be a member of our church."

Spencer took both her hands, looked kindly into her eyes, and told her she must not forget that she was still a part of the Church. The Lord wanted her to be a member and that we didn't have any "used-to-be" members. He also expressed his love for her.

She explained how she drifted away from the Church. Lovingly but firmly, he asked that she take time on Sunday to go to an LDS ward while she was visiting in San Diego. She agreed and departed.

Then President Kimball turned to Haymond and said, "What you did is just the way to magnify your calling. Remember to seek people like that out so that they can return to the kingdom."

He taught two people in one brief exchange.

Once as President Kimball entered a missionary meeting in West Berlin he overheard one missionary comment to another, "Today I

---

fund. Near Christmas two brothers gave him $25,000; another man gave $40,000; a high priest group gave $10,000, and a handicapped girl brought President Kimball two large piggy banks full of change—$137.

Greeting boys in the South Pacific.

converted two people to the Church and they're going to be baptized this next week."

Spencer put his hand on the startled missionary's shoulder and said,

"Young man, I couldn't help overhearing you say you had converted two members to the Church today. I want you to know that you've never converted anybody in your life. And what's more, you never will. Conversion is an act of the Spirit and you're only an instrument in the hands of the Lord to bring this person into acceptance of the gospel."

Then Spencer hugged him, kissed him on the cheek, and expressed appreciation for his good efforts.

On a trip to Tokyo, President Kimball taught humility and forgiveness to local leader Yoshihiko Kikuchi by example. Church leaders in Salt Lake had encouraged an American who served a mission in Japan to return to the country and start a business. The former missionary used referrals from Brother Kikuchi to start his company, but the poorly grounded venture failed. It nearly ruined Brother Kikuchi, who faced a lawsuit simply for introducing the American to his business associates.

As Spencer and Brother Kikuchi walked in the Imperial Palace gardens, Spencer took his arm and whispered, "Please forgive us and please forgive me. . . . We shouldn't have encouraged him to go back to Japan after his mission. Won't you forgive me?"

President Kimball often taught by asking questions. In interviewing a missionary he might say, "If you were writing a letter home to a younger brother, what would you tell him, to help him to become a qualified missionary?" or "Elder, what are the best qualities of your companion?" He asked Bruce Hafen, after he had been president of the Church's Ricks College for a year, "Well, Bruce, do the people up in Idaho love you?"

MISSIONARY MOMENTS

In May 1977 when Paul Dunn, who was responsible for military relations, brought a general to meet with President Kimball, the obviously well-prepared military official asked many factual questions about the Church, Brigham Young, and the pioneer trek. Spencer finally queried, "Aren't you going to ask the most important question?"

"I'm not sure I understand."

"Have you ever asked yourself why these people did what they did?"

"No," said the general, taken somewhat aback. "I really haven't thought about that."

After rehearsing the mobbing of Nauvoo, the crossing of the Mississippi on the ice, and the burial of children who died on the way West, Spencer told the general, "People don't do that to impress someone. They do it because they believe."

According to Elder Dunn, the general asked after they left the meeting, "What was it that I felt in there?"

"You were sitting with a prophet," answered Dunn simply.

"How do I keep that feeling?"

"Join us."

President Kimball could be very direct in his approach. In 1975 in Bogota, Colombia, when an airline representative met him at the airport, Spencer extended his hand and said, "Young man, I hope the next time I shake your hand you're a member of this church." The man looked him in the eye and replied, "Sir, so do I!" President Kimball then turned to the mission president and secured a commitment "to teach the man the gospel."

On another trip a reporter and his wife saw a clean-cut young man in his early twenties come down an airplane aisle and stop by President Kimball, who reached up and pulled him close. Twice during the conversation, President Kimball reached up and kissed him on the cheek.

The young man's eyes glistened with tears. Later, the reporter's wife struck up a conversation with the young man: "I suppose you're LDS."

"No," he said, "I'm Roman Catholic."

Surprised, she asked, "What did you talk about?"

"He asked me to join the Church."

"Are you going to do it?"

"Well, it is kind of hard to refuse what a prophet of God asks you to do."

After an area conference in Copenhagen in August 1976, Spencer and other General Authorities went to the Vor Frue Kirke (Our Lady's Chapel) to see the Thorvaldsen statues of Christ and his apostles. The building was closed, but a caretaker, a man of about sixty, allowed them in. As they left, he stood by the door to let them out. President Kimball shook hands, expressed his appreciation, and explained earnestly, "These statues are of dead apostles." He said, "You are in the presence of living apostles," indicating Elders Tanner, Monson, and Packer in his party. Then pointing to Elders Robert D. Hales and Rex E. Pinegar, he added, "Here are Seventies like those spoken of in the New Testament." He presented the custodian a Book of Mormon in Danish and bore witness of the Prophet Joseph. The custodian, moved to tears, said as they left the church, "Today I have been in the presence of servants of God."

Later that same month, after five area conferences, members of President Kimball's party were exhausted. On a bus headed to the Zurich airport, everyone relaxed except Spencer, who moved forward and sat on a low platform by the driver. As the bus sped along, Spencer engaged the driver in a conversation with Spencer's broken German and the driver's broken English. Spencer had singled out the only person on the bus not already converted. At the airport, President Kimball introduced the driver to the mission president and assured himself that missionaries would follow up.

In May 1980, Spencer agreed to travel in a small plane from Burbank, California, to San Diego to see a seriously injured stake president. Arrangements had been made for him to go directly to the tarmac without going through a security check. But as President Kimball and his party approached a door leading to the tarmac, a security guard, well over six feet tall, stood at the door with his arms folded. The pilot showed his airline badge and said, "We have permission to go out this way."

"Not with me, you don't!"

President Kimball reached out his hand and said, "My name is Spencer Kimball. What is yours?" The man unfolded his arms. President Kimball said, "What do you know about the Mormon Church? And would you like to know more?" The man relented, and he opened the door for them. President Kimball then turned to one of the stake presidents accompanying them, "Would you see that the missionaries make contact with this man?" When the pilot inquired some time later, he learned that the security guard had joined the Church and was then president of an elders quorum.

Spencer set an example of diligence as a member-missionary. He said that the responsibility to teach the gospel was one we "cannot escape. I accept my own part of that responsibility."

WITNESSING TO THE WORLD

MISSIONARY WORK

13

A Vision of Worldwide Missionary Work

"Do you know of any reason why I should send my sons but that you shouldn't send yours?"

ONE OF THE MAIN THEMES CHARACTERIZING President Kimball's administration is missionary work. As a newly ordained President, he made his first deep impression on the Church with his stirring calls for renewed vigor in this effort. Then in 1978 his dramatic revelation extending priesthood ordination to all worthy men opened new doors for missionary effort. Repeatedly, Spencer identified taking the gospel to all the world as one of three fundamental tasks of the Church.

Elder Ezra Taft Benson identified missionary work as President Kimball's central theme, and President Marion G. Romney concurred:

"I think there has never been a president of the Church who has moved the Church in missionary work as has President Kimball. His statements to 'lengthen your stride' and 'quicken your pace,' and his emphasis that 'every worthy young man should go on a mission,' are quoted and implemented from Alaska to South Africa, and from northern Norway to Invercargill in south New Zealand."

The primary effects of missionary service have always been two-fold—converting people to the gospel of Christ and giving missionaries experiences that mature them and strengthen their commitment to the gospel and the Church. Spencer told a neighbor that if a choice had to be made he thought a mission offered more value than a college education; it created a partnership with the Lord that affected the whole of one's life. He renewed his urgent plea to regional representatives several times, asking that they pour ever greater energy into missionary efforts.

His vision of the potential sweep of missionary work staggered his listeners:

"Suppose that South Korea with its . . . 7,500 members were to take care of its own proselyting needs and thus release to go into North Korea and possibly to Russia the hundreds who now go from the States to Korea.

"If Japan could furnish its own 1,000 missionaries and then eventually 10,000 more for Mongolia and China, then we would begin to fulfill the vision.

". . . Suppose that the United States and Canada awakened to their real responsibility, sending thousands of missionaries to join [those from Latin America], going east and north so that . . . [Europe] could be covered.

"Great Britain . . . should join that army and all together the army of the west would move across Western Europe and Central Europe and Arab lands, and . . . join their efforts with the missionary army from the east to bring the gospel to millions in China and India and other populous countries of the world."[1]

---

1. President Kimball's hard push raised concerns among some leaders who saw it as unrealistic and overambitious. In an April 6, 1971, memo to the Missionary Executive Committee, he

In March 1978, he again articulated his hope for increased commitment to teaching the gospel. "How can we be satisfied," he queried the regional representatives, "with 100,000 converts out of four billion in the world who need the gospel? . . . I wonder if we are doing all we can. Are we complacent in our approach to teaching all the world? We have been proselyting now one hundred forty-four years. Are we prepared to lengthen our stride? To enlarge our vision?"

In 1976, when Church membership stood at little more than three million, he envisioned the day it would become twenty million: "Now if only one-half the membership of the Church became wholly involved and assum[ing] they brought into the Church one convert [each], in one year they would bring in some millions of new members. . . . That would grow to three million, to five million, to seven million, and on until we would . . . have 20 million people." The suggestion seemed almost incredible then, but in 2004 membership already stood at twelve million.

EXPANDING THE MISSIONARY FORCE

When Spencer became President, 17,000 missionaries were in the field. He called for more: "Every boy *ought* to go on a mission. There may be some who can't, but they *ought* to go on a mission. Every boy, and many girls, and many couples." But he also pointed out the need for preparation: "When I ask for more missionaries, I am not asking for more testimony-barren or unworthy missionaries. . . . They must be physically well, mentally well, spiritually well." An expanded force of well-prepared missionaries was critical to a worldwide effort. "I can see no good reason," he once commented, "why the Lord would open doors that we are not prepared to enter."

In keeping with his vision, training of new missionaries was stepped up. In 1976 at Brigham Young University, President Kimball dedicated a new Language Training Mission for all missionaries assigned to learn a

---

had proposed much the same: call more missionaries from foreign lands, support them as need be from the general missionary fund; open proselytizing in new countries. "The Lord would find ways to knock down . . . iron curtains and bamboo curtains" when we have done all we can to make it happen. President Kimball urged publication of a book that would show the growing international character of the Church, and Church historian Leonard Arrington recruited Spencer Palmer to write *The Expanding Church*.

continued on p.2

Giving some boys a dollar to start a mission savings fund.

new language.[2] In 1978 the facility was enlarged and renamed the Missionary Training Center; all missionaries, including those going to English-speaking missions, went there for training in language, culture, scripture, and teaching methods.[3] In 1977 the Church created the first Missionary Orientation Center outside the United States in São Paulo for training missionaries from South America. By President Kimball's death in November 1985, there were nine such training centers.[4]

Missionary work was a major theme with Spencer long before he became President. He had served for many years on the missionary committee. As an apostle, Spencer frequently called up from the congregation of a stake conference all twelve-year-old boys. After asking what they would be doing when they were twenty and receiving the right answer, he would give each a dollar (or its equivalent) to add to or start a mission fund. Spencer later heard from many of these boys, one of whom wrote:

---

2. Groundbreaking for the LTM occurred in 1974; President Kimball dedicated it in 1976. In 1976 an estimated fifty-five hundred missionaries received training in twenty-three languages. In 2001 forty-seven languages were being taught for eight to ten weeks, depending on the difficulty of the language.

3. In 1976 the cost for eight weeks ran $290 per person. Whereas the Missionary Home had offered training for four days, the MTC involved four weeks of training for missionaries going to English-speaking missions. Study at the MTC included language, culture, scripture, and teaching methods.

4. By 2000 there were fifteen such centers: one in the U.S., seven in Latin America (Mexico, Guatemala, Colombia, Peru, Chile, Argentina, Brazil), two in Europe (England, Spain), three in Asia (Korea, Japan, Philippines), one in New Zealand, and one in the Dominican Republic. There were seventeen in 2004.

"President Kimball, you came to our stake conference when I was just a boy. You shook my hand and asked if I was going to be a missionary, and how much I had in my missionary bank account. At the time I didn't have a missionary bank account. You gave me a dollar and told me that was for my mission. My dad took me to the bank the next day to open an account. I wasn't able to answer your question then, but now I can tell you I have more than $3,300 in my account that I have saved for my mission. And I still have the dollar you gave me. . . . Someday I plan to give that dollar to the first of our children to open a missionary bank account, with an explanation the dollar came to them from you through me."[5]

Spencer's efforts were not confined to public occasions. At a wedding breakfast for Rick and Helen Vernon, Spencer sat across from Rick's younger brother.

"Eric, are you planning to go on a mission?" Spencer asked.

"Yes."

Spencer slid a silver dollar across the table and said, "This is to start your mission fund."

When someone remarked on the great numbers of missionaries serving in the field, Spencer said, "I am thankful, but not impressed." He wanted Church members to move on to still higher levels rather than bask in the warmth of their achievement. Carlos E. Asay, executive director of the Missionary Department, recalled a chance meeting after the Church reached an all-time high of 20,000 full-time missionaries: "I happened to meet President Kimball in an elevator and thought he'd be interested in this information, so I told him. He smiled, and without hesitation said, 'Wonderful. Now double it.' Later, when we reached 25,000 missionaries, . . . he pulled me down and kissed me on the cheek, and said, 'Now double it.'"[6]

President Kimball's enthusiasm for missionary work played a significant role in swelling the missionary ranks. Although the increase

---

5. Beverly W. Coyl said, "When my youngest son was about 12, Pres. Kimball came to our stake conference in Santa Ana, California. He gave all the young men a dollar bill for [their] missionary fund. My son who doesn't go to church at this time still has his bill. I keep praying that he will use it for what it was given to him for."

6. Spencer meant only to encourage, not to set a specific goal. For example, a 1976 plan for three-year stake goals reminded, "Goals should not be set by Regional Representatives, but should be set by stake presidencies."

Married couples expanded the missionary corps.

reflected in part a natural growth in the number of young men of missionary age, the percentage of eligible young men who accepted mission calls also increased. When President Kimball came to office, 24 percent of those eligible were serving. During his administration, the percentage fluctuated between 25 and 30 percent.[7]

An important factor in this growth was President Kimball's emphasis on the responsibility of young men outside the United States to serve. At area conferences he sought to change the expectations of Mormon young men and their families and leaders, encouraging them to think seriously about the young men as potential missionaries.[8] He could state his message starkly. In Buenos Aires he said:

"Do you know of any reason why I should send my sons but that you shouldn't send yours? . . . This is a great nation and great people, and it is your responsibility to teach the gospel in these nations. When

---

7. A survey in the U.S. and Canada for 1991 showed that 32 percent of young Latter-day Saint men in those countries go on missions between ages nineteen and twenty-one, the same as in a 1982 survey. Among sixteen- and seventeen-year-olds, 55 percent said they planned to go; many of them ultimately did not, principally because they had "lifestyles at odds with Church standards" or had career plans they felt were incompatible with missionary service.

8. John H. Cox noted that "he also made arrangements through special missionary funds to finance those who felt they could not afford to go. . . . The sacrifices, the experiences, and the strengthening of testimonies resulting from missionary service has done more, in my opinion, than anything else to strengthen families and priesthood leadership in Great Britain."

you have sent all the boys from this area on missions [here], we can send all the North American missionaries to India, or China, or Russia, or somewhere else."[9]

Nations across the world were positioned to supply more missionaries because the Church had been actively discouraging the emigration of members to the United States since the 1950s. This position was again articulated by President Kimball in April 1974: "The First Presidency and the Twelve see great wisdom in the [concept of] multiple Zions, many gathering places where the Saints within their own culture and nation can act as a leaven in the building of the kingdom." He suggested a different, smaller-scale gathering: scattered Saints should, where feasible, move to larger cities within their own countries in order to hasten the development of stakes.

The multigenerational Latter-day Saint families that developed in non-English-speaking countries produced missionaries of particular effectiveness from within their communities.[10] During President Kimball's administration, the missionaries coming from outside the United States and Canada increased nine times, from 975 to 8,628.[11]

Growth in the numbers of missionaries slowed temporarily in 1982 when the missionary term for young men was shortened from two years to eighteen months. The shorter time could make missionary service more feasible for young men subject to compulsory military service or trying to complete college or vocational training. A shorter term also would reduce the financial burden on families and thus make service possible for more young men. The experiment, however, did not

---

9. Son Spence served in Canada (1936–38), Andy in New England (1946–48), and Ed in the Netherlands (1949–52). When the missionary papers came in for one of Spencer's grandsons, Spencer Mack, on signing the letter calling his namesake grandson to serve in Japan, Spencer added a postscript, "I'm proud of you. Grandpa." When Ed's daughter Mary reported to Spencer that she had completed the interviews with her bishop and stake president for her mission, he asked teasingly, "Have you asked *my* permission?"

10. Chapels rather than rented quarters created a sense of stability for Saints outside of the United States and Canada. The increasing availability of translated printed materials enhanced teaching. Church magazines appeared in sixteen languages. The seminary and institute programs, begun in Europe in 1970, helped keep young people active and prepared for participation in the full program of the Church.

11. Missionaries from outside the U.S. and Canada were reported as 975 at the end of 1973, 891 at the end of 1974, and already 1,326 by June 1975. In 1977, 15.2 percent of all missionaries were from outside the U.S. Ten years later it was 30.5 percent. Local missionaries (3,900 of 5,000) received some financial support from the Church.

significantly increase the number of new missionaries. Furthermore, the eighteen months ended just when missionaries were reaching the peak of their effectiveness, because of experience and improved language skills. Two-year terms resumed in January 1985.[12]

Spencer also encouraged young women to serve missions: "Many young women have a desire to serve a full-time mission, and they are also welcome in the Lord's service. This responsibility is not on them as it is on the elders, but they will receive rich blessings for their unselfish sacrifice."[13] The number of women missionaries grew and their percentage of the missionary force increased from 6 percent in 1970 to 13 percent in 1979.[14]

In 1974 only about 320 older couples were serving missions. President Kimball chided, "We older people, who have been retired . . . have found an easy way to satisfy our . . . consciences. . . . We will send our boys, we say." But all older people, he noted, have the responsibility of serving if they are able, and "hundreds of thousands of Latter-day Saints are able." By 1980 about 1,000 couples were serving.[15]

In addition to urging more young men and women and older couples to serve full-time missions, President Kimball reiterated the pleas of his predecessors that all Church members personally accept missionary responsibility. Each member, he declared, should bring a friend into the Church. During President Kimball's administration,

---

12. Elders called for eighteen months were given the option to extend for six months. When missionaries were expected to learn languages in the mission field, the standard term of service had been two years for elders going to English-speaking missions, but two and a half years for those going to most foreign language missions and three years for those learning the more difficult Asian languages. When missionaries began learning languages in the MTC, their mission terms became uniformly two years.

13. President Hinckley in October 1997 said, "We need some young women. They perform a remarkable work. . . . I certainly do not wish to say or imply that their services are not wanted, [but] the First Presidency and the Council of the Twelve are united in saying to our young sisters that they are not under obligation to go on missions."

14. In the nineteenth century married women had sometimes served with their husbands, but only a few single women served regular proselytizing missions before the end of that century. The numbers remained small through World War II, even though during the wartime year of 1944, women missionaries outnumbered men. Women accounted for about 8 percent to 20 percent of all missionaries set apart during years in the 1930s. During the World War II era (1940–46), the percentages were much higher. After the war (1947 to 1961) the percentage of women varied between 5 percent and 15 percent, except for the Korean War years, when the percentage rose as high as 23 percent. In 2001 they made up about 16 percent of the total missionary force.

15. In 2001 couples made up about 9 percent of the missionary force.

Missionaries teaching an investigator.

members were given the additional responsibility before a referral was made of ascertaining that their friends were willing to receive a missionary visit.

The missionary program under President Kimball drew admiration for its scope and effectiveness. In April 1977, when he and Marion G. Romney were attending a stake conference in Fillmore, Utah, the White House operator tracked down President Kimball. But he was at the pulpit speaking, so President Romney took the call from U.S. President Jimmy Carter, who was preparing to speak at a Baptist convention about missionary work. He asked many questions about the Mormon program: How many missionaries? What salary do they receive? How long do they serve? Where do they come from? Where are they sent? He complimented the Church on an inspired program and asked that he be sent additional information.[16]

---

16. The Church made up an eighteen-page booklet answering the president's questions: Why, who, how long, finances, where, how called, what message, how to teach, who to teach, how trained, languages, supervision, success. President Carter had his own experience witnessing as a short-term Baptist missionary.

The Tabernacle Choir singing at the Lincoln Memorial.

SETTING MISSIONARY GOALS

Spencer encouraged missionaries to boost their effort and to baptize more, but he also told mission leaders to focus on high-quality, enduring conversions, not just on numbers of baptisms. He was aware of a period when many missions set up sports programs to attract investigators and baptized young people who had little understanding of what being a member of the Church entailed. The retention rate was abysmal, and the burden on local leaders to account for the numerous inadequately converted youth had a deadening effect.[17] The Church later deleted thousands of these names from its membership rolls.

President Kimball instructed mission presidents not to set baptism goals or quotas for missionaries. They might set mission-wide goals and encourage missionaries to set goals for themselves, but the presidents

---

17. Richard D. Poll describes President Moyle's encouragement of high-expectation proselytizing and his later concern about excesses. Spencer's journal from the late 1960s speaks of "hundreds of . . . improper baptisms of 1961 and 1962," "not all bad . . . there will be some salvage," but he clearly thought the results disastrous overall. In Britain there were "many thousands of inactive boys and girls who . . . came into the Church in 1961, 1962 and early 1963, through the so-called 'baseball baptisms.' . . . It is the screen behind which nearly all the leaders [making excuses for the low levels of activity] hide. Every time a suggestion is offered for improvement in any field, this army of inactives and 'lost' persons becomes the reason [for inaction]."

should not put undue pressures on those in their charge. A January 1976 letter from President Kimball and his counselors scotched a rumor that the First Presidency had called on missionaries to increase convert baptisms by a specified percentage:

"We have learned through experience that the use of such an arbitrary goal often leads to faulty teaching, done merely to achieve the goal, rather than to bring understanding and, hopefully, salvation to those being taught. This counsel is not intended to minimize the need to accelerate the pace and intensity of missionary work."[18]

Spencer wished to avoid the other extreme, as well:

"When we expressed some concern about many of these [sports club] baptisms, the pendulum swung the other way, all the way across, and there were many mission presidents who came to feel, mistakenly, that they should never discuss baptism with investigators. . . . We are not opposed to goals. We . . . expect . . . missionaries to set their own goals, and make them high enough to challenge their very best efforts, and work to achieve them."[19]

EXPANDING MISSIONARY TOOLS

When missionaries enter new countries there usually is no literature available in the native language. When President Kimball took office, investigators could read the full text of the Book of Mormon in only twenty-five languages. Just one translation of the Book of Mormon had been completed in the previous six years,[20] and on average each translation took about four years.

Beginning four years after President Kimball took office, full or partial new Book of Mormon translations averaged about four a year. Partial translations included major selections from the book, amounting to about 30 percent of the full text.[21] By the end of the Kimball

---

18. Excessively high goals can lead to cynicism or to overzealousness, as in "excessive or lengthy fasting," about which missionaries had to be warned.

19. Spencer concerned himself also with overreaction of some missionaries who were so worried about investigators' "complete" understanding that they unduly delayed baptisms. Numbers of converts declined, and missionary discouragement set in. In Guatemala from 1967 to 1978 average annual growth was only 1 percent, while from 1978 to 1990 the average rate was about 20 percent, after which the rate plunged again to less than 4 percent.

20. The pattern had been roughly one translation every five years since 1900.

21. In 1985, near the end of President Kimball's term, at least some basic teaching materials were available in ninety-six languages, used by 76 percent of the world's people. The Doctrine and

administration in 1985, the Book of Mormon or substantial portions of it were available in seventy-eight languages.[22]

Missionary work tended to be done in the cities. President Kimball proposed in 1974 that radio broadcasts, inexpensive transistor radios, and audio and videocassette players might one day open doors in rural areas, to be followed by the in-person testimony of missionaries, but this idea remains largely unfulfilled.

The Church occasionally organized missionary programs using notable LDS athletes and entertainers to draw a crowd. More than 19,000 people, two-thirds of them non-Mormons, turned out at Cleveland Coliseum in January 1976 for a special program on the Word of Wisdom called "What Makes Mormons Run?" In addition to the presence of President Kimball, noted Mormon athletes Vernon Law, Harmon Killebrew, and Marvin Bateman, politician George Romney, and astronaut Don Lind helped attract the large crowd. President Kimball delivered a message about the favorable consequences of living God's laws, particularly the Word of Wisdom.[23]

During this visit, Donald E. Kimball, a distant non-Mormon cousin, tagged along. As he accompanied Spencer and Arthur to the airport, Donald offered his highest praise: "Your church should make my cousin Spencer a saint." Spencer, sitting in the front seat, turned and responded, "Nobody can make me a saint. I have to do that for myself!"[24]

Wanting all to have equal opportunity to hear the gospel, he asked Elder LeGrand Richards to review what was being done to carry the gospel to the Jewish people. He was told that a special program

---

Covenants was available in twenty-seven languages. New languages were being added at about seven per year.

22. The twelve years before the Kimball administration produced four full translations; the twelve Kimball years produced eleven full translations and thirty-eight "selections"; and the twelve years that followed produced seven full translations and eighteen "selections." If allowance is made for time lag the disparity is even greater.

There had been only ten translations of the Doctrine and Covenants between 1851 and 1968, but seven more occurred between 1977 and 1984.

23. Eighteen thousand, half of them non-Mormons, attended; 378 families requested missionary discussions. In May 1977, the Kimballs flew to Louisiana to participate in another such program, "The Family Is Forever," attracting twelve thousand.

24. As an indication of Spencer W. Kimball's correspondence, his files include carbon copies of thirty-four letters to this man between January 1973 and January 1980.

developed for them had been discontinued.[25] Shortly afterward, in April 1975, Spencer commented to the regional representatives that he had never understood the reason for stopping the work among the Jews. He added, "This does not mean a proposed mission to Jerusalem. It means that we go to New York, Philadelphia, Chicago, and the other cities and spread the gospel to the Jews as we do to the Lamanites, as we do to the Gentiles, and give them an opportunity to hear the gospel."[26]

In November 1975 the Church called a task committee of Jewish converts, Phillip Rennert, Rod Zeidner, Harry Glick, and Elliot Landau. They developed pamphlets and three missionary discussions to bridge the differences between the culture and beliefs of the Jewish people and the basic missionary lessons intended for Christians. The resulting missionary effort, although not highly productive, was still a substantial improvement on previous efforts and continued for several years.[27]

The twelve years of President Kimball's administration saw a proliferation of other means of spreading the message, which resulted in thousands of missionary referrals. The open house for the Washington D.C. Temple attracted more than 750,000 people; 100,000 of them turned in a card asking to know more about the Church. Over a period of two years, missionaries visited them all, resulting in 1,900 baptisms. Of 105,000 who went through the Hawaiian Temple before its June 1978 rededication, 55,000 signed referral cards.

Many visitors' centers were constructed near temples and Church historic sites. The visitors' center at Expo '74 (in Spokane, Washington) was shaped like the gold plates. It received approximately 323,000 visitors. Cultural events also made friends for the Church. During President Kimball's tenure the Tabernacle Choir traveled overseas four times, in addition to tours within the United States and Canada. Previously, the choir had been overseas only twice (to Europe in 1955 and 1973). Some Brigham Young University student performing groups were televised in other countries and seen by millions. During the

---

25. In 1954, Elder Richards had written *Israel, Do You Know?* as a missionary message directed to Jews and had received authorization to organize small-scale stake missionary efforts directed at Jews in several large cities, beginning in Los Angeles. But success had been slim, and in 1959 the formal program had been discontinued.

26. The pilot program in 1975 had ninety-six missionaries in New York and Los Angeles.

27. When the Jerusalem Center became the focus of protest by Jews, the special program for proselytizing Jews in the United States was terminated by the Church.

summer of 1985, twenty-two countries enjoyed performances by these groups. The Polynesian Cultural Center at BYU–Hawaii, less obviously Church-oriented, also made a huge impact. By 1981 its personnel had greeted ten million visitors.

Concern for Missionaries

Spencer gave himself unstintingly to encourage missionaries in the field. Wherever he traveled, he insisted on meeting with them. If a meeting was not already scheduled, he asked that one be organized. He was glad to miss a meal if that meant he could hold such a meeting.

When his party arrived in Milan in 1977, Spencer asked Arthur when he would be meeting with the missionaries. Arthur replied that the missionaries would be at the general meeting that night. But Spencer persisted—he wanted a special missionary meeting. Finally Arthur confessed that one was not planned because it would demand so much time and energy. "I know what you are trying to do," Spencer responded. "You are trying to save me, but I don't want to be saved. I want to be exalted." Arthur got on the phone and scheduled a separate meeting with the missionaries in every locale they would visit, no matter how busy the schedule.

Returning weary from area conferences in Europe in August 1976, Spencer spent the layover in New York City visiting with six missionaries who were en route to Germany. "He inquired about their families [and] their personal feelings . . . [and] charged them to be the best missionaries in their mission."

In August 1975, at the end of an area conference in Manila, President Kimball made his way toward a waiting limousine. Throngs pressed from every side to shake his hand or see him up close. A young missionary worked his way to the President and said with tears in his eyes, "Oh, President, I have a terrible problem. Won't you please help me?" The elder's mission president, who was accompanying President Kimball, was chagrined by the situation, but Spencer stopped and gave the elder his full attention. The young missionary explained, "My companion, over there against the wall, has been here only two months and feels homesick and discouraged. He insists he is going home tomorrow, no matter what we say."

President Kimball went to the waiting companion, put his arm around the young man's shoulder, and said, "Elder, come walk with me for a moment." Others trailing along heard Spencer say, "You know, elder, I'm not going to tell you not to go home; others have already told you that. If you go home tomorrow the Lord will understand, and he will continue to love you despite your shortcomings. Your family will continue to love you, although they'll be disappointed. But if you go home tomorrow it won't be many weeks before the most serious problem will occur—you will be dissatisfied with yourself, and you may never fully recover from that."

They reached the car, and Spencer got into the back and said, "Elder, come in and sit with me a moment."

They talked together for several more minutes, and the missionary was tearful as he left the car. His anxious companion asked, "Well, are you going home tomorrow?"

"No, not until it's my time to go."

Though strenuous, missionary work was relatively safe, considering the thousands of missionaries in the field and the wide variety of cultures which they served. In rare instances, however, missionaries were injured or killed either accidentally or as the result of attacks motivated by hatred for the Church. President Kimball asked to be notified of such instances immediately. He felt a deep personal pain for each of these missionaries and their families.

In January 1974, three missionaries in Pennsylvania died when another car repeatedly bumped theirs, causing a head-on collision. Two missionaries were murdered in Texas by mentally ill Robert Kleasen, who had joined the Church in Austin, Texas, concealing his background of violence.[28] A seventy-six–year-old missionary in California was fatally stabbed, and two sister missionaries, ages sixty-five and sixty-six, serving in South Carolina, were battered and shot.

Other missionaries were held captive. In June 1976 members of a political group abducted two missionaries in Argentina for ransom. James E. Faust, then Assistant to the Twelve and area supervisor in South America, and regional representative Angel Fernandez offered themselves as substitutes, but the kidnappers ignored the offer. After five

---

28. His conviction was reversed for illegal search. Texas authorities said they might reopen the murder case, despite the lapse of time, now that DNA analysis would be available at a new trial. While awaiting extradition from England, Kleasen died of heart failure.

tense days, police freed them unharmed from a shack near Asuncion, Paraguay. A year later in England, Joyce McKinney and a male friend kidnapped a missionary who had rejected her. They kept him shackled for three days in a remote cottage.

Little could be done about these random acts of violence, but President Kimball acted quickly when known threats appeared. In late 1976 he heard a disturbing report through contacts in the U.S. military that the Soviet Union had begun a new arms buildup. He conferred with Marion D. Hanks concerning plans to evacuate missionaries quickly from Europe if the situation should become dangerous.

The Church did withdraw missionaries from Nicaragua in 1978 and El Salvador in 1980 during times of civil strife.

14

OPENING THE DOORS OF NATIONS

"Could you go by way of Portugal and establish the Church there?"

BY THE TIME SPENCER BECAME PRESIDENT, the Church had long had a presence in much of the world. He had predicted in 1967, when the Church had seventy-seven missions, that "we will have 185 missions by 1985." He hit the mark precisely; in July 1985 missions passed 185. Many were in places unfamiliar to Americans. Between 1978 and 1985 the number of nations with missionaries increased from about fifty to ninety-one.

But large areas—most of Africa, the Near East, and most of continental Asia—had no more than a handful of members, and many countries remained closed entirely. "When I begin to think there are 900 million people in one country that hasn't been touched yet," he once said, "that makes me feel the urgency. Eventually we've got to get them all."

In September 1978, Spencer told the regional representatives, "When we are ready, the Lord will use us for his purposes. There are almost three billion people now living on the earth in nations where the gospel is not being preached." He mentioned specifically the Chinese, whom he praised as "a disciplined, industrious, frugal, closely knit people. Their moral standards are very high by modern western standards. . . . Family life is strong." Spencer talked with as many people as he could who had lived in China, traveled there, or had connections. He hoped to gather the information and ideas that would hasten the opening of missionary work among that huge population. Once he inquired semi-seriously of the General Authorities, "How are you doing in learning Mandarin Chinese?"

With the faith typical of his approach to missionary work, President Kimball addressed the problem by launching a prayer campaign. He

Speaking at the dedication of a mural depicting Christ sending his apostles into all the world.

asked everyone in the Church—"parents, youth and children"—to join "in a serious, continuous petition to the Lord to open the gates of the nations and soften the hearts of the kings and the rulers to the end that missionaries may enter all the lands and teach the gospel in the approved way."

APPOINTMENT OF A CHURCH "AMBASSADOR"

Action was joined to faith. Early in 1974, President Kimball authorized his first counselor, N. Eldon Tanner, to pursue an idea President Lee had discussed but not implemented—calling a special assistant to focus on the closed countries. President Tanner invited former U.S. Secretary of the Treasury David M. Kennedy to come discuss with the First Presidency the possibility of having someone work on achieving official recognition for the Church in additional countries,[1] solve visa problems, and deal with U.S. and foreign government agencies in Washington, D.C.

---

1. Church leaders came to understand that "legal recognition" did not always mean the same thing. It might carry with it only the right to hold religious services, not the right to proselytize.

David M. Kennedy, Church ambassador, speaking in Hong Kong.

Kennedy arrived expecting to suggest how such a representative might serve the Church best and to name some people who could fill that role, but when President Kimball greeted Kennedy he went straight to the point: "Brother David, we want you to serve as ambassador for the Church. Are you willing to accept this call?"

Startled, Kennedy still offered the names of others he had come prepared to recommend, including three General Authorities. Presumably because he thought they did not have enough confidence in Spencer's vision of what could be accomplished, Spencer said, "They are too negative." "You have been working all your life in preparation for this job," he assured the sixty-eight-year-old Kennedy.

David Kennedy's background was, in fact, unique among Latter-day Saints. His career with the Federal Reserve Bank (1930–46) and Continental Illinois National Bank (1946–69) spanned forty years. He had served Richard M. Nixon as Secretary of the Treasury (1969–71), ambassador-at-large with cabinet rank (1971–73), and ambassador to NATO (1972–73).[2]

---

2. After President Kimball's death, Kennedy continued his service as Church ambassador until 1990, when he retired at age eighty-five.

Kennedy accepted the call gracefully. During the first two years as a special ambassador for the Church, Kennedy visited Lebanon, Greece, Portugal, Thailand, India, Pakistan, Yugoslavia, the Philippines, Hungary, Poland, the German Democratic Republic, Iran, and Egypt. The significance of his work in these countries was underscored by President Kimball, who asked Kennedy to report directly to him. Some members of the Twelve tried to get Kennedy's help in dealing with government problems in their administrative areas. When Kennedy reported this, President Kimball said, "Let me handle that." He told the Twelve that they should not divert Kennedy from his primary assignment.

Sometimes President Kimball asked Kennedy to accompany him, especially when trips included ceremonial visits to cabinet ministers or heads of state.[3] The prospect of these meetings filled Spencer with misgivings because he knew that subtle political land mines lay scattered about. With Kennedy along, President Kimball could talk of church, family, honesty, and loyalty of citizens to their nation, while Kennedy dealt with political questions. If Kennedy should say the wrong thing, the Church could disavow it. "What I say can always change. I'm dispensable," he said. For Spencer to misspeak would be a more serious matter.

In August 1977, President Kimball was scheduled to deliver a public address in Rome, and the Italian Mission sent written invitations to all members of Italy's Parliament except for Communist Party deputies. An uproar ensued in the press because of the discrimination against Communists. The action disturbed some Latter-day Saints as well. Many Italian Saints voted Communist because they believed that party was the only viable alternative to a corrupt majority party. The incident underscored the need for caution in political matters.

President Kimball avoided criticism of governments. He believed that if Church members enjoyed a few basic freedoms they could live under any form of government, even one that was oppressive. There had been a time of decrying "godless Communism."[4] While there is no

---

3. Spencer W. Kimball's journal lists twenty-one meetings with David Kennedy by appointment, plus trips together to South Africa, Poland, Hungary, and Peru.

4. Church leaders saw the Korean and Vietnam Wars as crusades to stop the spread of communism and thus were sympathetic.

David M. Kennedy and President Kimball met twice with Ferdinand Marcos, president of the Philippines.

doubt that Spencer also had anti-Communist sentiments, he thought it at this time more important to gain missionary access than to condemn Communist governments. He met with dictators of the right, such as Ferdinand Marcos, and with political leaders of the left, such as the minister of religion for Communist Poland. At all times, he stressed that the Church encouraged its members to be loyal to their countries.[5]

He continually asked, "Brother David, are we doing all we can to get into these lands?" And he instructed, "Always enter by the front door." But he was both persistent and flexible. He approved sending couples into lands where they could not openly proselytize but where they could respond to questions. When traditional missionary dress made missionaries look out of place, he authorized clothes more in keeping with local circumstances.

THE OPENING OF PORTUGAL

When President Kimball asked David Kennedy which closed countries could most easily be opened to missionary work, Kennedy put

---

5. President Kimball did not, however, volunteer the scriptural proviso that the duty to uphold governments persists only "while [citizens are] protected in their inherent and inalienable rights by the laws of such government" (D&C 134:5). The difficulties posed to Mormons living under actively oppressive governments finds stark illustration in Helmuth Hübener, excommunicated in February 1942 by his local Church authorities and beheaded by the Nazi regime for publicizing BBC broadcasts during World War II. Hübener was posthumously restored to Church membership in November 1946.

Portugal first on the list because of massive social change occurring there. The fascist regime that had controlled the country since 1932 was replaced in April 1974 by a military coup. The influence of the Catholic Church, which had been closely identified with the fascist government, sharply declined.

At the Stockholm area conference in August 1974, President Kimball asked Kennedy, "Where are you going when you are through here?"

"Home."

Spencer asked casually, "Could you go by way of Portugal and establish the Church there?" It was hardly on the way home, but Kennedy went to Portugal. He found that most of his friends from the former Portuguese government were jailed. But the American chargé d'affaires was to meet with foreign minister Mario Soares that same afternoon, and Kennedy went along. Soares in turn said he was having dinner that evening with Salgado Zenha, the minister responsible for religion, and would tell him about Kennedy.

The next day Zenha granted Kennedy an appointment, partly because he had a daughter and grandchildren in the United States. The men discussed Church recognition, and Zenha noted that the large number of "private cults" in the United States did not seem to have hurt national progress; indeed, they tended to dilute the excessive influence of a dominant church. However, he explained, under existing law a church needed five hundred members to obtain official recognition, and Kennedy knew of only three members in the country.

"But," said Kennedy, "you're a military government, still governing by decree. You have the authority to recognize the Church simply by order, haven't you?"

Zenha agreed. That same day he ordered recognition of the Church. Kennedy then urged him to extend to all churches the same recognition, and the minister agreed. In November the new parliament legislated freedom of religion in Portugal, and that same month the first Mormon missionaries arrived.[6]

---

6. Four experienced missionaries from Portuguese-speaking Brazil (Elders Camargo, Perisse, Thompson, and Topham) and W. Grant Bangerter, who had been mission president in Brazil, began the work. Despite the recognition edict, concern for possible opposition from the Roman Catholic Church caused the missionaries to confine their activities largely to contacting friends and relatives

In Poland with the Kennedys to dedicate the country for the preaching of the gospel.

THE DEDICATION OF POLAND

When President Kimball came to office, all of Eastern Europe had been under Soviet Communist domination since the end of World War II. The Soviet bloc excluded Mormon missionaries and generally oppressed actively religious people, although the degree to which each nation tolerated religion varied greatly. Of all the Communist countries, Kennedy thought that Poland and Yugoslavia offered the brightest prospects.

He speculated that the Poles would see recognizing an "American" church as a gesture of friendship to the West. The Roman Catholic Church in Poland was strong enough to have retained some freedom of religion despite the government's official atheism. For its part, the government may have wanted to see the powerful Catholic influence diluted. Pope John Paul II was Polish, a source of immense national pride, but he was also viewed as a potential outside threat to the stability of the government.

In 1975, Kennedy first visited Warsaw and quietly contacted the minister of culture and religion, Kazimierz Kakol. Kennedy avoided

of Brazilian Church members. Bangerter, who served seven months in Portugal before being called as an Assistant to the Twelve, established the policy that half the missionaries in Portugal should be Brazilians. By June 1975 there were approximately forty missionaries in Portugal. In the next ten years, half of the baptisms in Europe occurred in Portugal.

publicity to prevent premature disclosure, which could unsettle the sensitive situation. At their first meeting, Kakol offered him a tray with alcoholic drinks, but Kennedy chose currant juice. They met again in May 1976, and Kakol asked about the Church's teachings and governance. When Kennedy again chose currant juice from the array of alcoholic beverages, Kakol asked, "Is that part of your religion?" Kennedy told him about the Word of Wisdom. Kakol said, "I like that. We drink too much over here." At a third visit in November 1976, Kennedy found Kakol a receptive listener as he explained in more detail the Church's beliefs.

Several months went by, and Kennedy heard nothing. In May 1977, Kennedy and his wife were in Japan, but Kennedy was unable to get Poland out of his mind. He had planned to visit Korea next, but he wired Kakol, saying he was coming to Poland and asking for an appointment. Kakol wired him back, setting the day of the appointment. Arriving in Warsaw in the evening after a long flight, Kennedy learned the appointment was for 8:00 A.M. the next morning. He worked most of the night with an attorney and interpreter to put together a formal petition for recognition.

But Kakol had a surprise for him. "When I got your cable, I thought you would be wanting to talk about recognition for the Mormon Church. I pulled all of your information together, and we have done quite a bit of checking." With a smile he handed Kennedy a neatly bound folder containing a document of formal recognition. "We will have to have a celebration," he said, and he signed the document.

The recognition did not allow proselytizing because that would be "invading the freedom of the people." But it allowed freer communication with members, Church meetings, an information center in Warsaw, and permission to teach those who volunteered an interest in the Church.[7]

A few days later, when Kennedy reported the breakthrough to President Kimball, Spencer proposed traveling to Poland himself to dedicate the country for the renewed preaching of the gospel. He already

---

7. Translating the Book of Mormon into Polish began in 1975, and copies were available in 1982. Most of the copies from the first printing of three thousand were used among Polish-speaking people in the Chicago area.

Sightseeing in Poland as guests of the Polish government, August 1977.

had plans to be in England and Switzerland in August to install new temple presidencies, so he decided to include Poland in that trip.

In Warsaw the party received the most generous hospitality from a government they had ever experienced. Polish customs at the airport allowed them swiftly through, and they reached the Victoria Hotel earlier than expected. President Kimball felt ill, and Dr. Wilkinson advised him to go to bed immediately and excuse himself from the formal dinner the Church was hosting that evening for Minister Kakol and his staff. Instead of taking the advice, Spencer requested a blessing from Kennedy and Haycock. When Kennedy changed clothes and went downstairs for the dinner, he found Spencer already there, cordial and smiling.

The dinner went smoothly. Kakol told the gathering:

"At this table are people from two different lands who think differently. Some are staunch Communists and some are staunch believers in God. Some would say we could not get along, but we can. We of the government think high moral standards are very important in life as does your Church. We like those people who do right and are good human beings. With that in mind, we are happy to have your Church in Poland to help the people."

The next day the Ministry of Culture and Religion arranged a long day of sightseeing. Very late in the evening, they stopped at the cathedral in Warsaw, where a choir performed especially for them (the choir director having been recalled from vacation in Bulgaria for the occasion). The archbishop invited the party to his adjacent residence, and they were directed to go upstairs. Camilla looked up at the long flight and felt she simply could not manage with her aching arthritic knees. She sat down and said she hoped no one would be offended if she just rested there.

The next thing she knew, two sturdy priests had grasped the arms of the chair she sat in and prepared to carry her up. She jumped up in alarm, embarrassed, protesting, "Oh, no! Oh, no! I don't need anyone to carry me!" Sore knees notwithstanding, she hobbled up the stairs at double time.

Returning to the hotel near midnight, the group found a handful of Church members waiting to see them. Spencer held an impromptu testimony meeting with them. The next day the visitors rose early and, after another meeting in the Kimballs' room, they and the few local members walked across the public square to Ogrod Saski Park. They found a grove of trees, away from the traffic, and prayed and quietly sang a hymn as two police agents stood by and took notes. As Spencer concluded his dedicatory prayer, the sun shone.

For the next ten years, although proselytizing was forbidden, missionary couples maintained contact with the few members and managed the information center. A number of baptisms occurred, and friendly relations with government officials continued. In January 1988, the first young elders were allowed to enter Poland and begin proselytizing full-time.

A VISIT TO THE GERMAN DEMOCRATIC REPUBLIC

Immediately after President Kimball's visit to Poland in August 1977, he and his party flew to East Germany. The largest body of Saints behind the Iron Curtain, about 5,000, lived in East Germany (formally the German Democratic Republic). The Church had been recognized by the government in 1949 but was under continual scrutiny by the state police. Because the Saints behind the Iron Curtain were not members of the Communist Party, they experienced obstacles to attending college or gaining job promotions. As members of a Church headquartered in the United States, they were always under suspicion. Members met very quietly in small groups.[8] General Authorities occasionally were able to visit. Spencer had visited in January 1962, meeting with about eighty members who gathered secretly in East Berlin.

This time they arrived in Dresden late for a scheduled meeting, but 1,200 members were waiting patiently in a chapel that seated only 750. Some even stood on ladders placed outside the windows so they could hear the proceedings.

As the meeting began, two members of the Communist police entered and introduced themselves to the person conducting the meeting. They then asked two Church members in the first row to move somewhere else, and they sat through the meeting listening for seditious statements.

The meeting lasted from two until four. A fine choir performed, the congregation sang with gusto, and the talks communicated deep emotion. For forty minutes after the meeting, members greeted the President.

President Kimball encouraged local Church leaders to establish better relations with Communist government officials and obtain what concessions they could. Years of local effort—particularly by Henry Burkhardt—and the oversight of Elder Thomas S. Monson finally bore fruit. In 1978, the government invited the Church to build a temple in the German Democratic Republic.

CONTACTS WITH EGYPT

Missionary efforts in the Near East struggled. In 1975 businessman Lynn M. Hilton, inspired by President Kimball's sweeping view of missionary work, established a business in Egypt drilling water wells. The International Mission president set him apart as district president of Egypt and the Sudan, where a mere forty-four Latter-day Saints lived among sixty million people. Hilton filed papers seeking governmental recognition for the Church and was met with pleasant smiles but endless delays. The Hiltons were threatened with deportation if they proselytized any Egyptian, of whatever religion, so they could teach only expatriates. After they left in 1979, the Church continued to pursue

---

8. Although no *American* missionaries were admitted, a great deal of proselytizing was done by German members.

government recognition. The First Presidency met with Professor D. Delos Ellsworth, who represented BYU's Benson Agriculture and Food Institute and had the good will of government and university officials in Egypt.

President Kimball told him: "We are concerned that the Arab world not think that the Mormons are too pro-Jewish. We want the leaders of the Arab nations to understand we believe that the Arabs are children of Abraham and as such are entitled to the blessings of Abraham. In your meetings with any of these leaders would you please convey this to them."

President Kimball gave Ellsworth a new formal petition to the Egyptian government for recognition of the Church. As he left, Ellsworth asked, "Is there any advice you could give me?"

President Kimball looked him straight in the eye and said soberly, "Yes. Don't make any mistakes."

Egyptian president Anwar Sadat was personally cordial to the idea of recognizing the Church, but because of serious Christian-Muslim tensions, he found it impolitic to recognize another Christian church. After Sadat's assassination in October 1981, President Hosni Mubarak felt the same reluctance to grant recognition. The answer continued to be "Not yet."[9]

In a great many other countries beginnings were astir, sometimes through the touring of BYU entertainment groups, through Church members living abroad, through members converted abroad and returning to their home country, and through couples serving as "special representatives" of the International Mission, sent to make friends and to teach as permitted. Developments begun during these years matured in the years after the Kimball administration, leading to a truly worldwide Church.

---

9. The branch in Cairo was closed down by the government for several months in 1984. It consisted of about one hundred expatriates meeting in Cairo.

15

THE PRESIDENT AS
PUBLIC REPRESENTATIVE

"If it will help the Church, I am healthy, and I have the time!"

PRESIDENT KIMBALL RECOGNIZED THE VALUE to the Church of cultivating associations with government leaders and other notables. And despite his wariness about working with the press, he accepted that interviews were opportunities to dispel untruths and project Christian love. President Kimball further served as a key public representative of the Church by participating in ceremonial events and extending hospitality.

MINGLING WITH THE NATION'S NOTABLES

Over the years, Spencer received hundreds of guests from varied backgrounds, such as publishers, foundation executives, the president of Rotary International,[1] entertainers such as Art Linkletter and Dean Jagger (who had played Brigham Young in the 1940 movie of that title and later joined the Church), the chief of U.S. military chaplains, business executives, army generals, the Finnish consul general, a Libyan delegation touring the United States, U.S. senators, LDS featherweight boxing champion Danny "Little Red" Lopez, and Soviet cosmonaut Alexis Lyanov. They all considered meeting the head of the Mormon Church an opportunity not to be missed.

In January 1977, President Kimball and the Quorum of the Twelve listened together to the inaugural address of President Jimmy Carter, then sent him a telegram of greeting and support. The next June,

---

1. Spencer had been district governor of the Rotary clubs in the state of Arizona and attended the club in Salt Lake City occasionally as a life member.

A sculpture is presented to President Jimmy Carter during National Family Week, December 1978.

Church genealogists completed research into Carter's ancestry, and President Kimball had the two-inch-thick document delivered to the president. In December 1978, President Carter and his wife, Rosalynn, came to Salt Lake City for a program recognizing National Family Week. President Kimball met them at the airport and escorted them to the Tabernacle, where President Carter spoke and was presented with a sculpture by Dennis Smith titled "In the Family Circle."[2]

Three years later in Washington, President Kimball met with President Ronald Reagan and presented him a bound copy of his maternal genealogy. Reagan responded, "[I don't have] time to read many books these days, but this is one book I'll read with great interest." Spencer and Camilla had watched the television coverage of Reagan's inauguration as U.S. president. The Church was represented at that event by the Tabernacle Choir, which had been invited to be in the inaugural parade. The choir provided a grand finale by singing "The Battle

---

2. Heber Wolsey, director of Public Communications, had borne the worrisome responsibility for details of the Carter visit. He received a phone call that evening: "Heber, this is Brother Kimball. I want to tell you how much we appreciate all your efforts. Would you please let everyone in your office know that we are grateful?"

Hymn of the Republic" when their float stopped in front of President Reagan's reviewing stand.[3]

PROMOTING INTERNATIONAL GOODWILL

When President Kimball traveled to area conferences in foreign countries, he met, when possible, with the heads of state or with ministers concerned with religion. He always stressed the Church's values of loyalty in citizenship,

General Orlando Urbino presents to the Church a medallion in recognition of the Church's contribution to the welfare of Chile.

honesty and industry in employment, and commitment to family. His first such meetings as President were in March 1975 with President Ernesto Geisel of Brazil and Raul Sapena Pastor, foreign minister of Paraguay. Many other meetings followed, often arranged by Church members in diplomatic service or by David M. Kennedy, the Church's ambassador. Kennedy commented that the experiences were often stressful for Spencer:

"President Kimball is a very humble man. When we'd go to see heads of state, or to meet with the press for news conferences in foreign countries, he was afraid that he would say or do something that would . . . in some way embarrass the Church. He said this was the hardest thing he had to do.

"I'd see Sister Kimball before we'd go, and I'd ask how he was. She'd say, 'He's uptight.' So I'd go in and see him and he'd say, 'Oh, I'm fine. But what shall I say?' I'd say, 'President, be yourself.'

"Invariably when we'd get there, his tenseness would evaporate and he'd be very relaxed. He has such a love for people that it comes through with his expressions; and people, regardless of their station in

---

3. President Reagan had blinked away tears and later wrote that hearing the hymn was "one of the most touching moments Nancy and I have ever experienced." A letter to a missionary son of Sen. Jake Garn stated: "Although I am not a Mormon, I very much respect your Mormon values."

life, see what he has in mind. In every case, things worked out very well."

In February and March 1977, during eight area conferences in Latin America, President Kimball and David Kennedy met with the presidents of Mexico (Jose Lopez Portillo), Guatemala (Kjell Eugenio Laugerud-Garcia), Chile (Augusto Pinochet-Ugarte), and Bolivia (Hugo Bonzer Suarez).

When the party arrived in Santiago, Chile, President Pinochet sent his helicopter to fly President Kimball, David Kennedy, Arthur Haycock, and Dr. Ernest Wilkinson to the summer palace in Viña del Mar, sixty miles away on the seacoast. Kennedy, who considered himself well-traveled, was amazed at President Kimball's knowledge of the area from his previous visits: "As we flew along about tree-top height, President Kimball pointed to the various roads and told us about the things we were going to see. I asked him how he knew the country so well, and he told me, 'Oh, we've driven all through here.'"[4] In Bolivia, Kennedy was again impressed: "I had seen the airport. I had been in the hotels and government houses. But he had been in the Indians' tents. He had slept in different places throughout the country."

The next year President Kimball visited the presidents of Argentina (Jorge Rafael Videla) and Uruguay (Aparicio Mendez).

In late May 1981, President Kimball was scheduled to fly to Lima, Peru, to meet with dignitaries on his way to the groundbreaking for the Santiago Chile Temple. Learning that President Kimball had just had a heart pacemaker inserted, area supervisor Gene R. Cook called Arthur Haycock to see whether scheduled meetings should be canceled. "His doctors say he should not come, his counselors and his wife say he should not come," said Arthur, "but you had better not cancel the meetings yet."

Elder Cook later received a call from the President saying, "I am coming."

One of the meetings was scheduled with the Peruvian president, Fernando Belaunde-Terry, who had seen and been much impressed with the Washington D.C. Temple. He expressed his approval of the Church's

---

4. Spencer had supervised and visited all the missions in South America in 1959 and 1964–68.

News conference with David M. Kennedy in the Netherlands, July 1976.

plan to build a temple in Lima. Also at the meeting was United States ambassador Edwin Corr, who entertained the Kimballs at dinner and later commented that he "had not met anyone who could convey love so thoroughly to all people" as could Spencer.

MEETING WITH THE PRESS

In the United States, when Heber Wolsey, a Church public communications executive, told President Kimball about an Associated Press reporter's request for an interview, Spencer asked, "Should I do it?"

"President," Heber said, "we're concerned about your health and the tremendous pressure on your time."

"That's not what I asked you. Do you think this interview will help the Church?"

"Yes, sir. I believe it will."

"Just remember this, Heber. If it will help the Church, I am healthy, and I have the time!" D. Arthur Haycock saluted this determination by acknowledging, "He would do anything to build the kingdom, even attend press conferences."[5]

Spencer dreaded the ordeal of press conferences and interviews,

_____

5. His first major interview was on national television—the *Today Show.*

U. S. President Gerald Ford receives a sculpture of family and hears children sing, June 1976.

which were scheduled with major newspapers, wire services, and local radio and TV stations, when possible rationed to about one per month. Interviews sometimes focused on awkward topics. For example, at a June 1976 press conference in Great Britain, the reporters asked President Kimball about a sex scandal involving an American Mormon politician, the purported Howard Hughes will that named the Church as a beneficiary, and the restrictions on priesthood.

These issues frustrated Spencer, as they offered little chance to build understanding and goodwill. He also worried that he might say something that would be misinterpreted or used against the Church.[6] Despite his misgivings, he had a good public relations sense; in interviews he was "usually able to avoid quibbling and instead project Christian love."

Spencer learned wariness from one of his first experiences with the media after he became President. In January 1974, photographers for a French magazine wanted to photograph the First Presidency and the Twelve grouped around a table in a pose similar to da Vinci's *Last Supper.* Spencer rejected the proposal since his central position would cast him in the role of the Christ, but he did allow a group photo session. When he saw the photo in print, he realized to his chagrin that—despite his

---

6. Interviewers on the *Today* television show asked President Kimball about race and Church business involvements without even leading up to the issues.

Spencer and Camilla riding in the BYU centennial parade.

instructions—the photographers had managed to approximate the arrangement in the famous fresco.

PARTICIPATING IN CEREMONIAL EVENTS

As the bicentennial of the Declaration of Independence approached in 1976, attention focused on the nation's capital. On July 2, Spencer and Camilla flew to Washington, D.C., to meet with President Gerald Ford. They presented him with a statuette of a pioneer family. Together on the south lawn of the White House, they listened as a hundred Primary children from the area sang "I Am a Child of God." The next day the Tabernacle Choir sang in the Kennedy Center, where the Kimballs joined the Fords in the presidential box.[7] On Sunday evening, the fourth, the choir sang and Spencer spoke at a bicentennial service for 23,000 Saints in Landover, Maryland.

In 1977, the national president of the Boy Scouts of America (BSA), Arch Monson, attended the priesthood session of general conference to present President Kimball with the Silver World Award, the BSA's highest honor for service to boys on a global scale, given to three people that

---

7. The visit was more personal than with other presidents. They had met before, when Ford was vice-president and in September 1974, just weeks after Ford replaced Richard Nixon upon his resignation. In November 1977, ex-president Ford visited the First Presidency for half an hour.

year. Although Spencer had not been directly involved in Scouting since he left Arizona in 1943, he accepted the recognition on behalf of the Church, which had provided long-standing, international support for the Scouting program since Scouting's inception in the United States. Some years later, the BSA also awarded him the Silver Buffalo for "distinguished service to youth at the national level."[8]

Traditionally, the Church President and his wife rode in an open car in Salt Lake City's annual 24th of July parade commemorating the 1847 arrival of the first Mormon pioneer company. Each year from 1974 to 1981, they cheerfully smiled and waved under the blazing sun.

After the 1980 parade, they participated in the dedication of the reconstructed Social Hall in the Old Deseret Village, where buildings from the pioneer era had been restored or reproduced. At the Brigham Young Farmhouse, Spencer and Camilla climbed into a carriage, but something startled the team of horses and they bolted, jolting the passengers frighteningly. Arthur Haycock raced after them, trying unsuccessfully to grab the reins. After a few blocks, the driver regained control of the horses and returned his passengers to the Social Hall. Spencer and Camilla alighted safely, but a tangled harness spooked the horses again and they fled with the now-empty carriage, tipping and wrecking it. Thinking of his worldwide travel in jet airplanes, Spencer ruefully observed, "Wouldn't it be ironic for me to be killed in a buggy accident!" Spencer's grandfather Heber had, in fact, died in 1868 shortly after being thrown from a buggy.[9]

In April 1979, after twenty-five years, the Mormon Pioneer Memorial Bridge in Omaha, Nebraska, was paid for and about to be rededicated as a toll-free bridge. Spencer declined an invitation to represent the Church at the ceremony, but news media erroneously reported that he would be there. To avoid embarrassing the event's organizers, President Kimball arranged to come. He had participated in the dedication of the toll bridge in 1954, and now he would have the honor of being the last person to pay the toll.

The Church members in the area were greatly excited. The stake president's wife planned dinner for the Kimballs, but a short circuit in

---

8. Presidents Benson, Hinckley, and Monson also received the award.

9. It is thought that Heber died of subdural hematoma, the same condition as caused the three brain surgeries Spencer underwent in 1979 and 1981.

University of Utah honorary degree recipients Terrell H. Bell, Edward W. Clyde, Spencer W. Kimball, and Camilla E. Kimball, with university president David Gardner and commencement speaker Lord Eric Ashby, 1981.

her electric stove started a fire. Although the blaze was quickly controlled, an electrician told her it would take ten days to get parts to fix the stove. She explained her predicament and asked his religion. "Catholic," he said. She asked him, "What would you do if the Pope were coming to dinner at your house?" He conceded that he could probably rewire the stove for temporary service and did so.

The stake president's ten-year-old son Shane said he would not eat with the guests for fear he would spill something and be embarrassed; he changed his mind when President Kimball hugged him and took time to visit with him. Then Shane not only agreed to eat with the guests but asked if he could sit next to President Kimball.

Spencer planned to make only a brief statement at the dedication ceremony. But when he learned of the many people who were coming from afar to hear him, he arranged for a meeting at 3:30 P.M. the next day, just before the plane left. To avoid conflicting with the public ceremony, he asked that there be no publicity except word of mouth. That proved more than adequate; nearly two thousand members jam-packed the stake center with still others crowded around doors and windows. President Kimball talked about Church history events in the Winter Quarters area and preached the commandment to love one another. At one point he said plaintively, "We love you if you are righteous and we love you if you are not—but we wish you were."

After the meeting Camilla, unable to stand very long because of arthritic joints, waited in the car. Their hostess commiserated, "Wives find themselves waiting a lot for their husbands, don't they?"

Camilla responded, "They do, but there is no one I'd rather wait for than Spencer. There is nothing I have to do that is more important than this."

Spencer considered the several schools that awarded him honorary degrees as acknowledging the Church's importance in the state of Utah. They were Snow College (1974), Utah State University (1975), and the University of Utah (1981). Brigham Young University had conferred an honorary degree earlier (1969).

In March 1981, a major new building, the Spencer W. Kimball Tower, was dedicated on the BYU campus. An apocryphal story circulated that when the BYU Board of Trustees decided to name a building after him, Spencer requested, "Please don't let it be a short building." The Kimball Tower, at twelve stories, is the tallest structure on campus.

In May 1975, President Kimball flew to Arizona to speak at the baccalaureate service of Eastern Arizona College.[10] A sixty-first-year reunion of Spencer's high school class of 1914 was scheduled for that evening. The graduating class's gift to the school had been a pillar bearing a plaque with their twenty-one names inscribed. Because Spencer had been class president, his name headed the list. Arizona Supreme Court Justice Jesse A. Udall joked, "Back then I doubted the advisability of having a monument put up with our names inscribed in granite; but after I've seen how important we have become, I've kind of concluded it was the right thing to do."

---

10. Gila Academy, a Church-owned high school when Spencer attended in 1910–14, became a public junior college in 1933.

CONTROVERSIAL ISSUES

16

PUBLIC RELATIONS, PUBLIC ISSUES

"Just tell the truth."

A PROSELYTIZING CHURCH has reason to be concerned about the perceptions the public has of it. During the twelve years Spencer was President, the public relations efforts of the Church expanded greatly, sometimes in response to a crisis of bad publicity, but increasingly as an orchestrated effort to lay groundwork for the missionary message.

PROMOTING POSITIVE VALUES AND IMAGE

About a year before Spencer began serving as President, the Church established a public relations office headed by Wendell Ashton, vice president of a Salt Lake City advertising agency, with Heber Wolsey as his associate director. When Ashton left in November 1978 to become publisher of the *Deseret News,* President Kimball called Wolsey to take his place. Wolsey went on to initiate several successful programs, including the award-winning Homefront series (radio and television public service messages with family-oriented and often humorous themes)[1] and a series of eight-page booklet inserts in the monthly *Reader's Digest.*[2]

One of Wolsey's innovations, Church-developed TV specials, received President Kimball's personal support at a critical moment. In 1977 the Public Communications Department produced a sixty-minute

---

1. In one radio spot, for example, the phone rings. "Hello," says a man's voice. A girl's voice somewhat hesitantly replies, "Hi, daddy. I just, uh, called to tell you I love you and appreciate everything you do." There is a silence. Then comes the man's stunned response: "Who is this?" By 1989 Homefront spots appeared on 90 percent of U.S. television stations and were heard on 50 percent of radio stations.

2. In 1978 the magazine had a circulation of almost 20 million and an estimated 50 million readers.

The Osmond family brought good publicity to the Church. At left is seated Elder LeGrand Richards.

TV program, "The Family . . . and Other Living Things," which was about a divorced couple struggling to reconcile. A week before the telecast, President Kimball, his counselors, and the Quorum of the Twelve previewed the special. When the program concluded, there was absolute silence. Wolsey held his breath. Then President Kimball said enthusiastically, "Oh, may we not applaud?" and started clapping. The rest of the General Authorities then joined in.

Scheduled to coincide with the National Family Week proclaimed by President Ford, the special aired in prime time in fifty-four top U.S. markets. Viewers requested more than 100,00 copies of "It's Next Week," a free booklet about family values. The show was rebroadcast in 1978 to one hundred markets.

In 1980 the Church produced "Mr. Krueger's Christmas," starring Jimmy Stewart as an old man alone at Christmastime. The thirty-minute special featured the Mormon Tabernacle Choir, conducted in fantasy by Mr. Krueger. Jimmy Stewart worked six days on the film but charged for only one day's shooting. At the end of the filming, President Kimball and his counselors presented Stewart with a record of his genealogy, his own life, and stories of his ancestors. Greatly moved, Stewart commented, "This is the most wonderful thing I have ever received in my life."

That year more than 120 stations showed the program, and 40,000 viewers requested a free brochure and Tabernacle Choir tape recording offered in conjunction with the presentation. The film demonstrated exceptional staying power and reappeared each Christmas season.

RESCINDING ANTI-MORMON ACTIONS

During this period, several gestures of goodwill were proffered by governments that in the pioneer past had been hostile. Christopher S. Bond, governor of Missouri, sent a message that he had, in the words of President Kimball, "rescinded the 138-year-old executive order of Governor Lilburn W. Boggs calling for the extermination or expulsion of the Mormons from the State of Missouri." President Kimball announced this action at the October 1976 general conference.

Similarly, in June 1978, Governor James Thompson of Illinois sent a representative, Ilana D. Rovner, to the dedication of the Monument to Women in Nauvoo to express regret for the state's failure to protect Mormons when mobs expelled them from Illinois in 1846.[3]

In November 1978 the U.S. Congress repealed the provision in the 1862 Morrill Act that prohibited a church from owning real estate worth more than $50,000 in a territory of the United States. Intended to suppress plural marriage by attacking the Church economically, more than a hundred years later the law threatened the Church's plan to build a temple in the U.S. territory of American Samoa.

Another attempt at reconciliation demonstrated a still-intense antagonism against the Church. In 1982, Idaho voters repealed an anti-Mormon provision of the state constitution that disenfranchised members of any group that taught plural marriage. The provision had been a dead letter since 1890, but roughly a third of Idaho's voters voted against repeal.

---

3. In a converse situation, the Church owned and maintained the site at Mountain Meadows in southern Utah where, in the hysteria of the "Mormon War" in September 1857, local Mormon militia and Indian allies murdered approximately one hundred twenty men, women, and children, members of the Fancher party of emigrants to California. Spencer had received a report from Fred Baker that the site was "well kept up and . . . appropriately maintained," but more positive steps toward reconciliation were taken after Spencer's death. President Hinckley joined with Fancher descendants in a meeting of reconciliation in September 1990. In September 1999 President Hinckley dedicated a rebuilt monument, larger than the existing one built in 1859, and pledged Church maintenance.

THE "HOWARD HUGHES" WILL

In April 1976 a handwritten will attributed to the recently-deceased billionaire Howard Hughes turned up in an envelope left on a desk in the Public Communications Department at Church headquarters. Among other bequests, it named the Church as recipient of one-sixteenth of Hughes' huge fortune. The bequest had some plausibility because the eccentric and reclusive Hughes was surrounded by LDS guards and attendants whom he trusted. Nevertheless, Wendell Ashton, then department head, correctly foresaw that people would not believe such a story and expressed his concerns when he briefed President Kimball. Spencer's advice was simple: "Just tell the truth." Spencer had the will delivered to the officials in Clark County, Nevada, where Hughes had lived. The Church took no position on the will's authenticity.

The will named as another beneficiary Utah service station operator Melvin Dummar. He explained the unlikely bequest as an expression of gratitude from Hughes, whom he had once rescued in the Nevada desert. When police identified his fingerprint on the envelope, Dummar admitted he left the will at the Church Office Building. Apparently he hoped that association with the Church would give the will added credibility. He insisted, however, that he had not forged the will. Controversy lasted for two years, with the size of the Hughes empire guaranteeing both litigation and publicity. Because the media dubbed the document "the Mormon will," the Church received massive, free, worldwide publicity, nearly all of it neutral or positive.[4]

MX MISSILE BASING PROPOSAL

In October 1978 the Pentagon announced that Utah was a potential site for a system of intercontinental ballistic missiles, called MX, to serve as a deterrent against a first-strike attack by the Soviet Union. Seeing the issue as political, President Kimball and his counselors were silent about the proposal. Regardless of that reticence, several months later three Air Force generals made a presentation about the MX to the First Presidency, considering them important opinion makers.

---

4. The issue was resolved only when both a Nevada and a California court concluded that Hughes did not write the will.

" EXCUSE ME, BUT COULD WE BORROW A LITTLE WATER FROM YOUR TAP? "

In September 1979, President Jimmy Carter announced that the plan called for two hundred MX missiles to be moved about among 4,600 shelters in the Utah-Nevada desert. An October poll showed that 69 percent of Utahns favored the plan because it would create jobs and safeguard international peace by contributing to a strong national defense. But the opposition was very vocal and stimulated robust public debate in 1980 and 1981.

With the emergence of additional details—the MX plan would require nearly 10,000 miles of roads, occupy much of western Utah and eastern Nevada, and cost $60 billion dollars or more—public sentiment began to tilt against the proposal. Many objected to the negative environmental impact and to perpetuating the arms race with the Soviet Union. Utah's governor Scott Matheson, who initially supported the proposal, announced in June 1980 that he now opposed it.

Earlier that year, Elder Gordon B. Hinckley of the Special Affairs Committee asked Edwin B. Firmage, a law professor at the University of Utah, to provide a memorandum for the First Presidency analyzing the issues. His memorandum strenuously opposed the arms buildup, relying heavily on statements about peace by earlier Church leaders.

On May 5, 1981, President Kimball and his counselors issued a strong statement objecting to the proposal, a rare public stand on a political issue. However, the First Presidency believed it also had moral ramifications. The statement cited as reasons for the opposition that the MX missiles would escalate the arms race, would make the area a primary target for a Soviet preemptive strike, and would strain community and ecological resources. The statement also called for seeking "viable alternatives" to arms escalation.[5]

The statement did not represent a new position for Spencer. As an apostle, he had consistently opposed the arms race. As President, he had decried relying on gods of steel rather than trusting in the true God. Firmage believed that President Kimball's personal feelings about issuing the statement overcame concerns that some of the Twelve had.

Some of the news commentators expressed their opinion that the Church was motivated only by regional self-interest.[6] The analysts ignored the clear objection to the missiles "wherever based."

The military establishment responded with counterarguments, but the First Presidency statement accelerated the shift to negative public opinion.[7] In October 1981, President Reagan referred the proposal back to the military for reconsideration, effectively killing it. And by the decade's end, with the fall of international Communism, such a defense system was no longer considered necessary.[8]

CONCERNS ABOUT PUBLICLY STATED POLITICAL OPINIONS

As President of an international church, Spencer was keenly aware that any American statements critical of foreign governments might hamper the Church's missionary work, especially in Communist or fascist countries. He believed that, as long as members in a country were allowed to perform their religious ordinances and duties, the Church could operate adequately under any form of government.

As was widely known, not all of the General Authorities shared this

---

5. "We repeat our warnings against the terrifying arms race in which the nations of the earth are presently engaged," the statement said. "We deplore in particular the building of vast arsenals of nuclear weaponry. . . . History indicates that men have seldom created armaments that eventually were not put to use."

6. William F. Buckley criticized the statement as provincial and evidencing a "narrow view of national defense," in contrast with the usual perception of the Latter-day Saints as "super patriots."

7. Edwin B. Firmage said, "This statement, in retrospect, effectively killed MX basing as it had been proposed by the [Carter] administration, and in reality killed any other basing of significant scope, anywhere."

8. According to former governor Scott Matheson, the Utah congressional delegation grumbled about not being consulted. "Senator Jake Garn was extremely unhappy that the Church had not consulted him. He viewed himself as the defense expert in the state, but there wasn't anything he could do." In March 1985, nine of the twelve LDS senators and representatives in Congress voted in favor of MX missile funding.

A new Church-owned million-dollar press is examined by leaders Gordon B. Hinckley, Spencer W. Kimball, Marion G. Romney, and N. Eldon Tanner, May 1973.

approach or fully embraced President Kimball's international vision. Although Elder Benson made many noncontroversial speeches in favor of freedom, he also made some remarks so pointedly anti-Communist that others reassured Communist government officials in East Germany, "There is only one person who speaks for the Church and that is the prophet; everything else is a matter of individual opinion."

In 1974, when asked in an interview whether a good Mormon could be a liberal Democrat, Elder Benson replied, "I think it would be very hard if he was living the gospel and understood it." He also said that the Church might at some point endorse political candidates. When these remarks appeared in print, they caused a flood of calls and letters from Church members protesting his views.[9]

Spencer, who disapproved of public political statements by Church leaders as potentially divisive, discussed the matter with Elder Benson. Spencer understood his worthy motives and patriotic spirit, but reminded him that "as President of the Council of Twelve" he should

---

9. Spencer had Wendell Ashton collect official statements about Church leader involvement in politics in preparation for the meeting with Elder Benson.

avoid involvement in politically sensitive issues. Elder Benson apologized, and the interview closed on a cordial note.[10]

But in November, just before Election Day, Elder Benson's passion for his cause prevailed, and in a spontaneous expression he publicly endorsed the American Party. He noted that the Church was nonpartisan, but in his extemporary remarks he also said that he believed the American Party was established on divine, eternal principles.

"Never in decades have I read a set of principles of any party that come so close to the philosophy which I have and which I think my own Church people have."

He went on to assert that "the real hope" of a nation in crisis lay with people such as those gathered at the rally.

Newspaper accounts of these statements caused great consternation, heightened when a radio report erroneously said the statements had President Kimball's approval. Calls flooded the Church phone lines. Spencer hurried to his office to draft a statement reiterating, without direct reference to the incident, that "we take no partisan stand as to candidates or parties, and any person who makes representation to the contrary does so without authorization."

The next day the full First Presidency asked Elder Benson to meet with them. Spencer's journal notes that they "discussed at great length" his remarks. They reminded him that "all General Authorities must speak with one voice and . . . [not] take any partisan position."

Many people looked for political messages where none may have been intended. In February 1980, Elder Benson gave a talk at Brigham Young University titled "Fourteen Fundamentals in Following the Prophet." It emphasized that the living prophets' statements take precedence over those of earlier prophets. He also asserted, "Those who would remove prophets from politics would take God out of government."[11]

Spencer was concerned about the talk. He wanted to prevent any misperception that the Church espoused ultraconservative politics and

---

10. President Benson's biography does not mention the incident. Spencer recorded in his journal, "I doubt if he will get into politics any more."

11. The talk may have been an impassioned response to a full-page anti-Mormon advertisement in the *Salt Lake Tribune* two days before, trumpeting inconsistencies between latter-day prophets.

wanted to discourage an unthinking follow-the-leader mentality.[12] Church spokesman Don LeFevre told the press the day after the speech that it is "simply not true" that the Church President's "word is law on all issues—including politics." The uproar continued, however, and a week later President Kimball and his counselors issued still another statement to "reaffirm that we . . . exercise no constraint on the freedom of individuals to make their own choices in these matters."

While President Kimball himself was politically conservative, he was committed to allowing multiple political viewpoints to be heard within the Church. For example, he gave approval for the chairman of the Supreme Court of the Soviet Union to speak at the BYU law school.

Despite differing on the degree to which Church leaders should speak out on political matters, the personal regard President Kimball and Elder Benson had for one another never wavered. Each appreciated the unswerving commitment of the other to the cause they had both served as apostles since 1943. And after Elder Benson himself became President, he had little to say of a partisan nature.[13]

---

12. Camilla speculated that if one of the other apostles had given the same talk there would have been much less reaction.

13. Elder Benson's biographer suggests that by 1984, at age eighty-five, he rarely spoke on political and economic ideologies because he recognized the complications that could cause for spread of the Church in the United States and abroad. When he became President in 1985, those who expected him to use his position as a platform for political activism, and particularly anti-Communism, were surprised. He ignored those themes and concentrated instead on the importance of the Book of Mormon. Part of the reason may have been changes in national and international circumstances. A conservative president had been elected to the White House; the Cold War was over; international Communism was faltering and would collapse four years later. Perhaps his counselors influenced him away from political themes on the grounds that they were distractions from the Church's main objectives. Perhaps also he felt guided by the Spirit away from political themes.

17

ISSUES OF CONCERN TO WOMEN

"Let us speak of marriage as a full partnership."

WHETHER THEY CALLED THEMSELVES feminists or not, many Mormon women found that the women's movement, although unsettling, instilled self-confidence, gave incentive to grow to one's potential, and broadened the range of choices. But militant and even moderate feminists regularly criticized the Church for doctrines and policies that they thought denigrated women. With this feminist consciousness rising rapidly both within the Church and without, people began to recognize unrighteous dominion more often and speak out against it more vigorously. Some LDS men lent legitimacy to the criticism by behaving dictatorially toward their wives and children.

President Kimball acknowledged women's legitimate grievances, and he acted to clarify the LDS position. Throughout his presidency, he emphasized the service and sacrifice obligations of priesthood rather than its authority aspects. For him the model of the provider-father and the at-home mother was not a prescription for power relationships between husbands and wives. He stressed that women have no obligation to follow their husbands in unrighteousness.[1] In response to criticisms of messages that mothers should stay home with small children, he explained he was not speaking of a family where necessity required the mother to work for pay.

---

1. Spencer W. Kimball said, "No woman has ever been asked by the Church authorities to follow her husband into an evil pit. She is to follow him as he follows and obeys the Savior of the world."

Women and Priesthood Ordination

While in society at large many argued that political and economic equality for women required enactment of the ERA, within the Church some argued that spiritual equality required priesthood ordination for women.[2] After 1978, some members began to think that since there had been a change in the restriction on priesthood by race there could also be a change in the restriction by gender. They saw more and more denominations ordaining women priests and ministers. However, President Kimball offered no hint of change.

The question came up in an interview President Kimball granted shortly after the June 1978 revelation on ordination for all worthy males. He responded, "We pray to God to reveal his mind and we always will, but we don't expect any revelation regarding women and the priesthood."

President Kimball never engaged the argument made by some members that no scripture prohibits women from holding priesthood office. He, along with a large share of Latter-day Saint women, believed that faith, love, and service, not simply holding priesthood office, gave one honor before God. President Kimball reminded the members, "We should not overlook the fact that . . . a mother may pray with her children and call down the Lord's blessings upon them. She does not act by virtue of priesthood conferred upon her, but [she acts] by virtue of her God-given responsibility to govern her household in righteousness."

Some women had difficulty understanding but were resigned to the situation. Others were greatly upset by the exclusion of women from ordination. They had been taught that priesthood bearers held power and received respect and honor, things they saw themselves denied simply by virtue of their gender. They rejected the pairing of priesthood and motherhood. President Kimball was understanding toward those whose questioning seemed honest and loyal toward the Church. He was less sympathetic toward those who publicly criticized the Church.

---

2. A supporter of the ERA staged an ordination of his wife for the press. Both were excommunicated.

With sculptress Florence Hansen and Relief Society president Barbara Smith before a statue of Joseph and Emma Smith.

MOTHER IN HEAVEN

The women's movement turned the thoughts of religious women of many denominations toward the feminine in the divine. Many LDS women took solace in the Church's theologically unique teaching that there is a Mother in Heaven, though she is rarely spoken of officially and scant doctrine leaves her largely undefined and unknown. Her existence was apparently taught by Joseph Smith and she persisted in LDS awareness largely because of Eliza R. Snow's frequently sung hymn "O My Father." Brigham Young and Wilford Woodruff referred to the concept of Mother in Heaven,[3] but few other Church leaders mentioned her.

In April 1978 general conference, President Kimball made his one public statement on the subject. He said, "When we sing that doctrinal hymn and anthem of affection, 'O My Father,' we get a sense of the ultimate in maternal modesty, of the restrained, queenly elegance of our Heavenly Mother, and knowing how profoundly our mortal mothers have shaped us here, do we suppose her influence on us as individuals to be less if we live so as to return there?"

Many LDS women appreciated that he acknowledged her existence, but his statement offered no further insight about who she is or what role she plays. Ideas about her generated a lively discussion, including an outpouring of poetry and articles.[4]

---

3. In 1909, the First Presidency, then consisting of Joseph F. Smith, John R. Winder, and Anthon H. Lund, issued a statement titled "The Origin of Man" that said, "Man, as a spirit, was begotten and born of heavenly parents" and "All men and women are in the similitude of the universal Father and Mother, and are literally the sons and daughters of Deity."

4. The discussion largely terminated in September 1991. Noting that some women were

Bolstering Women's Standing in the Church

While opposing the ERA and priesthood ordination for women, President Kimball took several measures to emphasize to Church members and the world in general that women are equal to men. In 1976, an internal memorandum, probably sent with his approval, urged Church leaders to avoid referring to "priesthood correlation" when discussing Young Women and Relief Society programs because this phrase could be misinterpreted as indicating men are more important.

In a 1977 memo, President Kimball and his counselors also clarified the distinctive role of the premier LDS women's organization. They noted that "the Relief Society . . . plays a special, supportive role, different in purpose and magnitude than the roles played by the other auxiliary organizations." This memo was preceded by a statement that President Kimball's first counselor, N. Eldon Tanner, made to the Church Coordinating Council: "The presidency of the Relief Society, having a specific responsibility placed upon them by the President of the Church at the time they were organized, should be considered as a partner with the Melchizedek Priesthood in somewhat the same manner as a wife would work with her husband in directing the affairs of the family." This concept was later disseminated churchwide.

During President Kimball's administration, the Church also began publicly honoring young women in order to balance the attention given young men who receive priesthood advancements and Scouting awards. Wards were instructed to announce the presidencies of Young Women classes, recognize the graduation of girls from one age group to another, and present girls' achievement awards in sacrament meeting.

As chair of the Board of Trustees for Brigham Young University, Spencer encouraged more recognition for women there as well. In 1975, BYU's most prestigious academic scholarships (always named after the current Church President) were extended to women in numbers equal to those of men recipients. About the same time, the board approved BYU president Dallin Oaks's appointment of Marilyn Arnold as Assistant

---

praying to Mother in Heaven, President Hinckley instructed first the regional representatives and then the women's general meeting that such prayers were "inappropriate," and those who further this practice are "misguided." The scriptural admonition is to pray to the Father in the name of Christ (see 3 Nephi 18:20; Moses 5:8).

One of the sculpture vignettes in the Relief Society Monument to Women.

to the President—Special Projects, with attention to women's concerns. The administration dealt with inequities in hiring, promotion, and salary. With the board's backing, BYU began holding highly popular annual women's conferences and publishing many of the presentations. In 1984, the Board of Trustees began including in its membership the current Young Women general president (the Relief Society general president had been added in 1971).

In September 1978, President Kimball, his counselors, and the Quorum of the Twelve explained that a Church policy (set in 1967) allowing only Melchizedek or Aaronic Priesthood holders to pray in sacrament meetings had no scriptural basis and should be abandoned.

In 1980, the First Presidency began inviting the general presidencies of the Relief Society, Young Women, and Primary to sit on the stand at general conference. In April 1984, women spoke in general conference for the first time since 1930, though they spoke only briefly. Barbara Winder spoke on the occasion of her calling as president of the Relief Society and Barbara Smith upon her release, as did Young Women presidents Ardeth Kapp and Elaine Cannon.

Not all change moved in the same direction. Some women objected to the 1983 *General Handbook* instruction that leaders calling a woman to a Church position should first consult her husband, "to show respect for authority in the home," while at the time no consultation with a wife was advised before calling a man to a position in the Church.[5]

SPECIAL CONFERENCE FOR LDS WOMEN

Possibly as a response to continuing concerns about the status of women, the Church in 1978 held a conference for all women ages twelve and older, a conference that later became an annual event. Convened in the Tabernacle two weeks before the October 1978 general conference, this first women's meeting was broadcast by closed circuit communication to 1,400 locations in the United States, Canada, Australia, and New Zealand.

In preparing his address for this first meeting, Spencer thought and prayed, revised, worried, and prayed again. Because women's issues were a delicate topic, he knew that as a male leader keynoting the meeting he would be under scrutiny and his words would be doubly significant. He invited Emma Lou Warner Thayne, former member of the Young Women's general board and an accomplished poet and essayist, to review a draft of his remarks and make suggestions. Although her daughter was gravely ill in the hospital, she worked on the draft through the night at her daughter's bedside. She found a number of things that, while they reflected more a generational difference than any devaluation of women, were open to possible misinterpretation. The next day, she passed on her suggestions. When she heard President Kimball deliver the talk, she noted that, while he did not adopt all her suggestions, he had accepted a number of wording changes that reduced the likelihood of misunderstanding.[6]

Entitled "Privileges and Responsibilities of Sisters," the talk emphasized gospel basics but also included strong statements about equality of women and an acknowledgment of the difficulty of the times:

"When we speak of marriage as a partnership, let us speak of

---

5. More recent instructions recommend meeting with both spouses to extend any call.

6. An analyst of the talk commented that "rather than a narrow focus on mothering tasks alone, this speech is widely based, positively stated, and actively encouraging. It counsels women to make a broad range of choices, fulfill potential, and exercise agency. It clearly communicates love, appreciation, encouragement, and respect for women. This tone, which permeates President Kimball's address was, in my memory, a trend-setting approach to women that was generally typical of the addresses of other General Authorities and of the women leaders during the late 1970s and early 1980s."

marriage as a *full* partnership. We do not want our LDS women to be *silent* partners or *limited* partners in that eternal assignment! Please be a *contributing* and *full* partner."

"We want our sisters to be scholars of the scriptures as well as our men."

"Much is said about the drudgery and the confinement of the woman's role in the home. In the perspective of the gospel it is not so. There is divinity in each new life. . . . There is partnership between the man and woman in building a family which can last throughout the eternities."

"We hope our women as well as our men will be conscious of the philosophies of the world which would attempt to reverse the wisdom of the Lord when he told us that we can find ourselves only by losing ourselves."

A year later Spencer was in the hospital at the time of the second women's meeting, but he again had carefully crafted a talk sensitive to the times and had Camilla read it for him. The address began with expressions about the equality of women before God, despite the inequality they might experience in mortality:

"The scriptures and the prophets have taught us clearly that God, who is perfect in his attribute of justice, 'is no respecter of persons' (Acts 10:34). We know also that God is perfect in his love for each and all of us as his spirit children. When we know these truths, my sisters and associates in this divine cause, it should help us greatly as we all experience much less than perfect love and perfect justice in the world. If, in the short term, we are sometimes dealt with insensitively and thoughtlessly by others, by imperfect men and women, it may still cause us pain, but such pain and disappointment are not the whole of life. The ways of the world will not prevail, for the ways of God will triumph."

FAMILY GOVERNANCE

President Kimball clarified the separate but equal roles men and women have in the family. The scripture "Thy husband . . . shall rule over thee" (Genesis 3:16), he taught the Relief Society in 1975, means "Thy husband shall *preside* over thee." And presiding does not involve a power relationship but is merely a matter of family structure. He emphasized this point, emphatically declaring that a man who said, "'I hold the priesthood and you've got to do what I say' . . . should be tried for his membership." This interpretation tracked an earlier statement:

"Husbands are commanded: '. . . love your wives, even as Christ also loved the church, and gave himself for it' (Ephesians 5:25).

"Here is the answer: Christ loved the Church and its people so much that he voluntarily endured persecution for them, stoically withstood pain and physical abuse for them, and finally gave his precious life for them.

"When the husband is ready to treat his household in that manner, not only the wife, but also all the family will respond to his leadership."

This is a teaching he tried to follow in his personal life.

Speaking to the priesthood in general conference two weeks after the first women's conference, Spencer encouraged men to be "leader-servants" in their homes. He also made a statement that is often quoted to remind men in blunt terms how they should treat women:

"Our sisters do not wish to be indulged or to be treated condescendingly; they desire to be respected and revered as our sisters and our equals. I mention all these things, my brethren, not because the doctrines or the teachings of the Church regarding women are in any doubt, but because in some situations our behavior is of doubtful quality."

VIOLENCE AGAINST WOMEN

In 1979, for the first time temple recommend questions, approved by President Kimball and his counselors, asked whether anything in the conduct of the applicant within his or her family was "not in harmony with the teachings of the Church." This question, although not limited to men, appears to be in response to a growing awareness of the prevalence of men's physical or emotional abuse of wife or children. In 1985 the question was broadened further to inquire about faithfulness in providing financial support for one's family after separation or divorce. That same year, the Church made its most explicit statement of institutional concern about child abuse by publishing a booklet titled *Child Abuse: Helps for Ecclesiastical Leaders.*[7]

---

7. Gordon B. Hinckley said: "Any man involved in an incestuous relationship is unworthy to hold the priesthood. He is unworthy to hold membership in the Church and should be dealt with accordingly. Any man who beats or in other ways abuses his children will be held accountable before the great judge of us all."

A First Presidency letter of February 1985 made it clear that a rape victim bears no moral guilt and that a bishop should not undertake to judge the sufficiency of the victim's resistance. The 1989 *General Handbook of Instructions* added the caution:

"Victims of rape or sexual abuse frequently suffer serious trauma and feelings of guilt. Victims of the evil acts of others are not guilty of sin. Church officers should treat such victims with sensitivity and should help them regain their sense of innocence and overcome any feelings of guilt."[8]

REPRODUCTIVE ISSUES

Against strong social pressures in the country favoring population control, President Kimball felt that large families were desirable. He also believed that having a family should not be deferred until graduation from college or until finances became secure. This position did not, however, mean that a woman should have all the children she physically could bear. Her general well-being, more than just her physical ability to have children, should be considered in family planning.

There were questions concerning not only whether to limit conception but also how. Some urged that only "natural" means might be used, particularly abstinence. But Spencer once said to Dr. Homer Ellsworth,

---

8. J. Reuben Clark Jr. has been widely misinterpreted. He said, "Better dead, clean, than alive, unclean." But it is vital to note that the statement related only to voluntary unchastity. The victim of rape is not unclean.

a Salt Lake City obstetrician, "Abstinence for married people is not a good answer."[9]

Jay Todd, managing editor of the *Ensign,* asked Dr. Ellsworth to write an article—couched as a question and answer—about reproduction and fertility, but Ellsworth put him off. Later, when Homer was at the Kimball home, he mentioned the request and President Kimball said, "Why don't you write what you think and let me read it. I don't think a woman should have to have a baby every year."

Ellsworth submitted a draft to President Kimball and received a phone call from him, saying, "We've read your draft and you can publish it."

"I'm glad you approve it."

"That's not what I said. I said you can publish it."

Ellsworth later received a call from Todd saying that the article had been held up by the Correlation Reading Committee until Todd protested, "But it has been approved for publication by the Brethren."

"Who are 'the Brethren'?"

"I don't know who all, but President Kimball has seen it."

When the people involved received confirmation that President Kimball had seen it, the *Ensign* was free to publish. The question and answer, which appeared in the August 1979 issue, made the point that the important issue is whether it is time to have a child: "If . . . having another child immediately is unwise, the method of spacing children . . . makes little difference."

Speaking in a television address in January 1984, President Hinckley said God has not designated the number of children a family should have, "nor has the Church. This is a sacred matter left to the couple and the Lord."[10]

President Kimball stated in a *New Era* article his belief that sex was not just for conception but also a uniting bond between spouses,

---

9. The specific subject of discussion between Spencer and Dr. Ellsworth was whether nursing a baby operated as a contraceptive. Dr. Ellsworth's answer was that research showed nursing had little effect on conception after about five months.

10. The *Church Handbook of Instructions* states: "It is the privilege of married couples who are able to bear children to provide mortal bodies for the spirit children of God, whom they are then responsible to nurture and rear. The decision as to how many children to have and when to have them is extremely intimate and private and should be left between the couple and the Lord. Church members should not judge one another in this matter."

"divinely approved, . . . an expression of love." But, he said in another forum, "Sex experiences were never intended by the Lord to be a mere plaything or merely to satisfy passions and lusts. . . . No provision was ever made for indiscriminate sex."[11] Dr. Homer Ellsworth once asked what sexual conduct was acceptable for a married couple. Spencer replied that in his view anything mutually pleasurable and satisfying was acceptable, but neither should ask for conduct the other found offensive.

ABORTION

Increasingly abortion was being seen as merely a tool of family planning. President Kimball denounced abortion in nearly every general conference, fourteen times in all. In his first address as President, April 1974, President Kimball said:

"Abortion is a growing evil that we speak against. Certainly the terrible sin of premeditated abortion would be hard to justify. It is almost inconceivable that an abortion would ever be committed to save face or embarrassment, to save trouble or inconvenience, or to escape responsibility. How could one submit to such an operation or be party in any way by financing or encouraging? If special rare cases could be justified, certainly they would be rare indeed."[12]

He was reaffirming a First Presidency statement from 1972 that said:

"The Church opposes abortion . . . except in the rare cases where, in the opinion of competent medical counsel, the life or good health of the mother is seriously endangered or where the pregnancy was caused by rape and produces serious emotional trauma in the mother. Even then it should be done only after counseling with the local presiding priesthood authority and after receiving divine confirmation through prayer."[13]

In 1983, the stated exceptional circumstances under which abortion might sometimes be justified were expanded to include incest.

---

11. The *Church Handbook of Instructions* made the view official: "Married couples also should understand that sexual relations within marriage are divinely approved not only for the purpose of procreation, but also as a means of expressing love and strengthening emotional and spiritual bonds between husband and wife."

12. Spencer W. Kimball said, "Abortion must be considered one of the most revolting and sinful practices in this day, when we are witnessing the frightful evidence of permissiveness leading to sexual immorality."

13. Being party to unjustified abortion was mandatory grounds for Church discipline.

In 1973 the United States Supreme Court in *Roe v. Wade* overturned state statutes that would prevent a woman from obtaining an elective abortion during the first trimester. The Church spoke out against the decision and supported the unsuccessful efforts to reverse or overturn it by constitutional amendment. In March 1974 the First Presidency sent David Lawrence McKay, president of the Eastern States Mission, to testify before a Congressional committee in favor of such an amendment.

In 1976 the Church produced a filmstrip about abortion. In the audiotape accompanying the filmstrip, President Kimball expressed the view that in cases of pregnancy caused by rape, "abortion would greatly compound the wrong. An unborn baby must not be punished for the sins of his father." Ten weeks later, however, the First Presidency reissued its statement reiterating that abortion might be justified by "pregnancy . . . caused by forcible rape and produc[ing] serious emotional trauma in the victim." President Kimball's contrary statement was thereby identified as simply a personal view, without directly repudiating it.

MOTHERS EMPLOYED OUTSIDE THE HOME

As an apostle Spencer had made several strong statements that women should concentrate on family care and leave to men the responsibility of financial support. As President he still spoke of women rearing children at home as the most desirable situation.[14]

His views were shaped in part by his personal experience. He sorely missed his own mother after she died when he was eleven. His own

---

14. Early in his presidency he responded to questions by George Cornell, AP religion writer: "We want [women] to grow, develop and educate themselves so as to become really good mothers of families. Certainly wives are not slaves. They should read and study, but we think they also should bear children and have a home."

"They should go out and vote, read the newspaper and sometimes hold offices if it doesn't interfere with their primary duty to take care of the family. We believe that families are the basis of civilization."

President Benson's 1987 address to parents quoted generously from his predecessor and said that, without fathers' relinquishing their role as breadwinner, men should "help with the dishes, change diapers, get up with a crying child in the night, . . . help with the dinner . . . [and have an] equally important role . . . in nurturing, training, and loving . . . children." Bruce A. Chadwick and H. Dean Garrett found that LDS women generally accepted the advice as inspired, although many found it inapplicable to their own situation.

children, on the other hand, had been nurtured unstintingly by Camilla's focus on family.

Despite Spencer's general plea for women with children at home to avoid working outside the home, he recognized the need for exceptions. His own daughter was a case in point. Olive Beth had in midlife returned to the workforce after her husband, Grant, suffered a heart attack and blindness at age forty-five. Spencer sat down with his daughter and calculated her family's financial resources. He concurred in her conclusion that "there is nothing to do but go back to work." She had a degree in elementary education and had taught a year in the public schools before marriage. For nearly four years, Camilla cared for Olive Beth's youngest child, also named Camilla, until she was old enough for first grade.

When Grant recovered from his heart attack and, despite his blindness, returned to work as an insurance salesman, Olive Beth continued to teach third grade until retirement, nineteen years later. Her income helped pay for seven children's college and mission expenses. Spencer never suggested that she should quit, even after necessity no longer required her to work. He left her to apply the general principles to her personal situation.

During the Kimball administration the percentage of LDS women who worked outside the home increased. Inflation ate at husbands' incomes, and divorce increased, resulting in more single-parent families and more women in the job market.

A 1981–83 survey conducted by the research arm of the Correlation Department found that 50 percent of LDS women in the United States and Canada were in the workforce, a percentage almost identical to the figure for all women. LDS women were less often in the workforce in Britain, more often in Japan. Traditionally the Church itself had not employed married women at all, but by 1961 women working for the Church who married could continue only for six months. Then in the 1970s the Church decided to employ married women without any formal time restriction.[15] And when the Church Historical Department raised the issue in 1975, the First Presidency discontinued any special

---

15. Maureen Ursenbach Beecher reports that the Presidency further suggested that she be allowed to work at home as much as possible, to be with her new baby.

restrictions, allowing women to decide for themselves whether or not to keep working after having children. Women applying for jobs with the Church would not be turned away because of their motherhood.

18

THE EQUAL RIGHTS AMENDMENT

Inside the Tabernacle, three women shouted, "No—ERA policy—No!"

DURING THE KIMBALL PRESIDENCY, the women's movement in the United States became a major social force. The challenge for Church leaders was to help members benefit from the positive contributions of the movement without adopting the harmful aspects. Such balance was difficult to achieve. Often the emotionally charged issue of feminism became divisive, as was seen during the attempted ratification of the Equal Rights Amendment (ERA), a constitutional process that spanned nearly the whole of Spencer's presidency.

OPPOSITION TO THE EQUAL RIGHTS AMENDMENT

The proposed Equal Rights Amendment to the United States Constitution read, "Equality of rights under the law shall not be denied or abridged by the United States or by any State on account of sex." Beginning in 1923 the ERA was proposed repeatedly in Congress, but never adopted. However, when the ERA was raised again in 1972 on the heels of progress in civil rights for racial minorities, it sailed through Congress. Proponents saw passage as the way to achieve national commitment to women's full equality and to bypass myriad smaller legislative and judicial battles. Adoption required ratification by three-fourths of the states—thirty-eight—within seven years. By the end of 1974, thirty-three states had ratified the ERA, and it seemed destined for quick adoption.

President Kimball's journals give no indication how he felt about the issue or how his attitudes may have developed. As late as January 1975, a California newspaper quoted him as saying the Church had no official stand on the ERA. But one was developing.

Belle S. Spafford, Relief Society general president, delivered an address in New York City in July 1974 asserting that the worthy objectives of the ERA could better be achieved through legislation, without risking the unknown consequences of a vague constitutional amendment. Her successor, Barbara Bradshaw Smith, made the next public statement. After being sustained in October 1974, Smith, in consultation with the Church's Special Affairs Committee, decided to address the University of Utah Institute of Religion on the subject in December. In that talk, she supported equality in employment and property rights but repeated Spafford's concerns that the vague and overly broad ERA was not the best way to achieve those objectives.

Smith's talk stirred comment, much of it critical. Seeking a public indication that President Kimball did not disapprove of her stand, when they both attended a banquet soon afterward, she asked him to talk with her. He obligingly chatted with her throughout the meal. A few weeks later, the *Church News* ran an editorial echoing her remarks. With a Church leader and a Church publication weighing in, popular opposition to the ERA among Utahns quickly rose by 20 percent. And when the Utah legislature voted on the ERA in February 1975, the amendment was defeated 54–21.

Not until October 1976, with ratification only four states short, did President Kimball and his counselors release a formal statement. In it they proclaimed their support for women but opposed the ERA as the means for addressing injustices:

"There have been injustices to women before the law and in society generally. These we deplore.

"There are additional rights to which women are entitled.

"However, we firmly believe that the Equal Rights Amendment is not the answer.

"While the motives of its supporters may be praiseworthy, ERA as a blanket attempt to help women could indeed bring them far more restraints and repressions. We fear it will even stifle many God-given feminine instincts.

"It would strike at the family, humankind's basic institution. ERA would bring ambiguity and possibly invite extensive litigation.

"Passage of ERA, some legal authorities contend, could nullify many accumulated benefits to women in present statutes.

"We recognize men and women as equally important before the Lord, but with differences biologically, emotionally, and in other ways.

"ERA, we believe, does not recognize these differences. There are better means for giving women, and men, the rights they deserve."

In January 1977, Idahoans voted to rescind their ratification of the ERA. A few other states also rescinded.[1] But proponents continued their efforts, believing that rescissions were not valid and thus only three more states would be needed to reach the requisite thirty-eight.

In August 1978, President Kimball and his counselors elaborated on their position, saying that the ERA by "its deceptively simple language . . . [constitutes] encouragement of those who seek a unisex society, [and] an increase in the practice of homosexual and lesbian activities."[2] Only two months later, the First Presidency called upon Church members to do more than merely take a political stand, to instead "join actively with other citizens who share our concerns and who are engaged in working to reject this measure on the basis of its threat to the moral climate of the future."

In implementing this charge the Church's Special Affairs Committee encouraged LDS women to become activists in the crucial remaining states and urged members to contribute money to legislative candidates who opposed the ERA (the Church itself did not take institutional action

---

1. Nebraska (1973), Tennessee (1974), Idaho (1977), Kentucky (1978), South Dakota (1979). According to one scholar, Mormons helped "prevent ratification in Arizona, Florida, Georgia, Illinois, Maryland, Missouri, Nevada, North Carolina, Oklahoma, South Carolina, and Virginia." Their efforts failed "in California, Hawaii, Iowa, Montana, Texas, and Wyoming."

2. Since the amendment was not adopted, it is not possible to know how these concerns would have played out, but some of the issues were later pursued under the Fourteenth Amendment rubric of "equal protection of the laws." In 1994 the Hawaii Supreme Court held 3-2 that "the due-process clause of [its] state constitution" required recognition of same-sex marriages unless the state could establish a contrary compelling state interest. The decision was overturned when the state's voters adopted a state constitutional amendment. In December 1999 the Hawaii Supreme Court held that the amendment gave the legislature power to prohibit same-sex marriages. Utah and other legislatures acted in 1996 to decline to recognize same-sex marriages performed in other states, and Congress enacted the Defense of Marriage Act to free states from an obligation to recognize same-sex marriages contracted legally in another state. In April 2000, Vermont became the first state to allow same-sex couples to form "civil unions" entitling them to all the legal rights of "marriage." In 2003 the Massachusetts high court held that the right to same-sex marriage is guaranteed by the Constitution.

or make any donations). Members responded, and large numbers of women descended on their undecided state legislatures.

When it appeared that the required three-fourths of the states would not ratify the ERA by the March 1979 deadline, Congress extended the period for ratification by three years—to June 1982. In May 1978, President Kimball and his counselors issued a statement opposing this extension as an "unwise as well as unfair . . . tampering with and . . . abuse of the process of amendment itself." They also objected to Congress's decision to disallow rescissions. An October statement reaffirming the First Presidency's opposition to the ERA concluded with this conviction: "We express confidence that this nation is sufficiently strong and fair to be able to resolve problems of inequality and unfairness to women, or any other group in our society, without abusing the amending process of our most basic document, the Constitution, as outlined above, and without undermining our most basic institution, the family."

News coverage of the Church's position was often negative. What the Church saw as encouragement of like-minded individuals to speak out was interpreted as a case of Church leaders pulling puppet strings and meddling in politics. But President Kimball did not waver. "Because he considers the ERA a moral issue, not a political one," an interviewer wrote in 1979, "he sees nothing wrong with an organized church effort to prevent its passage." A 1980 *Ensign* article explained the reasoning:

"Since the First Presidency believes that basic freedoms pertaining to the family and society's moral climate will be eroded if the ERA is passed, the Church has a moral responsibility, validated by history and doctrine, to oppose the amendment."

PROTESTS

The stand taken by the First Presidency precipitated protest. When the vote to sustain President Kimball was taken in the October 1980 general conference, three women rose at the back of the Tabernacle to vote in opposition and shouted, "No—ERA policy—No." Previously alerted to this possibility, Elder McConkie stood and invited the women to meet with Elder Hinckley after the meeting. The women later reported that Elder Hinckley said they "were entitled to [their] opinion" and that no action would be taken against them.[3] Outside, thirty or so picketers chanted slogans—"Two, four, six, eight, / Ratify in every state" and "Not the church, not the state, / Women will decide their fate"— and an airplane towed a banner with yet another slogan. At least one anti-ERA picketer countered with a sign that read, "Equal work for equal pay, / but not with ERA."

During the October 1980 open house and the November dedication of the temple in Bellevue, Washington, women again demonstrated. When asked to leave the temple grounds, some complied; others chained themselves to the temple gate. During the dedication, police arrested twenty-one for blocking entry.

After one of the dedication sessions, the Kimballs and Elder Howard W. Hunter left in a downpour to return to their hotel. A woman approached and shouted a profane insult at President Kimball. When security personnel tried to intercede, she ran away through the rain. Despite the verbal assault, Spencer expressed concern that she was without an umbrella and was getting soaking wet.

SONIA JOHNSON

One of the principal protestors, Sonia Johnson, had become active in support of the ERA when a letter opposing the ERA was read over the pulpit in her Sterling, Virginia, ward. She co-founded Mormons for ERA and began speaking energetically in favor of the amendment and against the Church's role in supporting it. For example, she urged Montanans to "write and tell church leaders that you do not like what they are doing in ERA politics, and that if their missionaries come to your door you will say that you are not interested in a church that is fighting your civil rights." In a September 1979 talk to the American Psychological Association, she contended that "the Mormons, a tiny minority, are dedicated to imposing the prophet's moral directives upon all

---

3. The Church principle of "common consent" (D&C 124:144) called for officers to be subject to acceptance by the membership. Open opposition at general conference to sustaining Church officers was very rare. It occurred at least occasionally in local congregations. In a stake conference in 1960 at which Spencer presided, two members voted against the proposed stake president because he was a lawyer and one voted against the proposed stake clerk because he was a used car salesman, both following occupations some felt inconsistent with their honesty.

Americans, and they may succeed if Americans do not become aware of their methods and goals. . . .

" . . . One of the major purposes of Mormons for ERA has become to shine a light upon the murky political activities of the church, and to expose to other Americans its exploitation of women's religious commitment for its self-serving male political purposes."

President Kimball sought to encourage a course of action, but he did not mean to intimidate. He addressed the topic in a meeting with local Church leaders in South Carolina:

"We feel that members of the Church need to be reminded in appropriate ways of the position taken by the First Presidency, although we do not want . . . to injure the feelings of the members of the Church who do not wish to accept this counsel. . . . Every man in this room has his free agency, and every woman has her free agency and can vote as she pleases, but she will be wise, and he will be wise, if he will listen to the Brethren."

In spring 1979, Johnson tried to arrange a meeting with President Kimball, intending to urge him to "free" Church members to vote their preference. President Kimball declined to meet her because he suspected she would manipulate whatever he might say. But according to one report, he repeatedly prayed for her by name during temple meetings.

Johnson held that her statements and activities were political only, that they were not an attack on the Church or its leaders. But Church leaders viewed the statements differently. In November, Sonia Johnson's bishop, Jeffrey H. Willis, instituted Church court proceedings based, not on her outspoken championing of the ERA, but on her attacks against the Church.

Johnson made the Church court a media event. At a preliminary meeting with her bishop in November, thirty-five pro-ERA demonstrators stood outside carrying banners and signs. Two weeks later about two hundred supporters and reporters held a vigil outside during the three-hour bishop's court that excommunicated her.

Because Johnson had sought publicity, her bishop, in an unusual action, publicly explained to the press the grounds for her excommunication. He said they included her position that Mormon society and its leaders were guilty of "savage misogyny," her expressed view that missionaries representing such a church "should not be invited into people's homes," her teaching "that the Church is dedicated to imposing the prophet's moral directives upon all Americans," and her spirit of disharmony with the Church.

The bishop and, later, Church spokesman Don LeFevre explained the Church's stand: "It's all right to be pro-ERA; it's just not all right to be anti-Church." The bishop felt Johnson had stepped over the line; he also pointed out that he knew of no other ERA supporter whose Church membership had been called into question.

Sonia Johnson appealed her excommunication to stake president Earl J. Roueche, who upheld the bishop's action. She then appealed to President Kimball and his counselors, who also affirmed the bishop's action.

ERA supporters tried other tactics. In May 1981, the National Organization of Women sent a number of "missionaries" door to door in Utah to obtain signatures on pro-ERA petitions addressed to President Kimball and to the United States president, Ronald Reagan. In February 1982, a dozen demonstrators at the Seattle Temple expressed their "outrage" at Church opposition to the ERA by hanging in effigy President Kimball and President Reagan.

During this period, picketers popped up wherever President Kimball and other General Authorities convened area conferences in the

United States, and supporters continued their protests at general conferences. At the October 1981 general conference, forty demonstrators marched in the rain. Inside the Tabernacle during the sustaining of Church leaders, one woman shouted her opposition. Again an airplane flew overhead, a banner stretched behind it.

The next conference, about two hundred demonstrators marched from the state capitol to Temple Square.[4] President Kimball remained unperturbed. "This work is divine," he testified during the final session, "the Lord is at the helm, the Church is *true,* and all is well."

Despite the protests and pleas of proponents, no state legislatures ratified the ERA in the waning days of the extension, and in June 1982, the ratification effort expired.

---

4. Twelve ERA supporters attended the first session intending to shout "No" when asked to sustain Church leaders, but the sustaining was deferred to the last session.

19

PERSONAL AND INSTITUTIONAL HISTORY

"The truth should be told, but we should not emphasize the negative."

"FROM TIME IMMEMORIAL," President Kimball reminded the Church, "the Lord has counseled us to be a record-keeping people. Abraham had a book of remembrance, and Adam had one." In the Pentateuch Moses wrote a history of his people up to his time:

"Where would we be if Moses hadn't written his history of the world, those first five vital books of the Old Testament? He had the background, the data, the record, and the inclination, and he has blessed us throughout the eternities by the service he rendered in writing the first five books of the Bible.

"How grateful we are that Abraham wrote his own life story and that important segment of the history of the world and his own revelations, thoughts, feelings, and rich experiences."

"Remember," he warned the Church, "the Savior chastised those who failed to record important events" (see 3 Nephi 23:6–13).

KEEPING RECORDS

President Kimball led the way in fulfilling what he termed "a duty and a responsibility," describing for the general Church membership his own long-standing practice of journal keeping:

"On the bookshelves in my office at home there are thirty-three large, well-filled journal books. In my journal, a year for each book, I have written daily and filed in this library. It records the trips to many of the nations in the world and all around the world and meetings held,

Examining his journal with Andrew E. Kimball Jr. and Edward L. Kimball, authors of his 1977 biography.

people contacted, marriages performed, and all things of interest to my family, and, I hope, someday to the Church."

Countering those who would excuse themselves for not being important enough to keep records, President Kimball assured youthful members, "No one is commonplace. . . . You are unique, and there may be incidents in your experience that are more noble and praiseworthy in their way than those recorded in any other life." If members but keep a journal, "angels may quote from it for eternity." If angels do not, one's posterity will, he promised.

As a result of his urging, there was a great increase in writing of personal and family histories. Many Saints sent him a copy to demonstrate they had heeded his advice.

As to how to walk the fine line between honest depiction and undue confession, he counseled:

"Your journal should contain your true self rather than a picture of you when you are 'made up' for a public performance. There is a temptation to paint one's virtues in rich color and whitewash the vices, but there is also the opposite pitfall of accentuating the negative. Personally

I have little respect for anyone who delves into the ugly phases of the life he is portraying, whether it be his own or another's. The truth should be told, but we should not emphasize the negative."

CHURCH HISTORY

Spencer promoted Church history throughout the active years of his presidency. In 1972 April conference, a few months before he became President, the Church created a Historical Department and sustained its first professional Church Historian, Leonard J. Arrington. The next ten years produced an outpouring of Church-sponsored books and articles, as professional historians collected artifacts, gathered records, researched, and began to write.

The Historical Department faced several thorny issues, including how to handle less faith-promoting incidents and how to detect forgeries. After a decade of controversy, the department was reorganized, and the professional personnel were shifted largely to Brigham Young University. There they were housed in the newly created Joseph Fielding Smith Institute for Church History.

Whether President Kimball would have initiated this change is not entirely clear. He never spoke publicly about these matters. While he generally approved of openness and candor in writing journals, history, and biography, he also believed in accentuating the positive. When discussing his own biography, he agreed it should be candid but urged the authors, "Don't emphasize the warts." In 1975 he wrote to his relative Stanley B. Kimball, who was writing a biography of Spencer's grandfather Heber C. Kimball:

"I hope sincerely that you will not be influenced unduly by those who claim [that] . . . true historians must tell all of the questionable and improper things in a person's life. . . . Be sure there is no good work prostituted to pay tribute to the god of . . . historian . . . standards. There are many writers who would sell the soul of a good man to make the story realistic. . . . I have no tolerance for the muckrakers and the debunkers."

"The good biographer," President Kimball emphasized in an article the same year, "will not depend on passion but on good sense. He will weed out the irrelevant and seek the strong, novel, and interesting."

In 1974 Deseret Book asked the First Presidency to decide whether, as a Church-owned company, it should publish a manuscript that included discussion of polygamy, the Mountain Meadows massacre, and a serious disagreement between David O. McKay and George Albert Smith. Elder Kimball met with author Merlo Pusey and advised him that it would be "unwise" for the Church itself to publish passages dealing with "controversial" and "delicate and personal" matters. But he did not direct Pusey to abandon publication or require him to make changes, and BYU Press later published the book unchanged.

In 1976, Spencer discussed with Church Historian Leonard Arrington a proposed biography of Brigham Young. A large chest of Brigham Young letters and papers had been discovered when the Historical Department moved from the Church Administration Building into the new Church Office Building, and President Kimball was eager to have these materials used in writing a new biography of the pioneer prophet. President Kimball asked Arrington to write the book personally and before publication to submit the manuscript to three types of historians—"a non-Mormon reader, a *Dialogue*-type Mormon, and an orthodox Mormon."

Spencer approved of several Historical Department publications that other General Authorities found objectionable in certain respects. In 1976 he read and enjoyed a one-volume history of the Church titled *The Story of the Latter-day Saints*, written for an LDS audience and published by Deseret Book. A similar volume, entitled *The Mormon Experience*, but aimed at the general reader, was published by the University of Illinois Press. Both books were cleared in principle by the First Presidency. Two or three of the apostles did not like the way the first book seemed to treat some topics too naturalistically; they also raised concerns about Church-paid historians writing in ways that humanized the prophets or seemed to underplay revelation and God's intervention in human affairs.[1] For example, Elder Packer said to a meeting of some BYU faculty, "[A historian] seemed determined to convince everyone that the

---

1. Ezra Taft Benson to First Presidency: "Members of our staff have carefully read . . . and in accordance with your request, these are our impressions." They were very disappointed with a lack of spirituality, reliance on sources like *Dialogue*, portrayal of Joseph Smith as affected by the political, economic, and religious environments in which he lived, not taking the conservative side on issues like evolution, and calling the "Black issue" a matter of "policy" (paraphrase of several pages).

prophet was a *man*. We knew that already. . . . It would have been much more worthwhile for him to have convinced us that the *man* was a *prophet*." He and others felt uncomfortable publishing information that they thought diminished Church leaders or could be distorted to discredit them. Elder Stapley objected to the book's mentioning that Brigham Young used chewing tobacco.[2] Others were unhappy about naturalistic explanations of Church doctrine and practices, such as mention that, at the time the Word of Wisdom was received, other people in nineteenth-century America were embracing similar health concepts.

As a consequence the book was essentially unadvertised and it was not used in the seminaries and institutes as had been expected. Even so, the first printing of 30,000 was sold out after three years; but the book was allowed to go out of print. Several years later *The Story of the Latter-day Saints* was reprinted and has continued to be available since that time.

Though Spencer disdained the label "intellectual" for himself and was consistently orthodox in behavior and thought throughout his life, he also was sensitive to how those with sensibilities different from his own might approach the gospel. He generally was inclined to allow a fair diversity of thought on questions and issues of an unsettled nature.

When in 1977 an apostle and member of the BYU Board of Trustees began soliciting student reports of "liberal teachings" in social science courses at the university, President Kimball stopped the practice.

Several periodicals of various types for the Mormon audience arose or expanded during President Kimball's tenure, including *Exponent II*,

2. Young used chewing tobacco to deaden the pain of bad teeth.

Journal of Mormon History, Sunstone, and *This People.* (*BYU Studies* had begun in 1959, and *Dialogue: A Journal of Mormon Thought* had begun in 1966.) Some of these publications included news and discussions about the Church that official sources did not carry, much of it faith building but some of it exploring, rethinking, or questioning or criticizing Church leaders or beliefs. While some General Authorities wanted to suppress the less-flattering material if they could, Spencer was slow to interfere.

In 1983, after President Kimball became too ill to be actively involved, one of the apostles contacted at least fourteen stake presidents and asked them to interview members of their stakes who had written on Church subjects in *Dialogue* and *Sunstone.* The writers were cautioned to take care that their work not hurt the faith of members who might not be well grounded. Subjects that seemed sensitive included Church opposition to the Equal Rights Amendment, exclusion of women from the priesthood, unquestioning obedience to leaders, organic evolution, and Church history that noted leaders' human failings.

President Kimball's tolerance had limits. In 1974, he called in LDS historian Reed C. Durham Jr. after Durham presented a paper at the Mormon History Association conference about Joseph Smith's use of Masonic imagery. After the interview, Durham circulated a letter reaffirming his faith in the temple ceremony, the Church, and its leaders. He also indicated that he had been asked to say nothing more about the subject.

The Historical Department had an aggressive publishing plan that aimed to produce a multivolume set on the history of the Church to be available for the 1980 sesquicentennial of the organization of the Church. Eventually the series idea was discarded, although some of the volumes were published separately.

Although President Kimball personally liked the Historical Department publications that some other Church leaders criticized, he never publicly expressed his approval or curbed the critics. In private, he encouraged the Church historians and praised them for their efforts. On one occasion, Spencer embraced Arrington, saying he was aware of the complaints, and urged him to continue his work: "The Lord is pleased that you are the historian of his Church."

In 1982, when Church history writing was moved to BYU, Arrington was released as Church Historian. The Historical Department then came under the managing directorship of General Authorities, who changed every few years. The department returned for a time to its previous role of preserving records, rather than interpreting them. Access to the archives was greatly curtailed, and the view seemed to crystallize among Church leadership that awkward truths should not be allowed to damage immature faith. In the 1980s, Elders Nelson, Maxwell, and Oaks publicly expressed the cautionary view that Church historians should build testimony. Elder Oaks said, "Even though something is true, we are not necessarily justified in communicating it."

THE MARK HOFMANN FRAUDS

During this era of great productivity by the Church Historical Department, the study of Church history was greatly disrupted by the Mark Hofmann forgeries of early Church documents.

In April 1980, Hofmann, a student at Utah State University and a collector of Church-related historical documents, took to the Utah State University archivist Jeff Simmonds a Bible he said he had purchased from descendants of Joseph Smith's sister. From between two sealed pages, they together removed a folded paper with the signature "Joseph Smith" and vertical columns of characters and a circular design—just what Professor Charles Anthon had said Martin Harris showed him in February 1828 as copied by Joseph Smith from the golden plates. Within a few days, the handwriting, signature, paper, and ink had been tentatively authenticated. Before the end of the month, the likelihood of genuineness seemed great enough to bring it to the attention of the First Presidency.

Elder Hinckley, then serving as adviser to the Historical Department, asked Hofmann to leave the document with the Church for further testing. Hofmann agreed.

Further tests showed that the paper was old, the ink consistent with the document's purported age, and the handwriting consistent with Joseph Smith's known writings. And the document fit the Martin Harris–Charles Anthon story in every detail. The Presidency discussed the document with the Twelve, and the Church traded rare moneys and a first edition Book of Mormon, together worth $20,000, for the "Anthon transcript."

This was only the beginning. Hofmann soon "discovered" other "historic documents"—a blessing of Joseph Smith III by his father naming the boy his father's successor as prophet, a letter mentioning the blessing (thus providing corroboration), a Lucy Mack Smith letter about the Book of Mormon, a Joseph Smith letter about his digging for treasure, the contract to print the Book of Mormon, and then a letter by Martin Harris saying that Joseph Smith had received the gold plates from a spirit in the form of a white salamander. These masterfully forged documents all brought Hofmann profit, but the last also achieved a second purpose: to cast a shadow on the traditional story of the Church's origins.

Hofmann claimed to know of still other significant documents and borrowed $185,000 on the representation that with the money he could procure them. When time came to repay the money or deliver the documents, and he could do neither, he set two bombs. One killed Steve Christensen, who was marginally involved in the transaction, and the other killed the wife of Christensen's former business associate. The first was to buy Hofmann time, the second to disguise the motive for killing Christensen.

Hofmann was soon unmasked as forger, thief, murderer, and secret enemy of the Church.

THE REVELATION
ON PRIESTHOOD

20

THE QUESTION OF
PRIESTHOOD DENIAL

"We realize we do not know all there is to be known about this problem."

THE MOST DRAMATIC MOMENT of the Kimball administration and probably of Church history in the twentieth century occurred in June 1978 when the First Presidency announced a revelation allowing worthy men of all races to be ordained to the priesthood. Until then, Latter-day Saint men of black African ancestry had been denied the priesthood. They could serve as teachers and in other callings not requiring the person to be a priesthood bearer, but they could not serve as missionaries. After the revelation there were no restrictions. Where previously the only temple ceremony open to them was being baptized on behalf of their ancestors and others, now they could be endowed and sealed, opening the door to exaltation, without having to wait any longer for a promised future time when the priesthood would be available to them.

The 1978 revelation did not come easily to President Kimball and his associates in the First Presidency and Quorum of the Twelve, because they were all reared in an America where prejudice toward non-whites was the norm. They also were reared in a church in which most people were taught and believed that it was God's will that black men should not hold the priesthood, because they had been less valiant in their premortal life as spirits.

President Kimball was an old man when he set out to know with certainty for himself whether God wanted black men admitted to or excluded from the priesthood. Most would expect a man at his age to be firmly set in his ways, but instead he was able to reconsider the teachings of a lifetime and accept radical change.

ORIGINS OF THE PRIESTHOOD RESTRICTION

President Kimball's first steps toward the events of June 1978 were years of asking why the restriction existed. The explanations he found relied sometimes on strained scriptural interpretations and doubtful historical understandings.

The origin of the priesthood policy was unclear. While later Church leaders asserted that Joseph Smith instituted the practice, no contemporary record exists indicating Joseph Smith said anything directly on the subject of blacks and priesthood. A statement made by Zebedee Coltrin thirty-five years after Joseph's death attributed the restriction to the Prophet, but that statement is dubious, because Joseph was fully aware that in 1836 a black man named Elijah Abel (also spelled Able)

was ordained an elder and then a seventy, a calling in which he was active the rest of his life in Kirtland, Nauvoo, and Utah. Furthermore, Elijah Abel was ordained a seventy by the same Zebedee Coltrin.

It appears then that the practice was likely instituted during Brigham Young's tenure as president, whether instituted by inspiration or by misunderstanding of the doctrine of the priesthood and the principle of individual responsibility for sin. He said in 1849 of "the Africans": "The curse remained upon them because Cain cut off the lives of Abel. . . . The Lord had cursed

Elijah Abel, a black Latter-day Saint who was ordained an elder and then a seventy in 1836.

Cain's seed with blackness and prohibited them the Priesthood." Three years later he again attributed priesthood denial solely to a man's ancestry, not to color, appearance, or premortal behavior: "Any man having one drop of the seed of [Cain] in him Cannot hold the priesthood & if no other Prophet ever spake it Before I will say it now in the name of Jesus Christ. I know it is true and they know it."

By the early twentieth century, when Spencer came to adulthood, the restriction—whatever its origin—had become fully entrenched. Church members generally accepted without question that it was God's will that "colored" or "Negro" members of the Church could not receive the priesthood. They assumed without proof that the restriction must have come from Joseph Smith and that Brigham Young merely perpetuated the teaching.[1] The few Church members who were aware of Elijah Abel accepted his ordination as an exception or as an aberration resulting from Joseph Smith's still-developing understanding.[2]

The scriptures relied on to explain the restriction were ambiguous.[3]

---

1. Although the first known declaration of priesthood restriction dates from Brigham Young's presidency, many assumed he would only have done this if following a pattern established by Joseph Smith. In 1908, Joseph F. Smith stated his understanding that Joseph Smith himself declared Elijah Abel's ordination "null and void." However, President Smith offered no basis for that assertion and Abel himself did not believe that his ordination had ever been nullified. Indeed, twenty-nine years earlier, in 1879, Joseph F. Smith himself noted that Abel had two certificates identifying him as a seventy, one of the certificates issued in Utah.

2. Harold B. Lee also asserted that Joseph Smith had declared the ordination void, an assertion not supported by the evidence; Andrew Jensen wrote: "He [Abel] was intimately acquainted with the Prophet Joseph Smith."

3. The scriptural statements and the arguments drawn from them went more or less like this:

God cursed Cain for killing Abel and placed a mark on him, and Cain's descendants were black.
Inference: The mark of Cain was blackness, which passed to his children.
Response: The scriptures say that the curse upon Cain was personal, that he would be a "fugitive" and unable to derive a livelihood from the earth. If the mark placed on Cain was blackness, it was not a curse, because its purpose was to keep Cain from being killed (see Moses 5:39–40). There is no reference in these passages to priesthood.

The Canaanites were black.
Inference: The Canaanites were descendants of Cain.
Response: The Canaanites became black as a curse upon them, probably for their slaughter of the people of Shum (see Moses 7:7–8). Thus their blackness does not necessarily indicate their lineage. There is no reference to priesthood in these passages.

Pharaoh, who was descended from Ham and his wife, Egyptus, had Canaanite blood and was black.
Inference: Cain's blood line survived the Flood through Egypt.
Response: It was the Canaanite black line that survived the Flood, not Cain's black line, if there was such a line.

Although Brigham Young offered only descent from Cain as justification for the restriction, later Church leaders began to find in the distinctive Mormon doctrine of a premortal spiritual state a justification for the policy that otherwise seemed unjust. The reasoning ran this way: We know that blacks are denied the priesthood and that a just God holds individuals accountable only for their own shortcomings; therefore, withholding priesthood from blacks who have lived worthily in mortality must reflect some kind of sin committed before they were born.

David O. McKay, counselor in the First Presidency, explained his views in a 1947 letter:

"I know of no scriptural basis for denying the Priesthood to Negroes other than one verse in the Book of Abraham (1:26); however, I believe . . . that the real reason dates back to our pre-existent life.

"This means that the true answer to your question (and it is the only one that has ever given me satisfaction) has its foundation in faith— (1) Faith in a God of Justice, (2) Faith in the existence of an eternal plan of salvation for all God's children."[4]

Other Church leaders generally concurred. Although they differed about when it would be, Brigham Young and other Church Presidents posited that eventually righteous blacks would receive all the blessings now available to others. This ameliorated the restriction somewhat by characterizing it as time-limited and subject to divine oversight.

Although Pharaoh was righteous, he was of a "lineage by which he could not have the right of Priesthood" (Abraham 1:27).

Inference: The denial of priesthood was because of Pharaoh's descent from Cain as marked by his blackness.

Response: In a patriarchal society Pharaoh could trace his lineage back to Noah only through a maternal line, whereas Abraham laid claim to priesthood leadership through his paternal line back to Noah, saying that he "became a rightful heir, a High Priest, holding the right . . . through the fathers" (Abraham 1:2–3).

Some premortal spirits were noble and great (see Abraham 3:22).

Inference: There were spirits of all qualities in the premortal sphere, among them spirits unworthy to bear the priesthood in mortality. These must be the ones without "the right to the priesthood."

Response: This inference depends on the premise that there is a black lineage group that should be denied priesthood and that being denied the priesthood was a penalty rather than a challenge.

4. It should be noted that Joseph Smith, who translated the Book of Abraham, probably in 1835, never connected the references in the Book of Abraham to premortal life and a priesthood curse.

A number of black congregations sprang up in Africa and asked that missionaries be sent.

EFFECTS OF THE POLICY

Because of the priesthood restriction, missionaries were instructed not to proselytize in black areas, although they were not to refuse teaching blacks who expressed interest.[5] The experience of blacks who did join the Church varied from place to place, but at times they were not accepted in full fellowship. For example, when black members Len and Mary Hope moved to Cincinnati, the branch president asked them to hold meetings in their own home because some white members objected to their presence in the chapel. They complied. A later branch president invited them to attend district conferences.

Although the priesthood restriction deeply disturbed many members of the Church, particularly after the civil rights movement of the 1960s raised consciousness about issues of racial discrimination, the matter remained largely abstract. So few blacks joined the Church that most white members never personally saw the effects of the ban. Most white Americans did not accept blacks as their equals, so those Church members who also did not were in the comfortable majority and they had available to them a pat religious basis for their different treatment of blacks.

---

5. The Council in Jerusalem arrived at a somewhat similar practical compromise, allowing teaching the gospel to the gentiles but asking them to keep part of the Mosaic law.

Those blacks who did accept baptism implicitly accepted their restricted status. If converted, they believed in the Church's prophetic leadership, and they could not easily challenge the Church's settled practice. Mary Hope, speaking the feelings of many black Saints in 1947, said, "We are not too much worried about the priesthood. We know that the Lord will take care of it. There is so much of the Gospel for us to live up to that we have a great responsibility and about all we can do."[6]

The policy repeatedly required the Presidency to deal with difficult borderline cases. For example, in 1948, during the George Albert Smith administration, missionaries in the Philippines did not know how to handle natives of a group called "Negritos," who had black skin but no known African ancestry.[7] The First Presidency authorized ordination, saying descent from black Africans was the disqualifying factor, not skin color or other racial characteristics.

President McKay was more concerned that no eligible person be excluded than that no ineligible person be ordained. His approach was to err on the side of inclusion. In South Africa, for example, converts had been required to trace all ancestral lines out of Africa to establish they had no black African forebears. The requirement proved burdensome and impossible in some cases, and in 1954, President McKay discontinued it.[8] In some areas of Brazil, 80 percent of the population was thought to have at least traces of Negroid ancestry, but records were generally not adequate to provide evidence one way or another. In 1965,

---

6. Spencer W. Kimball quoted Sister Hope as saying, "We are not worrying about the priesthood. We have so many blessings now to live up to that we have our hands full, and we are deeply grateful, and we are expending our every energy to magnify our present opportunities."

7. While in the Philippines to dedicate the land for proselytizing, Joseph Fielding Smith observed native peoples who appeared to be negroid. Despite this, he said in the dedicatory prayer, "I bless the native inhabitants both black and white with the blessings of the gospel and the priesthood—Amen." When asked about it then, he responded, upset, "That is what the Lord required me to do." He confirmed several years later that the event occurred and said, "I would not want it to be supposed that I gave the priesthood to the negroes."

8. Gregory A. Prince wrote, "[David O. McKay] thought that unless the requirement was changed the increasing inability of converts to accomplish this genealogical task would eventually leave the Church without sufficient men to assume the necessary leadership roles. He also thought that in the overwhelming majority of South African cases there was no black ancestry, and that errors subsequently discovered could simply be corrected." President McKay made the change "without consulting anyone." Afterwards, President McKay notified his counselors and the Twelve and received their endorsement.

President McKay directed that male converts in Brazil should be assumed qualified to receive the priesthood in the absence of evidence to the contrary. Soon afterward he extended that policy to all countries.[9]

President McKay said several times in private conversations that the restriction on priesthood was not doctrine but was a policy and thus subject to change. But he did not mean that such a change could come by a simple administrative decision. With a century of precedent, change would require divine intervention. President McKay is said to have wanted and sought such a revelation, but he did not receive it and "finally concluded the time was not yet ripe."

INTEREST IN THE CHURCH BY BLACK AFRICANS

For a church that seeks to take its message to every corner of the earth, the priesthood restriction was a particularly vexing problem in Africa. In South Africa there was a Church presence but understandably very little interest among blacks. Ghana and Nigeria had no Church organization but produced a stream of letters, at least as early as 1938, begging for missionaries to come teach large numbers of blacks already converted to the Restoration message by reading Church literature.

LaMar Williams was sent to Nigeria in 1961. As secretary to the Church Missionary Committee, he had answered dozens of letters from Africa. He was met at the airport by ten pastors he had been corresponding with and discovered that many of them were unaware of one another. Williams returned with the names of 15,000 unbaptized converts who were said to be waiting for the Church to come to them. In December 1962 newly ordained apostle N. Eldon Tanner spent two weeks in the Lagos area, visiting three groups that used the Church's name, one claiming 4,000 adherents. Elder Tanner reported to the First Presidency "cautious optimism" about missionary work, and in early 1963 President McKay called five couples to serve missions in Nigeria. He set LaMar Williams apart as presiding elder of Nigeria with tentative plans to establish Sunday schools headed by Nigerians, supervised by white missionaries who would teach and would administer ordinances.

---

9. Missionaries first went to Fiji itself in 1954; a decision was rendered in 1958 that Fijians, though black, could be ordained. The abandonment of genealogical proof was intended to be Churchwide in 1954 but was applied in Brazil only in 1965 and announced more generally in 1967.

The plan, however, foundered when a March 1963 editorial in the newspaper *Nigerian Outlook* condemned the Church as racist, and the Nigerian government denied visas to the missionaries. Not long afterward the Biafran civil war broke out in Nigeria. And after the war ended, political instability continued until a peaceful military coup in July 1975.

BACKLASH

As awareness of the priesthood policy grew in the United States and Europe, many white potential investigators found it offensive and refused to listen to the missionaries. Technically the ban was not inconsistent with full civil or legal rights for blacks,[10] and the policy did not affect men of all other races, including blacks not of African descent. But these distinctions did not persuade most people. Also largely ineffectual was the argument that those who did not believe in the truthfulness of the Church should have no interest in who had access to its priesthood anyway.

In 1963 the Utah chapter of the NAACP threatened to picket October general conference but dropped the plan when President Hugh B. Brown indicated to NAACP leaders that he would read to the conference a statement supporting full civil rights. The statement, approved by President McKay, said that the Church had "no doctrine, belief, or practice that is intended to deny the enjoyment of full civil rights by any person regardless of race, color, or creed. . . . We call upon all men . . . to commit themselves to the establishment of full civil equality for all of God's children."

Between 1968 and 1970 at least a dozen demonstrations or violent acts occurred when Brigham Young University athletic teams played other schools. Opposing players refused to participate or wore black armbands. One spectator threw acid, and another threw a Molotov cocktail that failed to ignite. Stanford University severed athletic relations with Brigham Young University.[11]

---

10. Among those most dogmatic about the priesthood restriction, Joseph Fielding Smith affirmed in about 1952 to Sterling McMurrin his belief in equal civil rights. However, integration, with its increased likelihood of intermarriage, worried Elder Smith. As race became diluted, it would be difficult to know whether a prospective marriage partner had some negroid ancestry so that temple marriage would be barred and children of such a marriage would be ineligible for priesthood or temple blessings.

11. These athletics-related demonstrations generated enormous negative publicity for the school and the Church. Heber G. Wolsey, BYU's public relations director, visited several universities

CHANGING PERCEPTIONS OF THE POLICY IN THE CHURCH

The possibility for changing the policy increased subtly as scholarly efforts to trace the restriction to its source showed uncertain beginnings and shaky reasoning in support of the practice. A 1967 article by Armand L. Mauss pointed out the speculative nature of the explanations based on premortal conduct and the "curse of Cain." He concluded that the policy rested on tradition, not on scriptural mandate.

A 1970 book by Stephen Taggart proposed that the policy began in Missouri in the 1830s to reduce the tension between abolition-tending Mormons and their slave-holding neighbors. Lester E. Bush Jr. responded to that argument in 1973 with a lengthy study concluding that the earliest clear evidence of priesthood denial dates only to Brigham Young's presidency.[12]

As the doctrinal foundations of the policy grew increasingly problematic, members focused on its social aspects. Armand Mauss, Eugene England, and Marion D. Hanks, among others, hypothesized that changing the policy perhaps depended on LDS members' developing a willingness to accept black men and women in true fellowship.[13] Lowell Bennion, highly regarded Institute of Religion teacher at the University of Utah, encouraged members to pray for change. In 1963, he said:

"God's revelations . . . depend upon our minds, our eagerness, upon

---

where demonstrators planned protests and defused the situation, in most cases, by explaining the Church's position on civil rights more fully. He took with him Darius Gray, a black Church member.

12. Bush suggests also that the Church should feel no embarrassment that a nineteenth-century prophet held nineteenth-century secular views about race. Bush suggests that even if Joseph did not believe in racial equality, he did not carry that view so far as to deny all black men the priesthood. Bush further points out that Brigham Young did not use the premortal-conduct rationale that later Church leaders saw as crucial to the "justice" of the policy.

13. Mauss wrote, "Perhaps . . . the chief deterrent to a divine mandate for change is not to be found in any inadequacy among Negroes, but rather in the unreadiness of the Mormon whites, with our heritage of racial folklore; it is perhaps we whites who have a long way to go before 'the Negroes will be ready' for the priesthood." Eugene England urged that God was waiting for the general membership of the Church to change. Marion D. Hanks said, much later, "For me it was never that blacks [were unqualified but that] the rest of us had to be brought to a condition of spiritual maturity . . . to meet the moment of change with grace and goodness." In 1964, President McKay explained that to change the policy then would be divisive in the Church, like the question among early Christians of preaching to the Gentiles. In like manner, Matthew 19:8 explained that Moses allowed divorce "because of the hardness of your hearts." And God gave Israel a king because of the people's insistence, not because it was a good thing to do (see 1 Samuel 8:18–22).

our search, upon our questions, upon our moral disturbances, if you will, upon our needs. . . . It may be that the Lord can't get through to us sometimes on things. Therefore we ought to be thinking and searching and praying even over this Negro problem."

But others thought it presumptuous for members to do anything but wait patiently and faithfully defend the Church's position. Spencer W. Kimball, to whom loyalty was an article of faith, placed himself in this latter group. In letters to his son, he explained:

"Perhaps what the prophet needs is not pressure, not goading, not demands. He needs in every city and place defenders—a million men and women to encourage patience, understanding and faith . . . saying: 'President, we realize we do not know all there is to be known about this problem. We have faith and confidence in you and in the Lord that if relaxation is to come, it will come when the proper time comes. We shall stand and defend as did Peter, 'though the whole world be against us.' . . . The very fact that he has not yielded to the public clamor sets him up in my mind as a courageous person, for it would be relatively easy to yield if it were his decision. . . . I have never heard any of the brethren say that the Negro is inferior as a man, nor have I felt the inference. We all know that there are many Negroes who are far superior to numerous whites. . . . The conferring of priesthood, and declining to give the priesthood is not a matter of my choice nor of President McKay's. It is the Lord's program. . . . When the Lord is ready to relax the restriction, it will come whether there is pressure or not. This is my faith. Until then, I shall try to fight on. . . . I have always prided myself on being about as unprejudiced as to race as any man. I think my work with the minorities would prove that, but I am so completely convinced that the prophets know what they are doing and the Lord knows what he is doing, that I am willing to rest it there."

Elder Harold B. Lee, convinced that the ban was doctrinally fixed and wishing to reaffirm the traditional Church position at a time when President McKay was incapacitated, persuaded First Presidency counselors Brown and Tanner to send a letter to that effect in December 1969 to bishops and stake presidents. This statement included strong affirmation of civil rights,[14] but it also attributed the policy on priesthood to

---

14. President Brown signed reluctantly and then only after insisting that a statement about civil rights be included.

Joseph Smith and explained that the reason for the exclusion "antedates man's mortal existence" and is "for reasons which we believe are known to God, but which He has not made fully known to man."[15]

Despite defending the policy, Church leaders sought to make the Church a more welcoming place. In June 1971 three black Mormons in Salt Lake City—Ruffin Bridgeforth, Darius Gray, and Eugene Orr— petitioned the Church for help in keeping and reactivating the relatively small number of black members in the city. A committee of three apostles, Elders Hinckley, Monson, and Packer, met with them a number of times, and in October they set Bridgeforth apart as president of the new "Genesis" branch, assigned to the Salt Lake Liberty Stake.[16] Gray and Orr became his counselors. Genesis members attended sacrament meeting in the wards where they lived but came together weekly for Relief Society, Primary, and youth meetings. Once a month they met to hear speakers and to bear testimony.[17]

Spencer and Camilla attended a Genesis picnic, visiting with the adults and holding little children on their laps. While President of the Twelve, Spencer personally took Christmas gifts to the homes of the Genesis presidency.

During the time Harold B. Lee was President, the civil rights movement was in full swing, and the issue unquestionably occupied his mind.[18] He asked Marion D. Hanks what answer Elder Hanks gave when asked about the policy on race and priesthood. Elder Hanks responded that he believed change would come through inspiration when whites

---

15. President Brown said, "As to the consensus, the Brethren are all united now that the time has not come until the President speaks on it."

16. The first meeting took place on October 19, 1971, with 175 in attendance.

17. The idea for something like the Genesis Group had been suggested in the Quorum of the Twelve at least as early as 1954. A survey in the Salt Lake area showed about fifteen active black members and perhaps one hundred thirty others who were inactive or were family of members. After a brief lapse in interest after the 1978 revelation, the group resumed its activity. Bridgeforth led the group until his death in 1997, when Darius Gray was called by the First Presidency to succeed him. Genesis meets monthly and has Primary and Young Adult activity programs, as well as Relief Society compassionate service.

18. Arrington asserts that President Lee, shortly before his death, sought the Lord's will on the question of blacks and priesthood during "three days and nights [of] fasting in the upper room of the temple, . . . but the only answer he received was 'not yet.'" Arrington relied on an unidentified person close to President Lee, but President Lee's son-in-law and biographer found no record of such an incident and thought it doubtful, although President Lee did say, "It's only a matter of time."

had sufficiently matured spiritually. President Lee approved a general policy that black children could be sealed to non-black adoptive parents, whereas such sealings had been previously approved ad hoc.

In December 1973, President Lee died unexpectedly, and the thorny issue of restriction on priesthood passed to his successor, Spencer W. Kimball.

SPIRITUAL PREMONITIONS OF OTHERS

Looking back after the revelation a number of people identified unusual experiences that seemed to signal the change to come. In a 1973 patriarchal blessing, Oscar L. McFarland, patriarch of a stake in Covina, California, promised Theodore Britton, a black Sunday School superintendent, that if he remained faithful he would one day enjoy all the blessings of the priesthood. It was clear from the context that "one day" meant in mortality. Frightened by what he had said, the patriarch called his stake president, who told him, "Send me a copy. I'll send it on to President Kimball." The blessing transcript later came back with a red question mark by the passage in question but no annotation. The responsive note from President Kimball said only, "A fine blessing."

Blessings received by other black male members indicated that they would have opportunities not presently available to them—promises that included priesthood, missions, or temple blessings. People generally accepted these promises as things that would occur in the next life or in the Millennium, not as a prophecy of imminent change.[19]

In 1974, Helvécio and Rudá Martins and their son Marcus received extraordinary patriarchal blessings that promised things that seemed impossible. The patriarch told Helvécio and Rudá that they would be privileged to live on the earth in the joy of an eternal covenant. He also promised their son Marcus that he would preach the gospel, and the language the patriarch used suggested to them a full-time mission. Despite their uncertainty the Martinses opened a mission savings account for Marcus.

---

19. There is no way of knowing whether the frequency of such promises increased in the time just before the revelation or whether the promises were merely reported more often in light of their quick fulfillment. In a solemn assembly in December 1975, President Kimball instructed, "One of our patriarchs in a blessing promised a black man the priesthood. The patriarch made a mistake. The man should be treated with full respect, but he cannot have the priesthood."

In 1976, Bishop Fujio Abe, a high councilor in the Greensboro North Carolina Stake, heard a knock late one evening. He found black member Joseph Freeman and his wife, Isapella, standing on his doorstep, carrying their one-year-old son, Alexander, who had a high fever that would not respond to medicine. While Brother Freeman held the child, Bishop Abe administered a blessing. Halfway through Brother Abe felt impressed to say that the child would one day hold the priesthood and serve a mission. Both men felt the fever leave the child as the blessing was pronounced. His temperature dropped to normal.

The bishop had scarcely said, "Amen," before Sister Freeman asked, "Do you realize what you just said?"

"Yes," Brother Abe replied, "I do. Those were not my words. I suggest that it be something private and sacred, between us. Others would not understand."

In March 1978, Jae Ballif, president of the New England Mission, interviewed a black woman and her young son for baptism. They knew the racial restrictions, and she confided, "After I was told of it, my son and I wept and prayed. Then as I prayed by myself a voice came to me that said, 'Just leave it alone.'" They both sought baptism, trying to prepare themselves emotionally for a lifetime, if need be, without some of the blessings of the priesthood. Also, in May 1978, while confirming a black nurse who had just been baptized, Ballif felt inspired to promise her things not possible under current Church policy.

In the spring of 1978, shortly before the revelation announcement, F. Briton McConkie was in Manila by assignment, giving patriarchal blessings. To a woman of African descent, he promised she would receive the blessings of the temple. To Alonzo Harris, a black man, he promised that he would receive the priesthood and the blessings of the temple in his lifetime. Upon his return to Utah, Briton told his brother Bruce McConkie about the unusual blessings, and Bruce responded noncommittally, "I am glad to know you have given those blessings."[20]

---

20. In conversation after the blessing, the patriarch also predicted that Brother Harris would be called upon to ordain a member of the patriarch's family to office in the Melchizedek Priesthood. In about 1982, Daniel McConkie, nephew of patriarch McConkie, was attending law school and received a calling to be stake mission president. Rather than personally ordain Daniel a seventy, the stake president felt impressed to ask Alonzo Harris to ordain him. Elder Harris was noticeably moved emotionally as he performed the ordinance. Afterward he related the prophecy made by Daniel's uncle four or more years earlier.

Several people in Africa experienced premonitions of the coming change. In the spring of 1978, Joseph William (Billy) Johnson, the leader of a number of congregations of unofficial Latter-day Saints in Ghana, felt impressed to tell them that soon the leaders in Salt Lake City would recognize the Church in Ghana and send representatives to help them. It was an extraordinary statement.

In only a few days, these mystifying events would be seen as a foreshadowing.

21

THE QUESTIONER

He had the direct, personal responsibility to discover the Lord's will.

IN HIS FIRST PRESS CONFERENCE, held shortly after his ordination, President Kimball faced a number of predictable questions. In response to questions about the restriction on priesthood for blacks, he answered straightforwardly:

"[I have given it] a great deal of thought, a great deal of prayer. The day might come when they would be given the priesthood, but that day has not come yet. Should the day come it will be a matter of revelation. Before changing any important policy, it has to be through a revelation from the Lord. But we believe in revelation. We believe there are yet many more things to be revealed from the Lord. . . . We are open to the Father on every suggestion that he gives us, to every direction he gives us, to every revelation of [his] desire for change."

At the time, no one saw this statement as a harbinger of change. Similar statements had been made before and had been interpreted as a kind of hedge: change could come, but it would take a miracle, so don't count on it.

It is difficult to know President Kimball's inner feelings as he made these statements, whether he was putting the best face on a policy he believed was right or if he was expressing a deepening hope and desire that the time for change had come. Although he was sensitive to the concerns of minorities and although in speech and action he did not denigrate blacks, he also gave no encouragement to others who pressed for change. "I decided long ago that I would be loyal to the Brethren," he once said in reference to this issue. He reacted especially negatively to militant protests against the Church and to coercive attempts to change the policy, particularly when those protesting had no interest in becoming priesthood holders. Spencer believed that external pressures made revelation even less likely to come.[1] Force invited resistance.

During his life Spencer had few close personal contacts with blacks. Inevitably, he absorbed general social prejudices against blacks, but they were vague, based on assumptions and the attitudes of other people. His twenty-five years as an apostle working closely with native peoples in North and South America did give Spencer a greater degree of comfort with ethnic and racial diversity than that of many Church members.[2] He was the first Church President to call non-Caucasian General Authorities: Adney Y. Komatsu, a Japanese-American; and George P. Lee, a Navajo.

His response to individuals was generous and compassionate. As a stake president in Arizona, he approved the use of the Lebanon Ward chapel for graduation ceremonies of a black school, despite some member opposition. In 1959, he recorded meeting a member in Brazil who had a remote Negro ancestor, giving him about 5 percent negroid heritage. "My heart wanted to burst for him," Spencer wrote. He sympathized with and admired Monroe Fleming, who worked at the Hotel Utah for many years and who had suffered with patience and dignity the scorn of other blacks for his faithfulness to the Church. Of a faithful black LDS family in Brasilia, Spencer wrote, "My heart went out to them and I thought of . . . many people who almost ignore their priesthood when this man would give his life for it."

In the April 1954 general conference Elder Kimball made an impassioned plea for respect toward Native Americans. When these sentiments were reprinted in *Faith Precedes the Miracle* in 1972, Elder Kimball broadened the language by adding:

"Some members of the Church would justify their own un-Christian discrimination against blacks because of that rule with respect to the priesthood, but . . . it is not for us to add burdens upon the shoulders of our black brethren. . . . And those who remain faithful to the end may

---

1. An exception is the 1890 Woodruff Manifesto (Doctrine and Covenants, Official Declaration 1), which gives the government's imminent threat to confiscate the Church's property, including the temples, as a motivator for Wilford Woodruff's seeking further guidance.

2. Arrington expressed the personal opinion that of all the General Authorities Spencer was the most personally inclined to disregard race.

expect that God may finally grant
them all blessings they have mer-
ited through their righteousness."

Spencer's personal position
toward blacks was the uneasy
and ultimately unsatisfactory
one of "separate but equal." He
opposed interracial marriage
with blacks because the partners
could not be sealed in the temple
and their children would be similarly limited. In contrast, while
advising couples about other
types of interracial marriage (in
his experience most often of a
Native American with a Cauca-
sian), he frankly pointed out the

social and psychological risks for the couple and their children but reassured them that the decision was personal and involved no theological
issues.[3]

Spencer affirmed his good will but always returned to the traditional
position.

"If I did not believe in the pre-existence and in the scriptures, I
think I would be inclined to fight strongly for the colored man even to
Priesthood and temple privileges. I think I have never abused nor been
unkind to a colored person. I think I have never rejected one on the
grounds of his race or color."

To an unbeliever the Church position looked like simple bigotry; to
Spencer there seemed no way to explain the policy without being misunderstood, so he talked very little about it:

"I never bring up the subject, not because I am afraid of it but
because it is futile. Many cannot understand because of their limited
knowledge of spiritual things; many will not understand, since they feel

---

3. In 1977 "it was the sense of the discussion that while the Brethren will counsel against
interracial adoptions for the same reasons they counsel against interracial marriages, there will be
no prohibition against Church adoption agencies arranging interracial adoptions where there
appears to be good reason for doing so."

their superior training or brilliance entitles them to make their own independent deductions."

Obviously, however, it weighed on his mind for years, and on occasion he did raise the question. In 1967, when he reorganized a stake presidency in Salt Lake City, he called Arvil Milne as a counselor to the new stake president. Expecting questions about his worthiness, Brother Milne was startled when Elder Kimball's first substantive question was, "Brother Milne, what do you think about black people receiving the priesthood?"

Milne reflected for a moment and then responded, "I suppose when the Lord decides it is time he'll let the prophet know. Until then they'll have to get along without it."

Elder Kimball said, "Thank you." That ended the questioning, and he went on with making the call.

In April 1969, while interviewing James Polve for employment as a professor of engineering at Brigham Young University, Elder Kimball asked him only one question, "What do you think about whether the Negroes should receive the priesthood?" Surprised, Polve assumed the question was a test of his orthodoxy and knowledge of Church teachings. He responded with a traditional answer. The interview so mystified him that he did not dare even write it in his journal.

Perhaps such questions were intended to probe loyalty; if so, they also reflected how much the question was on Elder Kimball's mind.[4]

Elder Kimball always responded to questions about policy and doctrine with traditional, orthodox explanations, even within his family. But it appears from these and other incidents that inwardly he struggled with the priesthood issue and wished the Lord would permit a change. He felt compassion toward those excluded and perhaps guilt that faithful men were banned from a responsibility and blessing he himself prized.

THE PRESIDENTIAL YEARS BEFORE 1978

From his statements to the press at the time he became President, few expected any change. Probably President Kimball himself did not.

---

4. In 1966 when a stake was first organized in Brazil, Antonio Camargo was called as a counselor in the stake presidency. In the interview, Elder Kimball asked him, apparently as a testing question, "What do you think about polygamy?"

But one huge factor was different; now the ultimate responsibility for the policy fell to him. His duty was no longer to be a loyal supporter. He had the direct, personal responsibility to discover the Lord's will by study, faith, and prayer, and he was determined not to be motivated by earthly pressures. He had a hundred other things that demanded his immediate attention, but the matter of priesthood continued to hang heavy on his mind.

Spencer had maintained a notebook full of correspondence and clippings about blacks and priesthood. The range and extent of the notebook's content show that the matter concerned him greatly. But the latest item is dated about 1975, well before the 1978 revelation. Perhaps his presidential schedule did not allow him to maintain the notebook, or perhaps he turned more to internal seeking.

By the time Spencer became President, external pressures to change the priesthood policy had waned, although they did not disappear. For example, substantial national publicity came from the excommunication of Douglas A. Wallace in 1976 for ordaining a black man in Seattle in defiance of Church policy. Wallace continued his protest at the next general conference by storming down the Tabernacle aisle with two associates, yelling, "Make way for the Lord! Don't touch the Lord!" Ushers swiftly escorted him and his two companions out. Outside he announced to news representatives that he was endeavoring to put President Kimball "on trial." Other protests kept the issue alive.

When in 1975 President Kimball announced a temple in São Paulo, Brazil, there was speculation about how the Church would determine who, in such a racially mixed country, would be eligible to enter. He later said that at that time he "was not thinking in terms of making an adjustment." He thought, rather, that the Church would simply have to inquire carefully into the racial background of members seeking recommends.

As President, Spencer consistently authorized granting the priesthood when circumstances were unclear. The family of John L. Pea, for example, came to October 1976 general conference to be sealed in the temple after the First Presidency rescinded an earlier denial. Spencer recorded:

"Forty-three years ago Brother Pea was judged by the mission president to have some possible Negro lineage. As a result he and 4 sons never had the Priesthood and none have been to the temple. Recently the Genealogical Society investigated the circumstances and the First Presidency then reviewed the facts and determined that there was no justification for withholding the Priesthood from Brother Pea and authorized the bishop and stake president to ordain the brethren and give approval for temple recommends for those worthy.

"Thirty members of the family came for conference and to be sealed. The whole group met with the First Presidency and sang for them."

A First Presidency letter of February 1978 reaffirmed to local leaders the principle established by President McKay that "the fact that there may be some question as to a man's ancestry cannot be rightfully considered as evidence that he has Negro blood. . . . If there is no evidence to indicate that a man has Negro blood, you would not be justified in withholding the priesthood and temple blessings from him, if he is otherwise worthy. However, if you find convincing evidence that he has Negro blood, then the priesthood and temple blessings should be withheld."[5]

---

5. In spring 1978, black male members in Brazil could be assigned as home teachers to accompany priesthood holders. In times past blacks had sometimes been appointed "acting deacons." Black members could be auxiliary leaders, and black men could attend priesthood meetings.

22

DECISION AND CONFIRMATION

"It was as though another day of Pentecost came."

THE DAYS LEADING UP TO JUNE 1978 offer a classic illustration of the pattern that often precedes revelation—an urgent question, intense consideration, a prayerfully formulated tentative answer, and a spiritual confirmation.[1]

"Here was a little man," President Hinckley is reported to have said, "filled with love, able to reach out to people. . . . He was not the first to worry about the priesthood question, but he had the compassion to pursue it and a boldness that allowed him to act, to get the revelation."

SEEKING REVELATION

President Kimball said in a news interview that his predecessors had sought the Lord's will about the priesthood policy, and for whatever reason "the time had not come." But now that the ultimate responsibility

---

1. A major source of information concerning the 1978 revelation is a July 5, 1978, interview by the author with Spencer W. Kimball, a month after the announcement of the revelation. The author's description based on that interview was read and amended on July 8 by Spencer W. Kimball and Camilla Kimball. Additions were made on July 12, after interviews with President Marion G. Romney and Elders Boyd K. Packer and Gordon B. Hinckley. Nearly four years later, on May 12, 1982, the author met with Elder Bruce R. McConkie and with Francis M. Gibbons, secretary to the First Presidency, to discuss the 1978 Draft. Neither pointed out any errors. Gibbons provided additional information by reading from the June 1978 council minutes in his possession. The resulting composite document is found in Edward L. Kimball, Journal, May 12, 1982. Another important recital is a document by Bruce R. McConkie, "The Receipt of the Revelation Offering the Priesthood to Men of All Races and Colors," June 30, 1978, which Elder McConkie sent to President Kimball with a cover letter stating, "Pursuant to your request I have prepared the attached document. . . . It summarizes what I said in the home of Dr. LeRoy Kimball in Nauvoo on Wednesday, June 28, 1978." President Kimball made minor editorial changes on nearly every page of the document, suggesting that he agreed with the text, as amended. Six times he changed "priesthood" to "priesthood and temple blessings" as having become available to all worthy men.

was his, it was no longer enough to rely on the understandings of previous prophets or to wait for the Lord to take the initiative. He wanted "to find out firsthand what the Lord thought about it."

Years earlier, writing about revelation in general, Spencer said in a letter to his son Ed:

"Revelations will probably never come unless they are desired. I think few people receive revelations while lounging on a couch. . . . I believe most revelations would come when a man is on his tip toes, reaching as high as he can for something which he knows he needs, and then there bursts upon him the answer to his problems."

He prayed long and intently, trying not to prejudge what the answer should be. Should we maintain the long-standing policy, or has the time come for the change? He received no immediate answer. President Kimball also undertook to study the history of the policy and to ask for the perspective of others. He remembered well that the question had become divisive during the McKay administration. Hoping to maintain harmony as the question was explored again, he asked the apostles to join him as colleagues in extended study and supplication. In May 1975 he discussed with his counselors various statements by early Church leaders about the reasons black men could not hold the priesthood and asked for his counselors' reactions. In June 1977 he invited at least three General Authorities to write memos about the doctrinal basis of the policy and how a change might affect the Church. Elder Bruce R. McConkie wrote a long treatise concluding that no scriptural barrier existed to a change.

Francis M. Gibbons, secretary to the First Presidency, observed that during the year before the revelation was announced President Kimball seemed focused on the issue. The President repeatedly invited the First Presidency and Quorum of the Twelve to discuss the issue at length and urged them to speak freely. A few said little or nothing when the topic was raised, and President Kimball invited them to talk with him in private. He could not let the matter rest. He seemed so intent on resolving the issue—with full unity among the leadership—that others worried. Elder Boyd K. Packer said to him, "Why don't you forget this?" But he quickly answered his own question: "Because you can't. The Lord won't let you."

President Kimball went to the temple after patrons and workers had left. Some days he went more than once, always alone. He obtained a key so he could enter the temple night or day without troubling anyone else. He later recounted those months:

"Day after day, and especially on Saturdays and Sundays when there were no organizations [sessions] in the temple, I went there when I could be alone.

"I was very humble. . . . I was searching for this. . . . I wanted to be sure. . . .

"I had a great deal to fight . . . myself, largely, because I had grown up with this thought that Negroes should not have the priesthood and I was prepared to go all the rest of my life until my death and fight for it and defend it as it was."

Few knew about his contemplation in the temple except the security men who watched over him. One of them mentioned it to President Kimball's neighbor, who told Camilla. So she knew that much, but she had no idea what problem so preoccupied her husband. He always maintained strict confidentiality where Church business was concerned. She sometimes good-naturedly complained that he could not remember what was confidential and what was not, so he solved the problem by never telling her anything. She had to read about new developments in the *Church News*. Now, with her husband as consumed as she had ever seen him, she remembered Spencer's anguish over the excommunication of an apostle thirty-five years earlier and worried that something similar might be happening again. When President Kimball learned about the security officer's breach, he gently suggested to the security supervisor that his men should be careful about what they divulged.

On March 9, 1978, three months before the policy change, the topic was again discussed when the First Presidency and Twelve met in their regular meeting in the Salt Lake Temple. The apostles unanimously expressed the view that any change would require revelation received and announced by the prophet. President Kimball agreed but also wanted them to learn the will of the Lord for themselves. He urged them to fast and pray individually over the question.

Through the many days in the temple and through the sleepless hours of the night, praying and turning over in his mind all the consequences, perplexities, and criticisms that a decision to extend priesthood would involve, President Kimball gradually found "all those complications and concerns dwindling in significance." They did not disappear but seemed to decline in importance. In spite of his preconceptions and his allegiance to the past, assurance came that a change in policy was what the Lord wanted—"there slowly grew a deep, abiding impression to go forward with the change."

SEEKING UNITY

On March 23, President Kimball reported to his counselors that he had spent much of the previous night in reflection and his impression was to lift the restriction on blacks. His counselors said they were prepared to sustain him if that were his decision. They went on to discuss the impact of such a change and decided there was no need for prompt action; they would discuss it again with the Twelve before a final decision.

Francis Gibbons sensed that President Kimball had already come to know God's will and was now struggling with how to unify all Church leaders in support.[2] President Kimball wanted more than anything to have his fellow servants share with him a witness of the Lord's will. He sensed resistance from some, which he fully understood. He knew that others did not always fully share his views, and he may have feared that this change in policy would be seen as his personal objective. He did not push, lobby, pressure, or use the power of his office to induce compliance. Instead, he increased his visits to the temple, imploring the Lord to make his will known to these good men who all their lives had quoted other Presidents of the Church that it was not yet time. The

---

2. Elder Gibbons has confirmed that his description of "events leading up to and surrounding the revelation on priesthood are based upon personal, eyewitness knowledge and are supported by my diary entries made soon after they occurred."

wisdom of the dead often seems loftier than the word of an imperfect living spokesman.

Camilla noted that in their prayers together at home, where he had always asked for "inspiration" or "guidance," he began to plead for "revelation."

He continued to spend many hours alone in prayer and meditation in the temple's Holy of Holies. He later described the burden of his prayers in an extemporaneous talk to missionaries in South Africa:

"I remember very vividly the day after day that I walked over to the temple and ascended up to the fourth floor where we have our solemn assemblies, where we have our meetings of the Twelve and the Presidency. And after everybody had gone out of the temple, I knelt and prayed. And I prayed with such a fervency, I tell you! I knew that something was before us that was extremely important to many of the children of God. And I knew that we could receive the revelations of the Lord only by being worthy and ready for them and ready to accept them and to put them into place. Day after day I went and with great solemnity and seriousness, alone in the upper rooms of the Temple, and there I offered my soul and offered our efforts to go forward with the program and we wanted to do what he wanted. As we talked about it to him, we said, 'Lord, we want only what is right. We're not making any plans to be spectacularly moving. We want only the thing that thou dost want and we want it when you want it and not until.'"

On May 4, at the end of the joint meeting of the Presidency and the Twelve, when the priesthood policy had been discussed, Elder LeGrand Richards asked permission to make a statement. He then reported:

"I saw during the meeting a man seated in a chair above the organ, bearded and dressed in white, having the appearance of Wilford Woodruff. . . . I am not a visionary man. . . . This was not imagination. . . . It might be that I was privileged to see him because I am the only one here who had seen President Woodruff in person."

To friends Spencer appeared worried or distressed. And Spencer's counselors shared his anxieties. President N. Eldon Tanner's family saw him during this time "greatly concerned, as though he carried the burdens of the world."

The question was still open for discussion. On May 25, Mark E. Petersen called President Kimball's attention to an article that proposed

220 THE REVELATION ON PRIESTHOOD

the priesthood policy had begun with Brigham Young, not Joseph Smith, and he suggested that the President might wish to consider this factor.[3]

On May 30, President Kimball read his counselors a tentative statement he had written in longhand; it removed racial restrictions on priesthood. He said he had a "good, warm feeling" about it. They reviewed past statements and decided to ask G. Homer Durham, a Seventy supervising the Historical Department, to research further the historical basis of the policy.[4] They also concluded to alter the pattern of their next Thursday meeting with the Twelve by canceling the traditional luncheon in the temple and asking the council members to continue their fasting while they sought an answer.

CONFIRMATION

On Thursday, June 1, 1978, President Kimball left home early, as usual, so engrossed that he left his briefcase behind and had to send back for it. His journal for the day records, with striking blandness:

"After meeting with my counselors for an hour this morning from eight until nine o'clock, we went over to the temple and met with all of the General Authorities in the monthly meeting we hold together.

"Returned to the office for a few minutes and then went over to Temple Square for the dedication services of the new Visitors Center South, which was scheduled to commence at 3:00 P.M.

"The services lasted for about an hour, after which we returned to the office where I worked at my desk until six o'clock."[5]

The day proved far more significant than this entry suggests. On this first Thursday of the month, the First Presidency, Twelve, and Seventies met in their regularly scheduled monthly temple meeting at 9:00 A.M., all fasting. As usual, they bore testimony, partook of the sacrament, and participated in a prayer circle. The meeting lasted the usual three and a half hours and was not notably different from other such meetings until the conclusion, when President Kimball asked the Twelve to remain. Two had already left the room to change from their temple clothing in

---

3. The reference almost surely is to the 1973 article by Lester Bush in *Dialogue*.
4. Events overtook that request, for confirmation of the rightness of change came just two days later.
5. One suspects the entry was made by Arthur Haycock.

preparation for the regular business meeting of the Presidency and the Twelve that normally followed. Someone called them back. Ten of the Twelve were present. Elder Delbert L. Stapley lay ill in the hospital, and Elder Mark E. Petersen was in South America on assignment.

As men present later recalled, President Kimball said:

"Brethren, I have canceled lunch for today. Would you be willing to remain in the temple with us? I would like you to continue to fast with me. I have been going to the temple almost daily for many weeks now, sometimes for hours, entreating the Lord for a clear answer. I have not been determined in advance what the answer should be. And I will be satisfied with a simple Yes or No, but I want to know. Whatever the Lord's decision is, I will defend it to the limits of my strength, even to death."

He then outlined the direction his thoughts had carried him—the fading of his reluctance, the disappearance of objections, the growing assurance he had received, the tentative decision he had reached, and his desire for a clear answer. Once more he asked the Twelve to speak freely and without concern for seniority. Elder McConkie spoke in favor of the change, noting there was no scriptural impediment. President Tanner asked searching questions as Elder McConkie spoke. Elder Packer also favored the change, speaking at length, quoting scriptures (D&C 124:49; 56:4–5; 58:32) in support. Eight of the ten volunteered their views, all favorable. President Kimball called on the other two, and they also spoke in favor. Discussion continued for two hours. Elder Packer said a few weeks later, "One objection would have deterred him, would have made him put it off, so careful was he . . . that it had to be right."

They then sought divine confirmation. President Kimball asked, "Do you mind if I lead you in prayer?" He had reached a decision after great struggle, and he desperately wanted the Lord's confirmation, if it would come. They surrounded the altar in a prayer circle. President Kimball spoke to the Lord at length. If extending the priesthood was not right, if the Lord did not want this change to come in the Church, he said, he would fight the world's opposition. Elder McConkie later recounted, "The Lord took over and President Kimball was inspired in his prayer, asking the right questions, and he asked for a manifestation" confirming the decision.⁶

During that insistent prayer, those present felt something powerful, unifying, ineffable. Those who tried to describe it later struggled to find words. Elder McConkie said:

"It was as though another day of Pentecost came. On the day of Pentecost in the Old World it is recorded that cloven tongues of fire rested upon the people. They were trying to put into words what is impossible to express directly. There are no words to describe the sensation, but simultaneously the Twelve and the three members of the First Presidency had the Holy Ghost descend upon them and they knew that God had manifested his will. . . . I had had some remarkable spiritual experiences before, particularly in connection with my call as an apostle, but nothing of this magnitude.

"All of the Brethren at once knew and felt in their souls what the answer to the importuning petition of President Kimball was. . . . Some of the Brethren were weeping. All were sober and somewhat overcome. When President Kimball stood up, several of the Brethren, in turn, threw their arms around him."

Elder L. Tom Perry recalled:

"While he was praying we had a marvelous experience. We had just a unity of feeling. The nearest I can describe it is that it was much like what has been recounted as happening at the dedication of the Kirtland Temple. I felt something like the rushing of wind. There was a feeling that came over the whole group. When President Kimball got up he was visibly relieved and overjoyed."

Elder Hinckley said soon afterward that the experience defied description: "It was marvelous, very personal, bringing with it great unity and strong conviction that this change was a revelation from God." Ten years later he said:

"There was a hallowed and sanctified atmosphere in the room. For me, it felt as if a conduit opened between the heavenly throne and the kneeling, pleading prophet. . . . And by the power of the Holy Ghost there came to that prophet an assurance that the thing for which he

---

6. "It was one of those occasions when the one who was mouth in the prayer, prayed by the power of the Spirit and was given expression and guided in the words that were used." —Elder Bruce R. McConkie

prayed was right, that the time had come. . . .

"There was not the sound 'as of a rushing mighty wind,' there were not 'cloven tongues like as of fire' as there had been on the Day of Pentecost. . . .

" . . . But the voice of the Spirit whispered with certainty into our minds and our very souls.

"It was for us, at least for me personally, as I imagine it was with Enos, who said concerning his remarkable experience, ' . . . behold, the voice of the Lord came into my mind.'

" . . . Not one of us who was present on that occasion was ever quite the same after that."

As President Kimball arose from his knees, he first encountered Elder David B. Haight, the newest apostle, and they embraced. Elder Haight could feel President Kimball's heart pounding and his intense emotion. The President continued around the circle, embracing each apostle in turn. Others spontaneously embraced.

President Kimball was overjoyed that his Brethren now knew, as he did, that the time was right. Elder Perry said:

"I don't think we've had a president more willing to entreat the Lord or more receptive since the prophet Joseph. We knew that he had received the will of the Lord. . . . It was just as though a great burden had been lifted. He was almost speechless. It was almost impossible for him to contain his joy. Nothing was said or had to be said. We sensed what the answer was, the decision was made. There was a great feeling of unity among us and relief that it was over. As I have talked with other members of the Twelve since then, they felt the same as I did. I don't think the Twelve will ever be the same again. It was a once-in-a-lifetime experience."[7]

After their experience—so sacred that some would not discuss it and the thought of it brought tears—every man stood resolute in support of the decision.

---

7. President Kimball later said, "Finally we had the feeling, we had the impressions from the Lord who made them very clear to us that this was the thing to do to make the gospel universal to all worthy people." And: "This revelation and assurance came to me so clearly that there was no question about it."

23

ANNOUNCEMENT AND REACTIONS

"Have you heard?"

ORDINARILY, AFTER THEIR PRAYER CIRCLE the Presidency and Twelve would change out of temple clothing and continue meeting to conduct Church business. Because of the spiritually charged experience they had just had, one suggested that they cancel the further meeting. But President Kimball, intent on moving the Church forward, asked them to continue. They did so, but because of their intense feelings they were reluctant to bring forward any business that could wait. They set no immediate course, and the Twelve received no instruction. They separated.

Among the undecided business items was how to announce the decision, and President Kimball asked Elders Gordon B. Hinckley, Boyd K. Packer, and Bruce R. McConkie each to propose in writing a course of action.[1]

PREPARING THE ANNOUNCEMENT

Though the decision had been made and the Twelve were unified, President Kimball continued to go to the temple, praying that the rest of the General Authorities would accept this momentous change. During the next week, Camilla thought he was as agitated as she had ever seen. She still had no idea what was causing him such concern.

On Wednesday, Francis Gibbons presented to the First Presidency his composite draft of the three proposed announcements from Elders

---

1. President Kimball said, "There was a gradual and general development of the whole program, in connection with the Apostles." Without understanding the whole story, this comment could be taken as a description of an essentially rational, administrative decision-making process, but with a deeper understanding of the usual revelatory process, the description meshes well with a spiritual explanation.

Packer, McConkie, and Hinckley. The First Presidency spent substantial time in revising the language.[2]

On Thursday, June 8, the Presidency presented the proposed announcement to the Twelve. Discussion resulted in minor editorial changes.[3] Then they discussed timing. Some thought it best to wait for October general conference. Others suggested making the announcement at the mission presidents' seminar the next week. But Elder McConkie urged immediate release. Despite tight security, employees at the Church Office Building sensed that something important was afoot, although no one knew exactly what. Rumors had already begun to spread. "It will leak," said Elder McConkie, "and we have to beat Satan. He'll do something between now and then to make it appear that we're being forced into it."

After discussion, the First Presidency and Twelve adopted Elder Packer's suggestion that they announce the change in the form of a letter to local Church leaders throughout the world. Before sending the letter, they would release it to the media, making the new policy known to the whole world simultaneously.

After the meeting, Spencer felt tremendously weary but pleased at the sense he had of continuing unity.

About 4:00 P.M., President Tanner went to see Heber Wolsey, managing director of public communications. He asked Wolsey to be standing by at 7:30 the next morning to handle "an important announcement."

That same afternoon Bill Smart, editor of the *Deseret News,* attended an unrelated meeting with Elder Thomas S. Monson, who quietly told him, "Reserve space for an important announcement tomorrow."

"What is it?"

"I can't say anything now; it is confidential."

"Can you tell me whether to put it on the front page or on B-1?"

"You'll know when you see it!"

SEEKING FINAL UNITY

Two of the Twelve had not attended either Thursday meeting. Mark E. Petersen was still on assignment in South America, and

---

2. "President Kimball dictated the declaration [in final form] to Arthur [Haycock], who took it down in shorthand and transcribed it."

3. Bruce R. McConkie says that during this process he felt a renewed assurance of the rightness of change.

Delbert L. Stapley was seriously ill in the LDS Hospital. President Kimball telephoned Elder Petersen in Quito, Ecuador, and informed him what had happened. He had Francis Gibbons read him the announcement about to be published, and Elder Petersen approved. All three of the First Presidency visited Elder Stapley in his hospital room. He, too, approved. Support from the Twelve was unanimous.

Now President Kimball wanted the support of the remaining General Authorities. He asked them to come Friday morning, fasting, to the fourth-floor temple council room. They were asked to postpone travel if possible and cancel any conflicting appointments without advising their secretaries or anyone else of the meeting. The regular monthly meeting of all the General Authorities had been held in the temple just the week before, so the purpose of this special meeting generated considerable speculation.

On Friday, June 9, 1978, the meeting commenced at 7:00 A.M. All were dressed in their temple clothing. After the hymn President Ezra Taft Benson offered the prayer. Elder Neal A. Maxwell, then a Seventy, later said, "I had no inkling what was going on. And as we knelt down to pray, the Spirit told me what it was going to be . . . and after that prayer, President Kimball began the description. I began to weep."

As Paul H. Dunn recalled, President Kimball said:

"Thank you for making the necessary arrangements to be here. I want to tell you about some important things. As a boy in Arizona I wondered why the Indians were so poor and looked down upon. I asked my father, who was kind and never too busy to answer my questions, and he told me about the Book of Mormon and its connection with the Indians and their condition. My father never lied to me. Later I asked him about blacks and the priesthood. My father said that the time would come when they would receive the priesthood. I believed him, although it troubled me. I was called as a stake president. When one of the Twelve came I asked him. He said, 'I don't know, but the time will come.' I became a General Authority and asked President Grant, 'If I am to represent you and the Lord, I need to be able to answer questions about race and priesthood.' He said that the time would come when that restriction would change."

By now, the General Authorities realized where President Kimball was going. They were first stunned, then ecstatic.

According to Elder Dunn, President Kimball continued:

"Then one day the mantle fell on me. Brethren, you will never know how many times when you have gone home at night, instead of going home I have come to this room and poured out my heart. Now the Lord has answered me and the time has come for all worthy men to receive the priesthood. I shared that with my counselors and the Twelve and after getting their response I present it to you. But I won't announce it to the world without first counseling with you. We are not in a hurry. I want to hear from you."

Francis Gibbons read the text of the proposed announcement, and President Kimball asked for comments. President Marion G. Romney said:

"Brethren, . . . I have a confession to make. I knew President Kimball was searching for an answer and whenever we discussed the question, I told him, 'If you get an answer I will support you with all my strength,' but I did not expect him to get an answer. If the decision had been left to me, I would have felt that we've always had that policy and we would stick to it no matter what the opposition. I resisted change in my feelings, but I came to accept it slowly. I have now changed my position 180 degrees. I am not just a supporter of this decision. I am an advocate. When the revelation came I knew the mind and the will of the Lord had been made manifest."[4]

Another said, "I would have voted against such a proposal until I experienced the feeling that I did in this room this morning." Others called on endorsed the proposal. Elder Hanks, nearly overcome with

---

4. President Romney made a similar statement a few weeks after the events: "I knew President Kimball was moved in his spirit with the problem of permitting blacks to receive the priesthood. This had been going on for months, at least. . . . We as his counselors encouraged him to get it off his mind, to rest. The idea of change was new to me. I had gone eighty years defending the Church position. I am a Romney, you see, and a stubborn man. I was personally slow to accept change. I prayed hard that the Lord would give the president the right answer, but I did not presume to urge that the answer be yes or no. I was most interested that *he* be sure. And from the experience we had in the temple I was sure that he had the answer. I got a witness in my own soul; I would not have gone along without a witness that he had received the answer he sought. I felt a quiet warmth and whisperings of the Spirit. I didn't want to get excited; I wanted to be rational. It was not an emotional thing with me, but I was as sure as I have ever been of anything. This is the most far-reaching event of his administration, an historic event that opens up to vast numbers of people all the blessings of the gospel. It ranks well up with Wilford Woodruff's Manifesto in importance in Church history."

emotion, said, "I thank God I lived long enough to see this day." A vote approved the decision unanimously.

President Kimball put his hand on President N. Eldon Tanner's knee and said, "Eldon, go tell the world."

President Tanner returned in a few moments and reported, "It's done."

The General Authorities were instructed not to interpret or editorialize but to let the announcement speak for itself. The First Presidency would not be available for media interviews concerning the revelation.

By the time the General Authorities had dressed and returned to their offices, phone lines were jammed.

THE ANNOUNCEMENT: JUNE 9, 1978

Without addressing questions of history or justification, the announcement said simply that God had revealed that the day had come for granting priesthood and temple blessings to all who are worthy.[5] The critical part of the final text, canonized as Official Declaration—2 in the Doctrine and Covenants, read:

---

5. The revelation itself was not reduced to text. A forged document purporting to be the revelation itself is in circulation, phrased as an answer from God that he had heard the cries of his dark-skinned children, who had borne the burdens of others; that the Church should without delay extend missionary efforts to them; that priesthood should be given to those who are worthy; that racial intermarriage was "for the present" inadvisable because of social prejudice; that the end-time is near; and that the faithful will receive exaltation.

The document is typed, headed "A Revelation," and labeled in pen on the upper left corner "First Draft." At the end appears a signature block: "Faithfully yours," signed by President Kimball. Shadows of paper edges on the photocopied document show it to be a composite of four segments: the letterhead, two poorly aligned parts of the body, and the signature block (which appears to be from a different typewriter). The ending, "Faithfully yours," hardly fits a revelation purporting to be the words of God. Richard E. Turley Jr., managing director of the Church Historical Department, reports that copies of unknown origin circulated as early as October 1978.

"[The Lord] has heard our prayers, and by revelation has confirmed that the long-promised day has come when every faithful, worthy man in the Church may receive the holy priesthood, with power to exercise its divine authority, and enjoy with his loved ones every blessing that flows therefrom, including the blessings of the temple. . . .

"Sincerely yours, . . .

"The First Presidency"

Earlier that morning Heber Wolsey waited for the announcement President Tanner had told him to expect. When President Tanner handed him a copy of the letter and he read it over, he wept. "You're not the first to shed tears," said President Tanner. He then instructed Wolsey to release the statement.

Back in his office, Heber said to colleague Jerry Cahill, "What would you consider 'an important announcement'?"

Perhaps a new temple, said Jerry. Then Heber joyfully handed Jerry the letter. At his first free moment, Jerry Cahill closed the door to his office and knelt to pray, overwhelmed by a feeling that swept through him like a wave. He could not utter a formal prayer but experienced the most striking expression of divine power he had ever felt, confirming to him the revelation.

Despite their emotions, all the employees in the Public Communications office had to deal with the business at hand. They were under instructions to get the widest possible dissemination of the full text of the letter but to offer no explanations or commentary. Primary concerns were accuracy, simplicity, and dignity.

When Duane Cardall, religion reporter for KSL-TV, got the call that an important announcement would be made, he queried, "What is it?"

"We can't tell you."

"Come on, what is it?"

"The blacks are going to get the priesthood."

"Come on, what is the announcement?"

"No, it is serious."

"Really?"

"Yes."

Cardall rushed in a microwave truck to the Church Office Building, ran into the building, and hurried to the Public Communications office on the twenty-fifth floor. With a copy of the statement in hand, he sped downstairs and broadcast a news bulletin, standing on the street, interrupting regular programming.

By late morning all the news media had copies of the release. With no advance notice, the story hit like a bolt out of the blue. It was a stunning, revolutionary development.

INITIAL REACTION

The word spread like lightning through official Church channels, over radio and television, and by word of mouth. In some heavily Mormon communities, the telephone circuits became so overloaded that it was nearly impossible to get a call through. Exultation, gratitude, and excitement competed for place.

While Camilla was working in the garden late that morning, the telephone rang, and she came in to answer it. Her daughter, Olive Beth, asked excitedly, "Have you heard the news?"

"What news?"

"About the revelation that all worthy men can receive the priesthood!"

Camilla sat down on the floor and wept in joy and relief—joy for the revelation and relief for her husband. She understood now what had weighed so heavily on Spencer's mind. She went into the bedroom and poured out her heart in a prayer of gratitude and in hope that this development would not burden Spencer with new controversy. She worried that it might cause a schism in the Church, that there would be those who could not accept a change.

Spencer tried soon afterward to call Camilla with the news, but she was back in the garden and did not hear the telephone. He then called Olive Beth to ask if she knew where her mother was. Olive Beth did not know but said, "I just heard the wonderful news. It is marvelous!"

Spencer responded, "It is the most earthshaking thing that has happened in my lifetime."

That evening the story led the national NBC News broadcast. The story ran on the front page of major newspapers across the country—the *New York Times, Boston Globe, Washington Post. Time* and *Newsweek* stopped their presses to include the news in their weekly runs. Most newspapers reported neutrally: "The Mormon Church announced

Friday a revelation from God will give its priesthood to all worthy male members." Some commentators scorned the "convenience" of a "revelation" that allowed a way out of an embarrassing bind, but others noted that it had been some years since there had been any significant demonstrations against the Church or Brigham Young University. External pressure was the lowest it had been for years.

Because Church leaders declined to comment, reporters began to interview leaders of other local churches, NAACP officials, and men and women on the street for reactions. The responses were almost uniformly positive. The media next turned to black members of the Church, who fielded questions—sometimes barbed—with tact, patience, and humility. An elderly lifetime member said, "We have all waited for this, but I didn't think it would come in my lifetime." Monroe Fleming expressed his happiness by saying, "It's like not feeling you're a guest in your father's house anymore." Joseph Freeman said, "What a difference a day makes! All those years that I'd desired more than anything else to be a minister."

Among members the news brought nearly universal rejoicing. They were grateful the full blessings of the priesthood would now be available to worthy families who had been denied them. They were also thankful for dramatic evidence of the Church teaching that revelation continues to the present. As the news spread through Utah and beyond, people embraced and cried and rejoiced. As with such events as Pearl Harbor and the John F. Kennedy assassination, Latter-day Saints remember where they were and what they were doing when they heard the news.

A local television reporter who had been somewhat antagonistic to the Church later said, "I sensed a lot of happiness at the Church offices . . . a great burden being lifted. There was a sense of joy; people were genuinely thrilled." He understood then that Mormons had not been acting out of bigotry, as he supposed, but out of loyalty to their leaders. "I experienced a change in feelings toward the Church that day."

Mary Frances Sturlaugson, a young black woman, recorded that she was in a downtown Provo office when a friend told her the news. She responded, "Please don't joke with me about something like that."

"At that instant a young man who had been talking on the phone stood up and, with his fists stretched above his head, shouted, 'All right!'

Cold chills went completely through my body. All I could say was, 'I don't believe it's happened.' An older man beside me kept repeating, 'I'll be darned, I'll be darned.'

"As I walked outside, crying like a happy kid at Christmastime, horns were honking like crazy. I stopped for a red light and a car pulled up. The driver asked me if I had heard what he had just heard. I half mumbled and half nodded a disbelieving yes. He whooped and started blowing his horn as he drove off. When I arrived at my apartment my roommates ran out to meet me, and we jumped up and down screaming with joy. Finally we went inside and each said a prayer, sobs punctuating every one."

In Brazil, Helvécio Martins returned home from work to find his wife Rudá ecstatic. "I have news, amazing news!" The wedding invitations for their son, Marcus, had already been distributed when the announcement came. But he and his fiancée, Mirian Abelin Barbosa, decided to postpone the wedding because he now could serve a mission. He became the first black missionary called after the revelation.[6]

A week after the announcement, Ruffin Bridgeforth, leader of Genesis, had not yet been ordained because his local leader with that responsibility was out of town. Elder Boyd K. Packer discussed the situation with President Kimball and asked whether Brother Bridgeforth might properly be ordained a high priest rather than an elder in light of his long and faithful service. "Yes, that's right. You do that," said President Kimball. After being ordained by Elder Packer, Brother Bridgeforth asked him to give his wheelchair-bound wife, Helena, a priesthood blessing. Elder Packer later recalled, "I laid my hands on her head and just as I was to speak, I thought, 'Ruffin, you can now give this blessing.' And when he began that blessing—and he needed no coaching—'by the authority of the Melchizedek Priesthood,' that . . . was a moment in Church history."

For Latter-day Saints who harbored racial prejudices, the revelation came as a shock. A few people did reject the revelation and left the Church, and some lapsed into inactivity out of dissatisfaction. But there

---

6. Soon afterward Jacques M. G. Jonassaint, of Haiti, was called to the Florida Spanish Mission, and Mary Sturlaugson, of Provo, Utah, went to the Texas San Antonio Mission as the first African-American woman missionary.

was no schism. Most of the Mormons who might have protested tended to also have a strong commitment to obedience, and they did not object publicly. One white member had for years made his position clear: if blacks ever receive the priesthood, "that's the day I walk out the door." But the Sunday after the announcement, he showed up at church, explaining, "A lot of people didn't [expect to see me here], but they never gave me any credit for growing up."

Within a few days of the announcement President Kimball received a large number of positive letters, nearly all from members expressing elation and gratitude. He also received about thirty negative letters, nearly all from non-Mormons,[7] most calling him a fraud in claiming revelation[8] or a traitor to his race.[9] President Kimball took the criticism in stride: "We do not expect the people of the world to understand such things, for they will always be quick to assign their own reasons or to discount the divine process of revelation."

The day after the announcement, as Spencer's barber trimmed his hair in preparation for a trip to Hawaii, he found Spencer "happy, buoyant, and warm . . . [with] a great weight off his shoulders."

When reporters in Hawaii asked about the revelation, President Kimball answered, "It is a different world than it was twenty or twenty-five years ago. The world is ready for it." They asked him for details about receiving the revelation, but he said it was "a personal thing."

President Kimball desired that people not sensationalize the revelatory experience. "Some people would try to figure it out that I had a

7. The few protesting Church members wrote to President Kimball vituperatively: "You senile old bastard. . . . [They] are laughing at us and even planning for the 'take over' as they call it. . . . You stupid fool. . . . Our Church shall curse the day you were born."

"I request that my name be taken off the LDS Church records. You gave the N_____ the priesthood. This tells that you are liers [sic] and The Book of Mormon is a fraud."

"I could have accepted and respected your decision if you had been honest enough to make the following statement: 'The doctrine is being changed due to changing times and pressures from the bureaucratic government.' To claim a vision and lay the church open to further ridicule I can't accept with a clear conscience. . . . My only wish is to have my name removed from the records of membership."

8. For example, "You ostensibly had a 'revelation'—opportunistically, one fears." "I and many others really got a big laugh about your recent revelation." "Kimball, you faker." "A senile old man claims he had a revelation."

9. For example, "The N_____ and the Jews they taking over the world." "You are setting a path of distruction [sic] and caious [chaos?] for the Mormon Church." "Christian-white societies are inundated with parasitic colored." "God 'changes not,' and he does not accept Negro race priests." "You are a traitor to your own race."

personal visitation from the Almighty as in the First Vision. I would not want to make the revelation different from what it was." Still, he had no doubts that he had received a revelation and that its source was divine. The strong, distinct, sacred impression he experienced banished for him even the thought of questioning its source.

Speaking to seminary and institute teachers a few months after the revelation, Elder McConkie described the events in poetic language that some misunderstood. He said of the experience:

"From the midst of Eternity, the voice of God, conveyed by the power of the Spirit, spoke to his prophet. . . . And we all heard the same voice, received the same message, and became personal witnesses that the word received was the mind and will and voice of the Lord.

"President Kimball's prayer was answered and our prayers were answered. He heard the voice and we heard the same voice."

His ecstatic phrasing left some with the mistaken impression that the group had heard an audible voice speaking specific words. When President Kimball read the talk as published in 1981, he asked Elder McConkie to revise the statement to avoid possible misunderstanding.[10]

A few weeks after the announcement, Elder Hinckley said, "It is a tremendous thing. It came as a result of great effort and prayer, anxious seeking and pleading. Anyone who does not think that is a part of receiving revelation does not understand the process."

Elder Packer said of President Kimball's role in the revelation: "I have feared we might lose him, now that this great work is done. I hope there is something else only he can do, to keep him here. No one else could have done this; there is none so innocent and open, so sensitive."

---

10. Alexander B. Morrison equates Elder McConkie using the phrase "voice of the Lord" with Enos's experience, but Elder McConkie said he did not experience a "voice in the mind" as Enos did. The change President Kimball recommended was not made.

24

AFTERMATH AND AFRICA

"We spoke with a limited understanding."

IN CONVERSATION WITH HIS SON ED soon after the revelation, Spencer talked about some of the consequences he anticipated would gradually come about. Missionary work would spread to more blacks in the United States and in Africa. Black members would augment the missionary corps. Some whites would join the Church who otherwise would not have. Interracial marriages would likely increase, despite the Church's expressed concern for the social consequences of interracial, intercultural, and interclass marriages. Blacks would begin to hold Church administrative responsibilities. Some Church members whose prejudices ran deeper than their faith might become disaffected. But, he concluded, "I think there will not be much, if any, criticism."

Allegations that the policy evidenced bigotry would decline, but Spencer predicted that those who had criticized the priesthood restriction would merely shift their attack to some other ground. Ultimately, he believed, their concerns were not tied to a particular issue but arose from the fundamental question of whether God guides the Church.

A 1988 study by Armand Mauss reported that before 1978 Latter-day Saints were not much different in their racial prejudices from other individuals. But after 1978 prejudice lessened in both groups, and Latter-day Saints were in some respects more favorable to blacks than the national population generally. Surveys of LDS students showed a consistent reduction from 1975 to 1979 in the students' social distance from other ethnic and racial groups, the reduction being greatest with respect to blacks.

INTERRACIAL MARRIAGE

After priesthood and temple ordinances were open to people of all races, Church officials continued to recommend marrying within one's race. Some members interpreted that counsel to mean interracial marriage was contrary to fundamental gospel principles.

When Mary Sturlaugson, the first black woman missionary, returned from her mission and began dating a white man, she was cautioned by friends not to get serious with him because marriage across racial lines was wrong. Troubled, she asked several General Authorities for their understanding. They told her the Church had no objection. But she wanted further reassurance and arranged an interview with President Kimball. She recorded his counsel and loving concern:

"I don't know if President Kimball knew the turmoil I had suffered, but as I expressed to him my sincere desire to know the Lord's will on interracial marriage, tears slowly rolled down his face. Reaching out, he gently embraced me as one would a delicate and small child. Then he quietly but emphatically whispered, 'My child, it is not wrong. It is not wrong. The only reason we counsel against it is because of the problems the *children* could face. As far as its being incompatible with the Lord's gospel, or with your Father in Heaven, it is not.' He paused, still looking into my eyes. I felt that he saw into my soul. Then with another brief embrace he uttered, 'Be of good cheer; the Lord loves you dearly.'"[1]

PERSISTENCE OF TRADITIONAL EXPLANATIONS

Once the policy changed, most Church members had little inclination to dwell on questions of the past or to wrestle with the reasons for the change. They wanted to move on. But some members, black and white, continued to wonder whether explanations traditionally offered for the superseded policy had validity. Brigham Young was clearly mistaken about when the restriction would be lifted; was he also mistaken about its origin? If the priesthood ban had been sanctioned by God for a shorter time than expected, what determined the shortening of that time? Or had the ban not been God's will but a mistaken understanding that he allowed to stand until both leaders and members of the Church could accept blacks as full equals in the kingdom? Or had the

---

1. She did marry a white man, John Eyer.

restriction been, not a curse, but a challenge, allowed by God but not imposed by him, to see how some premortal spirits would react to the disadvantage of being denied the priesthood because of race and how others would react to being "advantaged"? Would those born black still accept the truthfulness of the Mormon claim to unique status with God? Or does God simply move in unknowable ways (see Isaiah 55:8–9)?

The announcement of the revelation avoided questions of history or doctrine. But in a much-quoted statement to Church educators, Bruce R. McConkie acknowledged that previous statements by Church leaders—including himself—were made without full understanding. Rather than explain the basis for the pre-1978 policy, he focused on the fact that this new revelation overrides all previous statements on this subject:

"Forget everything that I have said, or what President Brigham Young or President George Q. Cannon or whosoever has said in days past that is contrary to the present revelation. We spoke with a limited understanding and without the light and knowledge that now has come into the world.

" . . . It doesn't make a particle of difference what anybody ever said about the Negro matter before the first day of June 1978. It is a new day and a new arrangement, and the Lord has now given the revelation."[2]

President Kimball's most pointed rejection of previous notions was made during an interview with Richard Ostling from *Time* magazine. Ostling reported in 1978 that President Kimball "flatly [stated] that Mormonism no longer holds to . . . a theory" that blacks had been denied the priesthood "because they somehow failed God during their pre-existence."

Despite this strong language from President Kimball and despite official criticism of racial prejudice, the traditional explanations, especially the notion that all blacks were somehow less worthy in premortality, lingered in some Church members. On the twentieth

---

2. Despite this sweeping language, it is possible that Elder McConkie changed his views only about *when* the curse should be lifted. In the 1979 revision of the second edition of his *Mormon Doctrine,* he continued to express the view that those of black African lineage descend from Cain and that at least those who lived before 1978 came to earth under a curse related to their premortal lives. While he said in "The New Revelation," "the ancient curse is no more," he also said, "We can only suppose and reason that it [the restriction of Blacks] is on the basis of preexistence and of our premortal devotion and faith."

Baptisms in the sea, Cape Coast, Ghana.

anniversary of the revelation, several members urged that the time had come to formally disavow the traditional explanations. The Church did not take any such formal action,[3] but people speaking for the Church clearly distanced present Church policy from the earlier statements. Alexander Morrison, a Seventy, said that not only the official explanation but the real explanation why priesthood was not given to all men before 1978 is that "we do not know." He also stated that it is a sin to discriminate against people because of their race.[4]

CONSEQUENCES IN AFRICA

The effect of the revelation in Africa was immediate. On June 9, 1978, Joseph William (Billy) Johnson in Ghana came home from work discouraged by criticism from some of his followers about his unfulfilled prediction that soon missionaries would be sent. In the midst of these

---

3. It may be that any such statement was made less likely by the fact that those urging a statement had "gone public" with the issue.

4. President Hinckley made this statement to an Australian interviewer: "I don't know what the reason was. But I know that we've rectified whatever may have appeared to be wrong at that time." The current student manual for the seminary system says only that from the beginning "there has been a group of people who have not been allowed to hold the priesthood of God. The scriptural basis for this policy is Abraham 1:21–27. The full reason for the denial has been kept hidden by the Lord. . . . On 1 June 1978 the Savior revealed to President Spencer W. Kimball that the ban . . . was lifted."

feelings, he began to experience an unexplained inner excitement. He felt an impression to try to listen to the BBC, something he had not done for a long time. Patiently he tuned his shortwave radio for an hour. Finally at midnight he made the connection. The first thing he heard amid the crackles of static was a BBC news flash that the Mormon Church had opened its priesthood to all worthy men of all races. He could scarcely believe what he heard—the fulfillment of his hopes after fourteen years of struggle.

During the months before June 1978, Dale LeBaron, mission president in South Africa, puzzled over the unprecedented number of inquiries about the Church he had begun receiving from black men and women. The number increased even more after the revelation, even though few of the inquirers knew anything about it. He saw the interest as evidence that "the Lord had poured out his Spirit upon Africans, who had long been deprived of the fullness of the gospel blessings and ordinances."[5]

FIRST MISSIONARIES TO NIGERIA AND GHANA

For many years the Church had received persistent requests from black West Africans that missionaries be sent to teach them the restored gospel. Nowhere in the world did the revelation on priesthood make as much immediate difference as in Nigeria and Ghana.

In President Kimball's discussions with David Kennedy, Kennedy had frequently reminded him that there was little point in working to improve missionary access to black Africa because the Church would not succeed there without priesthood leaders. When they conferred over an open atlas, Kennedy would put his hand over Africa and say, "There is no use talking about it." As President Kimball returned to his office from the temple on June 9, 1978, he stopped at Kennedy's door and said, "You're going to be a happy man. You can take your hand off Africa."

Speaking to the *Church News* immediately after the revelation, President Kimball said Africa would be the focus of new missionary effort. In a regional representatives' seminar, he spoke of going to "the

5. In September 1978, President Kimball said, "There seems to be a great movement afoot in many nations to prepare people for the further light and knowledge that only we can give them."

Priesthood leaders in West Africa, including twenty-one stake presidents, 1999.

African continent," where black Africans "have waited so long already."
"It is a large continent," he acknowledged. "Roads are at a premium, and
homes are usually far less than we are used to here. Poverty is widespread. Country after country has scarcely over $100 per year per per-
son income for an economic base. But can we ask them to wait any
longer? I believe that we cannot."

In September 1978, President Kimball called two couples, Rendell
and Rachel Mabey and Ted and Janath Cannon, to serve a one-year mission in Nigeria and Ghana, primarily among the several thousand individuals who knew something of the gospel and had already organized
themselves into groups.[6]

"How soon would you like us to leave?" Mabey asked.

The prophet promptly responded. "Yesterday."

By November 21 the Mabeys and Cannons had arrived in Nigeria,
where one-fifth of all Africans lived. The first person baptized was
Anthony Obinna, who had waited since 1970. Others had waited even
longer. The couples also made a trip to Ghana and performed many

---

6. In 1978 an estimated two thousand Nigerians met in twenty "LDS" congregations. By
1978 the instability following the Biafran War had declined, and opposition political parties were
allowed.

baptisms there.[7] Joseph William (Billy) Johnson had organized unofficial congregations in many villages within a seventy-mile radius of his home in Ghana. The two elders baptized two hundred in a single day.[8]

Very soon black men were ordained and could perform baptisms.[9] By March nearly a thousand persons had been baptized in the two countries. Assimilating so many proved difficult because very few had any experience that would help them in Church administration.

By the end of a year, 1,723 people had been baptized. Nigeria had thirty branches in three districts; Ghana had five branches in two districts. Others who desired baptism were asked to wait until the first wave of new members had become settled.[10] On July 1, 1980, the Africa West Mission was organized with Bryan Espenschied serving as president. Because of Espenschied's earlier work with him on Lamanite issues, President Kimball trusted him with this challenging assignment.

President Espenshied sharply slowed the rate of baptisms by requiring the teaching of the missionary lessons as a prerequisite to baptism and disallowing baptism for anyone under eighteen unless another Church member lived in the same household. He assigned his few missionaries to find the thirty-three hundred members already baptized in Nigeria and Ghana and, if necessary, reteach them before seeking more new members. His strategy was "to strengthen the foundation without expanding the base." He felt that too many of those baptized, however genuine their desire, had no real understanding of what Church membership entailed.[11] As a consequence of these policies, the total

---

7. Sam Bainson said, "My baptismal interview was 1:30 in the morning because there were so many of us that had to wait in line. And I was in the first group of converts there, baptized in the Atlantic Ocean in December of 1978."

8. Christian missionaries had laid a groundwork of faith in Christ.

9. The missionaries had been instructed not to confer the Melchizedek Priesthood on converts immediately after baptism, but they did ordain some former ministers to the office of elder.

10. Wholesale baptisms were "ultimately counterproductive. Every individual had to be taught, every individual had to make commitments." The Church gained government recognition in Ghana in 1980 and in Nigeria in 1982.

11. Teaching and worthiness had suffered in the missionaries' responding to the urgent demands for baptism. The numbers baptized may be misleading because African religions are characterized by great fluidity; people joined and left church congregations easily. Some continued to engage in immoral conduct and had to be expelled for lack of repentance. However, overall the faithfulness is very high. Sacrament meeting attendance in Africa now is very near the highest of any area in the world.

Working on a Church farm, Cape Coast, Ghana.

membership at the end of President Espenschied's service was smaller than at the beginning, but those who remained were stronger.

Missionaries expended tremendous effort on leadership training, overcoming language and tribal barriers, building meetinghouses, and helping members with basic survival. Many members struggled with inadequate water, food, sanitation, and medical care.[12] In 1983, the Church sent two shipments of rice, corn, beans, oil, sugar, milk, and salt from Welfare Square to Ghana for members and for relief agencies. In January 1984, the Church announced it would no longer supply direct food aid but would provide a tiller for each branch so that members could plant gardens and establish cooperatives. Members were instructed to sun-dry surplus food and fish for times of need.

All these actions were in keeping with President Kimball's vision for Africa, whose poverty had concerned him from the first. "We will need to help educate the youth of these congregations and teach them the principles of growth and development."

12. Deseret Hospital, established in the 1980s by Dr. Emmanuel Kissi, a counselor in the mission presidency, received otherwise unobtainable medicines through Friends of West Africa, a group organized by and made up mostly of American missionaries returned from West African missions.

SOUTH AFRICA AND NEW MISSIONS

South Africa presented a special situation because of apartheid, a form of racial segregation legally established in 1948. Apartheid continued to be the law until the 1990s, although in the later years it was not generally enforced in Church meetings.

Some observers had expected that white South Africans would leave the Church en masse if it opened congregations to blacks. But they were wrong, mission president LeBaron reported. "I was not aware of a single instance of anyone leaving the church over the issues, and as leader of the church for all of South Africa, I would have been aware of any such actions." That did not mean there were no problems. Some white members did cease active involvement in the Church, although they might not officially leave it.

Because LDS Church units are geographical, they tended to be in either black or white areas in South Africa, leading to a high degree of incidental segregation. However, in stake meetings or in the temple, blacks and whites met and worshipped together with no apparent difficulty. Considering the racial history of South Africa, the level of acceptance and cooperation was striking.[13]

For many years, black South African missionaries could not serve effectively in their own country because of the hostile reactions they received from many whites. And black members sometimes faced ridicule from other blacks for belonging to a "white" church. Nevertheless, the Church flourished in South Africa after 1978 in a way not possible before the revelation.

After 1978 the Church established new missions in other areas with large black populations: Puerto Rico San Juan (1979), Dominican Republic Santo Domingo (1981), West Indies (1983), Haiti Port-au-Prince (1984), and Jamaica Kingston (1985). Three new Brazilian missions created between 1979 and 1985 helped convert large numbers of members with mixed racial ancestry.

In some areas missionary work struggled under the continuing perception of the Church as racist. Almost a decade after the revelation, missionaries in Barbados faced organized opposition—including

---

13. In interviews with hundreds of black members, LeBaron found that there was almost no report of discrimination.

Helvécio Martins of Brazil, the first black General Authority, 1990.

allegations of racism—by other churches. Jamaica permitted the Church to operate, but the Church's petition for corporate status was delayed because of allegations of racism.

GREATER NUMBERS OF BLACK MEMBERS

By President Kimball's death in November 1985, seven years after the revelation, Africa had four missions: one in Nigeria, one in Ghana, and two in South Africa. A substantial number of the missionaries came from Africa itself. And members joining the Church in Africa were as a group zealous, remarkably well educated, and disproportionately male.

Because Church records do not identify race, it is impossible to know the exact number of black members at the time of the revelation, but ten years after the revelation there may have been 75,000 to 100,000 total, with 20,000 to 30,000 in West Africa, 28,000 in the West Indies, and many more in the United States, Brazil, and elsewhere. The revelation had opened wide a door through which a throng then surged.

INNOVATION FOR A
GROWING CHURCH

25

REVISING PRIESTHOOD ORGANIZATION

"We can't lick every postage stamp in Salt Lake City."

RAPID GROWTH IN THE CHURCH after World War II strained the Church's leadership resources. General Authorities found it increasingly difficult to supervise headquarters departments, maintain contact with local leaders, visit the proliferating stakes four times a year, and visit every mission periodically.[1] As President Gordon B. Hinckley told a group of new mission presidents in July 1984, "We can't lick every postage stamp in Salt Lake City. We have to do something about decentralizing authority." Administration-minded Harold B. Lee had begun addressing the problems with a two-pronged effort: first, implementing a correlation policy that simplified, streamlined, and subordinated a broad range of both headquarters and field operations; and second, applying management practices that were standard in the American business world. As a member of the Quorum of Twelve, Spencer had been tangentially involved in implementing these changes; as President, he pursued them with thoroughness and speed.

Chief among the changes in leadership organization during his administration were (1) transferring to others some of the Quorum of the Twelve's duties, (2) reconstituting the First Quorum of the Seventy, (3) redefining the duties of the Presiding Bishopric, (4) introducing

---

1. When Spencer became President, the Church had already adopted several major organizational innovations—Assistants to the Twelve in 1941, Regional Representatives of the Twelve in 1967 (to serve as intermediaries between the apostles and the 470+ stake presidencies), and the correlation program in the 1960s.

emeritus status for General Authorities, and (5) retiring the office of the Patriarch to the Church. Because of the First Presidency's health problems, President Kimball also called an additional counselor.

AN AGING PRESIDENCY

Since Brigham Young's time, Church Presidents have been elderly when they assumed office, and with the exception of Harold B. Lee, all have experienced a period of incapacity before their deaths. Elder Kimball observed in 1970, "We may expect that the Church president will always be an older man." Age, he noted, can be an advantage because it imparts "stability and strength and wisdom through experience and long communion with God."

A vigorous President can accomplish some things an aging man cannot, but even an aged President can lead effectively with the aid of counselors who are more energetic physically and keener mentally and who are chosen for strengths that complement his weaknesses. History shows that when Presidents have been incapacitated, the work of the presidency has gone forward relatively unhindered, with strong counselors taking over everyday leadership.[2]

When the First Presidency collectively suffer illness or the disabilities of old age, the Twelve play a greater role. Thus for a time President Kimball conferred with the Twelve on many issues normally considered the province of the presidency. Then in the summer of 1981, when all three of the First Presidency had health problems, President Kimball called Gordon B. Hinckley as a third counselor.

Although President Kimball's health limited him from September 1981 until his death in November 1985, he could generally respond, indicating his approval or disapproval. He did not, however, initiate action. The practice for managing such situations was described by President Hinckley, when he spoke in 1994 of President Benson's similar incapacity:

"When the President is ill or not able to function fully in all of the duties of his office, his two Counselors together comprise a Quorum of

---

2. J. Reuben Clark led during the last years of Heber J. Grant and George Albert Smith. Harold B. Lee led as first counselor to Joseph Fielding Smith. In David O. McKay's declining years, however, there was no clear leader among his four counselors.

the First Presidency. They carry on with the day-to-day work of the Presidency. In exceptional circumstances, when only one may be able to function, he may act in the authority of the office of the Presidency. . . .

" . . . But any major questions of policy, procedures, programs, or doctrine are considered deliberately and prayerfully by the First Presidency and the Twelve together. These two quorums . . . consider every major question . . . [and] . . . no decision emanates . . . without total unanimity."[3]

For the last four years of the Kimball administration, President Hinckley bore nearly the entire load of responsibility for the presidency. His role reflected the principle that the First Presidency is not constituted of simply a leader who has two assistants; it functions as a quorum.[4] President Hinckley explained his procedure to his biographer:

"It was a difficult period. But I was careful. I had no question about moving ahead where there was established policy. But with anything that called for new policy or decisions that weren't covered by policy, I

---

3. Gordon B. Hinckley said, "The president, after all, is just one of the fifteen prophets, seers, and revelators, so when the president is not functioning, we simply carry on with the remaining apostles. . . . There is abundant 'backup.'"

4. Joseph F. Smith said, "I have always held . . . that it is wrong for one man to exercise all the authority and power of presidency in the Church. . . . I dare not assume such a responsibility, and I will not, so long as I can have men like these [pointing to his counselors] to stand by and counsel with me."

went to see President Kimball when he was well rested and explained in great detail the things we wished to do. Arthur Haycock [or Francis Gibbons] went with me and kept a detailed record of every discussion we had. There were times when I returned to President Kimball several times to make sure he was clear about a decision on a given matter. Only when I was sure that he both comprehended our conversations and agreed with the course of action did we move ahead. I also discussed many issues with the Twelve."

President Hinckley publicly acknowledged President Kimball's disability while minimizing its significance: "He is the prophet of the Lord, and he will be with us for so long as the Lord wills. And as the Lord's appointed servant, no major decision concerning this work will be made without his consideration and his direction."

SHIFTS IN THE TWELVE'S ADMINISTRATIVE RESPONSIBILITIES

Administrative responsibilities of the Twelve changed because of the steady growth of the Church. Some tasks traditionally performed by the Twelve were shifted to stake presidents: setting apart missionaries (1970), ordaining seventies and setting apart the presidents of seventies quorums (1974), ordaining bishops (1975), and ordaining stake patriarchs (1983).[5]

As correlation gained momentum in the early 1970s, a study of Church administration by the management consulting firm Cresap, McCormick, and Paget recommended freeing the Twelve from direct supervision of Church departments. The suggestion was adopted. The Twelve became primarily a board of directors that sets policy and supervises rather than manages departments.

CALLINGS AND ADVICE FOR THE QUORUM OF THE TWELVE APOSTLES

The calling of new General Authorities and naming of counselors in the First Presidency has traditionally been the President's prerogative, though generally he consults with the Twelve about new apostles.

---

5. The authorization to ordain seventies in the stake became obsolete when the office was retired by the Benson presidency in October 1986.

During his twelve years as President, Spencer called seven apostles, the first four while he was still fully active: L. Tom Perry (April 1974), David B. Haight (January 1976), James E. Faust (September 1978), and Neal A. Maxwell (July 1981).

David B. Haight, an assistant to the Twelve, received a telephone call from President Kimball asking him to come immediately to meet with him in the temple. After satisfying himself concerning Elder Haight's worthiness, President Kimball stood up, took both of Elder Haight's hands in his, and said, "With all the love I possess, I am calling you to fill a vacancy in the Quorum of the Twelve."

President Kimball believed that a calling was incomplete until the person had obtained spiritual confirmation that the call was from God. After Elder Haight's ordination, President Kimball suggested he remain in the temple alone. There Elder Haight "pleaded with the Lord to bless [him] with an understanding of the call of an apostle," and there he received personal revelation that allowed him to testify as an apostle with full assurance.

In September 1978, after the Thursday temple meeting, President Kimball invited James E. Faust, one of the Seventy, to meet with him. He called him to fill a vacancy in the Quorum of the Twelve. Afterward, Elder Faust returned to his office for a meeting, and during the meeting his secretary interrupted, something she would not normally do, saying, "President Kimball is on the phone."

When he picked up the receiver, he heard President Kimball ask, "Have you called Ruth?"

"I'm in a meeting and haven't had the time yet."

"I think you'd better call her. Now."

The remaining three apostles were called during President Kimball's last four years, when President Hinckley largely acted for him: Russell M. Nelson (April 1984), Dallin H. Oaks (April 1984), and M. Russell Ballard (October 1985). In announcing the Nelson and Oaks calls, President Hinckley assured the assembled Saints: "I want to give you my testimony that they were chosen and called by the spirit of prophecy and revelation." He added, "While President Kimball is unable to stand at this pulpit and speak to us, we are on occasion able to converse with him, and he has given his authorization to that which has been done. We would not have proceeded without this."

On occasion, the First Presidency exercised considerable influence on General Authorities' personal lives. Mark E. Petersen's daughter reports that, after her mother's lengthy illness and death in April 1975, the First Presidency allowed "a suitable time" to elapse; then President Tanner called Mark into his office "to inform him of the First Presidency's wish that he remarry." Elder Petersen expressed reluctance, explaining that "for the first time in years, he could live totally for the Lord. . . . After a brief consultation, the First Presidency gave him permission to stay single." He did not remarry before his death in 1984.

ASSISTANTS TO THE TWELVE AND THE FIRST QUORUM OF THE SEVENTY

In 1975 the Church further decentralized by dividing the fifty missions in the United States and Canada into twelve areas, with an apostle as advisor and one of the Assistants to the Twelve as supervisor. Stakes and missions in the rest of the world were divided into six areas and came under the supervision of six more Assistants to the Twelve.

The most important step in reorganization was the reconstitution in October 1975 of the First Quorum of the Seventy, a body that had not been operational since the Church's early days but that was called for in the scriptures (see D&C 107:25–27, 93–97). The First Quorum of the Seventy had been represented only by its seven presidents, called the First Council of the Seventy. Operationally, by the mid–twentieth century the First Council supervised the local seventies quorums and (under the Twelve) had a special responsibility for missionary work.

The First Council of the Seventy had repeatedly proposed reconstitution of the First Quorum, but no action was taken. Then in 1974, the new Presidency asked for resubmission of the written proposal. This time President Kimball said, "Brethren, the Lord is pleased with your product and we are ready to organize the First Quorum and make some other necessary changes."

S. Dilworth Young provided crucial leadership during this period, particularly in his willingness to relinquish his position as the senior President of the Seventy, which position he had held since 1967. His widow later told friends that a few days before 1975 October general conference, President Kimball telephoned Elder Young at his office in the late afternoon and asked if they could meet. Although Elder Young immediately offered to come to the President's office, President Kimball insisted on going up to Young's office. Earnestly President Kimball asked, "Are you sure you want us to go through with this? We can wait until you are gone." Elder Young assured him that the change needed to be made and that he wanted to serve as an example to others who might feel ruffled by the change. As the two men parted, Young quipped in mock indignation, "And what do you mean, 'After *you're* gone'? You are two years older than I am!"

At general conference, the First Presidency announced the reconstitution of the First Quorum of the Seventy with ten members—the seven who made up the First Council of the Seventy and three men not previously General Authorities, now called as additional quorum members. Commenting on the new arrangement, President Kimball explained, "I think that the First Quorum of the Seventy will gradually do much of the work the Twelve has done up till now . . . because, after all, it's much the same."

In calling new members of the First Quorum of Seventy, President Kimball showed his commitment to broadening ethnic and national representation among the General Authorities. Of the thirty-seven Seventies he called during the next few years, eleven were not white Americans; they spoke eight different mother tongues. One of them was Navajo George P. Lee, who had long held special interest for President Kimball because Lee was a success story of the Indian Student Placement Program.[6] The others were Charles A. Didier (a Belgian), Adney Y. Komatsu (a Hawaiian of Japanese parentage), Jacob de Jager (a Canadian immigrant from the Netherlands), F. Enzio Busche (a German), Yoshihiko Kikuchi (a Japanese), Derek A. Cuthbert (an Englishman), Angel Abrea (an Argentinian), John Sonnenberg (a German who moved to the United States at age six), Hans B. Ringger (a Swiss), and Helio R. Camargo (a Brazilian).

A year after calling the first new Seventies, President Kimball and his counselors took a second major step. They released the twenty-one Assistants to the Twelve, then called them and three other men as

---

6. In 1989, during the Benson administration, Lee was excommunicated for apostasy. In October 1994 he pleaded guilty to attempted sexual abuse of a child, which had occurred while he was a General Authority, and the court placed him on probation with the requirement he have therapy.

members of the First Quorum of the Seventy. These, with the fourteen already in the First Quorum, brought its total membership to thirty-nine. A new presidency of the quorum, no longer to be determined by seniority, as in the First Council of the Seventy, was appointed to serve indeterminate terms.[7] (By 1977, the growing number of General Authorities required remodeling the multitiered stand in the Tabernacle to provide more seating.)

Almost immediately, Seventies were assigned to take over much of the Church's administration. Under direction of the Twelve, they became managing directors of major departments, including Church history, curriculum, priesthood and auxiliary organizations, temple, family history, missionary work, and correlation.

The Church in August 1984 was restructured once again, dividing the world into thirteen geographic areas, each with an area presidency of three members of the First Quorum of the Seventy who, like all other General Authorities except the Presiding Bishopric, were called for life, subject to the emeritus policy. In 1984 President Hinckley on behalf of the First Presidency announced the appointment of new members of the First Quorum and explained that they would serve from three to five years, a period later standardized at five years. By the end of the Kimball presidency, the First Quorum of the Seventy had fifty-two active members.

CALLS ISSUED TO SEVENTIES

During President Kimball's active years, he handled most calls to the Seventy himself. He routinely found that the men being called had great misgivings, much like those he experienced when he was called to be an apostle.

---

7. President Kimball invited the seven new presidents to join the First Presidency in ordaining the new Seventies in a room on the fourth floor of the Salt Lake Temple. Afterward, Marion Hanks and Paul Dunn lingered in conversation. When they pushed the call button, the elevator, which had been on its way down, for some reason came back, bringing the entire First Presidency. The two men deferentially stepped back and allowed President Kimball and his counselors to go down again. They waited until they thought the elevator had reached the main floor and the presidency had surely exited, then pushed the button. Again the temperamental elevator brought the First Presidency up to the fourth floor. This time the two Seventies blushed in embarrassment. When the same thing happened a third time, Spencer teased, "Brethren, why don't you two take the stairway?" They did.

In April 1975 he called a corporate executive, Robert D. Hales, to leave his profession and become an Assistant to the Twelve (he was called as a Seventy the next year). Thunderstruck, Hales responded emotionally, "President Kimball, I just don't know what to say."

President Kimball prompted gently, "I only want you to say yes."

Reflecting on his call to the First Quorum of Seventy in September 1977, F. Enzio Busche commented, "I think the Lord helps by not giving you the full understanding at the time. If you really understood all that it meant, you wouldn't be able to respond." He answered President Kimball's call by saying, "I can't see an honest way to escape." Spencer, amused, countered, "Could you put that in a positive way?"

Yoshihiko Kikuchi, a Japanese business executive and president of the Tokyo Stake, and his wife were interviewed by President Kimball in October 1977. President Kimball asked the Kikuchis about their health, family, and business. Then he paused, his expression serious. Looking steadily at Brother Kikuchi, he leaned over his desk and said, "The Lord has called you to serve as one of the General Authorities of the Church. Can you accept this call?"

Hesitantly, Brother Kikuchi said, "It is impolite to ask, but could you kindly repeat what you have just described?"

President Kimball repeated the question. The Kikuchis, too shocked to speak, could only weep. President Kimball waited patiently, then asked the question a third time. When they were still unable to speak, he said, "You stay here and discuss it; I'll leave you alone."

Just as President Kimball was leaving, Brother Kikuchi managed to say, "Please don't leave us." The President came back, smiling, and repeated the question a fourth time. This time Brother Kikuchi answered, "I am not worthy, President Kimball. I cannot accept this call."

"Do you have problems keeping the covenants you made in baptism and the temple?"

"No, President, but I know what a General Authority must be and I am not qualified."

"I went through this myself once," said President Kimball compassionately. "I can understand your feelings. Can you accept this call? We want to have you sustained in this conference."

Brother Kikuchi continued to point out his inexperience and inadequacies. But finally President Kimball said, "My friend, the Lord revealed to me that I must call you from the land of Japan to serve in his Church as a General Authority. Isn't that adequate answer to your feelings of inadequacy? The Lord will bless and magnify you so that you can serve as his humble servant."

Brother Kikuchi finally responded, "I will do what the Lord asks me to do."

President Kimball came around his desk, hugged and kissed Elder Kikuchi and said, "I love you and the Lord loves you."

President Kimball also showed sensitivity to personal circumstances. When he asked Seventy Paul Dunn to serve in an area presidency in Germany, Elder Dunn explained the difficulties it would pose for one of his teenage daughters to be uprooted. A week later, President Kimball gave him a different assignment.

President Kimball's attitude toward callings is illuminated by his comment when he called an old friend, L. Harold Wright, as a mission president. When Wright seemed overwhelmed, the President pulled out a file bulging with letters from men volunteering to be called as mission president. "We don't call any of them," he remarked. "We call men like you who don't want to go."

EMERITUS STATUS FOR GENERAL AUTHORITIES

An important innovation of Spencer W. Kimball's administration was the creation of emeritus status for General Authorities. The idea had been discussed as far back as 1941 but was never implemented. In the fall of 1978, the First Presidency and Twelve decided it was time. The new policy was that all General Authorities except the Presidency and Twelve would be named emeritus when they turned seventy or when they become too ill to serve.

Emeritus status would not be extended to the counselors in the First Presidency or to any members of the Twelve, presumably because they held in suspended form all authority necessary to function as President of the Church. Giving them emeritus status would logically affect succession to the presidency.

The decision to establish emeritus status took at least some of the General Authorities by surprise. Henry D. Taylor, a member of the First Quorum of Seventy, received only one day's notice to attend a meeting with the First Presidency on the Tuesday before October conference. Six other Seventies were also invited. President Kimball explained to them that, after decades of consideration, he would soon announce that as of January 1979 these seven would be designated emeritus—not released as General Authorities, but excused from active service. They might be given special assignments and would continue to have sealing power in the temples. They would also be given office space and would continue to receive financial support.

Eldred G. Smith, Patriarch to the Church.

PATRIARCH TO THE CHURCH

The office of Patriarch to the Church, first held by Joseph Smith Sr. (1833–40), was passed on his death to his eldest living son, Hyrum (1841–44), with the understanding that it was a hereditary office of great importance in the spiritual life of the Church. But its function remained ambiguous. Was the title properly "Presiding Patriarch," suggesting presiding authority over stake patriarchs, or "Patriarch to the Church"? What were the implications of each title? Must succession go to the eldest worthy son? Where does the patriarch fit within Church government?

At the October 1979 general conference, these issues were resolved in an unexpected fashion. The First Presidency announced the emeritus status of the Patriarch to the Church, Eldred G. Smith, without naming any successor. Although the office continued to exist in theory, the action effectively abolished it. The announcement noted only "the large increase in the number of stake patriarchs and the availability of patriarchal service throughout the world."

Since the Patriarch Emeritus could continue to give blessings and perform sealings—the only activities in which he was then engaged—nothing much changed for him. But the office itself went into limbo.[8]

---

8. Patriarch Smith retains an office and a part-time secretary in the Joseph Smith Memorial Building and has given more than 18,000 patriarchal blessings.

26

CHANGES IN AUXILIARY ORGANIZATIONS

"When the Lord asks this boy, 'Where is your wife?' all of his excuses . . . will seem very light."

THE MOVEMENT THAT CAME to be called "Correlation" was initiated in the 1960s to respond to problems created by Church growth and to strengthen the Church against the deleterious societal changes sweeping the nation. Correlation provided a prescription for all Church activities: that they be priesthood-directed, scripture-based, family-centered, simple, and economical.

To those ends, several sweeping changes were made: the auxiliary magazines were discontinued and replaced by the *Ensign, New Era,* and *Friend* (1970); the Relief Society and auxiliaries no longer reported directly to the First Presidency; the Relief Society and auxiliaries no longer raised funds themselves but were funded from the ward budget at the discretion of priesthood leaders;[1] instead of writing lessons for their own members, subject only to the approval of a General Authority, lesson materials were written by a correlation committee with the Relief Society and the auxiliaries creating the lesson outlines; and curriculum for the whole Church was coordinated and based on scripture.

Although correlation was largely completed by the time Spencer became President, it continued under his leadership. However, in a 1978 meeting attended by the First Presidency, Church leaders recognized that with "increased emphasis upon priesthood direction and

---

1. In 1956, only half the women belonged to the Relief Society, a voluntary, dues-supported organization, and only one-third of them attended.

control . . . the pendulum has swung too far and that there is a need to give more recognition, authority, and responsibility to sisters."

Correlation Department

In 1975 a separate Correlation Department, supervised by General Authorities, was established. To better determine needs, Church leaders established about 1977 the Research and Evaluation Division of the Correlation Department. This division researched a number of concerns: women's issues, the Young Women's program, the conversion process (including stake missionary work), factors correlated with religious activity or inactivity, factors predictive of whether boys would serve missions, effectiveness of a bishops' training program, bishops' workloads, Church statistical record keeping, and submission of records for temple work.

Auxiliary Conferences and Activities

The all-Church annual auxiliary conferences held in Salt Lake City to instruct stake and ward leaders and teachers ended in 1975. The conferences had gradually been reaching a smaller and smaller portion of the people as Church membership outside the U.S. West increased. More responsibility was shifted to regional and stake leaders. The Relief

Barbara Smith turns over the Relief Society wheat storage to the Church.

Society Conference was replaced in 1979 with the annual General Women's meeting, conducted by and presided over by the male leaders of the Church.

In May 1977, Church, stake, and ward activities committees took over from the auxiliaries responsibility for planning social activities and running the sports program.

TRANSFER OF RESOURCES

In 1978, the Relief Society and all auxiliaries were asked to turn any separate financial resources over to the General Church Fund. For more than one hundred years the Relief Society had run a grain storage program to provide wheat for the poor. By 1978 the program had 225,000 bushels of wheat, worth $1.6 million, in granaries it owned. Other wheat fund assets were worth more than $750,000. In the October 1978 welfare session of general conference, Barbara Smith presented these assets to President Kimball, and he asked her to call for a sustaining vote from the women present. Some gave only reluctant assent, seeing the wheat program as the last vestige of Relief Society independence.[2]

CONSOLIDATED MEETING SCHEDULE

In March 1980 the Church adopted the consolidated meeting schedule, a three-hour block of time on Sunday that encompassed sacrament meeting, Sunday School, Primary, Relief Society, Young Women, and priesthood meeting.[3]

The new schedule was especially welcome in areas where members had to travel many miles to attend meetings.[4] This moved weekly Relief Society meetings from a weekday class of ninety minutes to a fifty-minute slot on Sunday, plus a monthly "homemaking" session during the week.[5] The change to Sunday benefited working women who were

---

2. The transfer was triggered by a request from the Welfare Department for the wheat. Barbara Smith asked if wheat could be given as a gift, by vote of the women in conference.

3. Adoption followed a pilot program in fifteen stakes for the month of October 1979.

4. Previously an illustrative Sunday schedule would be priesthood meeting at 8:00 A.M., Sunday School at 9:30 A.M., and sacrament service at 4:00 P.M. Primary met Tuesday at 4:45 P.M., M.I.A. met Wednesday at 7:00 P.M., and Relief Society met Thursday morning at 9:30. The Church leadership intended that the change would allow more time for families, scripture study, Christian service, and community involvement.

5. In 1999 the name was changed to "Home, Family, and Personal Enrichment Meeting."

Relief Society general president Elaine Jack with African Relief Society members.

unable to attend during the week, but it excluded women who staffed the Primary and Young Women meetings, held simultaneously with Relief Society.

The new schedule produced a rise in attendance at meetings. A year after the change, average weekly sacrament meeting attendance had risen from 44 percent to 49 percent.[6] Relief Society attendance also jumped substantially. However, nonmember children who had previously participated in Primary on weekdays rarely came on Sunday.

The Young Women's program became a Sunday analog to the Aaronic Priesthood program, meeting at the same time and focusing on religious subject matter. Some joint weekday evening activities continued, but they were clearly subordinate to the Sunday program.

One of the unintended consequences of the new schedule was a reduction in the social and cultural bonding that helps hold converts while testimonies mature. Still, few members would return to the former schedule if given a choice.

---

6. A 1995 Princeton Religion Research Center survey showed LDS average attendance at 53 percent, with the national average at 40 percent. The LDS figures are the more remarkable in that they include everyone ever baptized and not excommunicated whose location is known, even when they might no longer think of themselves as Latter-day Saints.

SINGLE ADULTS

A Church demographic study in the 1980s revealed that being a member of a stereotypical LDS family (a temple-married couple with children at home) described only 20 percent of the Church membership in the United States, and strikingly less in the international Church. Active single women in the Church over thirty years of age outnumbered active single men five to one. At any one time about 30 percent of Church members over eighteen were single. About 3 percent never married. Of those who did marry, one-third became divorced and others were widowed.

Growing consciousness of these facts resulted in some general conference talks being directed to single parents and divorced or never-married women. Church magazines began including discussion of problems associated with singleness. Church programs specifically for single adults began in 1972 under the label "Melchizedek Priesthood MIA." In 1977 responsibility shifted to the Relief Society and priesthood quorums.

In 1978 President Kimball acknowledged the problems for singles in a Church that so strongly emphasizes marriage and family. He said, "When we speak of family life, it is not done to make [single women] sad or unappreciated. . . . Women in such circumstances include some of the most noble spirits of our Father in Heaven." A year later he added, "Please be especially thoughtful of the [unmarried] sisters, . . . so they do not inadvertently feel left out as we rightfully focus on family life."

On the other hand, President Kimball admonished single men who shun marriage for selfish reasons:

"Recently I met a young returned missionary who is 35 years old. He had been home from his mission for 14 years and yet he was little concerned about his bachelorhood, and laughed about it.

"I shall feel sorry for this young man when the day comes that he faces the Great Judge at the throne and when the Lord asks this boy: 'Where is your wife?' all of his excuses which he gave to his fellows on earth will seem very light and senseless when he answers the Judge. 'I was very busy,' or 'I felt I should get my education first,' or 'I did not find the right girl'—such answers will be hollow and of little avail."

27

ACCOMMODATING GROWTH

"Everything we do and think now is on an international basis."

RAPID GROWTH CHARACTERIZED the twelve years from 1974 through 1985. Membership grew to almost six million, an increase of nearly 75 percent, with the most vigorous growth occurring in Asia and Latin America.[1] When President Kimball died late in 1985, nearly half of the Church members had known no other President.[2]

The Church's quick growth produced broad-scale changes in Church membership and administration. At headquarters, the Church bureaucracy was growing. The membership was becoming more urbanized.[3] Internationalization and cultural diversification of the Church was increasing.[4] The Church was expanding in Third World countries, with a resulting decline in average member income. More members and missionaries were located in countries dominated by dictators at both ends

---

1. Membership figures do not tell the whole story, because some members of record are not just inactive; they are lost, their whereabouts unknown.

2.

CHURCH GROWTH, 1974–1997, AT 12-YEAR INTERVALS

	Jan. 1, 1974	Dec. 31, 1985	Dec. 31, 1997
Members	3,300,000	5,700,000	10,100,000
Stakes	630	1,582	2,424
Missionaries	17,000	29,000	56,500
Missions	108	188	318
Converts during the year	80,000	98,000	318,000
Countries with organized units	47	95	143
Operating temples	15	37	51
Temples under construction or announced	1	11	19
Endowments performed for the living during the year	37,000	55,000	Not available

Various sources do not all agree, so figures should be considered only approximate.

3. Armand L. Mauss posits that urban Mormons become less "peculiar." Missionary work was done almost exclusively in the cities.

4. In early 1996 members in the United States became a minority.

of the political spectrum. And the Church was facing the financial challenge of building greater numbers of meetinghouses and temples.

To deal with these pressures, President Kimball led the Church through what he termed "program adjustments"—numerous modifications of structure, expectations, and resources. In a regional representatives seminar, he outlined the fundamental goals of these modifications:

"We see ourselves as positioning our people so that the Latter-day Saints can give greater attention to family life, can focus more on certain simple and basic things, can render more Christian service, and can have greater effectiveness in all these things—through the process of simplification, scheduling, proper priorities, and by honoring the priesthood line."

Many new Church policies related to the structure and operation of the organization, where concern for efficiency loomed large.

THE BASIC UNIT PROGRAM

Trying to follow the entire Church program often overwhelmed the ability or commitment of small groups of members. To limit the organizational structure and thereby reduce the demands on those members, the Church in 1977 adopted the Basic Unit Program. Under this plan, the smallest freestanding unit was an "independent group" presided over by a single priest; its formal program consisted of a sacrament meeting and home teaching. A "small branch" required only two elders, one to serve as branch president and the other as elders quorum president. Its program consisted of sacrament meeting, priesthood meeting, a women's meeting, and home teaching. The Church published simplified guidebooks, manuals, and reports to support the Basic Unit Program.[5]

Citing Doctrine and Covenants 19:22—"For they cannot bear meat now, but milk they must receive"—President Kimball reported in 1980 that "where the program is being used as outlined, we are meeting with great success." He encouraged priesthood leaders to use the program "to bless people."

Unfortunately, while these changes simplified life for basic unit members, it actually made the overall Church organization more

---

5. In 1979 materials in thirty-five languages supported three hundred groups and small branches. The book *Gospel Principles* provides basic gospel instruction.

Dedication of the Church Office Building, July 1975.

complex by generating yet another kind of unit with its own set of materials and reports. On one occasion, President Kimball saw a display of the vast array of lesson books, manuals, handbooks, guides, and report forms printed by the Church and expressed dismay. "We have done it all with the best of intentions," he said, but it was simply too much. The typical headquarters solution to each perceived problem was more programs, more scheduled interviews, more assessments and reports.[6] The Basic Unit Program was effectively discontinued in the mid-1980s, leaving branch organizational structure and curriculum largely to the discretion of stake and mission leaders.[7]

HEADQUARTERS STAFF

The growing Church relied on burgeoning bureaucracy. In an interview for his eightieth birthday, President Kimball noted that in 1905 his father had brought him from Arizona to Utah and introduced him to President Joseph F. Smith and his two counselors, who shared a single office and secretary as they presided over a church of 320,000 members. In 1975 Church headquarters employed an estimated 3,160 full-time equivalent workers in thirty-five departments.[8] This growing bureaucracy was housed in a new twenty-eight story Church Office Building, which was dedicated by President Kimball on July 24, 1975.

To a significant extent, the Church was adopting the style of a

---

6. President Kimball reportedly said, "This is a perilous problem and must be solved."

7. Although the program had become obsolete in the 1980s, it officially ended in 1994.

8. While in fifteen years membership had increased 100 percent, headquarters' employees increased 173 percent.

corporation, including a chief executive officer, a board of directors, an internal research and evaluation capacity, creation of a Public Communications Department, and distribution of a continually refined *Handbook of Instructions* for local leaders.

The more Church operations became professionalized, the more Church leaders, called for their spiritual strength, benefited also from having administrative skills or reliable staff administrators. There was less room for leaders who might be gifted in other areas but lacked administrative skills. The more the Church was governed by rules and correlated curriculum, the less room there was for exercise of individual initiative and open dialogue.

While bureaucracy and dispersion of authority cannot be avoided in any rapidly growing organization, difficulties arise when policy articulated at the top must be interpreted and applied by thousands of individual Church officers and employees worldwide. And at the higher levels, leaders must depend heavily on others for information upon which to base policy decisions.

Additional layers of leaders automatically generated problems of distance and inconsistency. More and more, the General Authorities' work became administration and public speaking, less and less visiting in people's homes and counseling individuals. Members were increasingly reminded to consult local leaders with personal problems or doctrinal questions and not to seek out General Authorities. In 1977, Marjorie Hinckley mourned, "The brethren are getting farther and farther away from the people. It is a melancholy prospect. As we read [in Spencer Kimball's biography] of some of his mission tours [as an apostle], Dad longed for the good old days, hard as they were."

TRAINING AND RESTRUCTURING LOCAL PRIESTHOOD ORGANIZATION

Rapid growth created immense leadership training problems on the local level, which in turn brought about—in Elder Neal A. Maxwell's words—"unevenness and disappointments in connection with the expansion of the work."[9]

As President Kimball acknowledged in 1974, "We recognize our

---

9. President Hinckley identified training of local leadership as a critical problem.

greatest problem is our rapid growth. Our increase in numbers is phenomenal. . . . The monumental challenge . . . is to provide trained leadership for the fast-multiplying units of members and to help that membership keep clean from [the] world."

Local priesthood organizations were restructured. Beginning in 1974, a separate elders quorum was organized for every ward and independent branch, even if the unit had only a few elders.[10] Previously an elders quorum was organized at the stake level, although each ward had an elders "group" as a subunit of the quorum.

Simultaneously, each stake was given its own quorum of seventies, with dual supervision provided by the stake president and the First Council of the Seventy.

In 1985 the Church announced the policy that male converts should not be ordained to the Aaronic Priesthood immediately upon baptism by missionaries; rather, they should be ordained only after an interview by the bishop and a vote of the congregation. Males sixteen or older could be promptly ordained priests, but men should become elders only after having demonstrated worthiness over some unspecified period of service as a priest.

Priesthood meetings had traditionally been closed to nonmember men. However, beginning in 1980, nonmember and non-priesthood-holding male members were allowed to attend priesthood meetings as guests.

OTHER CHANGES AFFECTING LIFE IN THE CONGREGATIONS

During the Kimball administration, wards and stakes were split sooner, thus reducing the average size of local units. The average membership of wards and branches dropped from 509 to 429 and of stakes from 4,610 to 3,510.[11] A standard naming system was implemented for identifying stakes, wards, and missions by their geographical locations. Wards and stakes in the United States and Canada were authorized to purchase computers for keeping membership and financial records.

---

10. In 1986, under President Benson, "seventy" as a local priesthood office dedicated to missionary work was terminated.

11. Over the next twelve years from 1986 to 1997 the numbers rose again, averaging 3,860 in a stake.

Church, stake, and ward activities committees were created in 1977 with the charge to develop cultural arts and physical activities. The Church encouraged drama, dance, sports, camping, and other activities. The activities committees were to relieve other ward leaders from the responsibility of organizing many of these activities, which ranged from a ward "road show" skit with a few youths to a dance festival in the Rose Bowl in 1985 that involved 13,000 dancers from nearly eighty stakes in southern California and 100,000 observers.

A long-term project to revise the 1948 hymnal had languished. In 1974 President Kimball renewed the assignment. The Church music committee of thirty to thirty-five members was charged with making the hymnal's language more sex-neutral, ensuring that doctrine in hymn texts was sound, and including hymns that reflected the international character of the Church.[12] After many months the committee reported its recommendations. The most lively discussion concerned recommendations for deleting old hymns. Some complained about omission of songs they considered standards. For example, President Kimball championed "In Our Lovely Deseret," and it was saved. In one of his conference talks, he told how as a child he had enthusiastically sung its refrain

---

12. Between the 1950 and 1985 editions, seventy hymns were omitted and many others were changed some way in text or music; forty-four hymns were new.

"Hark! hark! hark!" He also objected to the proposed omission of "Don't Kill the Little Birds," saying, "It is a part of the Church to me." But he recognized this as a personal preference and bowed to the committee's judgment. The new hymnal was finally published in 1985.

During President Kimball's tenure, the First Presidency expressed concern about the financial and time demands on the general membership, recognizing that the load could become so heavy that it would harm family life, employment, or education.[13]

Elder Boyd K. Packer was the First Presidency's spokesman on this issue. Once he half-jokingly asked Spencer, "Shouldn't I just mimeograph my speech and save time in meetings?" President Kimball replied, "No! You are never to let go of it and never give it up."

As an aspect of simplification, in 1977 general conference was reduced from three days to two days (Saturday and Sunday), with two sessions each day plus the priesthood session Saturday evening. April conference no longer always included April 6, the anniversary of the Church's organization. Before this, when April 6 fell midweek, it had made for an awkward schedule, since general conference also always included Sunday.

In 1979 the Church reduced stake conferences from quarterly to twice each year. A General Authority would attend once a year; the regional representative would attend the other conference.[14] That same year the Church discontinued the practice of holding regular ward sacrament meetings on the same Sunday as stake conference.

Efforts were made to reduce the number of other prescribed meetings. Beginning in 1978, priesthood leaders' monthly personal priesthood interviews could be held "as needed" rather than monthly. Also other ward and stake leadership and training meetings could be held less frequently than before. Stake Relief Society boards were abolished.

When in 1980 all general ward meetings were consolidated into a three-hour block on Sundays, President Kimball hoped that members

---

13. In 1989 the Church abolished locally collected budget and welfare funds and provided from Church headquarters the money needed for building maintenance, welfare needs, and support of local activities.

14. Under President Benson, even a regional representative would not always be able to attend stake conference. Under President Hinckley, Area Seventies conduct most conferences.

would take his advice: "Either before or after your series of Sunday meetings, depending upon your particular consolidated meeting schedule, you will do what the Savior asked the Nephite disciples to do: After he taught them, he asked them to go to their homes and to ponder and to pray over what was said (see 3 Nephi 17:3)."

BISHOPS' WORKLOADS

A study in 1978 of bishops' workloads revealed that the *Handbook* characterized too many tasks as exclusively the bishop's. If a bishop did everything he was supposed to do, it would take him forty hours a week. Logs kept by a number of bishops showed they spent an average of twenty-eight hours weekly. Some became disheartened because they simply could not do it all. The study revealed that in the best-run wards the bishops did less administrative work and more ministering to individuals.

The study recommended that bishops have more help, freeing them to counsel with individuals. Consequently the Church gave more responsibility to high priest group leaders and elders quorum presidencies in taking responsibility for home teaching. Bishops' counselors were authorized to handle routine youth interviews. In addition, a policy of shorter terms of service for bishops (and stake presidents) was implemented (typically then five years for a bishop and seven for a stake president).

SPECIAL LANGUAGE UNITS

The bishops' task was complicated by trying to integrate members who live in the United States but are not fluent in English. Church policy has alternated over the years between providing separate Church units for non-English speakers and expecting them to participate in English-language units.[15] President Kimball generally favored allowing people to worship and socialize in their native language and to gain the leadership experience they often would not receive in an

---

15. In 1980 President Kimball said to the regional representatives about cultural and minority groups, "When special attention of some kind is not provided for these people, we lose them." A recent study confirmed that ethnic wards produce greater activity among non-English speakers. However, on the other side, separate branches may have weaker auxiliary programs, less experienced leaders, oversimplified teaching, and some diminution of incentive to learn English.

English-speaking congregation. He did not see membership in special units as permanent but as a transitional status for individuals in the process of adapting to the majority culture.[16]

Beginning about 1975, major missionary efforts among ethnic minorities in large American cities produced substantial numbers of converts. Church leaders more uniformly recognized that for people to engage meaningfully in Church programs, they needed the context of their own language. Learning English was essential to their social and economic well-being in the United States, but that was not reason enough to force converts into wards where they would still be uncomprehending observers.[17]

Insensitivity still existed in some places. In 1980 a returned missionary wrote to President Kimball that in the area where he had served, the stake president would not organize a second Spanish-speaking ward, citing as Church policy the notion that each stake should have only one such ward. President Kimball invited the young man to come discuss the matter, and shortly thereafter the stake organized a second Spanish-speaking ward. In 1981, Polynesian-speaking wards in New Zealand were discontinued in an effort to encourage assimilation. Some Samoans resented the change enough to establish a separate Samoan church. In 1983, under the influence of Elder Monson, the policy was rescinded and the rift healed.

---

16. President Kimball opposed stamping out expressions of native culture. He applauded, for example, the retention of Maori dances, except for those that were erotic or warlike.

17. In 1992 there were at least 405 foreign-language branches in the United States.

28

MANAGEMENT OF RESOURCES

Reporters have concluded that there is no corruption in the handling of Church finances.

THE EVER-INCREASING NEEDS that accompanied Church growth called for continual reassessment of how Church resources were managed.

SEMINARIES, INSTITUTES, AND SCHOOLS

High-school-level seminaries and college-level institutes of religion constituted a major budget item and grew rapidly under the leadership of Church Commissioner of Education Neal A. Maxwell (1970–76). In 1974–75 seminary enrollment (released-time classes, early morning classes, and home study for isolated students) stood at 174,000 and institute enrollment at 74,000. By 1985–86 enrollment was 226,000 in seminaries and 122,000 in institutes.[1]

The Church also supported Brigham Young University and other college-level institutions as a major expense. In some areas where little schooling was available, the Church tried for a time to provide general education for children. In the 1960s, the Church established experimental grade schools in South America, Mexico, and the Pacific. But beginning in 1981, after a period of vacillation, the Church changed its policy. In Mexico, it closed its only teacher's college, three secondary schools, and thirty-seven primary schools, although it continued to support two high schools (Juarez and Benemerito). Non-Church schools had improved in quality and become more available, and the Church could

---

1. The seminary system, Richard Ostling commented, "involves a major commitment of time unique in religious education."

neither afford to build schools everywhere nor justify maintaining schools in some Mexican stakes but not in other stakes and nations.

In 1973 the Church Educational System began making student loans through an International Education Fund, which over the next twenty-eight years helped more than 25,000 young people in fifty-five countries pursue educational opportunities before it was superseded by a much larger Perpetual Education Fund in 2001.[2]

BUILDING CHAPELS AND TEMPLES

The Church invested heavily in providing chapels for its growing numbers of members. Responding to the increasing financial outlay, Church architects over a period of years developed sixty standard plans. Some observers saw the similarities of chapels as something of a trademark. Others found the sameness stultifying. But standardization

---

2. The program of grants and loans operated first in Central and South America, then the Philippines and Africa, administered centrally by the Church Educational System. Failure to repay and jealousy over differences in benefits were problems. The new fund granted more than eight thousand loans in its first year, averaging $800.

resulted in substantial savings in architectural costs and greater speed in building chapels.

Where possible, several units shared a single chapel, meeting at staggered times. In poor countries, small congregations were housed in simple chapels rather than larger American-style buildings. For example, in 1979 in the highlands of Guatemala ten new, small chapels were built for $20,000 each, including land and furnishings. Five more were then under construction in Ecuador and Tonga. Smaller buildings were also designed for congregations meeting under the basic unit plan.

In the early years of the Church, local members bore the entire cost for constructing ward and stake meetinghouses. Later the central Church organization began to pay an increasing portion. In 1982 members received the welcome news that wards meeting a tithing-faithfulness standard would pay no more than 4 percent.[3]

As converts were baptized in increasing numbers in poorer nations and from the poorer part of those populations, the average income of Church members worldwide declined steadily, yet faithfulness in payment of tithes everywhere allowed the Church to carry the burden of the building program. In some places, even simple chapels looked luxurious, creating the impression that the Church was a wealthy American sect.

New temples were built, too, but to reduce expenses while at the same time making more temples available, most of these temples were smaller. Temples in Samoa, Tonga, and Tahiti, for example, had only 8,500 to 12,500 square feet of floor space. Like the chapels, new temples were built from a few standard plans.

HISTORIC PRESERVATION

With its reverence for pioneer and Church history, the Church often chose to preserve old structures. Sometimes, however, present needs conflicted with the ideal of preservation. When President Kimball returned from an extended trip to South America in March 1975, he faced this clash of values. Leaders at a Bountiful, Utah, stake priesthood meeting proposed demolishing the Bountiful Tabernacle because it no longer met the needs of the growing stake. The proposal was approved

---

3. After 1990, the Church bore all construction costs.

with four dissenting votes and a greater number of abstentions; the stake's women were not consulted.

Built from 1857 through 1862, the Bountiful Tabernacle was the oldest surviving Latter-day Saint church building in Utah and the state's finest example of Greek Revival style. Every Latter-day Saint President except Joseph Smith had spoken there. Consequently, many in and out of the stake objected to the plan. Objectors alerted the press corps, who covered the issue intensely. More than four hundred accounts, mostly critical of the proposal, appeared in various newspapers. The Utah State Senate even passed a resolution asking for the Church's reconsideration of the Bountiful decision.

Substantial antagonism had already been stirred up when the historic Colesville Tabernacle in Utah's Summit County was razed in 1971.[4] In response to the groundswell of popular opinion favoring preservation, President Kimball counseled with Florence S. Jacobsen, director of Historic Arts and Sites for the Church. She expressed strong support for preservation, telling him that the tabernacle would come down "over my dead body."[5] The First Presidency announced its decision to save the tabernacle, despite the considerable cost of making an architecturally compatible addition to the building. President Kimball dedicated the rebuilt tabernacle.[6]

SECULAR PROPERTIES AND FINANCES

The Church also owned many properties not directly connected with its ecclesiastical activities. In 1974 builders broke ground for an

---

4. There was no overall Church policy and each property was considered ad hoc, often by different Church agencies.

5. In President McKay's time, as president of the Young Women, Florence Jacobsen had responded to the proposed demolition of the Lion House (which was part of the Young Women's responsibility) by saying it would happen "over her dead body." President Moyle defended the proposal, saying the building would require major upgrading and it stood as a constant reminder of polygamy. She said, "Are you ashamed of that?" He said, "That is not a fair question." After Moyle's death she and others urged President McKay to reconsider, and he said, "I think it should be saved." Sister Jacobsen promised that the Young Women would repay the cost of upgrading and refurbishing the building out of income from the Lion House food services. President McKay said, "We can't go wrong with a contract like that." The Young Women did reimburse the Church.

6. The Church's oldest remaining mural in a church building, a tromp l'oueil bust of Joseph Smith in profile in a niche that had been painted in 1862 by Danquart Anthon Weggelend, was "lifted" from the adobe wall of the tabernacle, remounted on canvas at a cost of $10,000, and displayed in the Museum of LDS Church History and Art.

At Deseret Ranch in Florida. From left: Harvey Dahl, Spencer Kimball, Arthur Haycock, Camilla Kimball, Margaret Dahl.

addition to the Church-owned Hotel Utah, the city's premier hotel since 1911. The new space would increase guest rooms from 445 to 625 and add a grand ballroom, exhibit space, a new restaurant, and an apartment that could be used by the President of the Church for convenience and security. Completion of the multimillion dollar project took two and a half years.[7]

The most impressive single property the Church owned was the Deseret Ranch in Florida, a 300,000-acre commercial ranch that pays taxes. In 1977 the ranch had 50,000 beef cattle, 2,400 acres of citrus trees, and 150,000 acres of timber. It employed eighty people, a third of them Church members. Sixty-one families lived on the ranch itself. Ranch manager Harvey A. Dahl drew press interest in 1980 when he contacted the county assessor to report that the property taxes were too low because improvements had been made since the last assessment.[8]

As Church President, Spencer found himself automatically elected chairman of the board in many of the various enterprises which the Church owned or in which it had large interest: ZCMI department store, Zions First National Bank, Beneficial Life Insurance Company, Utah

---

7. Later the building was remodeled to serve multiple Church purposes and renamed the Joseph Smith Memorial Building.

8. Henry D. Moyle was a major force in acquiring and expanding the ranch.

Home Fire Insurance Company, KSL radio and television, Utah Hotel Corporation, Zions Securities Corporation, and Utah-Idaho Sugar Company, among others.[9]

After diligently attending board meetings and trying to keep up with the paperwork for a year, however, President Kimball concluded that the time he spent in such activities could better be used in direct service to the growing Church. He retained positions only in Deseret Management Corporation, a holding company for most of the Church's properties (agribusiness, real estate, publishing, insurance, and hotels),[10] and Bonneville International Corporation, which operated the communications network of television and radio stations. He considered these two corporations vital to the Church's economic and missionary activities. He also remained on the Church Board of Education, which oversaw the Church schools, institutes, and seminaries.[11]

Most of the Church's real property is not financially productive but provides sites for chapels, stake centers, mission homes, seminaries and institutes, temples, schools, administrative buildings, and historical sites. In the 1960s the Church acquired and began to develop substantial acreage in the land around Adam-ondi-Ahman in Missouri.[12] This Missouri Land Fund Program fell under the supervision of Alvin R.

---

9. Partly because of his experience in insurance he had already been a director of Beneficial Life (since 1958) and of Utah Home Fire Insurance Company, serving on the credit committee and attending monthly meetings.

10. Real estate: Farm Management Co. (1980) to oversee Deseret Ranches of Florida (1951), Deseret Land and Livestock (1983), Deseret Ranches of Alberta (1940s), Deseret Farms of California (1960s), Rolling Hills and West Hills orchards, Cactus Lane Ranch (1984), Zions Securities Corp. (properties near Temple Square), Deseret Title Holding Corp. (office buildings in Atlanta and Tucson), Utah Hotel Corp. (returned to Church uses in 1987), Hotel Utah Motor Lodge (razed for library and museum construction); Hotel Temple Square (from 1990 to 2005 known as The Inn at Temple Square).

Media and communications: Bonneville International Corp. (fourteen TV and radio stations with related advertising, programming, data transmission, news bureau, and satellite), Deseret Book, Deseret News Publishing.

Insurance: Beneficial Life Insurance (1905) and Utah Home Fire Insurance (1886).

Retail: ZCMI (1868). The Church had controlling minority interest until the several ZCMI stores were sold in 1999 to May Department Stores Co. David Van Biema reports estimated value of the 312,000-acre Church ranch in Florida at $858 million.

11. In January 1996, President Hinckley instructed all General Authorities to resign from corporate boards, including Church-owned corporations.

12. The Church acquired substantial properties in Jackson, Clay, and Daviess counties. In the 1980s couples were called as Church-service missionaries to improve Church-owned property in Missouri. By the late 1980s ten to fourteen couples served such Church-service missions, typically for eighteen months.

Spencer W. Kimball illustrating the satellite relay capacity.

Dyer, then Assistant to the Twelve. In 1977, when Elder Dyer died, President Kimball and his counselors called Graham W. Doxey to replace him.

Since 1956 the Church has not published reports of its expenditures, leading reporters to wonder whether leaders have something to hide. But after investigating intensely, reporters have concluded that there is no corruption in the handling of Church finances.[13]

COMMUNICATION NETWORK

The Church invested in a communication network, partly to reach the growing Church membership. By 1977 the Church owned sixteen radio and two television stations. Hundreds of other radio and television stations were carrying portions of conference as a public service.

The first limited experiment with satellite transmission of general conference occurred in 1975.[14] In October 1979 members in nine U.S. cities received conference through receiver dishes set up at stake centers.

---

13. The 1991 series in the *Arizona Republic,* "Mormon Inc.," on Church finances also drew major interest. The report of an eight-month investigation headed by Richard Robertson found rumors of corruption in the handling of Church funds groundless. The Church books are audited but figures are not made public.

14. This was just the latest in technological developments: 1924 (conference first carried on radio), 1949 (television), 1952 (priesthood session carried by direct wire), 1957 (videotape for delayed viewing), 1980 (simultaneous satellite broadcast).

Translators make possible communication with Church members across the world.

In 1981, Church-owned Bonneville International leased a channel on commercial satellite Westar I, stationed 22,300 miles above the equator. This lease enabled the Church to telecast meetings held in Salt Lake City to stake centers equipped with dishes.[15]

For the April 1982 general conference, one hundred stake centers had receiver dishes. By 1985, the year of President Kimball's death, nine hundred of nearly sixteen hundred stakes were equipped to receive transmissions. This system freed the Saints from dependence on the willingness of local stations to give public service time to one or two sessions of general conference. It also permitted presentations at special times, such as at Christmas and Easter; to specific groups, such as young women or single adults or priesthood leaders; or on defined topics, such as missionary work or Church history.

This capacity greatly enlarged the Church's ability to reach its members around the world and reduced the need for area conferences. "Everything we do and think now," President Kimball noted, "is on an international basis."

---

15. In 1981 there were about thirty stake centers with receivers; by 1983 more than seven hundred. By 1999 more than 3,500 buildings could receive the telecast, including those in fifteen European nations. Translation was made in thirty-seven languages.

29

POLICY AND PRACTICE

"Refuse all association with organizations that . . . foster racial prejudice."

MORMONS OFTEN HAVE QUESTIONS about daily life that their leaders sometimes attempt to answer by issuing statements about policy and practice that are tied in some way to doctrine or right conduct. For example,
if a member has invited a nonmember friend to church, is it all right for
that friend to take the sacrament? If a teenage daughter becomes pregnant, should she be pressed to marry? If a young man has a conscientious objection to military service, can he remain in good standing with
the Church?

Church leaders do not try to answer every question, but they have
sometimes given guidance by stating a policy in letters, publications, or
in the *Handbook of Instructions*. Without the status of doctrine, these
policies represent only present understanding, so they sometimes
change.

HEALTH ISSUES

In 1974, James O. Mason, the Church Commissioner of Health,
assembled the first systematic guidelines on medical issues. Many of
these guidelines appeared in subsequent editions of the *General
Handbook of Instructions*.

In 1983 the handbook for the first time explicitly condemned
euthanasia, but it also did not encourage using extraordinary means to
extend life. Rather, "when dying becomes inevitable, it should be considered a blessing and a purposeful part of mortality."

President Kimball and his counselors in 1976 publicly supported
vaccination against an influenza epidemic, and in 1978 they issued

another statement supporting childhood immunizations. The Church also advised expectant mothers "to get the best prenatal and delivery care available from medically and legally qualified practitioners." It avoided the debate about whether midwives or medical doctors provide better prenatal care, stating these decisions "are a matter of personal choice."

A *Church News* editorial in 1977 said the Church did not endorse the current herbalist fad; rather it encouraged ailing members to consult licensed physicians. The 1985 *General Handbook of Instructions* warned, "Local leaders should advise members who have health problems to consult competent professional practitioners who are licensed in the countries where they practice."[1]

ADOPTION

Policy statements went well beyond health issues. The previous strong counsel that in case of pregnancy teens should wed was tempered to suggest that adoption be considered when parents are too immature to make a good home for the child.[2]

FUNERALS

The Presidency and the Twelve discussed extensively whether viewing of the body at a funeral, with the attendant socializing, detracted from the dignity and solemnity of funeral services as occasions to preach the gospel. Some leaders urged that the Church recommend against viewings, but they failed to persuade the others that there should be an official policy on the subject.

DEDICATION OF A HOME

Traditionally, the dedicating of a home in order to invoke divine protection and to manifest the family's commitment to God required that the home be paid for,[3] probably by analogy with the policy that

---

1. It further forbade using Church fast offering funds for unproven medical care without approval of the First Presidency.

2. A First Presidency statement confirmed, "When the probability of a successful marriage is unlikely, unwed parents should be encouraged to place the child for adoption, preferably through LDS Social Services."

3. About 1952 the Kimball home, mortgage free, was dedicated by son Ed.

chapels could not be dedicated until they were paid for. However, in 1980 this policy was changed to allow any home to be dedicated.

PARTICIPATION IN THE SACRAMENT

The Church had a long-standing policy of announcing that the sacrament would be passed "to members of the Church." The 1976 edition of the *General Handbook of Instructions* said that no limiting announcement need be made. Further, although the sacrament is for members, should visitors partake "nothing should be done to prevent them, lest the prohibition give offense." The effect of this is a slight shift in perception of the sacrament from a rite exclusively for the baptized and for children to a rite that may be shared with other Christians.

CONSCIENTIOUS OBJECTION TO MILITARY SERVICE

Even though the Vietnam War ended officially in April 1975, and active war was not thereafter a pressing issue during Spencer's presidency, an unresolved question of conscientious objection to military service persisted. Spencer's two older sons and his son-in-law all served in the Navy in World War II.[4] With the inconclusive end of the Korean War and the ambiguities of the Vietnam War, the national mood shifted, and some Latter-day Saints began considering whether they could conscientiously participate in war.

While the Church has always left members free to claim conscientious objector status, it has also said that they cannot rely for that stance on Mormon doctrine, which does not reject or discourage military service. The Church position appears to be that war is evil, that defending one's country is excusable and even laudable, and that conscientious objection to military service is permissible but not encouraged.

FREEMASONRY

The relationship between Freemasonry and the Church was for a century and a half seriously strained. Since the settlement of Utah, Masons there had strictly excluded Latter-day Saints both as lodge members and as visitors. The Church, for its part, frowned on its members participating in an organization that seriously competed for time and

---

4. Because of the effects of childhood polio, Ed was classified IV-F during the Korean War.

loyalty. In 1984, Utah Masons relaxed their rule against admission of Church members, and the Church thereafter dropped its cautionary instructions to bishops about the possible incompatibility of being an active Mason and an active Mormon.[5] Even so, the question of primary loyalty remains relevant to temple recommends and leadership callings.

CIVIL RIGHTS

The First Presidency took a stand on civil rights. They counseled members in January 1982 "to refuse all association with organizations that would deprive citizens of their civil and religious rights." President Kimball and his counselors also "deplore[d] the efforts of organizations and individuals that foster racial prejudice, feed upon religious intolerance and resort to terrorism, crime and violent interference with private conduct and public activity."[6]

ENVIRONMENTAL PROTECTION

In an era of great attention to the natural environment, neither President Kimball nor other leaders said much about air and water pollution, conservation of nonrenewable resources, or wildlife protection. Speaking at the 1974 World Fair in Spokane, Washington, which had an environmentalist theme, President Kimball emphasized the Church's concern for the moral environment. He did, however, say in the October 1974 general conference, "We are a throw-away people. Trash piles grow faster than population by far. Now we ask you to clean up your homes and your farms. 'Man is the keeper of the land, and not its possessor.'" And in the next conference he said, "We recommend to all people that there be no undue pollution, that the land be taken care of."

TAX PROTEST

Some members of the Church (and many nonmembers) took the position that the Constitutional amendment permitting the federal income tax was invalid, and they refused on principle to pay income

---

5. The caution does not specifically name the Masons but "advises its members strongly not to join any organization that (1) is antagonistic toward the Church, (2) is secret and oath-bound, (3) would cause members to lose interest in Church activities or violate Church standards, or (4) would interfere with members' performance of their Church duties."

6. An earlier First Presidency had made a strong statement on civil rights in October 1963.

taxes. President Kimball and his counselors issued a statement in 1975 that refusal to pay taxes violated the law and therefore breached the twelfth Article of Faith. In 1983, they warned that anyone "who refuses to pay state or federal income taxes is in direct conflict with the law and with the teachings of the Church" and "may . . . be considered ineligible for a temple recommend" and "should not be called to a position of principal responsibility in the Church."[7]

CHURCH DISCIPLINE

This policy on tax protest was supported by threat of discipline, while others constituted merely advice. The frequency and rigor of Church discipline has changed over time, although detailed data are not available. The rate of excommunications was a fraction of one percent, about two-thirds for sexual immorality and most of the rest for apostasy.[8]

The 1976 edition of the *General Handbook* listed more extensive and explicit grounds for discipline than earlier editions. For the first time, some acts, such as incest and transsexual operations, called for mandatory excommunication.

In 1980 the Church sent out a replacement chapter on Church courts for the *Handbook*. It set out even more specific grounds for discipline and distinguished between grounds that justify convening a court and grounds that require it. The instructions emphasized that discipline should serve as a tool for redemption rather than as punishment.

CIRCUMSTANCES AND CHANGE

Although many Church policy positions may have moral implications, others concerning organizational structure, programs, and personal conduct are simply matters of judgment and can change without embarrassment.

Some additional policies that changed during the Kimball presidency can be identified by comparing the 1968 handbook (before the

---

7. The Presidency had no objection to good-faith challenges, but viewed these objections frivolous.

8. Until 1989 one wishing to resign Church membership was subjected to excommunication for apostasy. After Norman Hancock of Mesa, Arizona, sued, protesting that excommunication implied misconduct, the *General Handbook* changed the procedure.

Kimball years) with that of 1985 (at the end of those years). Comparison shows that in 1968 each stake was to pick a night for family home evening, while as of 1985 Monday night was designated Churchwide as the time. In 1968 sacrament meeting was to be ninety minutes; by 1985 it was seventy minutes. No programs should be presented by auxiliary organizations in sacrament meeting; the Primary may present an annual program in sacrament meeting. Prayers in sacrament meeting should be offered only by bearers of the priesthood; any man or woman may pray in sacrament meeting. Men and women are encouraged to marry within their own race; no such policy is formally stated.[9] Ordination of seventies requires the approval of the First Council of Seventy; the stake president can call seventies. Excommunication or disfellowshipment of Melchizedek Priesthood holders should be announced in stake priesthood meeting and disciplining of others should be announced in a ward Melchizedek priesthood gathering; only those who need to know should be informed about disciplinary actions.

Some critics see in the frequent change an indicator of human action. But Latter-day Saints accept change as a result of inspiration in dealing with altered circumstances.

---

9. In 1978 Spencer advised that interracial marriage, like other intercultural marriage, has risks, but it is not "wrong."

30

CHILDREN OF LEHI

"We feel a special responsibility to these good people."

ELDER KIMBALL WAS A NEW APOSTLE in 1945 when President George Albert Smith asked him to take responsibility for Church attention to Native Americans. Elder Kimball immediately and energetically committed himself to further their interests. He visited reservations in many states. He rallied help when Navajos faced starvation in the severe winter of 1947–48. He considered it his ongoing personal responsibility to support and extend missionary and humanitarian service to natives of North, Central, and South America.

In his first press conference as President, he noted, "I have been especially interested in the Indian program. . . . We feel a special responsibility to these good people." He included in his concerns "60 million people in this hemisphere that we call Lamanites." But Spencer found that the sweep of his new presidential responsibilities limited his ability to continue giving these people his personal attention. It troubled him. He felt no one else had quite the same vision of this work.

A change in the 1981 edition of the Book of Mormon[1] supported President Kimball's theme that these were a people of promise. In this edition, the passage that righteous Lamanites would become "a white and delightsome people" was changed to "a pure and delightsome people," consistent with Joseph Smith's editorial changes in the 1840 edition. The change suggested that the primary issue was moral purity, not color.

---

1. The preparation of a new edition began during the administration of Joseph Fielding Smith. As Acting President of the Twelve, Spencer had appointed the committee and remained involved.

PERSONAL INVOLVEMENT WITH TRIBES IN THE UNITED STATES

President Kimball took every opportunity to support good causes related to Indian peoples. In 1975, he was the first Church President to participate in Brigham Young University's Indian Week; in 1976 he attended the All-Indian National Finals Rodeo in Salt Lake City; in 1976 he hosted a luncheon in the Church Office Building for about a hundred leaders attending the National Congress of American Indians in Salt Lake City; in 1977 he met in Florida with Buffalo Tiger, chief of the 450 Miccosukee Indians; and in 1980, he traveled with the Lamanite Generation from BYU to Arizona, where they performed and where he talked in the Phoenix Indian School Branch to an audience of 3,000. As President, he addressed a number of special conferences for Lamanites.

He repeatedly challenged regional representatives and mission presidents to see that the Lamanites were not neglected. He lamented, "I am conscious of the fact that the Lord has not forgotten the Lamanites, but sometimes I think maybe *we* have."

President Kimball welcomed individual Indians to his home and office. In August 1976, Clem Bear Chief, a Blackfoot, reported his experience with the President: When the "humble, ordinary looking man" said, "Brother Bear Chief, I want you to know that I love the Indian people," the chief related, "I melted inside. I felt as if I had found a long-lost father."[2]

In November 1980, two Indian girls who attended the dedication of the Seattle Temple lingered on the grounds until late. About 9:30 P.M. they impulsively knocked on the locked door. When a man answered their knock, they asked if they could talk with President Kimball. The man left, then returned and invited them inside. Despite the late hour, Spencer talked with them, autographed their journals, and gave them blessings.

In 1982, when Spencer was frail and no longer active, Cherokee James Ketcher and his family visited with him. Ketcher, a professional baseball player, was married to a third-generation Mormon from Florida. Ketcher, six feet two, lifted the fragile, short Spencer off his feet in an emotional embrace. Ketcher talked about his grandfather's surviving the Cherokee "trail of tears." Spencer told of his father's missionary service in the Indian Territory Mission. When it was time for the Ketchers to leave, Spencer wanted them to linger. "Oh, do you have to go?" he said.

THE INDIAN STUDENT PLACEMENT PROGRAM

Spencer Kimball's most significant effort to help Lamanites was increasing educational opportunities for two generations of American Indian youth. He believed that the key to their long-term welfare was education. Schools on the reservations in the 1940s were wholly inadequate, and many Indian children, who had been promised schools in treaties, had no school at all. In 1947 he and Golden Buchanan of Richfield, Utah, started a program of foster parenting for Indian youth whose families wanted them to have an opportunity for better schooling. The Indian Student Placement Program became an official Church program in 1954. The program peaked at 5,000 participants in 1970,

---

2. George P. Lee wrote: "For many years, he was the only 'Indian voice' in the Church. For a long time, it seemed that Spencer W. Kimball was alone against the world regarding Indian affairs. On many occasions, he defended the Native Americans when it was not popular to do so. He was truly bold and courageous yet humble and compassionate. . . .

"He has assisted many Indians to acquire self-regard in their native culture as well as in the dominant white culture in order to transcend both. . . . [He is a] man of great physical and moral courage."

then declined from that point.[3] By 1977, the number had dropped to 2,750 because of improved schools on the reservations and because rising ethnic pride challenged the program as paternalistic.[4] Critics believed the students suffered psychological trauma, both from being separated from their families and from being placed in a school system based on competition

With Arlene, Lamanite foster daughter of Olive Beth.

rather than on cooperation, as in their native culture.

The American Indian Movement (AIM) actively opposed the placement program. Its representatives marched on Temple Square and demanded one million dollars in reparations. In April 1974, AIM warned the Church to withdraw its missionaries from Indian reservations. Spencer felt betrayed and angry that the unselfish motives of Church members had been misrepresented and that his own efforts over the years were now so unappreciated.

There were special programs at Brigham Young University to help Indian high-school graduates achieve higher education. In 1974–75 there were over 600 American Indian students from 74 tribes attending BYU. A 1977 government report characterized the BYU program as "the finest Indian education program in the country." While the national

---

3. Mangum and Blumell say over 70,000 youth were placed during the program's life.

4. Sondra Jones says: "Such open acculturation of Indian children by non-Indians has virtually ceased today. . . . Many tribes continue to struggle to balance modernization with the preservation of traditional values and heritage. Meanwhile, Indian tribes across the country have reasserted their rights to their children and have begun to actively fight against the raising of them by non-Indians. . . . Given the . . . rise in Indian nationalism, pride, and demands for self-determination, it is not surprising that tribal entities now emphasize the maintenance of an Indian identity over the seeming advantages of more affluent, non-Indian adoptive or foster homes."

The *Navajo Times* in 1978 devoted the equivalent of four full pages, almost all highly favorable, to the LDS programs among the Navajo.

college graduation rate for Native Americans was 3.4 percent, at BYU it was 20 percent and rising.[5]

As President Kimball's administration progressed, the emphasis shifted from North American natives to Lamanites in Latin America, where numbers and success were greater. American Indians received less focused attention from the Church. By the time President Kimball died, only vestiges of the Indian programs survived.[6]

The Church's efforts to improve the lives of American Indians through the placement program produced mixed results. Interviews with former participants conducted in 1991 suggest that many had felt loneliness, parental rejection, and the stress of being caught between two worlds. Some achieved college educations and improved life circumstances, including a role as builders of bridges between cultures, while others did not. Reactions ranged from bitterness to deep gratitude.[7]

THE CALLING OF GEORGE P. LEE

The first group of children in the Indian Student Placement Program in 1955 included twelve-year-old George Lee. In his autobiography, he remembers Elder Kimball's comments to that first group of foster parents and Indian children as "magnetic, . . . filled with love."

Elder Kimball followed Lee closely as student, missionary, and educator. In 1975, George resigned the presidency of Ganado College in Arizona and returned to BYU as a doctoral candidate in educational administration. One April morning he felt weak, almost ill, and remained in bed. His wife, Kitty, woke him to answer a call from President Kimball, who immediately began to ask him interview-like

---

5. It appears that from perhaps a dozen students in 1954 the number in the American Indian Services Program at BYU rose gradually until in 1971–72 it was over five hundred. The number then began to decline and in 1991 had fallen to about 100. This decline may be explained by greater competition from other schools and rising admission standards, but BYU also probably recruited less aggressively after 1979. Financial aid was not an issue. By 1995 barely a handful of students remained in the programs.

6. There were once about thirty seminary teachers on the Navajo reservation, but in 1988 only two.

7. Present-day emphasis on multiculturalism makes some see such a program as "tinged with imperialistic, antiquated values of assimilation and cultural mentoring." A related issue is whether Native Americans should be organized in separate church units or integrated into Anglo wards and branches.

questions. In a daze, almost as in a dream, Lee heard him say, "The Lord has called you to preside over the Arizona Holbrook Mission."

Catching his breath, Lee explained that he was trying to finish his dissertation by December. But President Kimball told him to finish the dissertation by July, when his mission would begin. Lee wondered how that would be possible, but he did not argue. Two

George P. Lee and his wife, Kitty.

weeks earlier he had dreamed of a telephone call from President Kimball that left him feeling uplifted. He now saw the dream as a portent fulfilled. With incredible effort, he completed the dissertation by July. President Kimball took great satisfaction in setting Lee apart to serve as president of the Arizona Holbrook Mission, which included the entire Navajo nation.

Only three months later, while preparing to leave for a zone conference, Lee felt impressed to remain in the mission home. Three times he got up, concerned about keeping the missionaries waiting, but the impression to stay persisted. The third impression to stay included the information that an important phone call would come. Fifteen minutes later, Arthur Haycock called to say President Kimball would be calling soon.

Anxiously, Lee asked himself, "What did President Kimball want with me? [Have] I done something wrong?" When the call came, President Kimball again asked in-depth, interview-like questions. Finally he said, "President Lee, the Lord has called you to become a member of the First Quorum of Seventy."

"What is he saying?" Lee thought. "Why is he calling me to be a seventy? . . . and which stake is it?" (At this time, October 1975, the First Quorum of Seventy did not yet exist.) President Kimball continued: "President Lee, this means the Lord has called you to be a General Authority."

Lee could not speak. He sat down in a daze and handed the phone to Kitty. After a few moments' conversation, she handed the phone back to her husband. Weeping, he tried to speak through his tears. He thought, "Why me? Why me? . . . Is the Church ready for an Indian General Authority?" But he accepted and determined to do his best.

For fourteen years, Elder Lee served as a General Authority. During later years, he became critical of the Church's approach to Indian affairs and fomented a degree of discord. He was excommunicated in 1989.[8]

FULFILLMENT

President Kimball saw the children of Lehi as having a marvelous future. At a dinner in Mexico City with five stake presidents in 1974, one stake president recalled to Spencer and Camilla Spencer's statement in 1947 that, although many Church members in Mexico then went barefoot, the day would come when many had professional training and the people generally enjoyed better times. Of these five stake presidents one had qualified as an attorney, another as an educator, and three as civil engineers.[9]

In 1975, President Kimball reflected briefly upon the "remarkable" manner in which a passage in his patriarchal blessing concerning the Lamanites was being fulfilled:

"My interest in the Indian people was nourished by a patriarchal blessing that came to me when I was a little lad of eleven years. . . . I quote just a few lines of it:

"'You will preach the gospel to many people, but more especially to the Lamanites, for the Lord will bless you with the gift of language and power to portray before that people the gospel in great plainness. You will see them organized and be prepared to stand as the bulwarks round this people.'

---

8. In a letter to the First Presidency and Twelve, he decried the termination of Church Indian programs and criticized the leaders for pride, unconcern for the poor, materialism, prejudice against Indians, and depriving Lamanites of their special place in Mormon theology. He said, "I feel like the only person who completely trusted me was President Kimball." In 1990, after his excommunication, Lee ran unsuccessfully for office in the Navajo nation. See page 255, note 6.

9. In general the percentage of working Church members in professional occupations is higher than the broader population, but this is particularly so in Mexico, where the percentages are 27 percent for Latter-day Saints and 15 percent for the national average.

"Certainly not a patriarch nor anyone else could ever have guessed that, because I was just a little ordinary country boy when I received that blessing. There was no evidence that I would ever go into the world and preach the gospel, and certainly not that I would go to nearly all the tribes in the world. So it was quite remarkable that these promises should come as they have. . . .

" . . . There are now more than 350,000 Lamanite members of the Church. They attend their meetings faithfully. They have the priesthood among them. There are branch presidents, quorum leaders, bishops, stake presidents, high councilors, mission presidents, and leaders in all phases of the work among them. They are attending the temple and receiving the ordinances necessary for exaltation. They are intelligent and faithful; they are a great people and a blessed people."

"We are relatives," he reminded Church members. "We are brothers and sisters under the skin. We should receive each other with great joy."

31

THE CHURCH WELFARE PROGRAM

"I'm not a member of the Mormon Church, but I sure know who my neighborhood bishop is."

THE CHURCH HAD A LONG-STANDING REPUTATION for taking care of its poor. And its principles of generosity, cooperation, self-respect, and provident living garnered favorable publicity.[1] But by the time President Kimball took office, Church leaders could see that the welfare model developed for the United States would not work in developing nations where explosive growth in membership was occurring. There the problem was not individual and emergency aid, but systemic poverty. Among possible solutions, he was reportedly encouraged by the potential of micro credit programs and cooperatives. When a Church employee suggested that the Church subsidize such ventures, President Kimball at first reacted positively but finally concluded, "Brethren, we can't do this yet; the timing is not right."

Even in the United States, where membership of the Church was increasingly urban and scattered rather than concentrated in the more rural Intermountain West, the welfare program,[2] with its concentration on agricultural projects, posed increasing implementation problems.

In 1976, President Kimball chose to involve himself more directly in welfare issues by assuming chairmanship of the General Welfare

---

1. The welfare program and the canneries manned largely by volunteers continue to bring favorable publicity to the Church. The storehouse on Welfare Square built in 1975 includes a visitors' center. In a conference to promote volunteerism, President Ronald Reagan cited his visit as governor to an LDS cannery in California. And in 1982 he toured a welfare cannery in Ogden.

2. In 1975, Church welfare farms comprised 143,000 acres. The Church had about 600 welfare projects, 78 storehouses, 20 canneries, and 12 Deseret Industries stores in the United States and Canada.

U.S. President Ronald Reagan touring a Church cannery in Ogden, Utah, September 1982.

Services Committee, which was previously headed by the Presiding Bishopric.

Under President Kimball's leadership, the Welfare Services Department was charged to redirect welfare efforts toward helping families prevent the causes of poverty, such as underemployment, and be better prepared for short-term times of need. The new program asked members to become self-reliant by preparing in six areas: obtain an education, develop a career, learn to manage finances wisely, store food to last a year, maintain physical health, and develop emotional and spiritual strength.

A study commissioned by the committee in 1977 suggested that in a widespread emergency "the existing welfare capacity would meet the basic needs of only 5 percent of the Church membership temporarily and 1 percent on a continuing basis." At President Kimball's suggestion many storehouses were expanded to include granaries. And the welfare committee decided to greatly expand the program's scope to make possible temporary emergency support of 30 percent of the members who lived in areas where welfare projects already existed (mostly in the western United States). Pursuant to this policy, by 1981 the Church owned 900 welfare farms, many of them very small.

But Presiding Bishop Victor L. Brown said in 1983:

Damage caused by the Teton Dam collapse, June 1976.

"The build-up of resources in Church preparedness has resulted in the building of a false sense of security among far too many people. . . . Church institutional resources will provide for a very small percentage of the Church population. They are for the poor and needy who will always be with us, who cannot take care of themselves."

There came a contraction in the number of Church welfare farms, particularly outside the West. The Church sold many of its small farms and leased others to farmers with the proviso the Church could reclaim their use in an emergency. The remaining farms were placed under professional management rather than run by volunteer labor.[3]

The previous expectation had been that every stake and ward should be involved with a welfare production project. But this proved unrealistic in many urban and foreign stakes. By 1983 the Church had disposed of all welfare farms outside the United States and Canada. And where previously the Church assessed each stake a certain amount annually in cash or produce for the welfare program, it now ended all such assessments and dealt centrally with most welfare financial matters. The restructuring meant that during the Kimball administration, welfare production projects decreased from 600 to 200, while other

---

3. This gave up the benefits which had come from individual participation in welfare production projects, a loss which Marion R. Romney regretted.

Arriving in Rexburg, Idaho, after the failure of the Teton Dam flooded the Snake River valley, June 1976.

facilities expanded: welfare canneries increased from 20 to 51, places for grain storage increased from a handful to 63, storehouses increased from 78 to 113, and Deseret Industries stores increased from 12 to 43.

RESPONSE TO EMERGENCIES

Two striking examples of the Church welfare program in emergency action occurred during Spencer W. Kimball's tenure, both close to Church headquarters—the collapse of Idaho's Teton Dam and the Salt Lake City flood.

The earthen Teton Dam gave way in June 1976, sending a deadly eight-mile wide rush of floodwaters through ten towns. The flood destroyed more than 800 homes and damaged another 2,500. It spoiled 30,000 acres of farmland, damaged eleven Church buildings, and killed 11,000 head of livestock. Only six people drowned because the communities had a brief warning, but 40,000 had to flee their homes, 90 percent of them Church members. Reimbursement for losses amounted to nearly $400 million.[4]

---

4. Compensation was based on replacement value, rather than fair market value, so in many cases people were better off financially after than before the flood. Some farms were destroyed, but others were improved by the new layer of silt. Claims officer Loyd Ericson also said that he never worked on a project that had fewer problems with claims; some people even returned money they had been paid when items turned up that they thought were lost.

Before nightfall, tents, bedding, and other supplies arrived in trucks from Welfare Square in Salt Lake City, 225 miles away. Church-owned Ricks College (now BYU–Idaho), situated on a hill above the flood, housed 1,400 victims in its dormitories that first night. The Church hierarchical structure and lay leadership, coupled with members' willingness, allowed quick and effective organization and extension of relief. As soon as conditions allowed, hundreds of buses entered the valley every day, bringing an average of 3,000 men and women, mostly Church members from Utah, Wyoming, Montana, and distant communities in Idaho, to help with the cleanup. When a call went out for 150 electricians, 450 electricians and helpers responded. An estimated 40,000 volunteers donated at least a million hours of labor over many weeks. Help went to LDS and non-LDS victims alike.

President Kimball visited the area a week after the flood to encourage the victims. In a special conference, he acknowledged their hardships and cautioned them to continue Christian action in the midst of fatigue and trial:

"Amid all the confusion and disorder, let us be orderly and courteous. Make no distinction between member and nonmember. We have heard inspiring reports of the Christian brotherhood in action. Preserve these good feelings in the challenging weeks ahead. Do not let jealousy or rivalry creep in. Act as the Savior himself would act."

Spencer stayed afterward and shook hands with all who came forward, including babies in arms. Because of the time it took, he canceled a scheduled talk with the priesthood leaders of the area.

U.S. President Gerald Ford declared the locality a federal disaster area.[5] The First Presidency discouraged people from going to the government for help with food and clothing, which the Church could readily provide, but endorsed taking loans and other government disaster assistance for rebuilding the communities.

Seven years later, exceptionally heavy rain and snow in northern Utah during the winter left the soil saturated. Near-record heat in May caused sudden melting of the snowpack, and water, mud, and debris flowed into the cities along the Wasatch Front. Some flooding had been

---

5. The often-repeated loss figure of $1 billion was just an immediate rough estimate to justify triggering disaster treatment.

State Street as a river, May 1983.

expected, but no one had foreseen the magnitude of the problem. The waters of City Creek in downtown Salt Lake City, normally contained in an underground conduit, overflowed and had to be diverted down State Street. Earlier general calls for volunteers had brought modest responses, but on Sunday, May 29, the city called on the Church for aid, and "within two hours an estimated 6,000 volunteers, most called out of church meetings, responded." By evening the volunteers had placed sandbags to create "State Street River," which ran south for two miles and then westward toward the Jordan River, effectively diverting water that otherwise would have done great damage. The city hastily built four temporary pedestrian bridges and two automobile crossings over the shallow stream so that traffic could get from one side of the city to the other. The water ran for a week before it gradually subsided. Four thousand volunteers then helped clean up.

Not only Church members responded. One volunteer told a reporter, "I'm not a member of the Mormon Church, but I sure know who my neighborhood bishop is." In the Salt Lake Valley an estimated 150,000 person-days of volunteer labor had augmented the public works professionals, who provided supervision.

The whole state suffered. Total damage attributed to all the flooding reached nearly half a billion dollars. Seven people drowned.[6]

In another emergency, farther away, the Church responded in

---

6. William J. Alder of the Utah office of the National Weather Service ranked the 1983 flood as Utah's most dramatic weather event of the century.

February 1976 to a disastrous earthquake that killed 17,000 in Guatemala, including 22 Church members. The Welfare Services Department rushed immediate aid and provided long-term assistance in rebuilding. Missionaries devoted their efforts to emergency help. One, Randy Ellsworth, suffered serious injury in the collapse of a Church building; another, Daniel Choc, died when a wall collapsed on him as he helped clear away rubble.

Over the next few years relief supplies were sent successively to Nicaragua (civil strife), Poland (martial law), Tonga (hurricane), Colombia (earthquake), Tahiti (hurricane), and Mexico (earthquake).

In 1985, when a long-term drought caused severe famine in Africa, especially in Ethiopia, the Church announced special fast days in January and November that produced more than $10 million. All the money from the January fast went to purchase food, the immediate need. But after the second fast, the Church set up a Humanitarian Services Committee, which channeled the money this time mostly to long-term projects—health care, literacy, food production and processing, small enterprise, reforestation, drinking water systems, banks, grain processing, irrigation, nurse training, and schoolbooks. For example, one project helped 1,100 families in fifteen Kenyan villages establish a water system. And a major irrigation project in Ethiopia watered 960 acres, helping to ensure the food supply for 10,000 people in three villages.[7]

Fast Offerings

Some needs of the poor, such as rent or medicine, can be met only by cash. The primary source of such cash is the monthly fast offering asked of all Church members. President Kimball urged in his first general conference that members should "be very generous and give, instead of the amount we saved by our two meals . . . ten times more where we are in a position to do it." Within a year of this plea, fast offerings increased by almost half. On another occasion he requested:

"Please don't assume that . . . individuals will always make their needs known. . . .

---

7. Efforts continued and grew after the Kimball administration—money for polio immunizations in Africa, earthquake relief in Iran, and relief for Rwandan civil war refugees. Aid went to riot-torn areas in Los Angeles, hurricane-devastated parts of Florida, victims of volcanic eruption in the Philippines, and also to Russia, Estonia, and Africa. After 1985 the Church encouraged contributions to a humanitarian aid account but did not call additional special fasts.

"The ones about whom I am particularly speaking are those who will suffer in silence because they are proud or because they do not know what to do. . . . I worry about our being unaware of such needs."

FAMILY FOOD STORAGE

Health missionaries teaching hygiene.

Families had long been encouraged to store food, clothing, and fuel enough to last for at least a year, but H. Burke Peterson of the Presiding Bishopric estimated in 1975 that "on the average 30 percent of the Church had a two-month supply of food; the remainder had little or none."

In the welfare session of conference in April 1976, Vaughn Featherstone, counselor in the Presiding Bishopric, challenged every family to have a year's supply of food by April 1977. He said that God gives "a warning before a calamity" and that those who are prepared would have the blessing of helping those who are not. President Kimball endorsed the challenge: "We must remember that conditions could change and a year's supply of basic commodities could be very much appreciated by us or others. So we would do well to listen to what we have been told and to follow it explicitly."

Many members interpreted these statements as prophetic warnings of impending disaster, and they scurried to increase their food storage. Emergency food suppliers did a brisk business until the bubble burst—when April 1977 passed without any unusual event or any renewed special emphasis on storage.[8]

---

8. Food storage suppliers like Rainy Day Foods expected sales to decline after April, but they did not anticipate the sudden halt and had to liquidate huge inventory at considerable loss.

WELFARE SERVICE MISSIONARIES

Over the course of years the Church had acquired fourteen hospitals in the intermountain area to provide adequate facilities for its membership. But in 1974 the Church decided to turn the hospitals over to a nonprofit corporation (Intermountain Health Care) rather than continue to support the costly institutions for the benefit of an ever smaller percentage of the Church membership. With the transfer completed in 1975, Dr. James O. Mason, Church Commissioner of Health Services, expanded the recently initiated program of health missionaries who were called to serve in areas of the world where Church members needed basic instruction in subjects like nutrition and hygiene. In summer 1971, two missionaries were called specifically to work on improving health—a nurse was sent to Tonga and a physician to Samoa. Within a few months, three pairs of nurses went to Latin America, and in 1972, forty-two health missionaries joined the work in many places. A mini–Peace Corps emerged. In 1979, 500 health and agricultural missionaries were serving. By 1980, more than 2,500 men and women had served welfare missions and 768 welfare services missionaries were then laboring in thirty-five countries.

In 1981, however, supervision of the health missionaries shifted from the Church Welfare Services Department to the Missionary Department. With its emphasis on proselytizing, the number of missionaries specifically focusing on health issues declined substantially.[9]

SOCIAL SERVICES

"Welfare services is the full program the Lord has provided us," President Kimball reminded the Saints in 1978. It includes not only "provident living, personal and family preparedness, home and visiting

---

9. After the collapse of Communism in Eastern Europe in 1989, humanitarian missionaries served in Poland, Romania, Bulgaria, Albania, Armenia, Belarus, and elsewhere. The Church also provided English teachers in Bulgaria at the government's request. A great number of these missionaries were single women.

A major enlargement in the concept of missionary work occurred in 1991 when regular proselytizing missionaries received instructions to involve themselves in some sort of community service for several hours a week. This policy both broadened the missionaries' own understanding of their responsibilities and countered the impression some nonmembers had that missionaries were there only to accumulate baptisms and had no interest in traditional Christian service. Efforts to fellowship and integrate new members into the Church community also received emphasis.

teaching, producing and distributing goods to the poor," but also "rehabilitating members with especially difficult needs or handicaps [and] restoring emotionally disturbed souls to full activity in the Church and society." His statement reflected the Church leadership's increased awareness of the need to address psychological concerns.

By the late 1970s, a growing demand for psychological counseling led to encouragement that Church members seek counsel from their bishops or volunteer local professionals. Bishops in turn were advised to urge emotional self-reliance. To aid local Church leaders, during the Kimball presidency Social Services prepared basic booklets on homosexuality (1974, 1992), suicide (1974), unwed parenthood (1981, 1985), infertility (1982), alcoholism (1984), and child abuse (1985, 1991).

SOUTH VIETNAMESE REFUGEES

A different challenge was presented by the collapse of South Vietnamese resistance to Communist forces in the spring of 1975. This resulted in a flood of refugees. Of approximately 250 Vietnamese Church members, about one hundred escaped and were evacuated by the United States because their involvement with an "American" institution exposed them to special danger.

In May 1975 Spencer and Camilla traveled to San Diego for meetings with some 300 Lamanite youth and their leaders from all over Southern California and with young adults from that area. As the last meeting ended, Spencer asked to visit Camp Pendleton, a military base forty miles north, to meet with the seventeen Mormon refugees from Vietnam who had arrived the day before.[10] Although the LDS refugees had had to leave nearly everything behind, some came to the meeting with their treasured LDS hymnbooks.

Camilla particularly empathized with them, recalling the time in 1912 she spent housed in an El Paso lumberyard and fed by the Red Cross as a refugee from the Mexican revolutionaries who caused her family to flee the Mormon colonies in northern Mexico.

At the next general conference, Spencer said of the incident:

---

10. Another 46 escaping from Saigon arrived a few days later. Still 65 more were expected soon.

"We personally met the first refugees, and as we saw them in their new surroundings in a foreign world, we remembered our own people of the schooner days and the handcart days as they came into this new land, bringing relatively little or nothing with them. We have several hundred Vietnamese brothers and sisters who are building a new life among us. Some are members; some are not. We have located them without the money that the government offered, but our compensation has been that mentioned by the Savior: 'Inasmuch as ye have done it unto one of the least of these my brethren, ye have done it unto me.' (Matt. 25:40.)"

Some members, left behind, spent time in brutal "reeducation camps." Over time most of the remaining Saints escaped as boat people or by crossing secretly into neighboring countries, where they found safety in refugee camps. The Church helped their resettlement in the United States over the next several years. A 1979 First Presidency letter urged members to help the refugees from Southeast Asia by becoming sponsors or providing volunteer assistance. In 1980 the First Presidency established the LDS Refugee Relief fund and urged Church members to contribute to it.

In 1980 Elder Marion D. Hanks, as administrator over Southeast Asia, assigned welfare service missionaries to the refugee camps with instructions that they were not to proselytize but to prepare the refugees (many of whom were "hill people") for life in a much different society. The service continued for ten years in the camps in Thailand, Hong Kong, and the Philippines, illustrating the Church's willingness and commitment to help beyond its own membership.

In 1977 President Kimball summarized basic welfare principles:

"While often seen as temporal in nature, this work is spiritual at heart! It is people-centered and God-inspired. Welfare Services is not a program, but the essence of the gospel. It is the gospel in action. May I rehearse to you what I believe are its foundational truths:

"First is love. The measure of our love for our fellowman and, in a large sense, the measure of our love for the Lord, is what we do for one another and for the poor and the distressed.

"Second is service.

"Third is work.

"Fourth is self-reliance.

"Fifth is consecration, which encompasses sacrifice.

"Sixth is stewardship. Because all things belong to the Lord, we are [only] his stewards."

ON GOD'S ERRAND

TRAVELING THE GLOBE

32

AREA CONFERENCES, 1974–1976

"Wilt thou heal him and deliver him here."

HAROLD B. LEE, AS JOSEPH FIELDING SMITH'S first counselor, proposed in 1970 that the Church hold an area conference in a location far from Church headquarters. Spencer liked the idea: area conferences would reach people who could probably never attend a general conference and never see or hear the President of the Church in person. The first area conferences were held by Presidents Smith and Lee in Manchester, England (1971), Mexico City (1972), and Munich (1973). When Spencer became President, one was already scheduled for Stockholm (1974). For 1975, rather than scheduling one conference, Spencer scheduled seven conferences—all in South America and the Orient. Between 1975 and 1981, when his ability to travel ended, fifty-nine more area conferences were convened all over the world.

The conferences, most often held on weekends, at first included a dinner with leaders and their wives, an evening cultural program presented by the local members, one or more general sessions, and concurrent separate sessions for men and boys in one hall and for women and girls in another.[1] Camilla often talked in the women's session. Instruction was very much like that given at general conferences.

A member of the First Presidency always presided, and several General Authorities spoke in each meeting. These leaders brought their spouses to exemplify solid marriage.

---

1. Of sixty-three total area conferences, nineteen spread over three days beginning with an evening cultural program the first day; thirty-eight lasted two days; six lasted only one day. In early conferences there were separate parent and youth sessions; later there were more often separate priesthood and mother-daughter sessions.

SWEDEN

In August 1974, Spencer traveled to Stockholm to hold his first area conference as President. Throughout the trip, Spencer displayed his characteristic warmth, concern, and personal attention to all. During a layover in New York on the way to Stockholm, KSL-TV religion reporter Duane Cardall found himself ushered into the airline's VIP waiting room. A dozen Church leaders and others chatted in small groups. Feeling awkward, he took a seat alone off to the side. Within moments, Arthur Haycock was at his side, saying, "President Kimball would like to have you join us." That invitation opened the door to a long personal relationship.

When conference planners had tried to rent the most suitable convention center, they found it booked solid for the next three years. But providentially, the dates they wanted came open.

Some 4,500 members from Sweden, Norway, Finland, and Denmark attended—30 percent of all members in those countries.

Elder Neal A. Maxwell took several family members with him to the conference, including a son just released from his mission. As Spencer was walking from the hotel to the conference center, Elder Maxwell fell into step beside him and said, "I have been a little worried about my family's taking seats that should be kept for the Saints."

Spencer rejoined, "Aren't your family Saints?"

President Kimball spoke at the first and last general sessions and in three special sessions. He redefined the principle of "gathering" by

Performing an Indian chant on the ferry "Viking" from Stockholm to Finland, August 1974.

urging the Saints to gather into cities within their own nations, concentrating their strength to form stakes. He promised that if they did, they would one day have all the blessings of the Church, including a temple in Scandinavia.

After Stockholm, Spencer planned to visit the mission in Finland and dedicate a chapel there. The schedule called for a flight the next day. But rather than wait, he asked the Church travel agent if the group could take a boat overnight. He was pleased by the prospect of a trip by sea.

It was arranged and the party went directly from the conference center to the harbor, driving onto the ferry along with railroad cars and buses. Instead of heading for their cabin or a deck chair, Spencer and Camilla explored the ship from top to bottom, then stood at the rail and watched other passengers walk up the gangplank, many of them Church members returning home from the conference. Spencer suggested that they have an impromptu fireside that evening on the upper deck. There he talked informally about his life and mentioned having sung a great deal in his younger years. Although throat cancer had put an end to his singing, he could still hoarsely perform a Navajo chant he learned when recuperating on the reservation from his 1948 heart attack. He borrowed Camilla's handbag and beat out the rhythm on it as he chanted, to everyone's surprise and delight, "Hei naa yaunga. . . ."

Spencer and others traveling to area conferences would have liked to interact more with the local members individually, but language barriers and limited time made it difficult. They typically went by bus from the airplane to a hotel, to a conference hall or sports facility, and back.

The large traveling party, seldom numbering fewer than thirty and sometimes as many as fifty, required complicated logistics handled by a travel agency under contract with the Church. Airlines gave the group special attention when they could and sometimes arrangements could be made to skip customs in crowded airports.

Spencer's counselors insisted that a physician accompany him on every trip. His cardiologist, Ernest L. Wilkinson Jr., traveled with him most often. He took care of Spencer's health but also stayed at his elbow as additional security. Dr. Wilkinson said of his charge, "I have never known a person who was so totally dedicated to the call that he has."

On the ferry "Viking" from Stockholm to Finland, August 1974.

Spencer allowed few restraints on his activity, even for medical reasons. The relationship involved mutual affection. Dr. Wilkinson treasured Spencer's comment: "Ernest, I want you to know that I no longer consider you just as my doctor. I consider you one of my family."

D. Arthur Haycock, Spencer's indispensable personal secretary and aide, always traveled with him. He and Dr. Wilkinson often ended up carrying the Kimballs' loose luggage, overcoats, briefcases, and last minute gifts. Spencer would beg, "Ernest, [Arthur,] please let me carry something." When they declined, Spencer would try to find someone else to help.

SOUTH AMERICA

The conference held in São Paulo, Brazil, in February 1975 had special significance because Spencer there announced the plan to construct a temple in São Paulo—the first overseas temple since the New Zealand Temple twenty years earlier.

At a meeting with local Church leaders, Spencer explained that the Presidency and Twelve had decided a temple should be built but had not settled on when. He asked each leader, in turn, "Is now the right time? Will your people support the building of a temple? How much could your people contribute financially?"

These men weren't prepared to say how much their members could contribute, but they answered as well as they could. Spencer wrote on a blackboard the amounts they suggested. He complimented them on what they felt able to do but then challenged them to triple the amounts, promising that the temple would be valued by the people in part by the sacrifice it represented. He also challenged the leaders to prepare the members to be worthy and eager to attend the temple.

Then Spencer asked the several General Authorities present to respond. Assistant to the Twelve ElRay L. Christiansen said he had planned to buy a pony for his grandchildren, but he would contribute that money in their name. Several pledged substantial cash amounts. A. Theodore Tuttle, who had been a modestly compensated teacher in the Church Educational System before his call as a Seventy, responded ruefully, "I feel I'm out of my league. When I was a boy in Manti, our bishop or stake president came to our home and asked what my family could pledge to the construction of a new building. My father said, 'I don't have any cash, but I'll sell our cow and give the proceeds to the building fund.' Now, I have a milk cow at home and I will sell it and give the proceeds to the temple fund. My sons who milk the cow won't mind."

A public relations error threatened to mar the conference. Jeremiah (Jerry) Cahill had just begun working for the Public Communications Department, and attending the area conference in Brazil was his first major assignment. President Kimball asked him to prepare a press release announcing the São Paulo Temple, for release only after the South American Church leaders had expressed their support for the project. Spencer did not want the South American leaders to feel they had traveled from far places simply to rubber-stamp a decision already made. He explained to Cahill, "We want their wisdom. We don't know everything. There may be reasons to delay the building of the temple and we do not want to predetermine when that should be."

The day Cahill left for South America, he asked a colleague to prepare the press release and hold it until instructed. The colleague misunderstood and released the announcement in the United States prematurely. Fortunately, the news did not get to Brazil until the announcement had already been made in the conference.

When President Kimball became aware of the blunder, he sternly asked Cahill, "Young man, what is going on?"

Miserable, Cahill explained the mistake.

Spencer said generously, "Maybe we did not make ourselves understood. . . . Perhaps I didn't make clear what was needed."

But Cahill accepted responsibility for the mistake. Then President Kimball said something that stung, "Maybe we can't trust you."

Cahill replied from the heart, "I hope that is not the case, because I can't serve you if I do not have your trust."

At 11:00 P.M., after the last meeting that day, Cahill boarded the bus to return to the hotel. He was still mortified. As he walked past the prophet, Spencer caught his arm, pulled him down, and kissed him on the cheek. He said, "Jerry, have you forgiven us yet?"

Cahill never met Spencer afterward that he did not receive a hug, a kiss on the cheek, or personal thanks.

Another area conference was to be held in Buenos Aires the following weekend. Between times, Spencer flew to Paraguay to dedicate a building. As the old airplane flew over the jungle, one of the four engines quit, and the pilot turned back. Spencer brushed aside apologies for the delay, commenting good-naturedly, "Well, this is better than being down in the jungle."

During the long, hot wait in the airport without any air conditioning, *Church News* reporter "J" Heslop interviewed Spencer about his impending eightieth birthday. Someone approached with two ice-cold bottles of fruit soda. He offered the first to Camilla and the second to Spencer, who, Heslop reported, "with one quick movement tilted his head back and took a long swig. The motion continued as his arm came down and swept the bottle right into my hand. 'We will share!' he said."

In São Paulo and Buenos Aires, Spencer gave twenty-two talks, answered questions in six press conferences, and held several meetings with government leaders, including Ernesto Geisel, president of Brazil.

In area conferences, security personnel grew adept at assuring that President Kimball, short and elderly, was not swept off his feet by affectionate members pressing near him. In South America a large local leader, nearly a foot taller than the President, hugged him vigorously four times the first day. On Saturday he hugged him vigorously eight times. On Sunday just before the meeting Earl Jones, chief of security,

With missionary grandson Chris and Pusan Korea mission president and Sister Han In Sang, 1975.

saw this man in his favorite seat on the aisle. He whispered to Spencer, "President, our friend is in his place."

Spencer responded, "Brother Jones, I love him dearly, but can you take the bear hugs today?" This time as the man approached Spencer Brother Jones stepped forward and hugged him.

Another time as Spencer and Arthur came out of a conference session they almost lost their footing in the excited crowd. Out of the corner of his eye, Arthur saw a child knocked to the ground, and he instinctively caught her by the wrist. He pulled her with them fifty feet to the bus to keep her from being trampled, then released her safely.

THE FAR EAST

In August 1975, President Kimball left on the most ambitious trip of his presidency to date, five area conferences in ten days in Tokyo, Manila, Hong Kong, Taipei, and Seoul.

Jerry Cahill was assigned to go to Japan. Spencer called him in and said, "We expect to announce the building of a temple in Japan; would you prepare an announcement that we can issue after the meeting with leaders in Japan?" He made no mention of the earlier mistake.

Each morning when the traveling party boarded the bus, Spencer shook hands with everyone, greeted each by name, and inquired about their well-being. Each evening, returning to the hotel, he did the same. Even with an exhausting schedule, he remained cheerful, witty, and tireless. While the others rested, he would often scurry off to meet with the local missionaries, ward or branch leaders, reporters, or political leaders. When Dr. Wilkinson cautioned him to take it easy, Spencer replied, "I honor and respect your training, Doctor, . . . but the Lord wants me to do this."

Japan had nearly 30,000 members in three stakes and seven missions. Spencer's remarks at the Tokyo conference included themes that he reiterated through all five conferences: family solidarity in this life and in the eternities, genealogical work, and family home evening. Although these themes remained constant, he gave a different talk at each city and each session, as many as six a day for as long as forty-five minutes each time. His health held up well. Good amplification made his weak voice audible. His translators communicated the words, but his presence invested the words with an aura of inspiration.

Here, as in São Paulo, announcement of a temple to be built in Tokyo produced an emotional response. As the announcement was translated, the audience spontaneously broke into tears and applause, despite traditional Japanese restraint. Yoshihiko Kikuchi, president of the Tokyo Stake, held up an architect's rendering of how the building would look. The people applauded again.[2]

On Monday the party flew south to Manila. Because of a terrific monsoon, the plane arrived several hours late. A group of children dressed in white had huddled together out of the rain, determinedly waiting to sing a welcome for their prophet.

In Manila Spencer paid a courtesy call on Ferdinand Marcos, president of the Philippines. They talked about religion, with Spencer emphasizing the Church's concern for families.

Local Church leaders provided traditional open-necked Philippine shirts for the General Authorities. For a Filipino, including Marcos, these shirts, without jacket, constituted formal wear. But while Spencer wore the gift shirt, he wore it with a tie and coat. He looked odd but kept to his own notions of propriety.

---

2. It was the younger Japanese who stood and applauded, while the older Japanese bowed their heads and wept.

The two-day conference drew an astonishing 15,000 of the nation's 24,000 members. Elder Hinckley reminisced about supervising missionary work in the Philippines during its 1961 beginnings, when he knew of only one native Filipino member and when missionaries could enter only on two-month visitor visas. Now the Church had one stake and two missions, and the Philippines would soon become the fastest growing area in the Church.

When the new temple in Japan was announced, the Filipinos' response was less enthusiastic than Spencer had expected. Bitter memories of the brutal Japanese occupation during World War II persisted. Some even indicated they might continue to make the longer trip to the Hawaiian Temple.

The visitors drove away from the conference arena each evening in three black limousines and a bus. An escort of as many as four motorcycle policemen waved other vehicles out of the way. Crowds stared, wondering who the VIPs could be.

Arrangements had been made Monday evening for a shop near the hotel to remain open late for the convenience of those in the visiting party who wanted to buy souvenirs. Spencer and Camilla retired to their room, but Olive Beth, who was accompanying them at her own expense, went shopping and stayed overlong. When she returned to the

Spencer and Camilla surrounded by crowds in Korea, 1980.

hotel, she found her eighty-year-old father pacing by the elevator, pajama top tucked into his trousers, anxious about his fifty-three-year-old daughter.

After the meetings in Manila, the group divided for simultaneous conferences. Spencer and half the party flew to Hong Kong. President Romney and the other half flew to Taipei, Taiwan. Midway through these conferences, the leaders exchanged places. Then they joined forces again in Korea.

In Korea, after a cultural program on Friday evening, the first full day of the conference was Saturday, a work day for Koreans. But 5,000 of the nation's 10,000 members still attended the morning meeting.

The Sunday conference drew an even larger crowd—between 8,000 and 9,000. An intense heat wave tested the members' commitment (Arthur Haycock said he felt "hotter than I had ever been in my life") but, to make things more difficult, in the morning meeting the Korean Church leaders had instructed men to walk through the stands with large signs that read in Korean, "Please Don't Use Your Fans." This was intended as a gesture of highest respect. When President Kimball learned what the sign said he had an announcement made that using fans would not be considered disrespectful. Even so, many members refrained from using fans.

Korean members reacted to the announcement of a temple in Tokyo with mixed emotions. Although the temple would be fairly close, government policy made it nearly impossible for couples to leave the country. President Kimball promised the Saints that if they would keep the commandments, the Lord would provide a way for them to go to the temple. About the time the temple in Japan was completed in 1980, Korean travel restrictions were relaxed.

Among those who attended the conference in Seoul was grandson Christian Kimball, a missionary in the Korea Pusan Mission. Chris would normally not have traveled out of his mission, but Spencer requested his grandson's presence. In a telephone call to mission president Han In Sang, Spencer apologized, saying he would not ask for himself, but grandmothers are different. Camilla wanted to see her grandson, and she hoped he could interpret for her. Chris's presence also served another purpose: Church members saw that the prophet had sent his own grandson to serve the Korean people.

As the trip ended, Spencer considered this series of conferences, with the large and enthusiastic audiences, an important mark of the Church's maturing in Asia.

1976 CONFERENCES IN THE PACIFIC

The year 1976 set a high-water mark with seventeen area conferences. In February Spencer spent three weeks conducting nine conferences in the South Pacific. He stopped first in Hawaii to lay the cornerstone of a new library at the BYU–Hawaii campus. Visiting in the home of Dan W. Andersen, president of BYU–Hawaii, Spencer drifted off in a brief nap in his chair while others chatted around him. Unconcerned by this apparent lapse in manners, Camilla observed, "That's what saves him."

Although Spencer felt exhausted at the beginning of the trip, he seemed to gather strength as he went along.

In the Pacific Islands, February was the middle of the rainy season, and normally it rained hard every day. For several weeks, the Samoan Saints had fasted and prayed each Sunday and Thursday that the Lord would hold back the rain for the conference.

Duane Cardall recalls that a member who worked at the airport in Pago Pago was responsible for a welcoming reception. The day of the

Presidents Kimball and Tanner with Eugene and Ruthdelene Reid, holding their new son named Spencer Eldon, Pago Pago, American Samoa, February 1976.

party's arrival, that member's superior suggested that the outdoor event be moved indoors because of the probability of heavy rain. The member replied, "It won't rain on the prophet. Tonight you'll see the moon and the stars!"

The boss scoffed, "If I see the moon, I'll join your Church!"

That night the moon shone brightly. In fact, beautiful tropical weather greeted the traveling party.

After the conference session, people lined up to shake the president's hand. Asked by someone whether he didn't find it exhausting, Spencer said, "I milked cows all my life so I could shake hands. I don't get tired."

As Duane Cardall returned to the parking lot for a ride back to the hotel, he commented casually to his driver that he was eager to get something to eat. The driver responded, "I can't eat yet. The prophet's still here." Cardall learned that some of the Samoan Saints fasted the entire time of Spencer's visit so that rain would not fall on their prophet.

Sometimes rain did fall—in torrents—but never during the outdoor conference sessions and never while the prophet was outside. A few members of the party got wet, but not the President. As he moved from one place to another, it would rain while he was inside and let up when it was time for him to go outside. Asked about the remarkable weather, the regional representative looked up at the sky and said humbly, "I only hope we can be worthy of this great blessing."

President Kimball explained here and at each conference, "This Church belongs to the people, so we bring the conference to you. We want people to stay where they are and build Zion there."

Eugene Reid, president of the stake, and his wife, Ruthdelene, had just had a son, and they named him Spencer Eldon in honor of the two members of the First Presidency attending the conference. When President Kimball heard this, he removed his hat and said, "I am honored." He then made his way through the crowd to President Tanner to inform him: "This good man named his son after you."

From Pago Pago, the group flew to Apia, in Western Samoa, larger but less developed than American Samoa. The people treated Spencer like one of their own royalty, holding a kava ceremony and a great feast featuring a huge roasted pig. After the meal, the Samoan members sang a song with many verses about their yearning for a temple. They gave

President Kimball an English translation so he could follow along. Afterward, Spencer said, to laughter, "Now, if I understand your Samoan well, I get the impression that you are interested in having a temple here. I'll have something to say about that at our area conference tomorrow."

The next day some 12,000 Saints gathered outdoors at Pesega, a Church-owned school near Apia. Clouds threatened, but the members here, too, had fasted each Sunday for the previous month, and again it did not rain on the prophet. At one session, ominous dark clouds clustered in the distance and rolled down upon the town. But shortly before reaching the conference, the storm seemed to split. It passed on both sides, leaving the meeting place calm and dry. The clouds reunited and produced a downpour on the island beyond the conference site.

President Kimball said the Saints needed to prepare for a temple by gathering genealogical information in a form that could be used in the temple rather than the traditional Samoan oral genealogies. They also needed to increase membership, "for it takes a lot of people to run a temple. . . . When you have done your part, the Lord will do his."

Western Samoa already excelled in providing missionaries. Of the 130 missionaries there, 104 were local elders and sisters.

While flying from Apia back to Pago Pago, Spencer suddenly fell ill with a high fever, coughing, and vomiting. His temperature climbed to 104° F. Then Camilla became ill, too. Both felt miserable. Dr. Russell Nelson and Arthur Haycock gave them blessings, and Spencer told Dr. Nelson to take his place with President Tanner on a television interview scheduled for that evening.

The next morning they left their hotel at 3:30 A.M. for a 5:00 flight to New Zealand. An official at the airport, seeing Spencer's pallor, urged him to go to the hospital. But Spencer would not consider it. He had appointments to fulfill.

On the flight to Auckland, Spencer and Camilla's high fevers persisted. A television interview and a meeting with Robert David Muldoon, prime minister of New Zealand, had been planned for as soon as they landed, and the worried General Authorities began to make contingency plans. But as the plane circled to land, Spencer broke into a heavy sweat and his temperature dropped to normal. He straightened his tie and asked Camilla to brush his hair.

Upon landing, the Kimballs left the plane first and greeted the line of people awaiting them. Soon afterward on television President Kimball gave an effective twenty-five minute explanation of the Church's history and mission. He had sent his regrets to prime minister Muldoon but changed his mind, joining the luncheon only a few minutes late. During dessert he excused himself and joined Camilla in their room. After the two-hour remission, his fever again climbed to 102 degrees. That afternoon, the Kimballs were driven to Temple View, near Hamilton, where the conference was to open that night with a cultural program. Spencer asked President Tanner to take his place in paying a courtesy call on Dame Teatairangikaau, the Maori queen, and in attending the evening's cultural program. He felt a need to preserve his strength for the Sunday meetings. He and Camilla went straight to bed, but he fretted, knowing that the people would be disappointed.

Spencer slept feverishly while Dr. Nelson sat beside him. After a few hours, Spencer broke into a heavy perspiration and woke with a start, pajamas soaked. "What time was that [cultural] program to begin?" he asked.

"At seven o'clock, President Kimball," Dr. Nelson responded.

"What time is it now?"

"Almost seven." Dr. Nelson checked Spencer's temperature. Once again, it was normal.

"Tell Sister Kimball we're going!" Spencer announced.

Dr. Nelson swallowed his impulse to give medical advice and notified Camilla. They hurriedly dressed and drove to the stadium where the cultural evening had just begun. Before they arrived, a young man offered a lengthy opening prayer and pleaded, "We are three thousand New Zealand youth. We are assembled here to sing and dance for thy prophet. Wilt thou heal him and deliver him here." As if on cue, Spencer's car entered the stadium and the crowd of 16,000 erupted in a deafening shout. Spencer and Camilla stayed through the evening, wrapped in blankets against the cool air.

Rain had fallen every day for the previous two weeks or more; but once again the Saints had fasted and prayed for good weather. The conference was held at a rugby stadium, the only site large enough for the expected crowd. Although clouds threatened, no rain fell until after the meetings. When one woman complained to her husband that it was too

hot and sunny, he replied, "See, I told you we only needed to fast half a day." The television weatherman commented on the unusual break in the weather and credited the people's prayers.

From Auckland they flew to Fiji. More than 1,000 Saints gathered in Suva for a Monday conference. The temperature was over 100 degrees, the discomfort intensified by dripping humidity. Camilla and Spencer, both still ill, soldiered on.

In Tonga the party was greeted by the eighty-piece Liahona High School band, two hundred dancers from Vava'u, and many others. The king was away, but the visitors met with premier and prince regent Prince Fatafehi Tu'ipelehake.

This time the rains came. The conference was to be held in the auditorium of the Church school, fifteen miles away. As the party arrived, rain-soaked students, dressed in white uniforms with green trim, lined the campus road to the school. Rain continued to fall during the conference, and the feast, planned for outdoors, had to be moved into the school cafeteria. At least the rain cooled the air. In the cultural program 1,000 dancers performed on the muddy rugby field.

All together more than 10,000 attended the conference. Approximately 100 were Tongans who lived elsewhere but returned to their homeland for the meetings. From Vava'u, far to the north, a boat designed to carry 300 passengers carried 1,000 men, women and children, crowded together for the twenty-four-hour journey.

During the first of three general sessions, the visitors admired a group of about 225 young Tongans dressed in white and sitting in the choir seats. When President Tanner announced the choir would sing, it was the entire center section of the congregation that rose. The Tongans in the choir seats were missionaries. All sessions were carried by the only radio station on the island.

The next conferences were in Melbourne and Sydney, Australia, and the first hour of the Sunday session, held in the world-famous Sydney Opera House, was carried nationwide on ten television stations. Network officials estimated that an audience of three million tuned in to hear the Mormon prophet speak about the role of a prophet in the modern world.

Tahiti was the site of the last area conference on this tour. The weather could not have been better—dry with a "cool ocean breeze." The dominant French and Catholic culture of Tahiti provided a difficult environment for the Church, and relations with the government had been strained. President Kimball called on the new governor, Charles Schmitt, who coldly expressed his hope that there would not be any trouble. But he warmed visibly as they talked, and he accepted Spencer's invitation to attend the last session of the conference. An impressive crowd of 2,300 Saints and friends attended. Talks were translated into both French and Tahitian.

In the poorly lighted auditorium, President Kimball could not see to read his text, so he laid it aside and spoke extemporaneously. Afterward he felt that he had done poorly and worried about disappointing the people.

After traveling 28,000 miles in three weeks, holding thirty-seven meetings and sixteen press conferences or interviews, Spencer and his party arrived in Salt Lake City about 8:30 in the evening. Still ill and exhausted, he stopped at his office and worked for a while before going home. Promptly at eight the next morning, he met in his regular Thursday meetings.

Chest X-rays showed that both President and Sister Kimball had viral pneumonia. Camilla's illness quickly cleared up with rest and medication, but Spencer's hung on. He refused to go to the hospital, telling his doctors, "You brethren just do not understand the urgency about the

work I must do. You must not hospitalize me and slow the work down."
Reluctantly, they agreed to manage his illness as an outpatient.

1976 EUROPEAN CONFERENCES

That summer of 1976 President Kimball held area conferences in
Europe. The first meetings were held simultaneously in Manchester and
London, with Spencer traveling between them. He returned to Europe
six weeks later for a third set of conferences, bringing the total for the
year to seventeen. This time in just nine days he conducted conferences
in Paris, Helsinki, Copenhagen, Amsterdam, and Dortmund.

Davis Bitton, assistant Church Historian, accompanied the party of
about thirty to Europe. It was a new experience for him to travel with
General Authorities. While waiting in the airport in New York City, the
others talked in clusters. Davis, not wishing to intrude, sat a discreet
distance away, reading. Then he saw President Kimball excuse himself
from a group and walk over to him. "I'm Spencer Kimball," he said. "I
guess I don't know who you are."

When Davis introduced himself, Spencer put his arm around his
shoulder and assured him, "It's wonderful to have you along. I hope you
enjoy the trip."

After the conference in Copenhagen, President Kimball asked to
visit the Church of Our Lady cathedral to see the famous statues by
Bertel Thorvaldsen of Christ and his apostles. Replicas of his *Christus,*
with Christ's arms outstretched to the world, stand in several LDS visitors' centers. The chapel was closed for renovation, but when they
knocked at the door an accommodating custodian admitted them.

They noted that the date inscribed above the *Christus* is 1821, and
an inscription reads: "Behold, this is my beloved son; hear ye him." In
1820, while Thorvaldsen worked on his marble statue, the young
prophet Joseph Smith in America reported he had seen Christ and heard
those very words from the Father (see JS—H 1:17).

Several members of the party listened to the caretaker, while others
examined the statue of Peter, holding large keys symbolizing his authority. President Kimball turned to Johan Bentine, president of the Copenhagen Denmark Stake, and said emphatically, "I want you to tell every
prelate in Denmark that they do not hold the keys. I hold the keys!"
(For additional detail on this experience, see page 108.)

33

AREA CONFERENCES, 1977–1980

"If he can do it, I can do it."

"AREA CONFERENCES," PRESIDENT KIMBALL told a Hong Kong audience, "dramatize as nothing else could the truly international character of the Church." Begun in 1971 in Manchester, England, area conferences brought the general conference experience to the people, thus solving two problems: transportation costs that exceeded the financial means of many members and limited seating for the general conferences. For the first time, members in more distant areas could meet with the prophet.

LATIN AMERICA

In 1977, President Kimball arranged eight area conferences in Latin America that reached a total attendance of 65,000. Typically, he pressed to fill every moment. Scrutinizing a proposed schedule of conference meetings and speaking assignments, he saw two meetings in La Paz, Bolivia, that he was not scheduled to attend and made red checks beside them. "What are these meetings? Why am I not attending?" he asked. Because La Paz's elevation was 12,000 feet above sea level, the conference planners had accepted the recommendation of Spencer's doctor that he rest for several hours as soon as he arrived while he became acclimated. Elder Robert D. Hales explained, "That's a rest period, President Kimball." President Kimball teased, "Are you tired, Elder Hales?"

The first conference, in Mexico City, brought together 25,000 Saints from as far as 1,500 miles away, the largest conference yet held. In the opening session, President Kimball related how in 1946, three years after his call as an apostle, he toured Mexico and found Church affairs in disarray. He went to bed that night sorely troubled. Restless, he awakened in the middle of the night, recalling a vivid dream, but he soon recognized the experience as perhaps more than a dream. The future of the Church in Mexico had passed before him, the members growing from poverty and obscurity to people of substantial standing in their community. He got out of bed, went to a writing table, and recorded what he had seen. Spencer said that now, thirty years later, he could see the vision partially fulfilled, and he hoped one day to see its complete fulfillment.

In Monterrey, general sessions convened in the Plaza de Toros, the city bull ring. About 8,500 attended even though the weather was chilly. As President Kimball stood with his interpreter to address the people, he began, "Mis queridos hermanos y hermanas." The interpreter paused in surprise and then translated, to the laughter of the Spanish-speaking audience, "My dear brothers and sisters."

Spencer had in that phrase nearly exhausted his Spanish vocabulary. But at each conference, Camilla read her women's meeting talk in Spanish. She had learned Spanish as a schoolgirl in the Mormon colony of Colonia Juarez, even though the colonists there spoke English among themselves. At age eighty-one she remembered little Spanish and had asked Eduardo Balderas, one of the Church translators, to help her get it right. She knew that her pronunciation was faulty, but the women seemed to genuinely appreciate her effort.

In Guatemala the conference met in the National Gymnasium. A cultural program occupied the first evening. The finale depicted a carnival with dancers in masks, one wearing a large bull mask that covered his upper body. Suddenly fireworks came shooting out from the mask in all directions. Roman candles blazed up over the scenery and into the audience. The place filled with smoke, and the visitors, sitting in the front row, ducked. A Roman candle zipped under L. Tom Perry's legs; another singed Lenora Kennedy's eyebrow and Marjorie Wilkinson's hair.

The general sessions on Tuesday offered sedate preaching, no fireworks.

In Guatemala, as in Mexico, President Kimball met with the head of state, President Kjell Eugenio Laugerud-Garcia, and told him about the principles that guided the 15,000 Mormons in his country.

Just a year earlier an estimated 22,000 Guatemalans had died in an earthquake that measured 7.6 on the Richter scale. Many mountain villages had simply disappeared with all their inhabitants. In the areas of greatest destruction, people were still living in shanties of cardboard and tin.

In Patzicia, the worst-hit area, the LDS chapel had collapsed. A fifty-ton central concrete beam fell across the back of missionary Randal Ellsworth of Rockville, Maryland. During the long struggle to free him, one member, Domingo Mitch, crawled into the wreckage where the elder lay trapped and wiped the blood and vomit from his face. When the man's wife begged him to leave the dangerous place, he said, "Be quiet. The Lord is big amongst us. If this missionary dies, I will stay here with him."

It took seven hours to free Elder Ellsworth by cutting away the floor beneath him and more hours to get him to a hospital already overwhelmed with victims. The doctors there said he would be paralyzed from the waist down and would always need hemodialysis. But during six months of rehabilitation in Washington, D.C., the elder regained feeling in his legs and walked again with crutches. By the time of President Kimball's visit, Elder Ellsworth had returned to Guatemala and was working in a remote village, walking with the aid of braces. To get to the special meeting for missionaries, he and his companion had walked four hours to a town where they could catch a bus, then had ridden through the night to Guatemala City. At the lunch served in connection with the missionary meeting, he sat next to President Kimball. Noticing the missionary's stubble, President Kimball rubbed his cheek against the elder's in empathy and appreciation.

In Santiago, Chile, 6,800 Latter-day Saints gathered. Elder Bruce R. McConkie delivered a prophetic sermon. As he expressed his love for the people of Chile and extolled their devotion, he wept, trembling. Then, with intensity, he prophesied that some of those present would live to see not just seven stakes in Chile, but seventy times seven stakes, that they would see a temple atop the hill on the eastern part of Santiago overlooking the city, and that they would become a great leavening agent for all of South America.[1]

---

1. There were then about 37,000 Chilean Saints. By the end of 1999 there were 116 stakes, 8 missions, and about 500,000 members, although of course not all were active. Latter-day Saints made up 3.6 percent of the population.

Afterward Elder L. Tom Perry commented, "That was quite a prophecy you gave today."

Elder Bruce R. McConkie responded, deadly serious, "You write it down, because it will come to pass." The Santiago Temple was dedicated in 1983.

At the end of the conference, President Kimball asked to see the children. A great silence followed as he greeted hundreds of children one by one, shedding tears as he shook their hands or kissed them or put his hands on their heads. Hushed, many of the children also wept. President Kimball said he had never before felt this kind of spirit.

When the visiting group arrived in La Paz, Bolivia, the highest major city in the world, everyone felt ill from the effects of the high altitude. Duane Cardall collapsed on his bed at the hotel but was soon disturbed:

"There was a knock; it was the bellboy with my bags. I went back to bed. After five minutes there was another knock; it was one of the traveling companions just wondering how I was. I said, 'If I can just get some rest, I think I'll be OK.' I went back and lay down on the bed and there was a knock at the door; I got up with a harsh word on my lips, just wanting to get some rest. I had taken off my shirt and didn't bother to put it back on. I went to the door and, as I opened it, there standing before me was a prophet of God. And he said, 'How are you doing?' I said, 'I'm fine. Don't worry about me, President.' He said, 'Is there anything I can do for you?' . . . He went from door to door checking on some of us who were not feeling well. . . . I shut the door and immediately got dressed. I said, 'If he can do it, I can do it.' And I went about my duties."

In an hour or so, Cardall accompanied President Kimball and David Kennedy to see the Bolivian president, Hugo Bonzer-Suarez, at the presidential palace.

Spencer was not immune to the altitude. He later recalled, "I didn't feel too good either. You just can't go there [to La Paz] without feeling it."

Just before the last session of the conference, as the General Authorities waited in a room behind the stage, President Kimball told them, "Before we leave tonight I would like to shake hands with and express my appreciation and love to all the Lamanite people here at the conference." Thinking of the number in attendance, President Romney

Personal secretary D. Arthur Haycock, President Kimball, and Dr. Ernest L. Wilkinson Jr.

urged, "President, I don't think that is very wise. When we announce this we will have a real problem with security. We will have a problem with discipline. People will be stumbling over each other in order to shake your hand. You are already tired and have been on the road all this time. You need your rest."

President Kimball sat silently for a few moments, then, without responding to President Romney's objections, simply repeated that he wanted to touch the people. His advisers repeated their advice. Again he was silent. They looked to Dr. Ernest Wilkinson for help. "Doctor, how do you feel about this? Do you think he is up to it?" The doctor said it was unwise, considering all the recent travel, the altitude, his fatigue at the end of a long day, and the security problem. Again President Kimball sat silent a moment, then repeated his wish. The others, realizing finally that he had made up his mind, yielded.

As President Kimball concluded the conference, he announced, "I want to shake the hand of every person here." An audible gasp came from the crowd. After the prayer, pandemonium ensued. Many of the crowd could not believe he would shake everyone's hand, and they wanted to reach him before he quit. But once they realized he was serious, they stayed in an orderly line. They came—humble people, the well and the crippled. Some smiled, some wept, many gave him an *abrazo*. Some got in line a second time. President Kimball freely poured out his time and energy to greet each one, despite the altitude, his fatigue, and his old heart.

The other five General Authorities lined up with him while Dr. Wilkinson, Earl Jones, and Arthur Haycock stood by anxiously. At one point, Dr. Wilkinson quietly approached and asked whether he could stop soon. Barely glancing at him, President Kimball said, "If you knew what I know, you wouldn't ask me that question." The only help he would accept was from Elder McConkie, who stationed himself just beyond the President. As soon as a member had shaken President Kimball's hand, Elder McConkie would reach out, take the person's hands, and pull him or her along with his own greeting, lest the person stop to talk to President Kimball and make his promise to greet everyone impossible.

Before arriving in Colombia, President Kimball's talks had followed the usual themes: temple worthiness and temple ordinances, missionary work, and rearing families in righteousness. In Bogota for some reason he broke that pattern and spoke about revolution:

"[Christ] said that he who lived by the sword would perish by the sword. . . .

"Today, many are becoming extremists and are losing balance and effectiveness and are missing the results which they would desire to attain. Wouldn't they be far better off to align themselves with the constructive forces and attempt a slower, more peaceful way to reach the same ends?"

Although Jesus felt anguish at the world's ills, he sought to change the world by teaching correct principles, not by use of force.

President Kimball also spoke about the Savior's disapproval of class distinctions. Some seventy-five Otavalo Indian members had traveled fifty-six hours from Ecuador to attend. Most spoke only Quichua. Rafael Tobongo-Pastillo, president of the Otavalo District, offered one of the prayers. Along with long black hair in a braid to the small of his back, he wore traditional Indian dress—a white shirt, dark vest, white linen trousers, and sandals. There seemed to be a magnetic attraction between him and President Kimball, two physically small, highly spiritual men.

At the conclusion of the Bogota conference, Spencer acquiesced for one of the few times to his doctor's advice to forego shaking hands with every person.

This series of conferences concluded with a long flight south to São Paulo, Brazil, where President Kimball laid the cornerstone of the new temple under construction. Before the ceremony began, Helvécio Martins, a black member who had been baptized in 1972 and was serving as public relations director for northern Brazil, glanced up and saw President Kimball looking in his direction and beckoning. He assumed the gesture was for someone else and looked away. Glancing again, he saw President Kimball beckoning. Although they had met earlier, he still did not believe the gesture was meant for him. President Kimball then whispered to Elder James E. Faust, who repeated the gesture and mouthed, "Helvécio, come here."

When Brother Martins approached, Spencer stood up, hugged him, asked about his welfare, and introduced him to President Romney. Then the prophet put his arm around Helvécio, looked him in the eye, and said, "Brother Martins, what is necessary for you is fidelity. Remain faithful, and you will enjoy all the blessings of the gospel."

Warmed but perplexed, Helvécio returned to his responsibilities. At the ceremony's end, President Kimball, passing by Helvécio, stopped, took his hand and, laying his other hand on Helvécio's arm, said, "Don't forget, Brother Martins, don't forget."[2] This incident would assume great significance to Helvécio a year later when the revelation on priesthood was announced.[3]

Hawaii, South Africa, and South America

Just two days after the announcement of the 1978 revelation on priesthood, Spencer and Camilla traveled to Hawaii for the stake conference of the Kauai Hawaii Stake, the rededication of the temple in

---

2. A few months later, at the conclusion of stake conference in Rio de Janeiro, Elder Faust sent a note to Helvécio, "Could you please accompany me to the airport?" When they got in the car, Brother Martins drove fast, assuming there was a rush, but Elder Faust said, "You don't need to go too fast. We have enough time." Before they reached the airport, he asked Helvécio if he remembered President Kimball's counsel. Yes, he remembered, but he remained puzzled. Elder Faust explained cryptically that the Lord expected the same level of faith from everyone, even the prophet. "The promises of the Lord will be fulfilled only in the lives of faithful servants."

3. Elder Martins served in the Second Quorum of the Seventy from 1990 to 1995.

The Kimballs and the Tanners with Alice Okkers, a member since 1920, in South Africa, 1978.

Laie, a solemn assembly, and a brief area conference, the first area conference held in the United States.

In October 1978, President Kimball departed on a long, multi-purpose trip. Travel of 24,000 air miles took him to Washington, D.C.; London; South Africa; and South America, for four more area conferences. For the only time, the Kimballs took the supersonic Concorde across the Atlantic, marveling at the shortness of the three-and-a-half hour trip.

In Washington, D.C., and London, President Kimball installed new temple presidencies and conferred special blessings.

After the first conference session in Johannesburg, Spencer and Camilla sneaked away from their two security men so they could walk on the street without others trailing behind them.

At dinnertime Spencer chose to lie down in his room rather than join the others in the hotel dining room. As Ernest Wilkinson began his meal, a security man interrupted, "Doctor, the president just came out of his room and asked if we could find you." Dr. Wilkinson hurried upstairs. But Spencer was not in need of medical attention. "Ernest," said Spencer, "I just wanted you to come up and have dinner with me." A local Saint who knew Spencer's food preferences had delivered a loaf of still-warm bread and a bottle of milk.

"Let me fix it for you," Spencer continued. He broke a chunk from the loaf, stuffed it in a drinking glass, poured in some milk, and handed a spoon to Ernest, who did not have the heart to say that he had left prime rib of beef on his plate in the dining room.

The conference planners arranged a missionary meeting for Monday morning at 8:00 A.M. without telling President Kimball, intending to let him sleep in and join the meetings at 10 o'clock. At 7:15 A.M., mission president Dale LeBaron arrived at the hotel to take the other General Authorities to the meeting. He ran into President Kimball, fully dressed, who asked him, "Where are you going?"

President LeBaron, under instructions not to tell President Kimball about the early meeting, said, "I have an early meeting."

"With the missionaries?"

Not willing to lie to the Church President, LeBaron said, "Yes, but your meeting with them is at ten."

"Would you let me come now?" He hugged LeBaron and said, "Thanks. I'd like to go now," and he did.

On Tuesday the area conference continued, with 3,500 of 7,200 members attending. Some came 1,000 miles from Rhodesia (now Zimbabwe) in two buses, carrying automatic weapons to protect themselves against Marxist guerrillas.

Before leaving Johannesburg, President Kimball learned that his flight to South America had been cancelled, requiring a ten-hour layover in Cape Town, at the far end of the country. He asked mission president LeBaron whether there were missionaries in Cape Town who had not been able to attend the conference in Johannesburg. The mission president said there were ten, so a meeting was arranged to be held in the local chapel in Cape Town. The ten missionaries sat on the first row, matched by ten on the stand: President and Camilla Kimball, President and Sarah Tanner, Gordon and Marjorie Hinckley, Neal and Colleen Maxwell, and James and Florence Cullimore.

Each of the missionaries bore his testimony, and President Kimball spoke extemporaneously for about half an hour. He gave each missionary a hug and a kiss on the cheek and told each, "I love you."

The party flew then to South America. After meetings in Uruguay and Argentina, they stayed in São Paulo for a full week for ten temple dedication sessions and an area conference. The planning committee expected 8,000 people for the area conference but had been forced to reserve an inadequate 5,000 seat facility for $30,000. The 20,000-seat

Ibirapuera Stadium they had hoped for was booked by a Czech ballet troupe. But about four months before the conference, the ballet appearance was postponed and the stadium became available. Because it was a state-owned facility, the only cost was a fee for maintenance and cleaning.

In connection with the conference, about 1,200 missionaries attended a missionary meeting, 70 percent of whom were Brazilians. In the last general session, Elder Faust, who was scheduled to speak just before President Kimball concluded, leaned over to whisper that he would leave the President plenty of time. President Kimball replied that he wanted only ten minutes. Elder Faust said, "I'll be sure you have more." President Kimball rejoined, "If you don't take enough time, I'll call on you again."

1979 AREA CONFERENCES

In July 1979, Spencer suffered an attack of dizziness. The diagnosis was a transient stroke, with only temporary effect, but it was ten days before he could engage in any significant activity again and three weeks before he was spending full days at the office. As a result, he missed the August area conference in Madison, Wisconsin—the first time he missed an area conference.

At the end of August, Spencer had recovered enough to travel to the area conference in Toronto, Canada. He first flew to Ottawa to present the prime minister and the queen's representative with copies of their family genealogy. Doug King, a red-coated Canadian Mountie assigned to escort dignitaries, accompanied President Kimball in Ottawa. He observed:

"We are taught in the Mounties to respect a privacy zone of four to five feet while escorting a VIP. Dignitaries . . . expect respect and distance. But when I walked beside President Kimball, . . . he put his arm through mine, breaking right through the privacy zone. He patted me on the hand like a father would his son. The experience literally blew me away."

In the fall President Kimball missed the next seven area conferences, including five in New Zealand and Australia, because of surgery.

Dedicating the replica of the Peter Whitmer cabin as part of a general conference telecast, April 1980. Seated behind him are descendants of brothers Joseph Smith Jr. (Lorena Normandeau), Hyrum Smith (Eldred G. Smith), and Samuel Smith (Melvin Smith).

1980 AREA CONFERENCES

But he recovered enough to attend the twelve conferences planned for 1980 in the United States and the Orient.

In celebration of the Church's sesquicentennial, the closing session of April 1980 general conference was telecast from Fayette, New York, to television viewers and to an audience in the Tabernacle on Temple Square watching the proceedings on two seventeen-foot-high screens. President Kimball spoke from Fayette and dedicated a replica of Peter Whitmer's small, log farmhouse, the site of the formal organization of the Church in 1830.

An area conference was scheduled in nearby Rochester, New York, the next weekend, so Spencer and Camilla, accompanied by Arthur Haycock, spent the next five days at the home of son Andy and his wife, Phyllis, in Fairfield, Connecticut. It was an unusual break in Spencer's administrative routine. He and Camilla visited with the family, rested, played games, went to an ice cream shop, attended a performance of *Fiddler on the Roof,* and looked up a nephew who lived in the area.

At the priesthood session of the Rochester area conference, Tony Marren, a young adult, was seated on the stage as a member of the choir.

Tony had been baptized eighteen months earlier, although he acknowledged in the baptismal interview that he did not have a testimony that
President Kimball was a prophet. The man who interviewed him still
found him worthy and bore witness that he would one day "be
endowed" with a sure knowledge of President Kimball's prophetic role.

After the meeting, well-wishers surrounded President Kimball, some
weeping, others reaching to shake his hand or touch his clothing. Tony
watched in amazement. Suddenly the crowd parted, and President
Kimball came over to speak to him.

He said ordinary things, like "I'm so glad to see you. Are you feeling
okay? How is your mother? (She had been recently released from a hospital.) Can I help you? I'm so glad you took the time to join me."

Tony's stunned reply was simple, "President Kimball, I love you."

President Kimball answered, "I knew it already. I came over to tell
you that, too." President Kimball gave him a hug and a kiss on the
cheek.

In May 1980 an area conference for southern California convened
in Pasadena at the Rose Bowl, where an estimated 75,000 members
broiled in the sun through the Sunday morning session, the largest gathering in the history of the Church.

The previous Tuesday, May 13, Bishop Jimmie Lakey had called

*Aided by Ernest L. Wilkinson Jr., Earl Jones (head of Church security), and D. Arthur Haycock at
the area conference in Pasadena, California, May 1980.*

President Kimball's office to tell him that stake president Jordan Naylor in San Diego had been severely burned. To the bishop's surprise, President Kimball himself answered the telephone. The Naylors had been close neighbors to the Kimballs in Arizona, and Spencer had watched Jordan grow up. Jordan was the victim of a freak accident when he was siphoning gasoline out of his car to put in his lawn mower. The gasoline fumes ignited, and in a flash he suffered seared lungs and second and third degree burns over 60 percent of his body. President Kimball asked if there was anything he could do.

Bishop Lakey, who was employed by Pacific Southwest Airlines, suggested, "If I provide a plane could you possibly come to comfort the family?"

President Kimball responded, "Let me think." Within an hour, five members of the Twelve had called the bishop to say, "President Kimball can't do things like that. He is President of the entire Church."

But soon President Kimball called back: "Bishop Lakey, I know you have been inundated with calls, but don't you mind. I'll make the decision. I will be in the Rose Bowl in Pasadena on Saturday and if you could pick me up at the Burbank airport and get me back to Burbank the same night, I could do it."

Bishop Lakey's company made available a twin-engine turboprop airplane that he himself piloted to fly Spencer to San Diego. Spencer found Jordan conscious but unable to speak because of his burned trachea; he communicated by blinking in Morse code.

Spencer gave Jordan a blessing. Afterward he said, "I couldn't bless him to recover, but he needed a blessing of comfort."[4] Spencer spent an hour at the hospital with the family, then flew back to Burbank, subdued. Someone expressed concern for Spencer's well-being and suggested perhaps it was not wise for him to have gone to San Diego. Spencer retorted feelingly, "I *should* have gone. I was doing my Father's work and that is where I belonged." They arrived in time for the President to get to the evening session of area conference only a little late.

A series of six area conferences in Asia was timed to coincide with the dedication of the Tokyo Temple. Five years had passed since the

---

4. Jordan died a week later, remarkably free from pain.

earlier set of area con-
ferences had been held
in the Far East. In that
time the Church had
grown significantly—
especially in the Phil-
ippines, where it grew
from two missions to
five and from 19,000
members to 41,000.

With missionary grandson Spencer Kimball in Taiwan,
October 1980.

While in the Philip-
pines, President Kimball
examined possible sites
for a temple that had
just been announced.
He met a second time
with President Ferdinand E. Marcos, who went out of his way to accommodate the visit by coming into his office on Saturday. Marcos agreed
that religion added strength to his people. He did nearly all the talking,
with David Kennedy responding. President Kimball sat nearly silent,
looking haggard. While Spencer held no brief for despots like Marcos,
he believed that as long as freedom of religion was allowed, the Church
could continue to grow under any form of government. For that reason
he sought to foster good relations everywhere.

In Hong Kong, after the meetings had ended about 10:30 P.M.,
Spencer learned that his hotel was only a few blocks from the Star Ferry.
Although he had visited Hong Kong a number of times, he had never
seen much more than the airport, hotel, and meeting place. He wanted
to cross the bay to downtown, and this would be his only chance. He
set off walking, with others trailing behind, exhausted from the long day.

Arthur hovered anxiously at his shoulder, trying to reason with him.
"President, you don't want to do this. Think a minute," he insisted. "It is
too late in the evening."

Spencer replied, "I not only want to do it; I'm going to do it." But
by the time they got to the ferry, the passenger gates had closed.
Disconsolately, Spencer returned to the hotel.

From Hong Kong and Taiwan, the visitors went to Korea, following the pattern of the visits to the Far East five years earlier. By eight in the evening, all the visitors had settled in their hotel rooms. Elder Yoshihiko Kikuchi (a member of the First Quorum of the Seventy) and his wife, Toshiko Koshiya, occupied a room two doors away from the Kimballs. Exhausted and knowing that the next day would be strenuous, they prepared to rest. The doorbell rang. Through the peephole, Elder Kikuchi saw an old man with bare feet and no necktie. He did not recognize the man as President Kimball until he rang again. Elder Kikuchi dressed quickly and opened the door. President Kimball held out flowers he had received at the airport and asked, "Could you please help me find a vase? These flowers need water." That problem solved, President Kimball left.

Ten minutes later, the doorbell rang again, and President Kimball asked, "Are you folks free tonight?"

"Yes, sir," Elder Kikuchi promptly replied.

"Would you like to visit us? Would you like to come to our room?"

"We're more than happy to do so, President, but you must be tired!"

"I am not tired," said President Kimball. "Everybody is telling me that I must rest, I must rest. But I'm not tired; I had enough sleep on the plane and I would love to visit with the two of you if you don't mind."

Because the Korean Saints could not rent an adequate hall due to political considerations, the area conference was scheduled to be held outdoors in the mission compound. It was late October and bitter cold. The ward chapel in the compound seated only seven to eight hundred; overflow seating with a public address system was set up outside. Before the conference began, the rain and snow stopped, but temperatures were below freezing and a stiff wind blew.

In the afternoon President Kimball insisted on speaking outside despite the cold. The leaders wrapped him and the other visitors in large blankets. When President Kimball stood to speak he was exposed to the icy wind, which blew so hard that, despite the blankets, all the visitors felt chilled. After the meeting he greeted many of the Saints who had braved the cold. The second day it was again cuttingly cold, but President Kimball again insisted on speaking outside at one of the sessions.

In Japan, President Kimball dedicated the Tokyo Temple in seven sessions and held an area conference in Osaka before turning home-ward. The journey to Asia covered 18,000 miles and included thirty major addresses. Attendance in the five nations amounted to 35 percent of the total membership in those lands, despite the cost and difficulty of travel. Spencer had started out the three-week trip tired and his voice weak. But during the trip, his voice and eyes and vitality improved.

The Osaka area conference was the last of its kind. It was the sixty-third. In 1983, multistake or regional conferences took their place. The first of these, held in London in October 1983 for four stakes, was attended by apostles Boyd K. Packer and Neal A. Maxwell. By then, most areas around the world could receive general conference broad-casts by satellite transmission or radio-phone lines, removing one of the motivations for area conferences.

Multistake and regional conferences had many advantages. Because they did not draw such enormous crowds, it was easier to find facilities. Shorter travel distances reduced the financial burden in attending. Fewer sessions were easier to organize, and usually only two General Authorities attended, thus reducing the manpower required.

As with other organizational programs, area conferences had their time, only to be replaced. But for a decade they played an important role in "taking the Church to the people."

34

SOLEMN ASSEMBLIES
AND OTHER TRAVELS

"What better time and place for a father to show his love?"

IN ADDITION TO GREATLY EXPANDING the use of area conferences, President Kimball used the solemn assemblies as a device for reaching out to the local leaders, on whose loyalty and faithful service so much depends.

SOLEMN ASSEMBLIES

Traditionally solemn assemblies are convened to sustain a new President of the Church, dedicate a temple, or instruct priesthood leaders. President Kimball took the seldom-used "instructional" solemn assembly and expanded it so that he could personally reach tens of thousands of local priesthood leaders. Between 1975 and 1978, about sixty such gatherings were held across the United States and Canada.

These assemblies expressed the commitment of President Kimball and his counselors to be among the people, instructing and inspiring greater efforts at building the kingdom.

Solemn assemblies frequently lasted from three and one-half to four hours. Except for a few places where the assemblies could be held in a large temple room designed for that purpose (as in the Manti, Logan, Salt Lake City, and Los Angeles Temples), they convened in a stake center. The men came fasting and were admitted upon presentation of a temple recommend. The assemblies included prayer, music, the sacrament, and instruction. They were usually held in one city on Friday and another on Saturday, but the schedule could vary. For example, one meeting was held in Roanoke, Virginia, on Saturday and the next in Minneapolis on Sunday.

In each assembly General Authorities blessed and passed the sacrament of the Lord's Supper to all present. Normally the three members of the First Presidency and two other General Authorities spoke, addressing assigned topics. Instruction ranged over many issues, including abortion, gambling, incest, adultery, abuse, and dealing with apostates.[1]

The meetings had their intended effect. Local leaders gained a sense of unmediated connection with the top leadership. The limited audience allowed greater candor than would be comfortable in a public meeting. These meetings also built unity among priesthood leaders and a sense of belonging to a larger and more powerful movement than is easily felt in the smaller units where members experience most of their lives in the Church.

In August 1975, Church leaders flew to Calgary, Canada, for a solemn assembly. As they deplaned, Spencer reached over to carry Elder LeGrand Richards's briefcase for him. Spencer was eighty, but Elder Richards was nearly ninety. Outside the stake center, hundreds of children sang for them. Inside more than nine hundred priesthood leaders from nine stakes and from the mission covering that area had assembled fasting for the four-hour meeting. While the men listened carefully to all of the speakers, they responded with special attentiveness when the prophet spoke. Using only a few notes, he instructed them for an hour.

That evening the Presiding Bishopric had arranged a youth fireside. Although President Kimball was not scheduled to participate, he asked Bishop Brown during dinner if there would be any objection to his attending. When he came in during the meeting, the five hundred young people stood, many wiping tears from their eyes.

Saturday, December 6, 1975, was a long day for Spencer. From 7:00 to 10:30 A.M. he held a solemn assembly in the Logan Temple for priesthood leaders from northern Utah. That afternoon he held a similar meeting in the Salt Lake Temple for leaders from the Salt Lake area. In the evening he held in the Salt Lake Temple yet another session for

---

1. The subjects addressed in some specificity in a 1971 solemn assembly were the importance of temple work; responsibilities of husbands; attempts to legalize gambling, prostitution, and sale of liquor by the drink; homosexuality; Sunday buying and selling; polygamy; parents' teaching of children; chastity; interviewing; Church discipline; keeping confidences; family organizations; temple marriage; abortion; birth control; and wearing of temple garments by servicemen.

leaders from the Utah Valley area. Among the thousands of men in that last session, his son Ed sang in a choir organized for the occasion. At the end of the meeting, the audience stood respectfully, waiting for the First Presidency to leave. On his way out, Spencer spotted Ed and uncalculatingly crossed over to embrace and kiss his son. At first Ed felt embarrassed at the public display of affection, but then he thought, what better time and place for a father to show his love?

In June 1978, President Kimball traveled to Hawaii for a solemn assembly. As he arrived at the meeting place, he asked his driver, Ben Nihipali, "Are you coming in?"

"No, I am just an elder and membership clerk in my ward," responded Brother Nihipali. "I was not invited."

"Do you have a temple recommend?"

"Yes."

"Then you can come in."

Spencer then told Arthur Haycock to check with the other drivers and the police providing security, and "if they have recommends, have them come in."

Brother Nihipali let President Kimball out, parked the car, and returned to the stake center, planning to slip into the back of the hall. But as he entered, he found Spencer waiting for him just inside the door. Spencer led him and the other drivers to the front row, squeezing bishops and stake presidents who had been waiting since 6:00 A.M. Then he went on the stand, sat down, and winked at them.

TRAVEL TO THE MIDDLE EAST

President Kimball underwent brain surgery in early September 1979, but he recovered quickly enough to travel to the Middle East for the dedication of the Orson Hyde Memorial Garden in Jerusalem in late October. The Kimballs had been to Jerusalem twice before, in 1960 and 1961.

Spencer and Camilla and a party of fifteen flew to Athens, then boarded the cruise ship *Stella Solaris* along with more than six hundred members of a BYU travel-study group. Because Spencer was still recovering from the surgery, people had been warned not to bother him. Spencer joked about "being ostracized." It felt strange to be left alone so much.

When the ship docked at Alexandria, Egypt, it was greeted by a seventeen-piece band (including a bagpiper) dressed in white uniforms. A sign read, "Egypt Welcomes President Spencer W. Kimball." Representatives of the governor of Alexandria and of Jiran Sadat, Egyptian president Anwar Sadat's wife, greeted them and presented a bouquet of red roses.

While some of the party went to Cairo and the pyra-

With Ernest L. Wilkinson Jr., in Mykenos, Greece, October 1979.

mids, a smaller group, including the Kimballs, traveled through the Nile delta. Along the road they saw such sights as an ancient waterwheel—turned by a blindfolded cow—lifting water onto the fields. The ship next sailed to Haifa, Israel, where the party went ashore and traveled by car through lush fruit groves and towns with neat, substantial houses. They had four days before the dedication to play the unfamiliar role of sightseers. This freedom was particularly rewarding to the Kimballs, who for years when traveling had seen little but airports, hotels, and meeting places. They visited the Mount of Beatitudes, the Sea of Galilee, and Mount Carmel, where Elijah confronted the priests of Baal.

At Mount Tabor, one of two sites proposed by scholars as the Mount of Transfiguration, Spencer was not content merely to view this symmetrical round mountain. He wanted to stand on its summit, 1,843 feet above sea level. Early in the morning, they drove up the steep, winding road that switches back and forth across the face of the mountain to the top, where two churches stand. President Kimball climbed steps to the top of a flat area and looked out across the valley. He seemed preoccupied. Visibly moved by what he saw and felt, he spoke of a strong impression: "This is why we came to Israel. This is the highest point in all the world."

At a sacrament meeting held for the group in Shepherds' Field the next day, he commented again on Mount Tabor:

"I feel very sure that this was the spot where Jesus had taken his three disciples, Peter, James, and John, to this 'high mountain apart' and there had given certain blessings. I know there has been some disputation and difference of feeling about it, since there are some other possible places, but I have always felt this is [the place]."

However, he did not consider the question of location authoritatively settled by this feeling.

Spencer preferred going to places he had not already seen, but that did not apply to the Garden Tomb, the place he believed Jesus' body had lain until resurrected. Spencer recalled that during earlier visits "we sat here for hours and read the scriptures." He listened in each place to both the guide assigned by the Ministry of Tourism and to BYU religion professor Daniel Ludlow, who accompanied the group. Spencer never seemed impatient. At the Garden Tomb, Spencer said to the guide:

"We accept this as the burial place of the Savior. We realize people have different ideas about these places, but this seems to be the logical place.

"I feel quite sure that this is the spot where his body was laid. It gives me such a sacred feeling just to be here."

A *Church News* photographer wanted a picture of President Kimball walking alone in the garden by the tomb, and he consented. Arthur Haycock, concerned about the uneven flagstone paving underfoot, cautioned the President to be careful. Spencer replied quietly, "It's all right, Arthur. . . . I'm used to walking on holy ground."

The Orson Hyde Garden

President Kimball dedicated the Orson Hyde Memorial Garden on the anniversary of Elder Orson Hyde's 1841 prayer dedicating the land of Palestine for the return of the Jews, as prophesied in scripture. The history of the garden went back to 1972, when President Harold B. Lee discussed with Jerusalem Mayor Teddy Kollek the possibility of erecting

In the Orson Hyde Memorial Garden, October 1979. On the right is Jerusalem mayor Teddy Kollek.

a monument on the Mount of Olives to commemorate Elder Hyde's dedication. The mayor thought something might be included in a greenbelt being established around the city. The Jerusalem Foundation, a charitable organization headed by Mayor Kollek, obtained the five-acre site for the garden on the slope of the Mount of Olives overlooking the Old City. The Orson Hyde Foundation, headed by LeGrand Richards, undertook to raise $1 million from Church members to develop the greenbelt, including the Orson Hyde Memorial Garden. The municipality of Jerusalem agreed to maintain the garden perpetually.

Despite his ninety-three years and poor health, LeGrand Richards flew to Israel to join President Kimball and others for the dedication. In a meeting concerning final arrangements, Elder Howard W. Hunter said to Mayor Kollek, "We haven't finished paying the $1 million for the garden."

"We trust you," the mayor replied.

"We don't like to dedicate anything that isn't paid for," Elder Hunter said, "and Elder Richards has the last installment of the money." Elder Richards then presented a check for the last $225,000.

About two thousand people attended the dedication ceremony. When President Kimball spoke the dedicatory prayer, he chose his words carefully, acknowledging that Orson Hyde dedicated the land "for

Selecting the site for the BYU Jerusalem Center, October 1979. From left: Robert Thomas, Howard W. Hunter, Robert Taylor, Spencer W. Kimball, Ernest L. Wilkinson Jr., N. Eldon Tanner, Arthur Haycock.

the gathering of Judah's scattered remnants" but praying also for all of "Abraham's children," thus including the Arabs as well as the Jews.

The BYU Jerusalem Center

About a year earlier, David Galbraith, president of the LDS branch in Jerusalem, requested permission to secure property and develop plans for building a small chapel. At about the same time, Robert Taylor, director of BYU Travel Studies, submitted a proposal to Brigham Young University for acquiring a permanent facility in the Holy Land to house BYU Semester Abroad students.[2] When both proposals came to the First Presidency within a few months of one another, the Presidency assigned Elder Hunter to ascertain whether one building might serve both needs.

While in Jerusalem for the Orson Hyde garden dedication, President Kimball was to examine the properties being considered. First Robert Taylor and President N. Eldon Tanner reviewed a score of sites to decide which they should show Spencer. The most likely site was a five-acre parcel south of the Old City near the United Nations building compound. Another on Mount Scopus was suitable, though it had no

---

2. BYU began a Semester Abroad program in Israel with twenty students in January 1968.

view. A hundred yards farther on Mount Scopus was a property that offered a marvelous view of the Mount of Olives and the Temple Mount. It was ideal but not available. Mayor Kollek said it would never be available because it was already designated to be used either for the Israeli Supreme Court building or part of a greenbelt where no building would be allowed. Further, the site lay very near an earthquake fault line, and there was the possibility the site contained graves, making it unacceptable for building.

Notwithstanding all this, President Tanner told Taylor, "When you show President Kimball the possible sites tomorrow, come here last and show this view."

The next day, President Kimball reviewed each site, then said, "Drive on." Last, they came to the second site on Mount Scopus. They stood awhile, enjoying the spectacular view of the Old City. President Tanner said, "All in favor of this location?" All hands went up, including President Kimball's. That, then, was the impossible site they successfully set about to procure.

1981 Travels in the Caribbean

As Spencer's health permitted, he continued to hold special meetings in distant places but without the area conference format. No Church President had yet been to Puerto Rico, so he visited this U.S. commonwealth in May 1981. Missionary work in the racially mixed Caribbean islands had taken vigorous hold after the 1978 revelation on priesthood. Members and their friends crowded a large hotel ballroom in San Juan.

After the conference a woman, standing on a bench so she could see, seized Spencer's head as he passed by and turned him to kiss his cheek. He heard a pop and suffered a stiff neck for days afterward. Some recent converts, after shaking Spencer's hand, made the sign of the cross in a habitual gesture of reverence.

From Puerto Rico the presidential party flew to Santo Domingo in the Dominican Republic. Even though missionaries had been working in the country for only two years, membership was already nearly three thousand. A separate Dominican Republic Mission had been formed just two months earlier.

The nationwide conference of 1,600 Saints and friends met in a hotel ballroom, but the meeting began without 120 Saints from the Puerto Plata branch, located across the island. These Saints were traveling on two packed buses, but one of the buses had broken down. Over a stretch of twenty miles, the bus stalled a dozen times until the driver gave up and hitched a ride back to Puerto Plata to get another bus. The Saints in the second bus refused to abandon their friends, even though they wept as they realized they would likely miss the meeting. Some thought Satan had a hand in keeping them from seeing the prophet; others thought the Lord was punishing them for unworthiness.

The replacement bus did not arrive until 6:30 P.M. There was no way they could get to Santo Domingo in time for the seven o'clock meeting, but they continued on, often in tears, not even stopping to eat, in hopes of at least seeing the prophet. They finally arrived at the hotel about ten o'clock, long after the conference had ended. President Kimball had retired for the night.

When the Puerto Plata Saints told their story, Elder Joseph B. Wirthlin, Arthur Haycock, and mission president John A. Davis conferred. They first suggested that President Kimball meet with them in the morning. But the next day was Tuesday, and the Saints had to drive back through the night to be at their jobs in the morning. All three of the leaders were reluctant to tell President Kimball about the situation because they knew he would dress and come to meet with the members. But they also knew what his reaction would be the next day if they did not tell him.

Finally Arthur knocked at Spencer's room. Spencer opened the door in his pajamas. Arthur told him about the situation and asked if he could carry the President's message and blessing to the Saints.

"Oh, that wouldn't be fair, would it?" said Spencer. "You wait a couple of minutes and I'll dress, and then we'll hold another meeting." He and Camilla dressed quickly and met with the members. Despite the late hour, he delivered the full forty-five-minute message he had given earlier. "I felt we just couldn't let them down," he explained. A few of the Saints still around who had attended the earlier meeting listened again. At midnight the group boarded their buses, exhausted but content. They drove through the night and were back at their jobs in the morning.

OTHER MEETINGS

Throughout his presidency, Spencer talked at many special meetings, held sometimes for the public, at other times for missionaries or local leaders. In August 1977, he traveled to Europe, where he held public meetings (but not area conferences) in Milan, Padova, and Rome, and met with groups of leaders and missionaries in Switzerland, Austria, Italy, England, Poland, East Germany, and West Germany.

Building dedications provided another occasion to meet with the Saints. In August 1975, Spencer traveled to Tennessee for visits to four cities in three days. Bishop Philander K. Smartt had invited President Kimball to dedicate a chapel and speak at a public meeting in Chattanooga. Spencer had a special interest in the area because two of his uncles (Elder J. Golden Kimball of the Seventy and J. Golden's brother Elias) had served as presidents of the Southern States Mission.

The Chattanooga paper carried an article on the front page about his visit. On Saturday, after the chapel dedication, President Kimball spoke to the public in a beautiful downtown theater. Mayor Pat Rose, a Baptist deacon, presented him with a key to the city and introduced him warmly as a servant of the Lord. Two hecklers in the audience stood up and yelled at the mayor, "You have sold out the blood of Jesus to this apostate crowd." The men were ushered out and arrested for disorderly conduct and resisting arrest. Police found them armed with billy clubs.

President Kimball stood at the podium during the outburst but made no mention of it. Bishop Smartt, embarrassed at the disruption, asked whether he should pursue prosecution of the hecklers. Spencer said, "Leave them alone. They have their strong beliefs, just as we do." The city prosecuted anyway. The judge dismissed the case, but he scolded the hecklers and threatened them with jail if they caused any further public disturbance.

REDEEMING THE DEAD

35

A Burst of New Temples

"Instead of going to Switzerland, why don't you just have your own temple here?"

DURING PRESIDENT KIMBALL'S twelve-year administration, the number of dedicated temples rose from fifteen to thirty-six, with construction begun on five more and another six announced.[1] Before 1974, President Kimball had not been closely identified with temple work. His areas of focus included the Lamanites, missionary work, and Church finances, but aside from one special assignment, he had not had responsibility for temples or temple work. He was in the temple weekly, of course, for meetings with other leaders. He performed numerous temple weddings. He and Camilla belonged to a group of friends who met for dinner and attended the temple together monthly. The temple was an important part of his religious life, but after he became President the temple appears to have taken on a special focus for him, illustrated most dramatically by the burst of temple building.

---

1. President Kimball predicted in 1979: "I think we will have hundreds of temples. But not while I live, and it's too bad, too." Vigorous temple building continued under his successors. During Ezra Taft Benson's eight and a half years as President, nine temples begun or projected during the Kimball years were built and dedicated. In addition, President Benson announced plans for seven more.

President Gordon B. Hinckley announced in October 1997 general conference that, in areas where Church membership would not likely grow enough to support a traditional temple, the Church would build small temples. They would operate with a local member as temple president and function according to demand, perhaps one or two days a week. These facilities would not have laundries or kitchens, would share parking with a stake center, and could be expanded if more space was needed. The first three of these small temples were to be built in Anchorage, Alaska; Monticello, Utah; and the Mormon colonies in Chihuahua, Mexico. President Hinckley set and achieved as an objective having a total of one hundred dedicated temples by the end of the year 2000.

The First Presidency considered decisions about temples to be their province. When Paul H. Dunn was area administrator of the Southern United States, he told President Kimball about the strong desire of the people in the Southern states for a temple. He said they had even identified two possible locations. President Kimball responded, simply and straightforwardly, "Temples belong to the First Presidency." Elder Dunn understood the message: "Don't call us; we'll call you."

In June 1974, when President Kimball was to speak at Snow College's commencement exercises in Ephraim, Utah, he arrived with almost two hours to spare. He asked the driver to drive on to the temple in Manti, only a few miles farther. No one at the temple expected him, and when he arrived, they scurried around. He inspected the building from top to bottom, noting kindly that the office safe needed repair, the cafeteria could use renovation, and some areas should have more restricted access.

President Kimball involved himself directly in temple plans. When William Grant Bangerter became executive director of the Temple Department in 1980, he found that President Kimball called him in frequently, sometimes almost daily. The President wanted to know even small details about the groundbreaking, construction, and dedication of new temples and often offered suggestions or made decisions. For example, the São Paulo Temple originally was to have a simple baptismal font like those in stake centers, but President Kimball asked the architect, Emil Fetzer, "Can we manage a full baptismal font, with oxen?" The Atlanta Temple was well under construction when President Kimball reversed the First Presidency's decision to save costs by building without a tower. "I feel bad that there is no tower," he told Fetzer. "Is it possible still to add a tower?" Fetzer diverted the builder to working on other parts of the building while he planned a tower.

Temple building involved long-range planning and careful financial consideration.[2] Even before Spencer became President, temples in São

---

2. When Emil Fetzer persuaded President Kimball that a proposed Atlanta temple site was unsuitable, he received an annoyed phone call from an apostle who had helped select the site. The next call came from Spencer, apologizing for having let Fetzer's name slip in a discussion of the decision to seek another site. The apostle later accepted the reasons Fetzer urged (land conformation, lack of services and transportation in the area, and need for adjacent property that was not for sale) and apologized.

Paulo and Tokyo had been discussed.[3] The first thought was of a compromise, to build in Brazil a small "endowment house." But in January 1974, immediately after President Kimball took office, Church architect Emil Fetzer was sent to find a site for a traditional temple.

Modern construction technology and income from a growing Church membership made this boom in temple building possible. The prospect or presence of a temple also encouraged greater faithfulness in tithe paying.[4] In affluent areas a large part of the building cost (and in the case of the Jordan River Temple, the full cost[5]) was carried locally.

The First Presidency issued in October 1975 a policy statement encouraging people to contribute to the building of new temples rather than to raise funds for individuals to travel great distances to existing temples for their endowments and sealings.[6]

At the sesquicentennial general conference in April 1980, President Kimball announced seven new temples, all but one of them very small. In fall 1980, Emil B. Fetzer mentioned to President Kimball that he would be retiring as Church architect in January, when he turned sixty-five. President Kimball expressed surprise and asked whether Fetzer would do a few special projects for him before he retired: complete the Jordan River Temple, then under construction; remodel the Assembly Hall on Temple Square; and design the new temples to be built in Samoa, Tonga, Tahiti, and Australia. Later President Kimball added the temple in East Germany to the list. Fetzer retired at seventy.

After the Jordan River Temple was dedicated in 1981, it quickly became one of the busiest in the Church. The Salt Lake Temple, less than fifteen miles away, maintained its level of activity, supporting the

---

3. As early as 1964, Spencer had urged a temple in South America. Under President Harold B. Lee's direction, Elder Gordon B. Hinckley, as chairman of the Temple Committee, looked in May 1973 for a temple site in São Paulo.

4. Alan Blodgett, former Church financial officer, said, "I have always believed that the temples (in affluent areas) never cost the Church anything, rather, they increased tithing and other donations far beyond their cost. . . . The faithfulness of the Saints is astounding, and one of the most faith-promoting stories of all time."

5. The fifteen-acre site, concrete, sixty altar cloths, wall coverings, locks, concrete, organ, chandelier, sod, trees, flagpole, other materials, and cash came from thousands of people as gifts.

6. A bus with forty-nine Saints going from Guatemala to the Mesa Arizona Temple was hit by a truck, killing one and injuring several more. Spencer, already in Mesa, met with survivors. Twelve such groups had already come from Guatemala in 1975, and thirty were scheduled for 1976.

With Betty Ford at an open house before the dedication of the Washington D.C. Temple, October 1974.

view that easier access to a temple increased the faithfulness of members in doing temple work.[7]

Two days before the April 1981 general conference, President Kimball announced nine more temples—Lima, Seoul, Chicago, Dallas, Guatemala City, Johannesburg, Manila, Frankfurt,[8] and Stockholm.

Construction of so substantial a structure as a new temple often brought objections. Neighbors were often concerned about lights, traffic, and alterations to the character of the neighborhood. Simply the fact that Mormons were building the structure sometimes triggered anti-Mormon reactions. For example, the site of the Denver Temple, first announced in March 1982, shifted twice because of objections. A third site was found, and ground was finally broken in May 1984. Even then, opponents urged residents to boycott the temple open house.

Despite the objections, the chance to go through a temple before it closed to the public drew huge crowds of both the curious and the

---

7. The rate of temple work (endowments per member) remained relatively constant from 1965 to 1980, despite the fact that the greatest growth in membership was in areas where no temple was available.

8. It was four years before a suitable location in or near Frankfurt would be procured. Of fourteen potential sites, eleven were rejected by the government. The ultimate site was an abandoned noodle factory on five acres in Friedrichsdorf.

receptive. The media publicity and visitors' favorable reactions to what they saw and heard greatly aided regular missionary work in those areas.

Each temple had its own story. The first one dedicated by President Kimball was in the nation's capital.

WASHINGTON D.C. TEMPLE

In September 1974 the Washington D.C. Temple, rising ethereally above the Beltway, stood ready for occupancy. Although begun six years earlier, under President McKay, it fell to President Kimball to lay a symbolic cornerstone in the presence of three hundred invited guests—public officials, Church leaders, and news representatives. In connection with the occasion, the Tabernacle Choir sang four concerts in Washington's Kennedy Center. The Kimballs attended the first concert, accompanied by President and Mrs. Gerald Ford.

While in the capital, President Kimball accepted an invitation to offer the prayer at the day's opening of the U.S. Senate. When the time arrived for the prayer, only a handful of senators were present. Someone apologized for the small attendance, but Spencer answered, unperturbed, "That's all right. I wasn't going to pray to them, anyway."

Seven weeks of public tours then began. Before the dedication in November, three quarters of a million visitors had examined the beautiful building, a record for prededication visits to any temple.

In November 1974, President Kimball returned to Washington, D.C., to give final inspection to the temple and to preside at ten dedicatory sessions. His dedicatory prayer contained words that would be appreciated more and more as the years went by:

"Father, we are concerned with the political world of today and that nations seem to need only the lighting of a match to bring war and desolation and destruction. Bless, we pray thee, the leaders of nations, that they may rule wisely and righteously and give thy people freedom to worship thee in truth and righteousness. Stay the powers, our Father, that would bring us to the brink of annihilation.

"Bless all people, our Father, that they may prosper, but not more than their faith can stand.

" . . . There are national gates which seemingly need to be unlocked and doors that need to be opened, and hearts of kings, presidents, emperors, and ministers, which need to be softened, that they may

Accepting a gold medal for heroism from Oscar Novaco as a contribution to building the temple in Brazil, June 1975.

permit the gospel to be taken to their people.

" . . . Bless the missionaries on whom the sun never sets, that nothing will prevail against them . . . and bless especially, our Father, the children of Thy people in overseas countries, that they may devote their sons to this holy work."

Two weeks after the dedication, Wilfred and Marylee Kimball (not known to Spencer) traveled from Enid, Oklahoma, to be sealed, having been misinformed that the temple was open. They wanted particularly to be sealed before their baby's imminent birth, and they had just enough money to make the trip. When they arrived in Washington, they learned to their dismay that the temple was open only for baptisms, not endowments or sealings, because the veil had not yet been installed.

When they met with temple president Edward Drury and explained their situation, he tried to reach the Church Temple Committee but could not. Finally he called President Kimball directly. When Spencer heard the story, he was greatly touched. He responded, "Don't let them go without the sealing ordinance. What are temples for?"

The temple staff then worked until 2:00 A.M. installing the veil, and the first, special endowment session and sealing occurred the next day.[9]

---

9. A week before their trip, Wilfred woke one night to a voice saying that he and his wife, Marylee, would be the first to be sealed in the Washington Temple. He assumed this reflected his own preoccupation with their plans, but again in Washington, the night before their appointment with the temple president, Wilfred awakened to the same voice with the same message.

São Paulo Brazil Temple

Only a few months later, President Kimball announced the next temple, to be built in São Paulo, Brazil. This was the first outside the U.S. since the London Temple was dedicated in 1958.

President Kimball traveled to São Paulo in March 1977 to lay the cornerstone. Elder James E. Faust hosted the President's party at his home. After dinner Elder Faust brought out a velvet bag and emptied its contents. Out came wedding bands, diamond rings, brooches, a gold medal awarded for bravery, and even a gold dental bridge. "These will be sold to raise money for the temple because that's what the people wanted," he explained. At first the contributions by members in the countries served by this temple to their one-third share of the cost had been slow coming in. But when President Kimball reportedly instructed Elder Faust, "Tell those folks that if they don't want a temple, we'll build it somewhere else," the people responded. Their President had asked for sacrifice, and members gave generously.

Despite inflation ranging from 40 to 600 percent a year, members raised the needed amount. A young couple gave the money they had saved for furniture. Others worked two jobs so they could contribute. A widow donated her home and moved to rented quarters. Families gave money saved from food, transportation, and children's allowances. One missionary asked his parents to sell his only valuable possession, a microscope. In 1978 the temple was completed.

Tokyo Temple

The next temple to be announced was in Tokyo. Search for a temple site in Tokyo was delegated to Church architect Emil B. Fetzer. He looked at possible sites ranging in cost from $2.5 million to $10 million. Then it occurred to him that if the Tokyo Third Ward chapel were replaced by a stake center and a new mission home, the property of the present mission headquarters could be used for the temple. President Kimball and his counselors approved his plan. Members of the Tokyo Temple district, including all the Far East countries, pledged $1 million toward construction, and they raised the money even before architectural drawings were complete.

Leading the vote in favor of building a temple in Tokyo, 1975.

Seven dedication sessions were held in October 1980 for this first temple in a non-Christian nation. The initial session, with 860 attending, was held in the temple. The other six convened in the Tokyo stake center, where many more people could be seated. The temple could accommodate only a small choir, but to Elder Mark E. Petersen "it seemed that there was a far larger choir singing than was present." Those who wept included the forty choir members, who had to sing "through their tears." As President Kimball offered the dedicatory prayer at the first session, Elder Yoshihiko Kikuchi says he heard and saw spirits and experienced an indescribable feeling of joy.

The sixty visitors from Utah stayed in a hotel about fifty minutes away from the stake center. On the bus one day, President Kimball began talking to the driver as Elder Kikuchi translated.

"Are you LDS?"

"No."

"Would you like to know more?" They conversed, and when they reached the stake center, President Kimball invited the driver to attend the dedicatory service even though he was not a Church member and, of course, had no recommend. The driver attended three sessions, tears streaking his face.

After one session friends led a blind man to a rope barrier along which President Kimball walked, shaking hands. As the man sensed the prophet approaching, he held out his hand, and President Kimball took it. Neither spoke as they embraced.

Yukus Yokiyoshi Inouye, first counselor in the new temple presidency, felt self-conscious about how much time Spencer spent with him and how Spencer held his hands and hugged him. Just before setting him apart, President Kimball said, "You're going to run that temple," a statement that surprised Brother Inouye. He did in fact later run the temple for a substantial period because temple president Dwayne N. Andersen was ill for several months.

Mexico City

When the Presidency felt ready to build a temple in Mexico City, they gave the matter no publicity until it could be considered by the Mexican stake presidents. As with the São Paulo Temple, they did not want the leaders to feel that they were being asked to rubber-stamp an already-made decision. President Kimball announced the temple in April general conference, 1976.

A high councilor in Mexico City summed up many Mexican members' feelings about a temple in their midst: "When President Kimball said years ago that we would have a temple here, we never doubted it, but we could hardly imagine being part of it ourselves. We felt the temple would be completed in another generation."

Mexican law added complications. It required that title to all church buildings be held by the government, and it required that all government buildings be open to the public. After the Mexico City area conference in February 1977, President Kimball conferred with Minister of Interior and Education Reyes, who had jurisdiction over church property issues. President Kimball found the reception "very formal and rather cool." After a few minutes the minister stood up and abruptly terminated the interview.

The next week President Kimball again flew to Mexico City with President Romney and David Kennedy for a fifteen-minute audience with President Jose Lopez Portillo. As at all such meetings, President Kimball explained to President Portillo that the Church teaches its people to be loyal citizens. He further explained how the proposed temple related to the Church's belief about eternal family relationships. On the subject of limited entry, he emphasized that not even all Mormons could enter. President Portillo became so engaged in the discussion that the meeting went far over its allotted time. Finally he said, "Of course, officially I can do nothing for you, but, understanding what you are doing for our people in Mexico, unofficially I shall do all in my power to see that you can proceed."

Outside the presidential office, Señor Reyes, the Minister of Interior and Education who had been so cool the previous week, waited with the other cabinet ministers for a cabinet meeting with President Portillo. The waiting men paced up and down, puffing cigars. As President Kimball and his companions left the presidential office, Señor Reyes, seeing how President Portillo received the visitors, went out of his way to greet them warmly.

An accommodation was later achieved. The government kept technical title to the temple, but as a practical matter access could be limited to holders of temple recommends.

Among six alternative plans presented to the First Presidency by Church architect Emil Fetzer was a temple exterior that used Mayan details and proportions. President Kimball and his counselors smiled and nodded. The President put his arms around Fetzer and said, "I love that design and I love you."

Freiberg, East Germany

After many other temples were announced, the one with the most complex background rose in Germany. In 1968, Elder Thomas S. Monson met behind the Iron Curtain with a small group of Saints in Görlitz in the German Democratic Republic (GDR). He felt impressed to promise them that if they lived worthily "every blessing any member of the Church enjoys in any other country will be yours." At that time the GDR had no wards or stakes, no patriarch, no formal missionary activities,[10] no temple, and no freedom from the ever-present monitoring by the secret police.

The promise was gradually fulfilled. J. Henry Burkhardt led the Church and its 4,600 members in GDR for many years. The government regularly held him to account for the actions of Latter-day Saints in his country and for anti-Communist statements of Church leaders in the United States.

---

10. After the war, full-time local missionaries served until 1961, when the government made it practically impossible. The Germany Dresden Mission was organized in 1969 to give administrative structure to the Church in the German Democratic Republic. The Dresden Mission ended in June 1984 when all of the GDR was covered by two stakes. The mission was reopened in 1989 when outside missionaries could enter.

The Freiberg Germany Temple open house, June 1985.

In April 1975, President Kimball met with Burkhardt in Salt Lake City and expressed his own philosophy: that the world was changed most effectively when individuals changed. He challenged the local leader:

"Now, Brother Burkhardt, if you want to see a change of things in East Germany, it must begin with you personally. It must begin with you because you are the leader of the Saints there, and you must have a change of heart, which means you must force yourself to befriend the Communists. You cannot hold any grudges against them. You must change your whole outlook and attitude."

President Kimball advised him to go to the government and ask, "What must we do to get full rights to operate as a church?"

It took time and personal struggle, but Elder Burkhardt was able to change his attitude.[11] He then witnessed miracle after miracle—greater respect for the Church, more frequent granting of requests, and ultimately, permission to build a temple.

In 1978 Elder Burkhardt was seeking to persuade the East German government to allow six couples to travel to Switzerland to be sealed in the temple. It was hoped that when these couples kept their promise to

---

11. Henry Burkhardt indicated that changing his approach was the hardest thing he had ever done, but it worked. In the 1970s a few individuals were allowed to leave the country briefly to attend general conference.

return, the government would allow others to go. However, the government refused to allow both husband and wife to leave the country at the same time; only one could go. That meant they could be endowed as individuals but not sealed as a couple. During this same time, President Kimball and his counselors considered authorizing sealings in East Germany outside the temple, with or without prior endowment, as had occurred in the previous century when travel was difficult. A study by Elder G. Homer Durham had found ample precedent.

In May 1978, when Burkhardt broached the question again, the German officials made a suggestion, "Instead of going to Switzerland, why don't you just have your own temple here?" Later Elder Monson reported the statement to the First Presidency,[12] and in just a few weeks, he returned to Germany to show local Church leaders drawings of a possible temple. President Kimball and his counselors were closely involved at every stage. Because of the unsettled situation, only they and a few others necessarily involved knew about the proposal.

Brother Burkhardt approached the German government with the sketches. He reported to Elder Monson in March 1979 that the officials were pleased with the plans so long as all the funds to pay for the

---

12. The Church leaders were still pursuing the six-couples plan. Building a temple in a Communist country posed many uncertainties.

building were raised outside the country. The prospect of hard currency coming into the GDR improved cooperation markedly.

The GDR construction protocol was confusing and capricious. One applied for permission to build, and if the application was not denied, one simply went ahead. The government retained power to stop a project without cause at any point by saying that it had never given approval. After submitting its application, the Church received no answer and considered the application approved. It then began the process of obtaining land, a difficult project that took three years. In February 1982 a site was secured at Freiberg.[13] President Kimball and his counselors quickly approved the building of a small temple and a stake center, and in October 1982 they publicly announced the construction of this first temple in a Communist country.

Design was the next hurdle. State architects repeatedly rejected Fetzer's proposals. They in turn proposed unacceptable designs, all of which had the look of German Lutheran churches. On several trips to Germany, Fetzer showed twelve designs in all, and all were vetoed. After the twelfth veto, as Fetzer and the chief German architect crossed the plaza to lunch, Fetzer asked, "Isn't there one of these twelve that will do? If not, why?"

Looking about to be sure he was out of earshot, the chief whispered, "They look too Russian."

Fetzer then said he had one more design to show. The German architects liked it, saying that with its slate roof and arch in the tower, "it looks German," not "monumental" like the Russian buildings.[14] This was the design finally approved and adopted.

Church leaders knew that getting the temple film into the GDR posed a problem. Religious material was routinely confiscated during searches at the border. Just before Emil Fetzer made a trip to Germany to supervise construction, two men from the Temple Department came into Fetzer's office in Salt Lake City and put on his desk six copies of the temple video, three in English and three in German. They asked Fetzer to take them to East Germany.

---

13. The Church first sought permission to build in Karl-Marx-Stadt, where the largest branch of the Church was located, but local officials insisted that the building be located in much smaller Freiberg.

14. The temple was later doubled in size and an angel added.

"I can't do that," he said. "Every time I cross the border they go through my luggage with a fine-toothed comb. If the temple films were confiscated I would not want to be responsible."

The two men replied, "The Lord will bless you," and left.

With misgivings, Fetzer put the videotapes in an attache case and flew to Berlin, where he and a companion went to passport and customs control, a large warehouselike building divided down the center by an iron fence about eight feet high, with entry gates every so often. The serpentine line moved very slowly. Each person going through the one open gate spread out his luggage on big tables for inspection. As Fetzer got closer to the gate, he asked himself with growing anxiety, "What if the tapes are discovered? Should I back out while I can?" But the temple would need the films in order to operate.

As he passed along the fence, his eyes met those of a large woman in uniform. She opened a gate and said to him "Kommen Sie durch." Fetzer and his companion went through the gate into the area with tables. Many customs officials stood around. He expected one of them to ask him to open his luggage. But no one said a word. It was as though he and his companion were invisible. The two men walked deliberately along and past the tables, through the room, and out the door into East Berlin.

When the Freiberg Temple opened to the public for prededication tours in June 1985, many visitors came not out of religious interest but to see a beautifully wrought structure. Three thousand visitors came on the first day, a Saturday. The next day 7,000 came. Some people waited as long as six hours. Each morning when the gates were opened, a crowd was waiting. Some had slept in their cars. Even in rain and thundershowers they stood, soaked and shivering, pregnant or in wheelchairs, holding children in their arms, and huddling under umbrellas or newspapers. The visiting hours expanded to 8:00 A.M. to 10:30 P.M. One day, because of the enormous crowd, the gates stayed open until 1:30 A.M. During sixteen days, some 90,000 passed through the chapel and the temple before it was dedicated in June 1985 by President Hinckley.

TEMPLE-RELATED TRAVEL

In 1981 President Kimball made the last of his temple-related travels. In February he made a thirteen-day trip to the South Pacific, where he broke ground for temples in Tahiti, Tonga, and Western Samoa. In Tonga, King Taufaʻahau Tupou IV sent his private car and chauffeur to meet President Kimball, and the king himself attended the ceremony dedicating the temple site. Out of respect for the king, all sun shields came down, despite the intense heat. President Kimball presided at a missionary meeting the next day, where 235 of 247 missionaries were native Tongans. In Western Samoa, four thousand Saints attended the groundbreaking, ignoring torrential rain during the service. Even people with umbrellas got soaked. The chief of state,

Spencer and Camilla at the São Paulo Brazil Temple.

Malietoa Tanumafil II, attended. When President Kimball and he left the protected stand to turn the first shovels of dirt, the rain stopped.

In March, President Kimball broke ground for the temple in Atlanta. Georgia governor George Busbee attended.

In May, President Kimball flew to Chile to break ground for the Santiago Chile Temple. Although no one knew it, this would be his last trip. Only ten days earlier Dr. Nelson had installed a pacemaker for his aging heart, and there had been some doubt about whether he would be well enough to make the trip. But he was determined to go and kept up a relentless pace.

The morning of the groundbreaking ceremony brought an intense storm, but by 5:45 A.M., fifty people had already gathered for the 10:00 A.M. service. They wanted to be close enough to see the prophet well. They stood stoically in the mud as rain poured down and thunder crashed. Before the service a choir sang, its members soaked by the cold, steady rain. At last the meeting began. The leaders sat on a dais under a protective canopy and spoke to a crowd of more than six thousand. President Kimball offered to shorten the meeting, scheduled for ninety minutes, but the local leaders said the people would be disappointed.

When President Kimball stood to speak, the rain stopped, immediately and completely. A sunburst warmed the crowd. Umbrellas came down, and many of the people whose view had been completely blocked could now see.

At the conclusion of the President's address, the dignitaries stood on a mat and turned spades of mud to mark the start of construction. Before they had finished, the drenching rain began again in full force.

With President Kimball's decline in health, no further new temples were announced. It waited for Gordon B. Hinckley's presidency for a new season of temple building to begin, characterized by a large number of temples, many of them very small.

36

TEMPLE PRACTICES AND FAMILY HISTORY

"This work for the dead is constantly on my mind."

FOR INCREASING NUMBERS OF MEMBERS, talk about receiving the endowment and sealing was no longer an abstraction because all worthy members could participate fully and because temples were being built closer to where they lived. Indeed, the number of endowments performed in all temples increased during President Kimball's administration from 2.5 million during 1973 to 4.9 million during 1985.

ELIGIBILITY TO PARTICIPATE

In addition to the construction of new buildings, President Kimball addressed several other issues in his urgency to push temple work forward.

In 1978, the revelation on priesthood made men and women of every race eligible to receive the endowment and sealing ordinances. Previously those of African ancestry could participate only in baptism for the dead, although black children could be sealed to non-black adoptive parents. The privilege of the endowment was extended to an additional group of members in 1985. That year a policy change made the endowment available to a Church member married to a non-endowed spouse who gave consent, whether or not the spouse was a member.[1]

---

1. During President Benson's administration, policy permitted the sealing of a deceased woman to more than one husband on the grounds that she should have a choice of which marriage would be perpetuated by the sealing ordinance.

With granddaughter Paula, whose marriage sealing was the last one Spencer performed.

Temple recommend questions were first formalized into a list in about 1922. They have changed over time to emphasize matters of current concern,[2] to make explicit what had previously been assumed, to make evasive answers more difficult, and to discourage local leaders from injecting their personal criteria into interviews.[3] Such was also the case during the Kimball years. Instructions issued to bishops and stake presidents in 1976 added new questions and revised others to be more specific about the candidate's honesty, any major transgressions that had not been previously confessed and adjusted, and acceptance of the Church President as the only earthly holder of all priesthood keys.

In 1979 two more questions were added: whether there is "anything in your conduct relating to members of your family which is not in harmony with the teachings of the Church" and whether the applicant considered himself or herself "worthy in every way" to receive a recommend. In 1985 candidates were for the first time asked specifically, "Do you believe in God, the Eternal Father, in his Son, Jesus Christ, and in the Holy Ghost; and do you have a firm testimony of the restored gospel?"[4]

Although the First Presidency strongly encouraged members to attend the temple often, they disapproved of quotas and issued a

---

2. For example, bishops were instructed in 1976 to conduct especially searching interviews with the children of apostates, to assure their orthodoxy.

3. In 1976 bishops were reminded that long hair on men or tattoos were not by themselves reasons to deny a recommend unless they were so extreme as to be "unbecoming in the house of the Lord." In 2000, President Hinckley specifically decried tattoos and body piercings.

4. In 1996 an additional question asked about a testimony of the atonement of Christ.

statement to that effect in March 1979: "Leaders encourage . . . ; however, leaders should not set quotas." Temple participation should be voluntary, not coerced.

Some decisions about temple matters were made by the President. In June 1975 President Kimball met with a former stake president who had been excommunicated for adultery. He gave the man encouragement about rebaptism and eventual restoration of priesthood and temple blessings, but he said he could not foresee the man's ever being sealed to his present wife because of their joint responsibility for breaking up his first marriage. The *General Handbook of Instructions* in 1976 formalized this policy as a rule.[5]

Until 1977 men and women who had been sealed and later divorced required First Presidency authorization to receive a temple recommend. That year the policy was changed: First Presidency approval was needed only if the divorced applicant had been guilty of sexual transgression. In 1983 full responsibility for deciding worthiness in such cases was shifted to the bishops and stake presidents. The Church President remained ultimately responsible for acting on requests for sealing cancellations and restoration of blessings after excommunication, but President Kimball assigned preliminary review of these requests to other General Authorities.

TEMPLE PRACTICE

Special prayer circles had existed for generations. Local leadership groups, such as a stake presidency and high council, had previously sometimes convened prayer circles in a temple or in a dedicated room in a chapel or stake building. But in May 1978, President Kimball, together with his counselors, instructed leaders to discontinue the practice; the only prayer circles that should be conducted would be those that were part of the temple endowment or part of General Authority meetings.[6]

The First Presidency also addressed some temple-goers' practice of kneeling in private prayer in the celestial room, an area not arranged for private devotions. The 1983 *General Handbook of Instructions* stated that

5. The policy in the current handbook is that applicants in these circumstances must wait at least five years.

6. From the Nauvoo period to 1929, there had been private prayer circles, usually established by apostles, meeting regularly, often weekly or monthly, for united prayer.

Presenting President Ronald Reagan his mother's genealogy, Washington, D.C., March 1981.

members could "remain briefly in the celestial room and meditate in silent prayer," but should otherwise pray in their own homes.

Two major changes in garment styles also took place. A 1975 decision allowed temple patrons to use the same "new" style in the temple that had been used for daily wear since 1923, replacing the nineteenth-century style that extended to wrists, ankles, and neck. In 1979 the First Presidency authorized a two-piece garment as an alternative to the traditional one-piece garment.

EMPHASIS ON GENEALOGY AND FAMILY HISTORY

Temple work had a ritual aspect and a research aspect, linking families together. As an apostle, Spencer had set an example for Church members by working diligently on his own family history. In 1943, when he moved to Salt Lake City, he revitalized the languishing Heber C. Kimball family organization, supported an annual family reunion, republished the Orson F. Whitney biography of his grandfather Heber, gathered family history, and promoted genealogy research within the Kimball family.

Spencer stressed repeatedly the importance of temple work for the living and the dead. In 1977 he commented, "I feel the same sense of urgency about temple work for the dead as I do about missionary work. . . . This work for the dead is constantly on my mind."[7] In connection with the completion of the Washington D.C. Temple, he declared, "The day is coming, not too far ahead of us, when all the temples on this earth will be going night and day . . . because of the importance of the work and the great number of people who lie asleep in eternity and who are craving, needing, the blessings we can bring them."

President Kimball had long wished for official recognition of two revelations dealing with the state of the dead, for they gave added significance to genealogy work. The first, a vision received by Joseph Smith in January 1836, revealed that those who die without knowledge of the gospel but who would have received it had they had opportunity, will be judged by "the desire of their hearts." The second records the October 1918 vision of Joseph F. Smith about preaching the gospel to the dead. His vision showed that those souls who had had no adequate opportunity in mortality could be saved by repentance and by temple ordinances performed by surrogates. In 1976 these two visions were canonized as sections 137 and 138 of the Doctrine and Covenants, the first additions to that book since the 1890 Manifesto on plural marriage.

For 1977 stake conferences, General Authorities were instructed to teach Church members to write personal histories, support family organizations, complete genealogy research for at least four generations, and perform temple ordinances regularly. This drive was aided by a non-Church stimulus, the publication of Alex Haley's book *Roots* in 1975 and its dramatization as a television miniseries in January 1977. A "genealogy mania" swept the nation.

The Church had since 1938 assumed responsibility for microfilming records and making them available so that members and others could

---

7. In Latter-day Saint theology, ordinances essential for the living have equal importance for the dead. They can be performed vicariously by the living, both for one's own family and for others who have passed on.

do genealogy research without traveling to far places. To make these films accessible, in 1964 the Church started putting branch libraries in stake centers. Through these libraries, researchers were able to use microfilms borrowed from the central library. By 1976 there were nearly 200 libraries, and by 1985 there were 640 in thirty-one countries.

In 1977 Elder Boyd K. Packer and Ted Power of the Genealogical Society visited a contingent of nine archivists and scholars in Jerusalem to ask for permission to microfilm records in Israel. As Power later reported, Elder Packer candidly explained the Church would use the records to provide vicarious Christian baptism for deceased Jews who might, in the spirit world, accept it. An immediate uproar ensued until one rabbi, a university teacher of comparative religion, interjected, "You'll never make my grandfather, who is a rabbi, into a Mormon. . . . So why are we afraid? If we're afraid, we ought to join your Church. If we're not afraid we ought to let you use your money and help us pre-serve our records." The requested access was later granted.[8]

In 1980 the Genealogical Department, under the direction of the First Presidency and the Quorum of the Twelve, convened its second World Conference on Records (the first was in 1969). The program this time focused on pedigrees and family history. With about 11,500 participants from thirty nations attending, the conference proved hugely successful and cemented the Church's leadership in the field of family history.

In opening the conference, President Kimball announced plans to construct directly west of Temple Square a new genealogy library and a museum of Church history and art. When dedicated in October 1985, the genealogy building was said by library director David Mayfield to be "undoubtedly the largest, most modern and best-equipped genealog-ical library in the world."[9]

In 1962 the Church had begun to identify individuals from documents such as parish records and make their names available for vicarious temple work without requiring linkage to a particular family line. By 1975 this name-extraction program was providing three

---

8. In 1995 the Church agreed to discontinue vicarious baptism of deceased Jews who had died in the Holocaust unless requested by descendants who are members of the LDS Church.

9. In 1985 the library contained 160,000 volumes plus microfilm equivalent to another 5.5 million bound volumes.

quarters of the names for temple ordinances. In 1978 the Church shifted responsibility for this name-extraction program to the stakes. In 1985, 841 stakes involved 12,000 people in the assignment and produced nearly ten million names.

After a time it appeared that people were viewing the name-extraction program as a justification for halting their own ancestral research beyond four generations. Therefore, at the April 1980 general conference, President Kimball reaffirmed each person's responsibility to complete his four-generation assignment.[10] Individual research showed resurgence, and by 1985 the combination of extraction and family research provided enough names to supply current temple needs and create a backlog.

In December 1983, the Church genealogical department announced a family registry program as a means to bring together people working on the same family lines so they could coordinate their efforts. The Personal Ancestral File (PAF) computer program was introduced by the Church in 1984, and soon branch libraries in stake centers began making available for use compact discs that contained vast amounts of genealogy information. Family history work became much more accessible to everyone.

---

10. In 1976, Spencer urged that individuals be taught their personal responsibility to provide names and not rely on others. "Let us reinstitute the four-generation program . . . and then impress upon them the necessity of carrying on back through other generations as far as they can go. . . . It is imperative."

COMPLETING A LIFETIME OF SERVICE

37

The Struggle for Health

Suffering contributes to sainthood.

Anyone who lives long is likely to have a history of problems along the way, but Spencer W. Kimball's list of physical woes is much longer and more serious than most, ranging from brain surgery at the top to swollen feet at the bottom, with throat cancer, open heart surgery, ulcers, and prostatitis in between. A lifetime of health problems both tested and developed him. Patience and the ability to endure pain stoically proved to be among his strongest character traits.[1]

Despite the great pain he suffered periodically from various ailments and surgeries, he was slow to take medications, even aspirin. Among his belongings when he died were several old prescriptions for Darvon that he had not filled. He once said, "Suffering contributes to sainthood in people. I think the suffering of Christ as He neared the cross and as He died on the cross did not bring Him harm, but gave Him opportunity to become perfect [in the sense of having completed his mission]."

In spite of his history, when Spencer came to the presidency his heart surgeon assured him, "Your heart is better than it has been for years . . . you may consider this new assignment without undue anxiety about your health."

Spencer enjoyed reasonably good health for the next several energetic years. On his eightieth birthday in March 1975, he said, with a little bravado, "I can't believe that I am eighty years old. . . . I don't feel eighty, and I don't think in those terms. I feel like a boy." Even so, he continued to suffer from minor problems. He had skin cancers removed.

---

1. Jeffrey Holland mused in a talk at BYU, "Is it wrong to wonder if President Kimball has become what he is not only despite his trouble but because of it?"

He had pain in his thigh. His hearing declined, and his ears felt as though they had water in them all the time. He tried a hearing aid, but it proved to be more annoying than beneficial.

A plaque on Spencer's desk read, "Do It." This was a standard he held to with amazing determination despite constant obstacles. It was a work style that challenged his health. Dr. Wilkinson observed:

"He once came to me with the physical complaint that he was very tired. In trying to physically assess this complaint, I really could not find any specific new problem to explain this unusual fatigue. I then asked him if he would tell me about his schedule.

"He told me that it was his custom to arise each morning at 4:30. From 4:30 until 6:30 in the morning was his quiet hour. This was when he read the scriptures and petitioned the Lord in prayer. It was the time of day he had some privacy without interruption and could do some writing. Then, about 6:30 A.M., he would dress, have a very light breakfast, and arrive at his office by 7:00 A.M. While the composition of the days varied, depending on which day of the week it was, each was filled with appointments, committee meetings, and other activities, so that he rarely left the office before 5:30 or 6:00 P.M. He would then return to his home, have a light supper with his wife, and go into his study, where he would work for the next three hours, until about 10:00 in the evening, laboring on problems that he simply had not had the time to get to during the day. Well, if you count the hours from 4:30 A.M. until 10:00 P.M., you'll find he had a seventeen-and-a-half hour work routine."

1977

One morning in March 1977, after four years of grinding schedule, Spencer awoke and found his vision blurred. That day he gave a dedicatory address for new facilities at Utah Technical College in Provo, and he stumbled embarrassingly over his text. He did not know how much the audience noticed, but he felt depressed about his problems reading. General conference was approaching, and he wondered how he would manage to give all his scheduled talks. He tried having his talks typed all in capital letters a quarter of an inch high and found he was able to read the words with less difficulty. From then on all his talks were prepared in this large type.

Severe degenerative arthritis developed in his back, with sciatica in

Waving to daughter Olive Beth in the Tabernacle Choir.

his left leg and considerable low back pain that made travel distressing. He obtained a corset brace to support his back but disliked it and wore it only when the pain was intense.

During a meeting of the Church Board of Education in September, he suffered a sudden attack of severe dizziness. He whispered to President Tanner, "I'm in trouble." The meeting halted, and two men carried him, still seated in his chair, into his office and then to a lounge, where he vomited repeatedly. Dr. Wilkinson came immediately and found him ashen, sweaty, dizzy, and severely nauseated. His blood pressure was dangerously low.

Dr. Wilkinson took Spencer to the hospital in an ambulance and began tests. Dr. Nelson came directly and found President Kimball barely conscious. Examination showed no obvious explanation for the illness, and laboratory results were not yet available. When Dr. Nelson explained this to Spencer, he opened his eyes and asked, "Would you give me a blessing?" Dr. Nelson sealed the anointing, and he later reported:

"I felt the power of the Lord surge through me, prompting me to pronounce a blessing on his prophet that now was not the time for his life to be terminated. He was to continue to live! He would recover fully. . . . In fact, he would recover before the diagnosis was made and would not miss a single appointment of significance. . . .

"I knew that the words pronounced were not products of my own thinking."

By the next day Spencer began to feel better. Even though the doctors still had no diagnosis, that evening he returned home to sleep. At eight o'clock the next morning, he was back at work and, despite the concerns of his coworkers, he traveled that day to Cardston, Alberta, to install a new temple presidency. As Dr. Nelson had promised, he missed not a single appointment of significance.

1978

Camilla had been less prone to illness over the years, but a physical examination in August 1978, when she was nearly eighty-four, showed she had a hernia, an incipient ulcer, disintegrating vertebrae, and a low blood count. She and Spencer joked about "the old machines wearing out" and about the marvelous view of the Salt Lake Valley they would have from their waiting hillside cemetery plot. They both had a horror of dwindling usefulness, preferring a sudden death to cumulating disabilities. They were well aware of the last years of other Presidents whose physical strength and memory faded, and they hoped to be spared such diminishment. In her darker moments, Camilla wept at the thought of the two of them dragging on and on in the glare of publicity. Spencer dreaded especially the possibility that at some point he might not be able to pull his full share of the load and more.

Spencer felt frustrated at each new hindrance to his ability to carry on vigorously and resisted each limitation until it was forced on him. He had once written of President McKay, "He was always composed. He was not frightened [just] because he could not do everything. He accepted [the physical limitation of his last years] as it came." Spencer could not decline in health quite so gracefully.

1979

In July 1979, Spencer and Camilla went to Monterey, California, for the annual Beneficial Life Insurance convention. Just before getting up to speak, Spencer felt a wave of dizziness. He spoke only about fifteen minutes then had to be helped to his room by two men, one at each elbow. After a sleepless night, he returned to Salt Lake City and went directly to the hospital for rest and several days of tests. Camilla slept beside him on the floor on a pallet that she found less uncomfortable than the cot offered her. The doctor diagnosed Spencer's situation as a very small stroke, perhaps caused by tiny nylon fibers shed from his artificial heart valve.

When Spencer complained, "I have no balance," the doctor reassured him it would pass.

Celebrating 60 years of marriage, January 1978. On the right are daughter, Olive Beth Mack, and several of her grandchildren.

Spencer responded wryly, "What won't?"

He returned home with orders to rest. While he napped and worked at a reduced pace, Camilla bottled apricots, made raspberry jam, and juiced windfall apples from her backyard.

On July 21, Spencer got up from a nap and sat at the table with Camilla. He started to talk, but his speech was garbled. She could not understand him, but he did not seem to notice anything wrong. Frightened, Camilla said that she must call the doctor. Although he said, "No," she persuaded him to lie down, and she called Dr. Allan Barker, who came immediately. The doctor tentatively diagnosed the condition as another transient stroke caused by fibers from Spencer's heart valve. The confusion passed within a few hours, but the incident got Spencer thinking more about dying. "We have our bags packed," he explained, "We're ready to go."

When a third episode occurred three days later, Spencer felt exhausted and depressed, almost despairing. While trying to balance his checkbook, he made several errors in addition. "That makes me feel lower than a hole in the ground," he grumbled. The problem particularly galled him because he prided himself on accuracy. He, who had always been strong and independent, hated having to rely on others. "It makes me so *damned* mad to have to have someone with me every minute, even if I just go to the bank to deposit ten cents," he griped.

As might be expected of a stake clerk, bank teller, and businessman, Spencer had kept meticulous financial records. For a man with so many other responsibilities, his actions might seem compulsive, but each month he created a personal balance sheet of assets and liabilities and reconciled his bank statement to the penny, no matter how long it took. Except for an accountant to help with tax returns, he kept his own books until he forgot to pay his income tax on time and received a bill for interest and penalty. Berating himself for that, he turned routine financial matters over to Ed in 1979.

It was ten days after the third transient stroke before Spencer could engage in any significant activity. He missed the area conference held in Madison, Wisconsin, the first area conference he had missed since they began in 1971.

By late August, Spencer had recovered enough to travel to an area conference in Toronto. He had to ask Arthur Haycock to read his address because his cataracts made reading difficult and sometimes impossible, even with large print. His ophthalmologist, Dr. Richard Sonntag, proposed cataract operations, one lens to be removed right after October general conference and the other later. He offered two options, simple removal of the clouded lenses (which would necessitate thick glasses) or replacing the clouded lenses with artificial ones. Dr. Sonntag did not consider lens replacements well enough established yet to be a safe procedure in light of Spencer's glaucoma. Spencer's general physician, Dr. Wilkinson, urged Spencer to get a second opinion. Ultimately he did, but he delayed doing so for a long time because he did not want to offend the faithful eye doctor—who had served him well for fourteen years—by appearing to question his judgment.[2]

The operation was set for early September. A few days before that, Spencer went to BYU to deliver the traditional annual address from the

---

2. According to neighbor George "Sam" Parker, Spencer said, rhetorically, he would rather lose his sight than offend his doctor.

Church President to the students. He began his talk but soon had to stop. He explained his vision problem and turned his text over to President Dallin H. Oaks to read. After the devotional assembly, BYU provided a luncheon for Kimball family members who had attended. Despite feeling weak, Spencer's sense of humor had not left him. He expressed thanks "for the delightful repast. We're so glad to be able to eat with our family without having to provide the food."

The next day, Wednesday, in preparation for the cataract operation, Spencer stopped taking the anticoagulant medication that he had taken for years.[3] On Thursday he had difficulty getting out of the tub and needed help walking. He forced his way weakly through the day until 3:00 P.M., when he went to Brigham City to see his sister, Alice, whose husband had just died after years as an invalid. To walk, Spencer required the help of two men. The previous little strokes had left him temporarily confused and weak, but this time Spencer was mentally clear although very feeble. Arthur called Dr. Wilkinson to arrange for an examination as soon as they returned to Salt Lake City that evening.

After testing Spencer at his office, Dr. Wilkinson took him directly to the hospital for a CAT scan. It pinpointed a large collection of fluid inside the skull on the right side, pressing on the brain. Such hematomas develop after blood vessels rupture. Sometimes even slight jarring is enough to break aging vessels, and the effects can take time to develop.[4] No specific cause of Spencer's hematoma could be identified.

The situation called for immediate action. Arthur notified President Tanner. Arthur and others joined in giving Spencer a blessing. At 1:00 A.M., just an hour after the final decision to operate, the nurse wheeled Spencer off to the operating room. The absence of anticoagulant, providentially stopped in expectation of cataract surgery, greatly reduced the risk of uncontrolled bleeding during surgery.

Neurosurgeon Bruce Sorensen drilled a burr hole the size of a pencil through Spencer's skull two inches above his right ear. Nearly a cupful of fluid spurted out about two feet.

Recovering in the intensive care unit, Spencer, barely conscious,

---

3. In 1979 cataract surgery involved removal of part of the iris as well as the lens, requiring a much larger incision than now, posing a risk of bleeding.

4. Ironically, Spencer's grandfather Heber C. Kimball probably died of a similar subdural hematoma, resulting from a buggy accident.

Walking a hospital corridor after surgery.

struggled with pain and vivid hallucinations, common after such surgery. He thought he had died and the First Presidency had been reorganized, and that the hospital was burning.

Several hours after the surgery, he returned to full consciousness. He was relieved to find himself alive and not in great pain. Concerned calls and cards of sympathy poured in from family, friends, and hundreds of members. In two days Spencer had recovered enough to move to an ordinary room.

A few days later, John Warnick, who was visiting his wife in the hospital, happened upon President Kimball shuffling slowly in the hallway, assisted on one side by a nurse and on the other side by a security man. President Kimball greeted him and then asked, "Do you love the Lord?" This question from a prophet was electrifying. Warnick responded that he did love the Lord and, further, he said, "I love you." With a little smile, Spencer said, "But I only asked, 'Do you love the Lord?'"

Learning that Warnick's wife suffered from cancer, Spencer took both of Warnick's hands in his, kissed them, expressed his concern, and continued his slow walk down the hall. When Warnick returned from getting ice water for his wife, he saw President Kimball enter her room. Spencer offered to give her a blessing of comfort, and Warnick accepted. After the blessing, as Spencer left he whispered, "Life is eternal, Brother John. Life is eternal." Sister Warnick soon emerged from her semi-conscious state completely coherent, and in the four days before her death, she was able to converse with her family.

Spencer suffered a setback and sank into depression. His moroseness troubled Camilla as much as his physical weakness; it seemed so unlike him. But slowly he gained strength. Arthur came to the hospital daily, bringing mail and messages. Spencer's counselors consulted with him regularly. One of the best boosts to his morale was visiting other patients as he walked the corridor for exercise.

Twelve days after the operation, Spencer finally went home. Church Security stationed a man inside the house now, night and day. Although the help was welcome, his presence deprived Spencer and Camilla of privacy.[5]

Despite the traumatic experience, Spencer's sense of humor remained. When Dr. Sorensen checked on Spencer at home, the doctor asked, "Is there anything I can do for you?"

Spencer said with a smile, "How about a couple of conference talks?"

A woman friend, intending to reassure him, said, "Years ago I had the same problem and they put an extra hole in my head, too."

His teasing response: "I always wondered what was wrong with you."

Spencer's cataract surgeries were postponed indefinitely, and as matters turned out, he never had the operation.

Camilla, who had been plagued by stomach upset for weeks, finally took time out for a careful physical examination. She was greatly relieved when the doctor pronounced her in good health. She had secretly assumed that she had stomach cancer, which had killed her mother and sister. Asked why she had waited so long to get the examination, she said, "I didn't want to know."

On September 25, Spencer returned to his office for a few hours. His doctors felt he could probably attend the imminent conference but should not expect to participate actively. Spencer ignored their suggestion. He had spent part of his two weeks in the hospital planning for the conference with his counselors, and he would not sit back and simply

---

5. Though these men did not expect to be fed, Camilla normally insisted they eat right along with family.

look on. Drawing on reserves of strength no one thought he had, he delivered addresses at the regional representatives seminar, the opening general session, the priesthood meeting, and the closing session. His only concession to weakness was skipping the early Saturday morning welfare session.

He did slip once. He announced, "Marion G. Romney, First Counselor in the First Presidency, will be the next speaker." Second Counselor Romney whispered, "You've just promoted me." Spencer whispered back in mock contrition, "I'm sorry."

During the closing session Spencer told the story of the Israelites' arrival in Canaan and the request by Caleb that his inheritance be the mountain of Hebron, still occupied by giants:

"There are great challenges ahead of us, giant opportunities to be met. I welcome that exciting prospect and feel to say to the Lord humbly, 'Give me this mountain,' give me these challenges. . . .

"Humbly, I give this pledge to the Lord and to you, my beloved brothers and sisters, fellow workers in this sacred cause of Christ. . . .

"Earnestly and fervently I urge that each of you make this same pledge. . . .

"[For] we are on the Lord's errand."

It was an inspiring speech, even to those who did not know how ill he had been. To those who had seen him slowly fight his way back from incoherence and total weakness, the speech was doubly touching.

Shortly after conference, Spencer and Camilla traveled to Israel for the dedication of the Orson Hyde Memorial Garden. He held up amazingly well. In mid-November, numbness in Spencer's left arm and a sudden general weakness signaled renewed danger. Tests indicated another subdural hematoma, but it was not as severe as the previous one. When told he needed another operation, President Kimball said resignedly, "It's something that has to be done, so let's do it."

The surgery basically repeated the September operation. Dr. Sorensen entered through the same burr hole and relieved the pressure, removing blood that he surmised had been collecting for no more than a week.

Camilla sat beside the unconscious Spencer in intensive care all day. When consciousness returned, he was again disoriented. He thought he was in Australia for the area conference but that no arrangements had been made for him and no one knew him. At the large banquet no one had set a place for him; they ate and chatted among themselves, ignoring him. One man finally put a hot dog on the edge of the table for him. Spencer said plaintively, "You would think they would at least acknowledge my presence and say, 'Brother Kimball, we're sorry you're here,' but they didn't!" Such unguarded moments showed his great need for affection and support.

In what Camilla called "the most traumatic experience of my life," Spencer's personality after this surgery underwent a temporary change. Everyone became an enemy. He said hurtful things to Camilla. He castigated the doctor for letting him go on the trip to Australia when no preparations had been made. Camilla retreated to cry alone, although the doctors repeatedly assured her the outbursts were beyond his control and would pass. Spencer struggled, half knowing that what he said was unkind but unable to restrain himself. When his counselors came to the hospital, they agreed it was not a good time to visit. Instead, they gave Camilla a blessing that brought her comfort.

By the next day, Monday, Spencer was still disoriented but no longer angry. He was himself, sweet and mild, unless someone tried to tell him he was not in Australia. He stubbornly insisted that he was.

Each day in the hospital brought slow progress, although Spencer was visibly annoyed when people commented "How well you look!" One of the first signs of his returning strength was that he began expressing appreciation for the nurses' services.

On Sunday, Camilla suggested they listen to the Tabernacle Choir. Spencer sat up in a chair but immediately fell asleep. Camilla could not rouse him, nor could a physical therapist who had come in to treat him. Frightened, Camilla knelt beside him, holding his hand, weeping, and pleading with the Lord. She felt that he was sinking away to death. When Dr. Wilkinson arrived, he discovered that a nurse had mistakenly given Spencer a sedative rather than his blood pressure medication. It took six hours for the effect to dissipate, but the setback was minor.

From Australia and New Zealand, President Tanner telephoned Spencer each day, getting a report on his condition and giving him short accounts of the area conferences. After calling the hospital one day, President Tanner told his companions that he had nothing to report because President Kimball had not been in his room.

"Where was he?" they asked.

"They weren't sure; they couldn't find him. They thought he might have gone down to the next floor of the hospital to visit the sick."

On Friday, November 30, after two weeks in the hospital, Spencer once again went home. Less than a week later, Spencer spent a full six hours at work, returning home tired but happy. Camilla felt freed, too, exhilarated by the relief from weeks of anxiety.

During December, Spencer experienced minor problems. One day he could hardly feed himself; the next day his speech was slurred. Discouraged, he made a list of relatives to be informed in case of his death and said gloomily, "I wouldn't want a funeral if no one came." But the condition cleared up when the doctors increased his blood-thinning medicine. Then hiccoughs started and continued for four exhausting days and nights.

Another Christmas arrived. Despite family protests, Camilla, eighty-five, provided Christmas dinner. She stuffed a huge turkey, roasted it for seventeen hours, and served thirty family members who gathered to celebrate both Christmas and Spencer's survival after a difficult year.

1980

As the new year 1980 opened, Spencer dived back into a heavy work schedule. He tried to ignore his ill health as much as possible. One day Ed visited and momentarily set a box of books on a chair before taking it to his car. He turned to see Spencer with the heavy box, tottering off towards the car. Ed caught up with his father, wrested the box away, and said in exasperation, "You can't *do* that!" Spencer responded, almost plaintively, "Why can't I do what I want to do?"

During 1980 Spencer took his various chronic ailments to myriad doctors—ophthalmologist, dentist, cardiologist, urologist, otologist, oncologist, dermatologist, and internist. He had something for nearly everyone, although gratefully, for the moment at least, he had no need for the radiologists, cardiac surgeon, and neurosurgeon who had served him in the past.

For her part, Camilla required surgery to correct carpal tunnel syndrome, presumably caused by her long years of doing needlepoint, crochet, and other handwork. During that spring and summer, degeneration of her spine caused her constant pain, only partly controlled by

Clockwise from Camilla and Spencer: Andrew and Phyllis; Grant Mack and Olive Beth; Evelyn Bee and Edward; Kathryn and Spencer L.

medication. X-rays showed that she had a bone spur on a vertebra that pressed on a nerve. The doctor recommended both a back operation and knee replacements to solve her crippling arthritis. She decided to defer the knee surgery until the pain got so bad she could not stand it. She did agree to have her back repaired, but then she canceled the operation, unwilling to spend nine days in the hospital and several weeks recuperating. She said she would feel like a deserter if she made herself unavailable. Caring for Spencer was more important than her own health. She decided simply to endure the ongoing pain.

1981

In May 1981, Spencer performed the wedding for his granddaughter Paula Kimball and Teryl Gardner. He struggled slightly to read the text even though it was printed in large type. Usually at such ceremonies Spencer gave counsel to the couple being married. This time he did not, but later he leaned over to Teryl and whispered his only piece of advice: "Don't let on that you know how to do the dishes." It proved to be the last sealing Spencer performed.

Spencer went directly from the taking of wedding photographs to the hospital for the installation of a pacemaker. His usual daytime heart rate had dropped to forty-four beats per minute, only 60 percent of average, with resulting fatigue. He had deferred the operation for some days to avoid disappointing Paula and Teryl. Under local anesthetic, Dr. Nelson implanted the pacemaker under the skin of his upper left chest. Spencer left the hospital three days later, feeling much more energetic, his heart now beating merrily along at a clocklike sixty-eight beats per minute.

Less than a month later, Spencer's health resumed its decline. He had difficulty concentrating and making decisions. When signing books for people, he sometimes ended his name with three L's. When Camilla pointed it out, he passed it off as a joke: "That's worth extra." He needed help getting dressed. He was so weak that he rested two or three times a day on the couch in his office. At the funeral in July 1981 for Freda Joan Lee, President Lee's widow, he spoke for only a moment. At S. Dilworth Young's funeral a week later, he did not speak at all. He continued going to the office, but for only a few hours at a time. His world was rapidly shrinking.

38

DECLINE AND DEATH, 1981–1985

"See that I am buried—but not before I am dead."

THE YEARS 1974 THROUGH 1979 were Spencer's spring and summer as President, with freshness, warmth, and energy, and early harvest. A short fall of gleaning followed surgeries for intracranial bleeding in 1979. After 1981 only winter awaited him.

Before his two operations in 1979, President Kimball seemed vigorous for his age, and he recovered surprisingly well from the traumatic surgeries. But the next two years showed a clear downward trend. In retrospect, the summer of 1981 was pivotal. Spencer's condition declined rapidly despite his heroic efforts to get well. The body that had for so long responded to his will defied him now. He experienced increasing pain, discouragement, and disorientation and prayed for the Lord to take him. Ironically, Spencer's unremitting zeal for work— undeniably one of his greatest strengths—became a kind of curse to him during his final years, as his ability to work was taken from him.

In the early summer of 1981, he was interviewed for a documentary on the Dallas Temple, but the producer decided not to use the footage because "the film of the interview made him look very feeble and absentminded."

On July 13, Ed wrote about his father, "[He] is sometimes confused and has difficulty speaking. . . . He is discouraged and so is she [Camilla]. I begin to wonder whether he can last—but then I thought that seven years ago." Early the next morning, Spencer implemented one of the most significant decisions of his administration. He called D. Arthur Haycock, his personal secretary, into his office. As Haycock described the meeting, "The fog lifted. . . . He was clear in his decision."

Watching the screen at Spencer's 85th birthday celebration in the Salt Lake Tabernacle, March 1980.

He acted in a definite and controlled manner, as if the clock had turned back years. Spencer told Arthur he had decided after prayerful consideration and consultation with his counselors to call a third counselor and asked him to locate Gordon B. Hinckley. Arthur spontaneously lifted both hands high and exclaimed, "I can vote for him with both hands. I don't think you could ever make a better selection."

Minutes later, with Elder Hinckley sitting across the desk, Spencer indicated that he had decided to call another counselor in the First Presidency and asked what Elder Hinckley thought about that. Elder Hinckley's first reaction was to wonder why the President of the Church was discussing this with him, but he responded that other Presidents—Joseph Smith, Brigham Young, and David O. McKay—had done so and, in any event, it was surely within his authority.

Spencer then smiled, expressed appreciation, and said, "I would like *you* to serve as my counselor." Elder Hinckley was stunned but graciously accepted the new responsibility. Because of the poor health afflicting all three members of the First Presidency, this decision had a tremendous effect on subsequent events. A young seventy-one, Elder Hinckley brought renewed vigor to the First Presidency. He later served effectively as counselor to two more Presidents before he assumed the ultimate responsibility himself fourteen years later.

Spencer next asked Arthur to locate Neal A. Maxwell, one of the Presidents of the Seventy. When Arthur reported that he was still in the hospital following surgery, Spencer said, "Let's go see him." They drove to the hospital, where Elder Maxwell accepted a call to fill the vacancy in the Twelve created by Elder Hinckley's new assignment.

In a memo to President Hinckley, Arthur Haycock wrote:

"In my forty-six years of close association with the last six presidents of the Church, I can say unequivocally that, to me personally, this is the greatest testimony of direct revelation I have ever witnessed. . . . There is no doubt in my mind that the Lord strengthened President Kimball in mind and body and raised him up and inspired him to call [President Hinckley and Elder Maxwell]."

A week later, on July 23, President Kimball presented the nominations to the Twelve for their approval. He then called a press conference to announce the two new appointments. Immediately afterward, according to Arthur, Spencer "seemed to revert at once to his former condition and general ill health," and "the fog descended again."

The importance of the decision soon became apparent. On Thursday, September 3, Spencer arrived at his office about 7:15 A.M. but felt weak

The First Presidency with added counselor Gordon B. Hinckley, July 1981.

and went home two hours later. He needed help to get to his car. While eating lunch, he fell asleep in his chair and seemed disoriented. On Friday, he checked into the hospital for tests. A brain scan disclosed that he had yet another subdural hematoma. The bleeding inside the skull was creating pressure on his brain, causing the weakness.

Camilla as well as Spencer's counselors discussed with the doctors whether to operate again or let him slip away. Spencer had often said plaintively, "Why doesn't the Lord release me?" But it appeared he might recover well, as he had before, and Dr. Bruce Sorensen operated for the third time. This surgery lasted two hours and proved more extensive than the two earlier ones.

As Spencer began to awaken, there were no hallucinations or anger as with the previous surgery, just pain and restlessness. He looked terrible, his bandaged head covered by a stocking cap, eyelids purple from blood in the tissues, splotches of purple spreading down the right side of his face into his chin and neck, facial swelling, oxygen tubes in his nose, and an intravenous needle in his arm. Wednesday night he had two seizures, not unusual after brain surgery. But Camilla was alarmed, thinking once more that the end had arrived.

He recovered more slowly from this operation. He admitted he was "miserable" but also affirmed, "I want to get well!" Days passed before his sense of humor returned. On the tenth day, a nurse checking his consciousness and coherence asked him to scratch his nose. He rejoined, "It doesn't itch." Soon his teasing began.

"Cough for me."

"Cough, cough," he said.

"President Kimball, can you tell me when the Second Coming will be?"

"Why? Are you ready?"

Despite his improvement, rumors spread. One friend was told Spencer was "a blob." In another sacrament meeting, it was announced that the President was in a coma.

After three weeks, Spencer could walk in the hospital hallways. He needed steadying but bore his own weight. His memory was improving. But the general upward trend was punctuated with bad days of disorientation and sleepiness. The doctors finally concluded he was bleeding internally from a stress-induced stomach ulcer and ordered a transfusion. The nurse fretted over his arm for half an hour trying to locate veins, but none would accept the needle. Finally, she chose a vein in his upper right arm and probed several times before succeeding. Spencer flinched in pain. Placatingly, the nurse asked, "I guess you don't want this, do you?"

He roused enough to say, almost fiercely, "I *do* want it!"

Despite overwhelming weariness and weakness, he was willing to endure whatever pain was required to restore him to health.

When October general conference began, President Kimball was absent for the first time since his ordination as an apostle thirty-eight years earlier. That day he again had dangerously heavy internal bleeding in his stomach. He had to be forcibly restrained to undergo an endoscopy to locate and cauterize the bleeding. Afterward he said, "I never had anything make me so mad!"

His mental acuity was something like a radio signal, fading in and out. He managed small talk but had trouble recalling names, even of family members. Then a new blow fell. He had a blocked urethra and needed another operation. The pain from a spinal block was so excruciating that Spencer, ordinarily so stoic, screamed when he was moved. But he recovered quickly, and a week later, after a stay of forty-six days, he left the hospital.

This time he and Camilla did not return home. They moved instead to an apartment on the top floor of the Hotel Utah. It was large, comfortably accommodating full-time nursing and security. Since it was next to the Church Administration Building, his counselors had easier access to him than if he were in his home five miles away. The apartment was also easier for Camilla. It had no stairs to tax her bad knees, and she had housekeeping help. But it was not home.

Two weeks later, overwhelming midbody pain, back and front, attacked Spencer. X-rays showed that a thoracic vertebra had partially collapsed, compressing the nerve and causing agonizing pain. The doctor prescribed a back brace for support until the condition healed, which took several months.

At Thanksgiving and Christmas the hotel cooked a turkey the Kimballs provided, marking a poignant end to Camilla's years as matriarch preparing holiday meals for her family.

Life settled into a new routine. Ed and Bee drove up from Provo two or three evenings a week, bringing dinner and staying for a visit. Olive Beth or some of her older children usually brought dinner the other days. Camilla or one of the nurses fixed breakfast, made sandwiches or soup for lunch, or warmed up leftovers from the other meals. Camilla helped Spencer eat when his lethargy made him lose focus on the task of eating. Nurses provided care around the clock. Dr. Wilkinson came by often and called in specialists when needed, but the nurses had standing instructions from doctor and family to enhance the President's comfort but to take no heroic measures to extend his life. Church Security posted a man on duty twenty-four hours a day, both to protect and to help as needed, such as when Spencer needed help getting to his feet after kneeling to pray.

Spencer's role as President became primarily one of response, not initiation. He dealt with only those Church matters President Hinckley felt necessary to bring to him. Information or questions were also brought by Arthur Haycock, who was a constant visitor and looked after the President with the solicitude of a close friend.

As the winter of their lives closed in, neither Spencer nor Camilla left the apartment often. Spencer walked about the apartment and in the hotel hallways but remained weak. His vision remained cloudy and his hearing poor. Sometimes he could speak fluently, but other times when he tried to say one word, another word that made no sense would come out—a side effect of the brain surgery. The frustration was so cruel that he often simply lapsed into silence.

The communication problem precipitated discussions among family, Arthur, and Spencer's counselors about who should be allowed to visit him. Visitors usually stimulated and cheered him, but his counselors were concerned that Spencer's speech impairment might start rumors about his competency. Consequently, visitors were few.

President Kimball's first and second counselors were also living in restricted worlds. N. Eldon Tanner no longer accepted dinner invitations because Parkinson's disease caused an unmanageable tremor. Marion Romney's eyesight was dim, and his memory was fading. Meetings of the full presidency became increasingly rare.

The importance of having called President Hinckley as third counselor became clearer and clearer. It was the end of Spencer's active

With the Hollands at the dedication of BYU's Spencer W. Kimball Tower, 1982.

ministry.[1] By mid-1982, President Kimball was too weak to appear much in public, attend meetings, or go to his office more than sporadically. He had no choice but to accept a passive role. President Hinckley repeatedly acknowledged Spencer's condition in general conference, saying that President Kimball "is weak, and his body is tired" and that "advancing age and physical disabilities have in recent months restricted some of his activities." But, he said, the prophet meets intermittently with his

---

1. In one temple meeting President Hinckley asked Spencer whether he had anything he wanted to say. "I'd like to be released," was his poignant answer. But there was no precedent for such action.

counselors and the Twelve, and, he reassured the members, "No major decision concerning this work will be made without his consideration and his direction."

Spencer struggled to see even the headlines of the newspapers. Camilla read to him from the scriptures or from a book she was interested in. He took no pleasure in watching television. When he signed documents, his signature was a scrawl.

In March 1982 he was strong enough to make his first public appearance in nearly seven months. On a perfect spring day, sunny and warm, students at BYU began lining up before 7:00 A.M. at the closed doors of the Marriott Center. They wanted good seats for the 11:00 o'clock devotional at which the President was expected to make a rare appearance. The new twelve-story Spencer W. Kimball Tower was to be dedicated, a major landmark on campus. The dedication was originally scheduled for the previous September but had been postponed when Spencer's third subdural hematoma required surgery. More than 20,000 people filled the Marriott Center, including twenty General Authorities, who were present to pay the President honor and perhaps see how he looked after six months out of the public eye.

At the appointed time, Spencer and Camilla entered, walking side by side on their own but accompanied by Arthur Haycock, who kept a hand at Spencer's elbow. President Kimball's doctors and family had felt acute concern that he might become confused or fall asleep at some point during the day. But with the help of a mild stimulant he managed beautifully, walking into the Marriott Center with a sprightly step and listening attentively.[2]

The audience stood in respect as the visitors found their places. BYU president Jeffrey Holland convened the meeting. Expressions of love and respect were made by representatives of students, faculty, and family.

In brief remarks, son Ed told of asking his father, "Is there anything I can do for you?"

"Yes," his father said, smiling, "You can see that I am buried—but not before I am dead."

Camilla responded to the tributes, explaining that the doctors

---

2. Ritalin was used. Olive Beth wondered why that could not be given him routinely but was told it was inappropriate for continuing use.

At general conference, with a visible scar from 1981 operation on his head, April 1984.

thought her husband too fragile for public speaking just yet. After expressing thanks, she added her own tribute:

"No one has known Spencer Kimball as well as I. Perhaps, therefore, my assessment can have some weight. I can say, without hesitation, that in this man there is great virtue. It is too much to say that he is perfect, but he comes wondrously close. There is in him devotion, and consistency, and power. I have sensed his struggles to know God's will, and I have sensed his peace in receiving the answer. My testimony of his prophetic calling has come to me in the same way it comes to you—by the whisperings of the Spirit. I know and testify that God called Spencer Kimball out of obscurity to perform a great work. He has labored hard to bring the world to a knowledge of Christ and the Father and to persuade men to do good."

After lunch Spencer listened appreciatively as the BYU Indian Choir sang movingly. Some of the singers shed tears while they sang. As they filed out, two of the young women, unable to restrain themselves, broke ranks and hugged President Kimball. He looked surprised but pleased. The wearying day had been a satisfying one.

On the day of Spencer's eighty-seventh birthday, a family dinner party was planned for early evening, but at noon Spencer's strength suddenly flowed out of him like water draining away. He slumped back in his chair, muttering as he faded, "It doesn't matter. It's too late." He slipped into unconsciousness and could not be roused. Two doctors tried to wake him with pain—pins and pinches—but he did not respond. They were baffled. His reflexes, blood pressure, and heart function were normal. Camilla wept inconsolably. Members of the Twelve, who came to offer birthday greetings, went away, many in tears. Camilla, sure Spencer was dying, canceled the party. But after four hours, he began to regain consciousness. His eyes opened. Although he could not speak, he could nod or shake his head in answer to questions and tried to communicate with hand motions. After another hour he could speak a few words again, and he agreed to take a sip of milk.

The ten people present lit the candles on his cake and sang "Happy Birthday" with the feeling that there was really something to celebrate. Spencer managed to say, referring to what had just happened, "Don't let anyone be imposed on." He wanted no one put to trouble on his account. Later that evening he was up and about again. Surprisingly, he recalled things said and done while he appeared wholly unconscious and unresponsive.

A week later, rallying amazingly from the strange episode, Spencer attended the first and last sessions of conference. He even considered trying to read an address that Arthur had prepared for him, reiterating familiar themes, but he decided it would be too difficult. Arthur Haycock read the address for him. Then, unplanned, at the conclusion of the Sunday afternoon session, President Kimball took the pulpit. Painfully laboring over each word, he delivered his extemporaneous personal message. It was the first public speech he had given since his operation, and it would be his last. His words were brief but heartfelt:

"My beloved brothers and sisters, this is a great experience for me. I have waited for this day and hoped for it and believed for it. I have a great love for the people of this Church, and gratitude for the love expressed by them and by all of the people of this valley.

"So as I express that love for you and for the memory of the great experiences I've had with you, I bear my testimony: this work is divine, the Lord is at the helm, the Church is true, and all is well. God bless you, brothers and sisters, I pray in the name of the Lord Jesus Christ, amen."

A few days later, Ed arrived at his parents' apartment and found his

father agitated. Camilla had been reading aloud from a recently published book of talks by General Authorities. In one chapter, Bruce R.
McConkie described the climactic events of June 1978, extending the
priesthood to all worthy men. He had written, "We all heard the same
voice, received the same message." This language upset Spencer, since
it might give the impression that the First Presidency and the Twelve
had heard the voice of God audibly. He asked Ed to speak to Elder
McConkie about changing the text to avoid any possibility of mistaken
interpretation. Spencer had no doubt about the reality of the revelation.
"It *did* happen," he said, with an energy that belied his frailty. The
marvelous thing that had occurred did not need exaggeration.

In July Spencer served as grand marshal for the Pioneer Day parade.
In September Spencer and Camilla attended the season's first BYU football game in an enclosed loge of the university's newly expanded football
stadium. With his poor vision, he had no personal interest in attending
the game, but his counselors thought it would boost members' confidence to know he was well enough to be about. The long day proved
very stressful for him.

At October conference 1982, Spencer, looking very old, attended but did not speak. Arthur read a short talk prepared for him. President Romney gave a substantive address, his last. Within another month, he became housebound. President Tanner spoke briefly and died seven weeks later at age eighty-four. Marion G. Romney then became First Counselor, and Gordon B. Hinckley, Second, but President Hinckley continued to shoulder all responsibility.

No one expected President Kimball to endure much longer. The Church Public Communications Department quietly prepared and distributed background material for obituaries or media tributes to be used upon the President's death.

Two weeks after October conference, as Camilla prepared to leave the apartment, she turned sharply and fell to the floor with a broken hip. The next morning a surgeon replaced the head of her femur. Camilla stayed in the hospital for two weeks. Spencer visited her every day. It was a turnabout, after all the times she had watched over him as he recovered from his numerous operations.

Afterward, Camilla had to use a wheelchair whenever she left the apartment, a situation galling to someone of her independence. Inside the apartment she used a walker, as much for her arthritic knees as for her hip. She hated the walker, which she called her "burro." Sometimes she would get up from her chair and walk several steps without the walker until the pain stopped her. Stranded, she would have to call for someone to bring the walker to her. She thought back on the days when she feared a plane crash might simultaneously snuff out both their lives. Now she envisioned such death—together and quick—as the perfect ending.

Spencer's sight was further deteriorating. He now could see only outlines and thought of himself as blind. He often ate, whether alone or with help, with his eyes closed. His hearing, too, was failing fast. He could not rest, seldom sleeping soundly for more than an hour, even at night. He felt like a prisoner in a comfortable cell, surrounded by nurses and family whose care only made him feel more keenly his helplessness.

Still, his sense of humor endured. A visiting relative asked him, "Do you know who I am?" With his impaired vision and hearing, he did not recognize her. He said, "If you don't know who you are, how do you expect me to remember?" When nurse Ann Peterson shaved him with an electric shaver for several minutes without result, Spencer finally spoke up, "Perhaps it would work better if you took the cap off."

As April conference 1983 neared, Spencer's health again became a matter of greater public interest. For the first time he did not attend any conference sessions. Rumors abounded: President Kimball had had a stroke, two heart attacks, was bedfast, hospitalized, in a coma, about to die. During conference President Hinckley was direct and reassuring: "President Kimball is . . . not in a coma, as some have said. He dresses each day. But he is weak, and his body is tired. He . . . is feeling the effects of his advanced age and the cumulative effects of the surgical procedures he has undergone in the past."

Amazingly, in each of the next five general conferences President Kimball attended at least one session. However haggard and weary, he determinedly showed the flag.

Occasional up-times suggested he was not necessarily sliding quickly toward death but might go on for some time. In July he fell and suffered a small gash on his forehead. A CAT scan showed no bleeding inside the head, but he looked terrible for a time, with a huge black eye. Several months later he fell out of bed and required seven stitches to close two cuts on his head.

Typically, he attended the temple meetings of the General Authorities once or twice a month. Although he seldom participated, even that small degree of activity cheered him. In October 1983, he attended conference but did not speak nor was an address read for him. A warm moment occurred between sessions. A group of Korean Church leaders were dropped off by a shuttle in the Church Office Building parking garage to walk through the tunnel to Temple Square. As they moved along, President Kimball, who was being wheeled in his chair, came up behind them. They all stood respectfully to the side as he passed and were talking excitedly about their good fortune of seeing him up close when the wheelchair returned. Through their interpreter, Spencer apologized for passing them without stopping and asked their forgiveness. He had each one tell his name and calling, and he had each lean down so he could kiss him on the cheek. Then he apologized for having to rush off.

Mark E. Petersen died in January 1984, and President Kimball attended the funeral. It was his only public appearance between October

1983 and the next April. Following Spencer's expressed wishes, the family no longer prayed for his recovery but rather for his patience to endure until God should release him.

The winter of 1984 proved a particularly difficult time. Olive Beth, who lived nearest and on whom both Spencer and Camilla had always depended greatly for physical help and emotional support, had both knee joints surgically replaced. It was an operation that she had postponed as long as possible.

In April conference, President Hinckley announced new apostolic callings: those of Russell M. Nelson and Dallin H. Oaks. It was the first time two apostles had been sustained in the same conference since Elders Kimball and Benson were sustained in October 1943. President Hinckley carefully explained how the new apostles were called:

"I want to give you my testimony that they were chosen and called by the spirit of prophecy and revelation. There was discussion with President Kimball, the prophet of the Lord in our day. . . . There was a clear and distinct impression, what I choose to call the whisperings of the Holy Spirit, concerning those who should be selected to assume this most important and sacred responsibility.

"While President Kimball is unable to stand at this pulpit and speak to us, we are on occasion able to converse with him, and he has given his authorization to that which has been done. We would not have proceeded without this."

When Elder Benson conducted the Sunday afternoon session, he mistakenly announced that they would hear next from President Kimball. A buzz ran through the crowd. President Hinckley, the actual next speaker, handled the potentially awkward moment with grace, saying how wonderful it would be to hear from the President again. He then told the audience, "I said to him, a little bit ago, as we looked over this vast congregation, 'President, these people all love you.' He said, 'I love them.' I hope that you will accept that as his address to you." Those three words proved to be President Kimball's final message to the Saints.

At the next temple meeting after conference, Presidents Kimball and Romney sat for the ordination of the new apostles. Spencer seemed to be nodding and uncommunicative, but when President Hinckley asked whether he should charge the new apostles with their responsibilities, Spencer visibly roused and said clearly, "Yes."

With Gordon B. Hinckley at general conference, April 1985.

President Hinckley then asked whether they should proceed with the ordination. At first Spencer did not respond. President Hinckley touched his arm and repeated the question. Spencer again roused and said clearly, "Yes, I would like you to proceed."

"Should I be mouth in the ordination?"

"Yes."

It was reassuring to the General Authorities to witness that when it was important for President Kimball to respond, he could do so. The other apostles stood in the circle, and President Hinckley performed the ordination.

October conference 1984 brought a small spike in vitality. Ed wrote, "Dad seemed a little livelier than I've seen him in months. For the first time I could really see him attending conference. It is as though there is new vigor at conference time. I should not be surprised, yet I am each time."

The last year of Spencer Kimball's life, 1985, played out within the tight circle of a few hundred yards: the apartment, the temple, and the Tabernacle. Spencer had not been to the office for a long time. On March 28, the day he turned ninety, he attended the weekly meetings in the temple. He brightened in that familiar place, among men he loved and with whom he shared a special commission.

That evening he traveled to Olive Beth's home for a family birthday party. The trip of eleven miles was as extensive a trip as this world traveler had made in two and a half years. Although only a quarter of their family lived in the immediate area, Spencer and Camilla counted as their descendants four children, twenty-seven grandchildren, and fifty-one great-grandchildren, making eighty-two direct descendants plus twenty-six spouses for a total of one hundred eight. After dinner each person present had a chance to relate an anecdote about Spencer—their father or grandfather. Grandson-in-law Terry Johnson recalled hearing Camilla once say to Spencer at a family gathering, "If we had only bought that real estate up on the Avenues that we looked at when we first moved to Salt Lake City, we'd be rich."

Spencer had taken her hand and, indicating their family, said, "Mother, we *are* rich."

At BYU the Spencer W. Kimball Tower flew ninety helium-filled balloons from the roof, like so many candles on a cake. A giant banner draped the building, reading, "Happy 90th Pres. Kimball." A giant greeting card from BYU students contained hundreds of greetings:

"Happy Birthday! I was converted through one of your talks in the *Ensign*! Member now for 4 years! Love ya!"

"You have been a great influence in my life, starting with your baptizing my grandmother."

"Dear Sir, I'm not LDS but you seem to make a lot of people happy and do as people expect. So I wish you a Happy Birthday. A New Friend."

"I'll never forget the stories my mother told me of you and her playing piano duets in New Mexico when you were stake president!"

"Our birthdays are very close together—mine is March 29th. I'm getting baptized March 30th here at BYU. That is my birthday present to myself! Have a great birthday."

"You have probably had more impact in my life than any other person."

In April 1985 and again in October, Spencer attended four sessions of general conference, although he did not speak.

Before the month's end, Spencer developed a terrible rattle in his chest and throat. It was pneumonia. A few days later he had largely recovered, but on Monday, November 4, there was evidence that he was bleeding internally again. No major action was taken; the decision had been made nearly two years earlier to keep him comfortable but not to intervene with surgery or a transfusion. At 9:00 P.M., he drifted temporarily into unconsciousness.

That night he alternated between periods of alertness and peaceful rest. When disturbed, he waved his arms weakly. When a nurse tried to give him a drink, he clenched his teeth on the straw, refusing to sip. He gave no clear sign of recognizing family members but squeezed a hand when asked to do so. A nurse or security man sat by his bedside for the rest of the night while family members caught what fitful rest they could.

During these last days, Spencer several times said, "My life is at an end now. She's so happy, oh so very happy." When nurse Barbara Herrin asked, "Who?" he said he was talking of his mother, the mother he had lost when a boy of eleven and missed deeply all his life. Knowing that his parents joyously awaited him and that he longed to be with them comforted those who watched.

Early Tuesday, Dr. Duwayne Schmidt, substituting for Spencer's primary physician, Dr. Allan Barker, who was out of town, reviewed with the nurse the long list of medications: Demerol injections to relieve pain, Zantac injections to block the production of acid that exacerbated his ulcer, Maalox to sooth his stomach, Nistatin for thrush infection in his mouth, Digoxin for his heart, Lasix to control water retention, potassium to replace what he was losing by the diuretic, Bactrim as antibiotic, Theo-dur to aid breathing, and eyedrops.

For months Spencer had rarely slept restfully in bed and got up and down frequently, but all day Tuesday, with some sedation, he seemed content to stay in bed. By midafternoon his color seemed better, but at 9:30 P.M. his breathing became shallow, intermittent, and labored. His blood pressure dropped sharply, and he lapsed into unconsciousness. The nurse called Camilla in from another room. Camilla held Spencer's hand. Olive Beth returned from a speaking engagement and called Ed. Ed and Bee left Provo immediately for Salt Lake City but had not arrived when, at 10:08 P.M., Spencer W. Kimball's brave heart stopped and his last breath fled.

The nurses notified President Hinckley, who arrived quickly. After ascertaining the situation, he went to the telephone and called President Benson with the news.

"President Benson, this is Gordon. President Kimball has died. What would you like me to do?"

Thus the wheel of the presidency turned full cycle.

Ed and Bee heard of Spencer's death on the car radio as they entered downtown Salt Lake City. The KSL announcer said, "We will have a moment of silence at the passing of a great leader."

Ed helped the nurses, Leona Terry and Marsha Wright, prepare the body for removal. Ed had no sense that his father was present, just the body he used to live in. The jaw dropped, leaving the mouth agape. The ruddy face was pale. The body was still warm but cooling. The three washed him gently and dressed him in fresh garments and pajamas. Dr. Schmidt returned and signed the death certificate, listing as the immediate cause of death "cardiac arrest due to hypotension (shock), due to upper gastrointestinal bleeding (unknown cause)." He listed as indirect contributing factors "congestive heart failure, coronary artery disease, recent pneumonia, hypertension, etc." There were a lot of et ceteras.

Men from the Larkin Mortuary soon arrived. They covered the body with a white sheet, put it in a zippered bag, and rolled it away, accompanied by a security man.

Camilla had often wept for her husband's struggle; now she wept for her loss. But no one could regret his release from the long, slow process of dying. The keen anticipation Spencer had expressed for meeting his parents again warmed those who mourned him.

The family present had a preliminary discussion about funeral plans, then went to sleep as best they could in the apartment, which seemed suddenly incomplete.

The next morning Camilla wept anew. "I have no regrets except the void it leaves," she said. "The door has closed on my life." And bleakly, she added through her tears, "I'm here, but I wish I weren't."

39

FAREWELL

No short man ever had a longer stride.

SPENCER W. KIMBALL DIED ON ELECTION NIGHT, November 5, 1985. The KSL news staff was preparing to leave when the phone call came from Church Public Communications. A textual news flash ran across the screen of *M*A*S*H* while the television station scrambled to locate a four-minute generic obituary they had already prepared. As soon as possible, Duane Cardall went live on camera and made the announcement, followed by the brief obituary. Other television and radio stations followed within minutes.

The *Deseret News* headlined its November 6 edition: "President Spencer W. Kimball Dies at 90." Comments solicited by the paper echoed familiar themes: his courage, dedication, humility, kindness, love, hard work, and compassion. A *Church News* editorial spoke of his missionary zeal, his personal commitment to working at capacity, his concern for Native Americans, his power as a public speaker, and his love for all people.

The day before the funeral, 41,000 people filed past Spencer's casket in the Church Administration Building. They continued to come until the doors closed at 9:00 P.M.

At the service in the Tabernacle, President Benson praised his predecessor for a lifetime of devotion to serving the Lord. Elder Nelson, who had first operated on Spencer in 1973 and had often looked after him since, related, "When Sister Kimball asked that I speak at her husband's funeral, she . . . said, with a smile, 'No one knew his heart better than you. . . . You knew him at his worst moments.'

"I thought, how typically modest!"

People lined up to see President Kimball lying in state in the Church Administration Building, November 1985.

Other speakers were Barbara B. Smith, who served as Relief Society president during nearly all of Spencer's administration, D. Arthur Haycock, and son Andrew, representing the family. President Hinckley, who had borne the burden when Spencer could not, was scheduled to be the concluding speaker. But when his turn came, the time was gone, so he graciously forwent his remarks.

Spencer's grandsons carried the casket to the hearse. As the funeral cortege made its way from the Tabernacle, people on corners of the streets stood quietly with bowed heads. An old man in shabby clothes put his hat over his heart. Parents with children bundled up against the cold pointed out the procession, hoping their children would remember this moment.

Black clouds lowered over the city as the procession passed to the top of the Salt Lake City Cemetery. When the cortege arrived, snow began pelting down. The wind gusted, almost enough to blow away umbrellas. After Ed dedicated the grave, people pressed forward to greet Camilla. Ed urged her toward the car, out of the frigid wind, but she insisted on staying beside the grave to greet all comers, as Spencer would have done.

After the funeral, an outpouring of condolences continued for days.

Scores of letters and telegrams came from dignitaries, ordinary folk, friends, and strangers:

"Having read [his biography] and, of course, [having] heard Pres. Kimball many times and read his writings, I find myself feeling that he is my friend. And then I realize that I really don't know him personally at all. Yet, I feel, as thousands of persons do, that he really cared about me. . . ." Carol Crist

"The Prophet radiated so much love, it was like warming cold hands at a cheerful fire. . . ." Janet S. Norton

"As a church historian I would put him with Joseph and Brigham. Perhaps one should not rank prophets, but he gave us visions. He let us see ourselves as a world church, including China, India, and the Soviet Union, the 7/8ths of mankind we'd largely ignored in our thinking. . . ." Richard Oman

Letters from children proved the most poignant:

"Dear Mrs. Kimball, I sorry your husband died. But he was very old. . . . Your husband was a very nice guy. I like his talks he said at General Conference. . . . He did very good things in his life. But there's a time to go up and be with Jesus. . . . It was time for him to die. You guys made a great couple. Julie Peterson (age nine)"

"Dear Sister Kimball, I am sorry to hear that Spencer W. Kimball died. I just found out on wensday Nov. 6 1985. I would like to help you if you need me call 967–0266. I'm 9 years old I was baptized June 2, 1984. I have seen Spencer W. Kimball but you probly don't remeber. I danced with my cosin Tony. She's a girl. I wanted to write to you becase I very sad when I heard about the death of Spencer W. Kimball. If you are filling blue call me or just remember familys are forever. Love, Margarita Torres"

"Dear Mrs. Kimball, I am sorry your hussbund died. But thats life. He was a good man. Matthew Monson"

"he had a good Life. now he is in heven he must feel a Lot Better. Greg"

"Sister Kimball, I am really sorry about President Kimball, but I guess it was about time for him. I went to see his viewing he did not look pretty but he looked good. Love, Steve Simpson"

In late October 1986, almost exactly a year after the funeral, a monument was erected over Spencer's grave, bearing the simple inscription:

KIMBALL

Spencer Woolley   Camilla Eyring
1895–1985   1894–

The family's first thought was that their modest father would want a simple marker like those around his grave. But they decided that this was not *his* monument but rather their monument *to him*. The monument is six feet tall, taller than the man and woman it honors. The granite shaft is flanked by two pieces of petrified wood—perishable wood fiber that had been transmuted by the infusion of colorful and enduring minerals.

President Kimball was mostly a silent prophet during his last four years. Watching his slow and painful decline, many members wondered why the Lord would allow his prophet—who had already suffered so greatly during his long years of service—to suffer the indignities of a

debilitated body and an inability to communicate freely. But perhaps the Lord wanted to offer the Church an example of humility, love, and enduring to the end.

In one of the temple meetings just a few months before the end, the apostles came in turn to offer greeting. Elder Marvin J. Ashton, knowing that the aged prophet had difficulty in seeing, said to him, "President Kimball, I am Marvin Ashton." Spencer took his hand, paused, and then finally said softly, "Marv Ashton, I love you."

Spencer once said, "I still wonder what the Lord was thinking about, making a little country boy like me President of his Church, unless he knew that I didn't have any sense and would just keep on working." No short man ever had a longer stride.

CAMILLA'S LAST YEARS

With Spencer gone, the Church security men and the insurance-provided nurses ended their assignments. The nurses bundled up the equipment and supplies at the apartment to be returned to the LDS Hospital. Within a few days Camilla, almost ninety-one, vacated the rooms where she and Spencer had lived for four long years and returned to the home they had built in 1947. She began life without Spencer after sixty-eight years of marriage partnership. She missed him terribly, but it felt reassuring to be back in her own familiar surroundings.

She picked up intellectual pursuits again, reading and going to lectures and watching television (mostly nature programs on public television). She greatly enjoyed visitors. A rare exception was one woman who, she complained, had absolutely nothing to talk about besides her husband and children.

Although she tried not to give in to her health problems, they increased.

Nearly two years after Spencer passed away, Camilla died at home on September 20, 1987, a few weeks before her ninety-third birthday. Attending physician Allan H. Barker certified the cause of death as renal insufficiency resulting from chronic aplastic anemia. After the funeral, held in the Assembly Hall on Temple Square, Camilla was buried beside Spencer, with whom she had shared a long, productive, and loving life.

Appendix I

PERSONAL ENCOUNTERS WITH SPENCER KIMBALL

"Doesn't Brother Featherstone have pneumonia or something?"

THE ACCUMULATION OF SMALL ACTS best illustrates a man's character. Spencer Kimball was intently watched and well reported in the small and well as in the large.

PERSONAL SPIRITUALITY

Dr. Ernest L. Wilkinson Jr., Spencer's personal physician during the 1970s, sensed the President's dedication when, sitting next to him during the sacrament prayers, he heard Spencer say under his breath, "I do love thee. Oh, how I love thee."

Elder Packer, paying tribute to President Kimball as a revelator, commented, "I don't think we've had a period of revelation equal to the last several years except the opening years of the Church."

Barbara B. Smith, Relief Society general president, once asked Spencer, "When you create a world of your own, what will you have in it?" He looked at the surrounding Rocky Mountains for a few moments before he answered, "I'll have everything just like this world."

Spencer's ability to communicate love was unusual. He said in Taipei, "Somehow the Lord gave me from the time of my birth a spirit of love. I loved my companions in the mission field. I loved those against whom I played basketball as a boy. I loved people in all the world. I love you." President Hinckley noted that perhaps George Albert Smith was the President most like Spencer in his common touch and his warmth toward individuals.

Artist James C. Christensen was painting a portrait of Spencer and

Camilla and mentioned the fact that he was also working on a picture of Christ. The Kimballs invited him and his wife to come to the Kimball home to talk about the project. They sat around the kitchen table enjoying milk and cookies and looking at a variety of pictures portraying Jesus. Camilla expressed her opinions; Spencer said nothing. Christensen finally posed the question directly, "President, if you were going to hang a painting of the Savior in your office, what would you want that picture to be like?" Spencer took off his glasses and put his face a foot away from the painter and said, "I love people; that's my gift. I truly love people. Can you see anything in my eyes that tells you that I love people? In that picture, I would like to see in the Savior's eyes that he truly loves people. It is not affected; it is not his job. He truly loves all people."

WORK

It is uncommon to see Spencer's combination of deep caring for people and relentless work ethic. He followed with energy the sign on his desk that urged, "DO IT." Tributes following his death repeatedly praised his "incredible regimen of hard work." In his first five years as President, when he was fully active, he traveled 350,000 miles.

A nephew returning from a mission stopped in Salt Lake City to visit his Uncle Spencer. When he arrived at the Church Administration Building late in the day, Spencer was still in meetings. Afterward the two went home and talked until after midnight with Camilla. "It seemed like I had just barely fallen asleep when I felt a hand gently touching my shoulder, and I heard Uncle Spencer's voice telling me we needed to get up." It was pitch black as they drove to the office—not yet 6:00 A.M. Spencer's car had been one of the last out of the parking lot the night before, and it was one of the first in the parking lot in the morning. He was cheerful and uncomplaining, although he must have been weary.

Spencer's sense of urgency about working was so intense that he refused to let Camilla install new carpet in his home study when carpet was being replaced in the living and dining room, partly because he did not want to disrupt his work by moving the desk, two tables, three filing cabinets, a console phonograph, and piles of books.

When he was traveling, he or Arthur (sometimes both) always carried a briefcase; the minute the plane took off, he began to work.

With Rafael Tobango of Ecuador at the dedication of the São Paulo Temple.

Occasionally, he would lay his head back, nap for ten or fifteen minutes, then come wide awake and set to work again. All through his life his ability to nap enhanced his ability to work. During Spencer's organization of two stakes in Australia in December 1960, the man who helped in scheduling interviews saw Spencer start each day at 5 A.M. and work through the day until after midnight, but if there were a time between interviews Spencer would simply lie on the floor, saying he would sleep for, say, ten minutes. He appeared to fall asleep immediately and to wake in ten minutes, refreshed.

In St. Louis, Spencer conducted a long priesthood training session. When he became weary, he asked the stake president to carry on while he lay down behind a couch in the room for a nap.

A young historian spent four Saturdays at the Kimball home doing intensive research in Spencer's journal for a biography of J. Reuben Clark Jr. Spencer advised him to take a break every few hours "or you'll ruin your health," hardly persuasive advice from a man as driven as he.

When others gave him the same advice, he brushed it aside. To Olive Beth, he said, "You know, I'm not irreplaceable. I have to get in all the licks I can." A *Church News* reporter asked, "Do you ever worry about working too hard, killing yourself?" Spencer said, "A little, but not very much. Not enough to stop." When a friend asked about the two petrified wood stumps on his front porch, he answered, "Those are to remind me that if I sit down too long I will be like those pieces of wood—petrified, hard and worthless." To coworkers he commented, "My life is like my shoes, to be worn out in service," a fitting simile for one who urged a lengthened stride.

One day about noon, Arthur urged Spencer to have some lunch and then take a nap. When he resisted Arthur said, "If I can't get you to rest, Sister Kimball will scold me." Spencer grinned, "Well, I'd rather she scolded you than me!"

Spencer believed in a gospel of doing. He took pride in being the one who suggested to Naomi Randall, the author of "I Am a Child of God," that she change the phrase "teach me all that I must know" to teach me all that I must *do*," to emphasize action over mere knowledge.

To the Twelve, he once said, "I am not afraid to die, but I am concerned that when I meet the Savior, he might say to me, 'Spencer, you could have done better.'"

D. Arthur Haycock, who knew him intimately, said, "He never wanted the job as President; he would have been content to go along quietly and do any work to which he had been called. But having been given the responsibility as President, he ignited the Church with his common touch, simplicity, warmth, and prodigious capacity for work."

Humility

Greatness and humility do not always go together, but they did in Spencer W. Kimball. "For the first time in my life," observed Elaine Cannon, "I think I understand about Christ's love as I watch President Kimball deal with people. . . . One of the nicest things about him is that he isn't even aware how marvelous he is." Elder Maxwell also observed, "There's a kind of innocence about him in that he doesn't realize how special he is."

Spencer once said to his brethren, "There were many, many common people in the Church, untrained, unschooled, but with faith, and good people, and maybe . . . that was the reason that I was called. It has given me a little comfort that maybe there are people in the Church whom I can touch."

A regional representative said that he observed Spencer enter the rest room of a Brazilian chapel where he saw paper towels littering the floor. He picked them up and wiped the washbasin area dry with them. Seeing this, the regional representative, who had previously thought it beneath his dignity to clean up after others, made it a practice to pick up any litter before a meeting and tell the people what he had seen Elder Kimball do.

Spencer's charity extended to everyone but himself. He frequently chastised himself for being "weak," "limited," "incapable," and "insignif-icant"—though he was the only one who thought so. His concern may have stemmed from worry that his inadequacies would reflect badly on the Church. In that vein Elder Packer commented, "If he's ever uncom-fortable, it's around people that might be termed 'prominent.'"

When he learned that Mormon Tabernacle Choir director Jerold Ottley had received a devastatingly critical anonymous letter, Spencer recommended his own procedure for dealing with a letter from some-one without the courage to sign it: "I read it carefully to see if I can learn from it. Then I have a special file for it," and he pointed towards the wastebasket. "I file it there," he said, smiling, "and I also file away any hurt or anger.'"

Despite such advice to others, Spencer felt criticism keenly. Although few knew it, he was easily stung, suffered in silence, and yearned for approval, particularly from his family and his Church associates.

Spencer's humility made him virtually immune to the subtle arro-gance that all too frequently accompanies high office. When the admin-istration building was being remodeled and the President's office enlarged, Spencer said, "I don't need an office that big." Church architect Emil Fetzer responded, "You don't, but the President of the Church does."

He was as quick to greet the building custodian as the stake presi-dent. During the 1974 oil crisis, Spencer asked Church members to walk rather than drive where possible. For that time, he and Camilla walked to church. He signed up for tithing settlement along with other ward members, asking for no special accommodation of his schedule. He was among the first to contribute to the ward budget. And when the bishop visited the sick, he often found President Kimball had been there before him. When the Kimballs' home teacher brought a filmstrip about sharing the gospel with friends, Spencer insisted he wanted to see it, although he had seen it before and was himself in the presentation.

One spring day in 1974 while Spencer and Camilla visited Ed's family, Ed, who was a ward home teaching supervisor, received a call from a young man saying that his companion could not meet appointments that had already been made. Ed said, "Come over; we'll find someone." Spencer volunteered and went home teaching with the boy, to the pleased surprise of the families they visited.

Elder Faust, who was assigned as an area representative for all of South America in July 1975, was looking on behalf of the Church for a home in São Paulo for his family. The realtor showed him large, elaborate homes. Elder Faust said to himself, "No, that little man from Arizona, Spencer W. Kimball, is going to come down here and visit us, and he is not at all pretentious." So he selected the least expensive house they looked at. It was comfortable and near the temple site. When Spencer saw the house he said, "This is just right."

In New York City, President Kimball, KSL radio general manager Don Bybee, and announcer Spencer Kinard were in an elevator in the CBS Building. Don was the only one who knew where they were going. As they got off on the eighteenth floor Don said, "Spence, go to your left." President Kimball responded, "Anything you say, Brother Bybee." Smiling, he took Don by the arm and said, "You know, Brother Bybee, it's been a long time since anyone has called me Spence." Then to Kinard he said, "I've never really gone by Spence, so I'll be Spencer and you can be Spence."

When Belle Spafford and her counselors were released as the Relief Society general presidency, a dinner in their honor was held at the Hotel Utah. The children of counselor Louise Madsen held back from the buffet table to let the Church leaders serve themselves first. When Spencer noticed, he left the line, escorted them to his place in line, and went back to the end of the queue. Although embarrassed, they could not reject the gesture.

At a luncheon for regional representatives and their wives, Antonio Camargo's wife was delayed, so he waited by the door for her to arrive. When she finally came, the others had already been seated, and the Camargos looked around, wondering where to find places. Spencer, seeing them hesitate, walked over to the doorway where they stood and escorted them to the head table, where there were two empty chairs.

Spencer regularly had his hair cut in the Deseret Gym. One day he came in and, seeing the barber chair occupied, sat down to wait his turn. Customer Thor Leifson, uneasy at seeing the President waiting, whispered to the barber to find a stopping place and he would come back later for the rest of the trim. But the barber whispered that President Kimball would be unhappy if he saw that happen. It was apparent to Brother Leifson that Spencer had understood what happened, because when the haircut was finished, Spencer gave Leifson a hug and kiss on his cheek.

"I don't think we've ever had a leader with less ego to be administered to and who identifies himself more with everyone and likes everyone as well as Spencer W. Kimball does," commented scientist Henry Eyring.

KINDNESS AND LOVE TO OTHERS

Spencer was generous with his time and affection, both with those he knew and with those he met for the first time and who otherwise had no connection with him.

"He's completely selfless with his time and his energy," commented Marvin J. Ashton. "If there's a place where he is expected he thinks of the appointment and the people more than 'Should I go?' or 'Am I up to it?' He just goes."

He impressed visitors with the feeling that nothing and no one was more important than they. When he asked, "Tell me how things are with you," it was not small talk but genuine concern for another's well-being, conveyed by his tone, his attentiveness, his smile.

Between Saturday sessions of conference in April 1978 Spencer and Camilla attended a luncheon on the twenty-sixth floor of the new Church Office Building. In a well-intended effort to afford them a respite from people, the organizers set them off alone in a small room, but Spencer felt unhappy at the isolation.

In 1978, BYU–Hawaii gave Jack Sing Kong a "distinguished service award." Spencer was in Hawaii at the time, and at a garden reception the university president, Dan Andersen, introduced the two small men. Brother Sing, eighty-three, was being honored for his long service as

mayor and branch president at Kalaupapa, Hawaii's leper colony, where the wizened little man had lived for fifty-seven years. Despite the continuing stigma of leprosy and without hesitation or any apparent shred of self-consciousness, Spencer greeted the former leper with a warm embrace and kissed his disfigured face.

In a corridor of the Chicago airport a Church member recognized Spencer walking past and said to his companion, who often watched the Tabernacle Choir, "There goes the president of the Mormon Church." Spencer, aware that he had been recognized, came back, shook hands with the first man, looking up into the tall man's eyes, and said warmly, "It's good to see you again." Then he turned to the still taller companion and said, "Hello, I'm Spencer Kimball; who are you?" After an exchange of pleasantries, he wished them a good flight home and went on his way. It all took less than a minute but left an indelible memory of friendliness and warmth.

On a similar occasion his friendliness unnerved its recipient. One evening in the Church Office Building, H. David Burton, later the Church's Presiding Bishop, entered the elevator, saw a hand outstretched, and heard a voice that said, "I'm Spencer Kimball. Who might you be?" In his surprise at suddenly confronting one of his heroes, he was not quite sure who he might be but finally managed to mumble his name.

The love Spencer projected flowed back to him. Among his papers is an envelope on which a postal worker added a note: "Hi Pres. Kimball. I like to write a little note for you. So I working in U.S. post office at SLC. Anyway, I was born deaf. I really love to attend to deaf branch in Ogden. I really want to my goal to get marry in the temple. So I have to better go to work. Good luck in your life. I love you! Love, Pamela Tuckett"

Michael Rodriguez of *This People* magazine accompanied a photographer to the Kimball home to take pictures of Camilla for a story. When she answered the door, Spencer, wakened from a nap by the doorbell, came up behind her in his stocking feet. He took Michael's hands in his and smiled, filling Michael with warmth. He said, in his gravelly voice, "Brother Rodriguez, blessed are the valiant servants of the Lord." Then he leaned up to kiss the taller man on the cheek. Michael wanted at that moment nothing more earnestly than to be valiant.

In 1980, Spencer attended in Salt Lake City the annual football game between BYU and the University of Utah. After the game, L. Robert Webb, a young BYU administrator, approached him in the university president's box to shake his hand and express thanks for a recent article in the *Ensign*. Spencer drew him close and kissed him twice on the right cheek. "I love you," he said, then kissed his other cheek. Capturing the experience in his journal, Brother Webb wrote:

"I felt the texture of his face and even the strength of his aging arms, but more than that, I felt the love of the Savior radiating from him quite completely. No one else nor anything else seemed to matter to President Kimball just then. It was as if time stood still. The experience left me quite oblivious to all of the people about me. I realized anew the absolute power of love in its complete sharing with no second thoughts of embarrassment, acquaintance, or explanation. The experience touched me so completely that I had some difficulty re-entering the world of my surroundings. I felt renewed by the experience and consciously made an inward commitment to be more loving."

Young People

At a wedding reception in the Lion House, a young mother brought her two little sons to meet President Kimball. She said, "Children, this is the man you pray for every night." The small boys studied Spencer carefully as he gently greeted them. The older child finally spoke and said, "Do you have any candy?" "Why, yes," said President Kimball, ignoring the mother's chagrin. Unperturbed, he reached into his pocket and produced two wedding mints for the children.

A man with his eight-year-old son and the son's friend happened to see President Kimball on the street. On impulse, the man stopped the car and took the boys over to meet the prophet and shake his hand. Spencer warmly visited with the boys for several minutes. As they were leaving, he asked if he could kiss the boys and did so, providing a life-long memory.

Marion G. Romney, after long acquaintance, observed, "[Spencer] will put himself out any time to greet visitors that come with little children. He'll step out and shake hands with them, so that individual people from all walks of life love him more than any man I've ever seen."

Barbara B. Smith told President Kimball that her three-year-old grandson, who was accompanying her, had memorized nine of the Articles of Faith. Spencer asked, "Joshua, will you please say the first nine Articles of Faith for me?" Joshua did. Then Spencer invited, "When you learn all thirteen, will you come back and repeat them for me?" On Joshua's fourth birthday he was back. Spencer congratulated him: "Joshua, I'm proud of you." Then he issued another challenge: "When you have memorized the New Testament, come back again."

The 1978 centennial of Snowflake, Arizona, brought Spencer back to the state where he had spent more than half his life. It always felt like home. As his motorcade passed through the villages of Payson and Heber, dozens of people gathered along the road to catch a glimpse of their prophet. At one of the stops, Spencer noticed a small girl with leg braces; he picked her up as he had once carried his own small son in braces and kissed her.

On the same occasion, Spencer gave a hug and kiss to one of the law enforcement officers in the motorcade, then an inactive Church member. The officer later said, "That kiss changed my whole life."

He had an easy way with people, adults and children alike. When a little boy greeted him, "Hi, Kimball!" he responded cheerfully, "Hi, boy!" He visited a family home evening in a home in Mexico, bringing candy for the children and roses for the mother. On their invitation, he participated by telling them about his childhood and playing the piano while everyone sang.

In the summer of 1981, when Spencer was quite frail, a group of young women from Alaska and their leader drove in a van past the Kimball home just to see where the Prophet lived. When they stopped, a security man came to the van and explained that he was sorry, but the President could not come out to meet them. They had not expected that he would. But just then the door opened, and Spencer beckoned to the guard. The guard returned with the message that the President would like to greet them. So they lined the walkway to the house, and he shook each one's hand and made a personal comment. The leader had surgery scars on her throat not unlike his, and he asked about her condition. Then he walked back up the line, shaking everyone's hand again and telling them good-bye. As they drove away, the leader remarked that the house was "the most beautiful white cottage she had ever seen"—it literally glowed. Their driver disagreed, saying that the house was red, but his passengers unanimously agreed that the house was a glowing white. To settle the point, the driver drove back past the house. This time, they saw a small red-brick house partly covered with ivy.

On New Year's Day 1976, as many of the Kimball family as could gather had dinner together at the Kimball home. Four young men from California knocked on the door, wanting to meet the President. When Spencer learned that they had not eaten, he had Camilla prepare a meal for them and chatted while they ate. They stayed and stayed. After they finally left, Ed asked, "Was all that necessary?" Spencer replied mildly, "I belong to all the people, not just to my family."

Ed had heard his father use this phrase before. A week earlier, Ed's neighbors had entertained elders from the Missionary Training Center in Provo, Utah, for Christmas dinner. Knowing that the President was at Ed's house, the neighbors asked whether the missionaries might come and meet President Kimball. Ed responded that he preferred his father enjoy the holiday undisturbed. But when Spencer learned about the request, he said, "I belong to all the people, not just to my family," and insisted on walking to the neighbors' home to meet the elders.

A young convert at BYU, who because of parental opposition had had to wait for baptism until she was eighteen, supported herself by working in one of BYU's kitchens. When Spencer was at BYU and heard of her story, he insisted on being taken into the kitchen to meet her. He told her, "I love you and the Lord loves you."

President Kimball once received as a gift a set of books bearing the note "From the bindery girls at the BYU Press." After his talk to the BYU student body, he appeared at the Press building and said, "I came to see 'the bindery girls.'" He was ushered into the back work area and shook hands with each of the surprised and elated student workers.

A chorus of young people traveling through Salt Lake City decided, on the spur of the moment, to perform for the prophet at his office. Arthur explained that Spencer had a full schedule of appointments and also was not feeling well; he suggested they sing in the lobby where President Kimball would be able to hear them even though he could not attend their impromptu concert.

After singing two or three numbers, they sang reverently "We Thank Thee, O God, for a Prophet." As they sang, Spencer interrupted the meeting in his office, appeared in the doorway, and listened. Then he moved forward, thanked them all, and shook their hands, speaking to each one and encouraging them to go on missions and to marry in the temple. One of the young men in the group said, "President, I sent my mission papers in before we left California. I can't wait to get home and find out where I am going." Spencer, who had been returning to his office, stopped, turned back, and asked mischievously, "Would you like to know now?"

"I sure would," said the young man, "but they told me I would have to wait until I returned home."

Spencer smiled, "I think we might be able to tell you now." He asked Arthur to call the Missionary Department. A few minutes later, Arthur handed him a slip of paper. Spencer looked at it, then teased, "Are you sure you want to know?" He chuckled and announced, "Taiwan!"

At the Chicago airport, a disheveled young man with unkempt hair and beard kept looking at President Kimball. He apparently recognized him and asked a security aide if he could speak to him. After a few minutes of conversation, Spencer reached up, tugged the young man down to hug him, then kissed him on the cheek. The young man wiped away a tear as he went on his way.

A young man attending BYU–Hawaii fought off any suggestions he go on a mission and  let his hair grow to express his rebellious feelings. He tucked his long hair into a cap when he went to class. He felt unloved. One day President Kimball was on campus to speak to the students. Later, the young man sat on a bench by the temple, musing. He saw a cluster of people gathering around the temple entrance, and

President Kimball emerged. The first thought that came was anxiety that President Kimball would discern his rebellious spirit and chastise him for having long hair in violation of school rules. As the prophet came nearer, he left the group and walked directly to the youth, who later recalled, "A feeling of shame engulfed my soul and I wanted to run. When he reached me, he threw his arms around my neck, kissed my cheek, and whispered, 'I love you.' I could not dispute it—he loved me. I actually felt it. I cried. I couldn't control myself. I went behind the temple and continued to sob as his pure love melted away my anger and bitterness."

ASSOCIATES

Spencer showed great consideration for his fellow workers in the Church. When Spencer needed to see Church architect Emil Fetzer, he called and asked, "Would it be all right if I came over to talk with you?" Brother Fetzer responded, "I'll be there right away." Elder Maxwell confirmed Spencer's practice: "Sometimes . . . President Kimball would just show up at my office and ask, 'Is Brother Neal in?'" Similarly, when Spencer called Elder Maxwell to serve as an Assistant to the Twelve, he went unannounced to the Maxwell home.

Elder Vaughn Featherstone was serving as mission president when his son became engaged to marry. Normally mission presidents do not leave their fields of labor for such family events, but Spencer commented innocently, "Doesn't Brother Featherstone have pneumonia or something? Don't you think we ought to have him come home at conference time for a checkup? And while he is here he can perform the ceremony for his son."

When Thomas E. Brown, a stake president and Church employee, had occasion to confer with the President, Spencer would have him sit beside him. During their conversation, Spencer would hold his hand and tell him how much he loved him. Brother Brown remembered with deep emotion: "I would have climbed any mountain, swum any sea, crossed any desert for him. I believe he was the first man to ever say that he loved me; I never remember my father telling me that."

As they both sat on the stand in their home ward sacrament meeting, Spencer took Neal Maxwell by the hand and whispered, "Do you know that I love you with all my heart?" The next week Spencer renewed the sentiment: "Do you remember what I said to you last week?"

After one of the solemn assemblies, the visiting General Authorities attended a buffet dinner with local leaders at the home of a bishop. Spencer jumped up from his seat and trotted across the patio to where one of the wives sat. He said, "My dear, your chair is too close to the edge of the patio; I am afraid you will fall off." He helped her move her chair and stayed to visit with her and her husband.

It is not that Spencer was incapable of sharpness. In May 1981 he went to the St. George Temple to install a new president. In the solemn assembly when he was announcing the change in leadership, he got the names confused. Elder W. Grant Bangerter stepped up and whispered that he was making a mistake. Because the microphone was attached to Spencer's glasses people heard him say, sharply, "I'm in charge here." Elder Bangerter shrank back and began to weep. Spencer recovered his composure, got the names right, and proceeded. At the end of the meeting he undertook to repair the damage, announcing, "Before I conclude, we would like to hear the testimony of Elder Bangerter."

PEOPLE IN SERVICE

Because there had previously been a serious threat on Spencer's life in St. George, security was high during that May 1981 trip. When it came time for him to leave the temple for the airport about ten St. George police officers surrounded the waiting car, creating a shield to protect him. Arthur told Spencer to get in the car quickly, but Spencer went from one police officer to another and shook each man's hand, saying, "Thank you for being willing to give your life for me."

One Saturday evening in the late 1970s, after attending eight hours of conference sessions, Spencer stood by the back choir exit to the Tabernacle and shook hands with every member of the priesthood chorus that had provided music. He also often stopped by the translation booths in the Tabernacle to speak to the translators and thank them personally for their work.

In 1977, President Kimball went to Logan to attend the funeral of Elder Alma Sonne of the First Quorum of the Seventy. As soon as he stepped out of his car, he headed for a police car he saw waiting on the far side of the parking area. He surprised the police chief, Ferris Groll, who had assigned himself the task of overseeing security on the occasion, by coming over to express his appreciation for the concern shown by the police presence.

When Spencer traveled, local men were asked to serve as drivers and to provide on-site security. In June 1978, in Hawaii for rededication of the temple, the local Hawaiian driver asked Presidents Kimball, Tanner, and Romney whether they would consider stopping at his home for a moment to say hello to his family, and they agreed. The driver turned off the highway toward his home without notifying the security men, who were expecting him to follow their car to the hotel. While the driver ran into his home to get his family, Presidents Tanner and Kimball got out of the car. One of the family took Spencer around back to see the garden they had planted on his advice, and when a young man watering the garden with a hose turned around to see who was coming, he sprinkled Spencer's trousers, to the gardener's great embarrassment.

By now a crowd of neighbors had begun to gather. The driver, belatedly realizing the security personnel must have missed them, urged that they leave. Meanwhile, security men searched frantically for the missing car. When the Presidency's car caught up with them, men were leaning out the windows looking about anxiously for the "lost" prophet. The driver expressed concern, but Spencer said, "Don't worry. We had a nice visit." He made sure that no one chastised the driver.

Photographer Bill Duncan came to the Kimballs' home to make portraits of Spencer and Camilla together. Spencer struck up a friendship with him. He added Bill to their Christmas card list and even looked up his children in the Church records and sent each an autographed copy of the Book of Mormon.

Gerry Avant, a *Church News* reporter, accompanied the presidential party to the Midwest in September 1978 when Spencer was dedicating a stake center in Independence, Missouri. When they reached Kansas City her suitcase was not among the luggage. Spencer expressed his concern when he learned of the problem. About midnight that evening a local member knocked on Gerry's door and asked what size dress she wore. President Kimball had arranged for someone to lend her clothes for the next day's activities.

In June 1978, Janet Brigham, the *Ensign's* news editor, went to Nauvoo to report the dedication of the Relief Society Monument to

Women. From a distance she observed President Kimball was always surrounded by an entourage and people crowding in to shake his hand and talk to him. She hung back, collecting quotations and fighting off mosquitoes, feeling puzzled by a powerful desire to tell President Kimball that she loved him, particularly because of the recent revelation on priesthood. She thought of writing a letter but doubted it would get past his secretary. She felt so strongly about this impulse to speak to him that she even prayed about it.

The next morning right after one of the public meetings, she received instructions to take the *Ensign* photographer and hurry to Joseph Smith's red-brick store, where President Kimball was going. But at that moment the photographer was in a plane taking aerial shots of Nauvoo, so she decided to use her own camera and do the best she could. As she drove up across from the store, she saw a cluster of dignitaries around the President and dreaded being in yet another situation where important people would treat her as invisible. But as she started to cross the street, Spencer looked in her direction, broke away from the group, and walked over to greet her. She introduced herself and said, "You know, President Kimball, there's something I've wanted to tell you." She saw a slight look of apprehension on his face, as if he had heard more advice than he wanted, but he nodded politely and asked what that might be. She said, "I've wanted to tell you I love you." She then explained how deeply touched she had been by the announcement of the priesthood revelation. "Somehow I felt it was important for you to know that."

A tear came to his eye, and he held her hand for a long time, saying, "Thank you" and expressing appreciation for the love of Church members. She felt that just as his humility enabled him to be the messenger for the revelation, so his humility allowed him to receive the love of the Saints. Although she had been much in evidence as a reporter, of all the dignitaries only he spoke to her that day.

THE TROUBLED, THE SICK, THE NEEDY

A young woman in Spencer and Camilla's neighborhood was excommunicated after confessing serious misconduct. For a month, every night after their supper, Spencer and Camilla walked down the street to her house to visit and comfort, setting an example for their neighbors.

Elder Boyd K. Packer mused, "A lot of people like things clean and comfortable. He's always been willing to go out to where the people are and he . . . really relates to people, especially to the children.

"I couldn't name the times that I've been called in his office and have been asked the question, 'Are we doing everything we can? Is there something we should be doing and we're not?' He somehow keeps track of thousands of individuals. If there's something left hanging you'll get a telephone call."

People sensed his compassion. A woman related to Olive Beth that five years earlier her child had died. She suffered and grieved, unable to be reconciled to her loss. Then she dreamed that President Kimball came to her and took her hand comfortingly. When she woke from the dream, she said, she could still feel the comforting touch of his hand on hers.

In a somewhat similar experience, Adan Gutierrez, a father who was very troubled about his rebellious son, dreamed that he was in the temple. President Kimball, dressed in white, hugged him and said three times, "Everything is going to be all right." A few days later, his

Clockwise from top right: Camilla, Spencer, brother Dell Kimball, sister Alice Nelson, sister-in-law Clara Kimball, the last family members of his generation, about 1978.

priesthood quorum asked for volunteers to work at the temple. Brother Gutierrez volunteered and had a strong impression that he should arrive early, though he did not know why. As he entered the temple, the temple president met him and asked, "How would you like to meet the prophet? Look behind you; there he is." President Kimball put his arms around him as in the dream. No words were spoken, but Brother Gutierrez felt the words "Everything is going to be all right." Shortly after that, the son accepted a mission call.

A convert of two years, present in the Tabernacle to watch the choir rehearse, suddenly had a strong impression and told his cousin, excitedly, "The prophet is in the building!" Just then Spencer appeared on the stand from backstage, having come to the rehearsal to greet Donald Ripplinger, the new assistant director of the Tabernacle Choir.

Spencer spent a good deal of time in the hospital, both as patient and as visitor. In LDS Hospital, a nurse brought a woman ready to go home in a wheelchair to the elevator. When the doors finally opened, they saw President Kimball in the elevator. The nurse and he exchanged smiles, then she realized that the elevator was full. In that instant, Spencer stepped off the elevator, saying, "I'll get off here and you can get on." The nurse replied, "No, President, we can wait for the next one." Then someone in the rear spoke up and said, "If we all push together there will be room," and they did. As the elevator descended, the position of the wheelchair put the nurse face to face with President Kimball, and she thanked him. He took her hand and held it.

Dr. Frank Madsen, a young bishop, lay dying of cancer in LDS Hospital. His wife, Vivian, who had come down to the lobby for a newspaper, saw President Kimball and felt impressed to invite him to visit her husband, despite a reluctance to impose on him. Spencer agreed readily and seemed eager to meet her husband and to learn all about their family. Brother Madsen explained that he had already received an administration for his illness and had faith in its healing power; but when President Kimball asked if he would like another blessing, he said, "To have a prophet lay his hands on my head would be a great honor."

In describing the prayer, Brother Madsen said, "It was almost as if the Savior were standing there." The prayer asked the Lord to spare him, "but if it be thy will to have him come unto thee, we accept thy decision." Spencer also prayed for Sister Madsen to receive strength (she was pregnant with their seventh child) and for the children to be strong leaders in the Church. As he finished praying, he leaned over and kissed Frank on the forehead. Sister Madsen's concern about imposing on Spencer vanished as she sensed his kindness and concern.

The next day she answered a gentle knock on her husband's hospital room door and found President Kimball standing there. He said that in his earlier visit he had felt a strong impression this man had a very choice spirit. He kissed Brother Madsen again, visited a while, then kissed him again upon leaving. Frank told his wife, "Three times the prophet kissed me . . . All my suffering, all my pain, all my concern has been worth it, to have had this one experience."

A few days later, President Kimball wrote an encouraging letter to the Madsens, paid a third visit, and then a fourth. When Frank died in November 1976, President Kimball wrote to his wife, "We came to love Frank very much as we visited with him in the hospital. I could hardly understand how he could be so pleasant and smiling when he was so ill. We pray for you in your childbirth and with you in the rearing of those splendid children. May the Lord continue to bless you."

In February 1978 Spencer noted in his journal, "This evening on my way home I went by way of the LDS Hospital to see Brother Roy Simmons and Brother Noble; but after seeing them, word must have spread that I was in the hospital and about twenty others requested that I stop in to see them, which I did."

A young man in a wheelchair with a terminal illness came in 1976 to the Church Administration Building, wanting to meet a General Authority before he died. He was referred to the office of Rex E. Pinegar, of the Seventy. But Spencer, learning of the situation, hurried to Elder Pinegar's office so he, too, could spend a few moments with the youth.

Elder Monson took Bishop Hans Schult, from East Berlin, GDR, to meet President Kimball. In their conversation Spencer did not ask about organizational matters, but "Do our people have enough to eat? Are the widows cared for?"

NEIGHBORS

The Kimballs brought their small-town neighborliness to Salt Lake City. When Elder Didier's family moved into a house next to the

Kimballs in 1979, the first person to knock on their door was President Kimball, bringing a cantaloupe from Camilla's garden.

When Spencer was out in his yard, his neighbor "Sam" Parker liked to visit with him. Sam's wife, Saundra, once said, "You shouldn't impose on President Kimball to have to visit with you all the time. He deserves a little privacy." So Sam stopped going out to visit. After about ten days, Spencer appeared at the door with a plate of cookies. "I'm here to apologize," he said.

A shocked Sam exclaimed, "What for?"

"I don't know," replied President Kimball. "It is for whatever I did that made you mad at me. You used to come out to visit me, but now you seem to be avoiding me."

Spencer's gestures were remarkably open and physically affectionate. In mainstream American culture the emotional reticence of men is notorious. Ed asked his father why he kissed so many people. Thoughtfully, Spencer replied, "It did not seem right when I was an apostle." Now, however, he felt like everyone's grandfather, and it felt right to express affection that way.

HUMOR

Despite his serious responsibilities, Spencer had a great sense of humor, expressed mostly in quips, puns, and teasing rather than anecdotes or storytelling. In the Church Administration Building, a man once went up to Spencer's nephew, Nick Udall, who looked a great deal like Spencer, and addressed Nick as "President Kimball." When Nick reported the incident to Spencer, the response was, "Were you embarrassed?"

In 1975 when Spencer flew to Arizona for his brother Gordon's funeral, Nick drove him to the chapel. On the way Spencer protested, "The chapel is the other way."

Nick said, "I'll get you there."

"You're going the wrong way," insisted Spencer, who refused to believe that he did not know everything important about Arizona.

"Just wait."

At the chapel, a florist's van was making deliveries. Nick said, "You see?"

Spencer only smiled. "Somebody else must be having a funeral, too."

"But you see there, our relatives are going in."

"How can they go to two funerals at the same time?" he joked.

Before the October 1977 conference, photographers posed the First Presidency. When one asked Spencer to smile, he said, with a twinkle in his eye, "What, twice in one day?"

A Church member asked L. Tom Perry and Spencer to pose together for a photograph, promising to send a copy. When Spencer received the photograph, the top of the much taller Apostle's head was out of the camera frame. He forwarded it to Elder Perry with a droll note: "I think this is one of the best pictures ever taken of you."

When he and his friend John Simonsen attended a golden wedding anniversary party, someone said in tribute to the couple that they had never raised their voices at one another. Spencer whispered to John, "It must have been a little dull sometimes."

He teased Elders Perry and McConkie about their singing ability, commenting that at general conference, "with the Tabernacle Choir behind you, maybe you should just mouth the words."

After the new Seventies were set apart in the temple in October 1975, some of them and their family members entered the elevator at the same time as Spencer and Camilla. One joked, "Oh, we're safe on this elevator now because President Kimball is with us."

Spencer chuckled and replied, "Now don't be too sure about that. Last week in the Church Office Building I was trapped between floors for nearly an hour."

At the Hotel Utah late one night, a hurried Mitt Romney stuck his bag into the elevator door as it was closing. It opened again to reveal President and Sister Kimball. Embarrassed, Mitt introduced himself, and Spencer said, "You look like a Romney."

Mitt responded, "Thank you, I guess."

"What do you mean, I guess?"

Mitt said, apologetically, "Well, we Romneys have such huge jaws."

With a straight face, Spencer said, "Camilla is a Romney." Then, after a moment, seeing Mitt's discomfiture, he laughed.

His good friend and secretary Arthur Haycock was the object of many jests. On the drive from Cincinnati to the airport, Spencer claimed the reclining front passenger seat and went to sleep immediately while the stake president drove him and Arthur to catch their plane. Making conversation, the stake president said, "Brother Haycock, do you have any grandchildren?"

Arthur said, "Yes."

Spencer came awake enough to say, "For heaven's sake, don't ask him about them! We'll miss the plane."

Spencer and Arthur were the same height and build, so if Spencer went on a diet, he thought Arthur should do so, too. Some days, hungry Arthur would suggest lunch, at least a bowl of soup. Spencer sternly refused. But Arthur was puzzled. He was losing weight but Spencer was not. After a time, Arthur solved the mystery when he chanced across cookies, nuts, and other snacks squirreled away in Spencer's desk.

One evening Spencer stayed late at the office, so Arthur continued working at his desk. It turned out that Spencer was waiting for Camilla to join him for a 6:30 dinner next door at the Lion House. About 5:30, Spencer urged Arthur to go home, but Arthur said he would stay. When Spencer insisted, Arthur said, "I am torn between doing what I think I should and doing what you ask me to do." Spencer smiled and said, "They should both be the same, shouldn't they?'"

When Spencer learned that Dr. Homer Ellsworth had moved from Salt Lake City to the town of Lehi, President Kimball asked him, "Homer, how many acres do you have?"

"Ten acres."

"Do you have a year's supply?"

"Yes."

"If there were an emergency, how many people could you help?"

"With ten acres we could have a huge garden, if there were enough water."

"I was just checking," said Spencer solemnly. "If things get tough, I want to know where to come."

Long-time friend Harold Wright said that when he was mission president Spencer told him he could be released if, by putting full-time missionaries in the Big Horn area of Wyoming, he could create two stakes out of five mission districts. After some hard work, the two stakes were organized, and Harold reminded Spencer of his promise.

Spencer said, "Harold, do you ever eat gooseberry pie?"

"No," said the puzzled Harold.

"You must have, and it caused you to dream. I would never have said anything like that."

During a visit to the Kimball home, daughter-in-law Bee grumbled that the zucchini in her garden were not growing. The following week she said, "Last week when I came I was complaining about our zucchini, but now the vines are growing fine."

Spencer quipped, "You should have complained sooner."

On a trip to Hawaii, Elaine Cannon gave some fudge she had just made to the security man traveling with the party. The next day he said, "I shared the fudge with President Kimball and he wanted to know whether you had any more."

By then the fudge was gone, but when she returned to Utah, Elaine had the fifteen women of the Young Women presidency and general board each make four pounds of fudge with the same recipe. They then arrived for a meeting with the First Presidency rolling a cart bearing a beautifully wrapped box containing sixty pounds of fudge. Delighted but also somewhat appalled, Spencer protested, "I didn't know we were supposed to have a year's supply of fudge, too!"

An indication of how thoroughly Spencer depended on Camilla's homemaking occurred one Sunday while Spencer was working at home. His security guard came to the ward chapel to call a concerned Camilla out of Relief Society. He explained that President Kimball wanted to know where to find the thermostat.

Another day Spencer was chatting in the kitchen when Camilla stuck her head through the door from outside and said, "Spencer, would you please hand me the garbage container?"

He said, "Yes, but where is it?"

She laughed, "By the hall door, where it's been for twenty-five years."

One day Spencer started, uncharacteristically, to dry the dishes as Camilla washed. Saundra Parker, their next door neighbor, happened to be there, and Spencer announced, "Saundra, please mark down in your journal that I have done the dishes for Camilla."

CORRESPONDENCE

Spencer maintained a huge correspondence, official and private. Although he wrote some letters on his own typewriter at home, as

President he usually dictated them to a Dictaphone to be transcribed by his secretary. He often added a handwritten postscript.

While serving as a mission president in 1979 Elder Busche sent Spencer a Christmas card with a picture of his family. He soon received a letter obviously personally typed by Spencer thanking him for the card and noting, "You forgot to mention the names of your children."

Over the years he wrote to young cousin Stanley B. Kimball at least sixty-seven letters, some just a few paragraphs but many much longer, usually signed "Uncle Spencer."

He once chastised his namesake nephew, Spencer Brinkerhoff: "You don't write to me very often."

"But Uncle Spencer, my writing is an imposition on you, since you answer every one of my letters, and I know how busy you are."

He was diligent about expressing appreciation.

Over a period of years R. Quinn Gardner, who worked in the Church welfare department dealing with emergencies, received twenty-nine typed and two handwritten notes from President Kimball, expressing appreciation, asking questions, and making suggestions.

When Brother Schein, a convert of only a few months, lay dying of cancer, he called President Kimball's office and made an appointment to talk with him by telephone. But when he called, Spencer was not there because Brother Schein had forgotten to account for the time difference between Texas and Utah. In a few days, however, he received a personal letter and a copy of Spencer's talk "Tragedy or Destiny." In the short time remaining before he passed away, Brother Schein delighted to show visitors the gracious letter from his "head man."

A young engaged couple, happy to be married in the temple, put President Kimball at the top of their invitation list. They wanted their prophet to know that they were following his counsel, but they had no expectation of a response. To their great surprise, the mail brought a copy of The Miracle of Forgiveness. President Kimball had cut their picture from the invitation and pasted it inside the front cover and had written a personal greeting.

A friend in Arizona failed to contact Spencer when her husband died. She considered writing him a bit presumptuous. But Spencer learned of the death and sent a letter of condolence with an apologetic postscript: "I typed this myself. I will not have a steno till Monday, and that is too late."

When Elder Kikuchi was a stake president in Japan, he sent a wire to the Salt Lake Temple requesting that the name of a family member suffering with cancer be added to the prayer rolls. He soon received a personal letter from President Kimball expressing sympathy and concern for the family.

After Spencer's death, Camilla received many notes with messages of love and appreciation, mentioning how correspondence had linked them to Spencer:

"I joined the church eight years ago . . . Your husband wrote me after my baptism [Portland, Oregon]."

"He wrote us and our daughter when we first joined the church in 1979 [Walla Walla, Washington]."

"Though I am a sinner I could feel the love in his eyes. I was very fortunate to receive an answer to a letter I wrote to him [Honolulu, Hawaii]."

A friend, Quinn Gardner, expressed wonder, "Why do you answer your mail personally? How can you afford the time?"

Spencer replied, "This is my life, my joy!"

WHEN NO ONE IS WATCHING

If one anecdote were called on to represent the man's character, it should be one where he was anonymous. Almost all the stories about Spencer describe a man "on stage," with people watching who have high expectations of him. One anecdote does not. In October 1961, Sharon Morgan, a young mother, was on a direct flight from Utah to Michigan with a two-year-old daughter, LeaMarie. But bad weather forced her plane to land in Chicago, where she became stranded.

She found herself in the airport without food or clean clothing for the child and without money because she had left it all with her husband, who was driving a car loaded with their belongings, and she was to be met at the airport in Michigan. She was two months pregnant and threatened with miscarriage, so she was under doctor's instructions not to carry the child. Hour after hour she stood in one line after another, trying to get a flight to Michigan. The terminal was noisy, full of tired, frustrated, grumpy passengers, and she heard critical references to her crying child and to her sliding the child along the floor with her foot as the line inched forward. No one offered to help with the soaked, hungry, exhausted child until, as she later reported,

"Someone came towards us and with a kindly smile said, 'Is there something I could do to help you?' With a grateful sigh I accepted his offer. He lifted my sobbing little daughter from the cold floor and lovingly held her to him while he patted her gently on the back. He asked if she could chew a piece of gum. When she was settled down, he carried her with him and said something kindly to the others in the line ahead of me, about how I needed their help. They seemed to agree and then he went up to the ticket counter [at the front of the line] and made arrangements with the clerk for me to be put on a flight leaving shortly. He walked with us to a bench, where we chatted a moment, until he was assured that I would be fine. He went on his way.

"About a week later I saw a picture of apostle Spencer W. Kimball [in a film about the Indian Student Placement Program shown at church] and recognized him as the stranger in the airport."

Years later Spencer received a letter:

"Dear President Kimball: I am a student at BYU. I have just returned from my mission in Munich, West Germany. . . . I was sitting in Priesthood meeting last week, when a story was told of a loving service which you performed some twenty-one years ago in the Chicago airport. The story told of how you met a young pregnant mother with a young screaming child . . . waiting in a long line for her tickets. She was threatening miscarriage and therefore couldn't lift her child to comfort her. She had experienced four previous miscarriages which gave added reason for the doctor's orders not to bend or lift. You comforted the crying child, and explained the dilemma to the other passengers in line. This act of love took the strain and tension off of my mother. I was born a few months later in Flint, Michigan. I just wanted to thank you for your love. Thank you for your example!"

Appendix II

THE PRESIDENCY YEARS, 1974–1985: AN OVERVIEW

DURING THE FIRST SIX YEARS of his presidency (1974–79), Spencer W. Kimball approached the daunting calling with deep faith and commitment, extraordinary energy, sweeping vision of possibilities, and a depth and breadth of love that embraced everyone.

From 1979 to 1981 he maintained moderate activity; from 1981 to 1985 the effects of serious surgery drastically curtailed his ability to lead personally, but he had set the course, and his counselors carried on.

1974

In September hurricane Fifi caused the death of eight thousand in Honduras. The national political scene was largely dominated by the Watergate scandal, the subsequent hearings, and the rising clamor for impeachment of President Richard M. Nixon, which resulted in his resignation. President Kimball did not comment on this situation in his public addresses or his journal, apparently because he saw it as outside his area of greatest interest.

For Spencer, the year involved shouldering the weight of a new calling. The tasks themselves were not unfamiliar, but now there was no one to whom he could turn for answer except the Lord.

Early in his administration, he focused attention on missionary work, urging that all worthy young men should expect to serve and sharing a global vision that electrified those who heard it. As a result, the corps of missionaries grew, swelled not only by an increasing number of young men but by young women and older couples as well. He articulated a vision of missionaries coming not just from the United States, but from many nations, filling first the need for teachers of the restored gospel in their own lands and spreading across the globe into nations that did not yet allow proselytizing.

The Washington D.C. Temple was dedicated and Stockholm was the site of an area conference for the Saints in Scandinavia.

1975

In 1975 newspapers featured the end stages of the Vietnam War, from which the United States had earlier withdrawn, but this conflict went unreflected in Spencer's journal except indirectly, through his concern for the welfare of refugees.

Now that he had the responsibility for scheduling area conferences, he greatly increased the number held each year. In 1975 he traveled to São Paulo, Buenos Aires, Tokyo, Manila, Taipei, Hong Kong, and Seoul for such meetings, announcing in São Paulo and Tokyo that temples would be built there. Later he announced a temple for Seattle.

Some older temples, such as those in Mesa, Arizona, and St. George, Utah, underwent refurbishing, restoration, and, after a period of public tours, rededication.

As another aspect of President Kimball's "taking the church to the people" he held twenty-six solemn assemblies during the year, meeting in cities all over the United States and Canada to instruct stake and ward leaders on Church policies and their responsibilities.

Organizationally the Church outside the United States and Canada was divided into six and then eight administrative areas, each under supervision of an Assistant to the Twelve, later under a member of the First Quorum of the Seventy.[1] In 1976 the United States and Canada were also divided into areas. The Assistants became members of the Seventies quorums, with supervision a task of the First Quorum of the Seventy.[2]

Growth of the Church forced ever more decentralization. Stake presidents received authorization to ordain bishops. Church-wide conferences for auxiliaries ended.

The Church divested itself of the fifteen hospitals it had operated

---

1. In 1976 the United States and Canada were also divided into such areas, and in 1977 the areas became eleven zones with areas as subdivisions. The "area" label returned later.

2. In 1984 there were thirteen areas, each with three Seventies called as a presidency. By 1993 there were 23.

for years, and President Kimball resigned all corporate directorships except those few tied closely to the Church's main functions.

The First Quorum of the Seventy was reconstituted at October conference. At first it comprised only the First Council of the Seventy and three additional men. Two of the new men, among them Charles A. Didier of Belgium and George P. Lee, a Navajo, represented a beginning of national and racial diversity among the General Authorities.

Although President Kimball turned eighty years of age, he enjoyed reasonably good health during the year.

1976

A violent uprising in Soweto, South Africa, helped move that nation toward the end of apartheid. Viking II landed on Mars. And Mao Zedong, chairman of the Chinese Communist party, died. The nation celebrated the bicentennial of its Declaration of Independence.

As a major activity during 1976, Spencer participated in a continuing program of solemn assemblies and seventeen area conferences, held in the South Pacific, New Zealand, Australia, the British Isles, and continental Europe.

He announced a temple to be built in Mexico City, the largest outside the United States.[3]

In Church organization, the First Quorum of the Seventy more than doubled in size as all of the men then serving as Assistants to the Twelve were moved into this quorum. Among the new Seventies were Adney Y. Komatsu, a Japanese-American from Hawaii and the first non-Caucasian General Authority when he was called as an Assistant to the Twelve in April 1975, and Jacob de Jager, originally from the Netherlands. The Seventy became administrators of Church areas and departments under the supervision of the Twelve. The necessity of further delegation in the growing Church was underscored as stake presidents were authorized to ordain seventies.[4]

By vote of the conference, two revelations—a vision of the celestial

---

3. Even in the United States only the Salt Lake, Los Angeles, and Washington D.C. Temples would be larger than the one in Mexico City, although several temples were approximately same size (Provo, Ogden, and Seattle). The other new temples built over the next decade, except for the Jordan River and Bountiful Temples, were significantly smaller. Some remodeled older temples (e.g., St. George) had added enough floor space to be comparable to the large temples.

4. During President Benson's administration, the local office of seventy was terminated.

kingdom and work for the dead (given to Joseph Smith in 1836) and another about the Savior's ministry among the dead between his death and resurrection (given to Joseph F. Smith in 1918)—were added to the Standard Works.

A statement by the First Presidency put the Church officially in opposition to ratification of the proposed Equal Rights Amendment, opposition that continued energetically until the period for ratification ended in 1982. A drumbeat of criticism continued for the Church's policy of limiting the participation of members of African descent in priesthood and temple ordinances.

The Indian Student Placement program, which over the years had put thousands of LDS Indian children into the homes of LDS foster families during the school year, began to phase out. The 2,600 Indian children involved were down from a high of about 5,000 in 1970.

The Teton Dam in eastern Idaho failed, and the resultant flood made homeless 40,000 people, the great majority members of the Church. The Church Welfare program and innumerable Church members, bused in to work as volunteers, greatly aided the provision of relief.

President Kimball's health continued to be reasonably good, despite his age. He was able to ordain his older brother, Delbert, age eighty-six, an elder. Del had been inactive in the Church since he left home as a youth.

1977

The United States agreed to return the Canal Zone to Panama in 1999. "Star Wars" captivated the popular imagination. The worst airline disaster in history killed 574 people when two planes collided in the Canary Islands. The television miniseries based on Alex Haley's book Roots *stimulated an unprecedented interest in family history, giving the Church's genealogy resources wide publicity.*

During a trip to hold eight area conferences in Central and South America, President Kimball met with the heads of five nations. Upon the Church's receiving official recognition of the Church in communist Poland, Spencer traveled to meet with the Polish minister of religion and to dedicate the land again for preaching the gospel. This represented the first foray by a Church president behind the Iron Curtain.

General conference would hereafter last only two days and not necessarily include April 6, the anniversary of the Church's organization.

President Kimball's eyes began to fail him. He had his talks and reading matter typed in large print, but carried doggedly on. In September he had a sudden frightening attack for which hospital tests provided no explanation. After a blessing, he recovered enough to go home the next day, and in two days he left for Canada, resuming his work as though nothing had happened.

1978

Major news stories of the year included the mass suicide by poison of 917 followers of cult leader Jim Jones at Jonestown, Guyana. At Camp David the United States president Jimmy Carter brokered an accord between Egypt and Israel, a welcome step toward peace that President Kimball had long prayed for. John Paul II assumed the papal throne.

President Kimball conducted area conferences in Hawaii, South Africa, and South America. The Hawaii conference was the first of many held in the United States.

Announcement of the Jordan River Temple, a second temple in the Salt Lake Valley, reflected the population growth in that locality and the consequent increase in temple activity. A Church-wide name extraction program began to provide names for vicarious temple work. President Kimball dedicated the São Paulo Temple, the first of the temples announced and completed during his administration.

Semiannual stake conferences replaced the traditional quarterly meetings, and even so General Authorities could attend no more than half the time. The first all-Church women's fireside was held and telecast, becoming an annual event, followed soon by a Young Women's general meeting each spring.

A First Presidency statement recognized that the Church was not the only source of truth, that great religious leaders and philosophers over the centuries also received inspiration and transmitted divine wisdom. This positioned the Church to establish more cordial relations with the Islamic and Far Eastern worlds.

In June, the event occurred for which President Kimball's administration will always be best known. The First Presidency and Twelve received revelation confirming that the priesthood should be conferred on all worthy men and that persons of all races could share fully in temple ordinances. Probably no event in the century had the impact upon Latter-day Saints of this revelation overturning the long-standing restrictive policy. General Authorities, other than the Presidency and Twelve, were granted emeritus status, normally when they became seventy years old or suffered ill health.

President Kimball declined somewhat in health but continued to keep a vigorous calendar. He had been president of the Church five years. When a *Church News* reporter asked, "As you look ahead, what kind of things do you foresee or anticipate?" Spencer responded, "Well, I just see an extension of what we are doing. That's where I'm small, you see. I ought to be extending it. I ought to be seeing all the things that could happen."

And of his position as prophet: "I still feel that the Lord made a mistake, that He shouldn't have called me, that there were many, many men greater than I was who could have done a better job. That's very sincere. And I still wonder what was the Lord thinking about, making a little country boy like me [president of his Church] . . . unless He knew that I didn't have any sense and would just keep on working."

1979

During 1979, major news stories included a peace agreement between Israel and Egypt; an arms-limitation treaty with the Soviet Union signed by President Carter and Leonid Brezhnev, but still lacking approval by the Senate; and a leak of radioactive material from a nuclear plant at Three Mile Island. The United States and China resumed diplomatic relations after decades of separation. There was, of course, also the usual litany of crimes and airliner crashes. President Kimball saw international developments, when he commented on them at all, through the lens of missionary potential. The Shah of Iran suffered overthrow by the strict Islamic regime of Ayatollah Khomeini. Later in the year the Iranians took and held fifty-two hostages from the American embassy.

During 1979 the Church, which had six hundred stakes when Spencer became president, created again a stake in Nauvoo, timed to be the thousandth stake. A new edition of the Bible came from the press, with many new study aids.

President Kimball attended only two of the year's ten area

conferences in the United States, Canada, New Zealand, and Australia, because of deteriorating health. In September he underwent surgery to evacuate a life-threatening subdural hematoma, bleeding in the brain. He recovered enough, however, to participate fully in October general conference and then travel to Israel to dedicate the Orson Hyde Memorial Garden on the Mount of Olives. In November a recurrence of the hematoma required new surgery, an event marking the midpoint of his twelve years as president and the beginning of steep decline.

1980

The most significant news stories of the year included Iran's continued detention of fifty-two hostages from the United States embassy in Teheran, finally released in January 1981. The people elected Ronald Reagan president by a landslide. Economic recession with high inflation and a prime interest rate of over 20 percent shook the people. The ill-fated Soviet invasion of Afghanistan continued for years before withdrawal. Mount St. Helens in the state of Washington provided the greatest volcanic eruption in United States history. Labor strikes in Poland, though temporarily suppressed by Soviet tanks, set in motion a series of events leading to the breakdown of the Soviet Union. War over border territory that would last for years commenced between Iran and Iraq.

President Kimball recovered again substantially from the second brain operation and resumed his work with surprising energy. In the winter he participated in a series of area conferences held in the Far East, timed to coincide with the dedication of the Tokyo Temple.

The year 1980 brought the sesquicentennial celebration of the organization of the Church.

He dedicated the Seattle Temple and announced seven new, small temples.

A few missionary couples had gone to Nigeria and Ghana right after the 1978 revelation, but a regular mission was established in West Africa in 1980.

The Church adopted a consolidated meeting schedule and a unified curriculum on a calendar-year basis.

Mark Hofmann "discovered" the first of many controversial documents relating to Church history that he forged. His deceptions continued until 1985, when he committed two murders in an effort to cover up his unraveling scheme.

President Kimball turned eighty-five.

1981

The Iran hostage crisis ended early in the year. The Soviet Union crushed the Solidarity workers' strikes in Poland, but the Iron Curtain had begun to show its cracks. President Ronald Reagan was wounded by a mentally disturbed attacker. The first woman Supreme Court justice, Sandra Day O'Connor, took the bench. AIDS was first identified as a serious health threat and continued its spread.

The First Presidency issued a statement opposing the basing of a massive MX missile system in the Utah-Nevada desert, possibly the decisive step in halting the project.

The series of area conferences ended. Sixty of the sixty-three occurred during the Kimball presidency, and he missed only eight of those, all in 1979 because of illness.

Satellite dishes installed at 500 stake centers constituted a giant step toward making general conference sessions and general firesides available live to members in widely scattered areas.

The Church published a new edition of the Triple Combination.

In 1981, the Jordan River Temple was dedicated, ground was broken for several temples, and nine more new temples were announced.

At April conference, President Kimball noted that during the past six months he had traveled 50,000 miles in Church service. In July the president, conscious of his own physical difficulties and the fading abilities of his counselors, N. Eldon Tanner and Marion G. Romney, called as a third counselor Gordon B. Hinckley, a man capable and vigorous enough to carry the load of the First Presidency alone, if need be.

Spencer's sister Alice passed away, leaving him the last of his parents' family and one of the last of Heber C. Kimball's many grandchildren.

In May, President Kimball traveled to Santiago, Chile, for the ground-breaking of the temple to be built there. It proved to be his last major trip, because in September he required a third operation to remove another subdural hematoma. From this point on he was largely confined to an apartment in the Hotel Utah.

1982

The major news stories of the year included a suffering economy, with employment at a forty-two-year low. England and Argentina had a ten-week battle over control of the Falkland Islands in the south Atlantic. Israeli troops invaded Lebanon and later allowed a massacre of Palestinians there. The United States administration covertly supported the Guatemalan Contras in their opposition to the Sandinista government. Utah's legislature passed a Cable TV Decency Act, only to have courts rule that it was unconstitutional. And Barney Clark, an LDS dentist from Seattle, received the first artificial heart, developed at the University of Utah. He survived four months, connected to a machine. The Equal Rights Amendment was defeated after ten years of ratification effort.

In 1982, President Kimball gave his last talk at general conference. But the work of the Church went on. Church membership swelled to five million. Five more temples were announced, including one in Freiberg, in Communist East Germany.

The Church assumed responsibility for the costs of all chapel construction, leaving the local members responsible only for some operating expenses.

1983

The pope's visit to Poland lent support to the Polish workers' Solidarity movement. In Beirut a reported 241 American marines and fifty UN French peacekeepers died in a terrorist bombing. The United States invaded the island of Grenada on the premise that American students studying there stood in danger. Realization grew that an AIDS epidemic was spreading worldwide, with millions of victims.

President Hinckley dedicated six temples in 1983 as the only active member of the First Presidency.

Multistake (regional) conferences began, replacing area conferences. The first of these convened in London.

1984

The bloody war of attrition between Iran and Iraq dragged on. A major mining tragedy—fire in Utah's Wilberg Mine–killed twenty-seven men, nearly half of them Latter-day Saints. Ronald Reagan won a second term as president by a large margin. Personal computers had already become ubiquitous for word processing and record keeping; the Internet lay in the future.

It took only five years for the Church to grow from one thousand stakes to fifteen hundred.

A major activity for President Hinckley was dedicating the many temples coming to completion. Forty-seven temples were operating or in the planning or construction phase. The new Church museum opened.

Some new members of the First Quorum of the Seventy received five-year appointments, rather than the lifetime callings that had previously characterized nearly all General Authority callings.

1985

The announcement by Soviet premier Mikhail Gorbachev that "perestroika" or openness should characterize Soviet society marked a clear turning point toward the breakdown of the totalitarian Soviet state with its hegemony over all of eastern Europe and more.

President Kimball turned ninety years of age in March. He attended sessions in each conference, but only with difficulty, and he no longer took an active role in Church leadership.

Two Church-wide fasts raised millions of dollars for the benefit of famine victims in Africa, particularly Ethiopia.

The missionary force reached 30,000 again. The total number had declined somewhat during a period of two-and-one-half years when the term for elders was shortened to eighteen months rather than twenty-four months.

The interview questions for temple recommends added an explicit requirement of testimony. Four temples, including one in Freiberg, East Germany, were dedicated by President Hinckley before the death of President Spencer W. Kimball on November 5.

Three social movements permeated the whole period of President Kimball's administration. They were the ongoing civil rights movement, seeking to do away with racial discrimination; a feminist movement determined to give women equal treatment before the law; and an increased openness about homosexual orientation and a claim that, like race and gender, same-sex orientation should be accepted as normal because it was inborn. The first two, racial and gender equal rights,

President Kimball encouraged, though he resisted the Equal Rights Amendment as an inappropriate means to achieve equal rights for women. He believed same-sex orientation aberrant and felt that if it could not to be changed it must be suppressed. Same-sex orientation did not constitute sin, but sexual activities outside male-female marriage were immoral.

PHOTO AND OTHER CREDITS

Thanks is expressed to all those who graciously allowed their photographs to be used in this work. The numbers below indicate the page numbers where photographs are found.

Photographs courtesy of *Deseret Morning News* (where known, these photographs are © the individual photographer):

Gerry Avant: 278
Pat Bagley: 157
Don Grayston: 91, 211, 416
J. Malan Heslop: 312, 314
Claudell Johnson: 130
O. Wallace Kasteler: 9, 61, 433
Gerald W. Silver: 66, 362
Tom Smart: 301
Owen Stayner: 411
Dell Van Orden: 319, 347, 349, 390
Photographer unknown: 39, 58, 72, 143, 145, 321, 325, 387

Photographs courtesy of the Church Archives, The Church of Jesus Christ of Latter-day Saints:

Royce L. Bair: 80
Eldon Linschoten: 20, 154, 261, 281
Gerald W. Silver: 267
Glade Walker: 298
Ernest L. Wilkinson Jr.: 317
Photographer unknown: 6, 8, 12, 19, 44, 51, 55, 94, 122, 133,

135, 137, 146, 147, 196, 199, 229, 243, 263, 270, 280, 291, 293, 297, 299, 303, 319, 325, 335, 360, 367, 395, 398, 399

Photographs courtesy of the Visual Resources Library, © Intellectual Reserve, Inc.: 100, 118, 121, 245

Photographs courtesy of independent photographers:
Bill Duncan: 213
Richard Holzapfel: xiv, 35, 92
Nyle Leatham: 84
Kenneth R. Mays: 166
Steve Nissle: 339
Mark A. Philbrick: 403
Fred Schwendiman: 350
E. Gary Smith: 259
J. H. Warner: 217
Eric W. White: 64

We are indebted to still other photographers whom we have been unable to identify.

Political cartoon courtesy of Calvin Grondahl: 157

INDEX

Abe, Fujio, 207
Abel, Elijah, 196, 197
Abortion, 43, 172
Abrea, Angel, 255
Activities committees, 270
Adam-God theory, 95
Adoption, 33, 43, 283; of blacks, 206
Affirmation, 87
Allred, Rulon, 16
American Indian Movement, 291
Andersen, Dan W., 321, 428
Andersen, Dwayne N., 365
Anderson, Guy, 104
Anderson, Tom, 14
Anthon transcript, 190
Area conferences, 311–43
Arnold, Marilyn, 165
Arrington, Leonard J., xiv, 99, 186–90
Art museum, 52
Artificial insemination, 85
Asay, Carlos E., 117
Ashby, Lord Eric, 149
Ashton, Marvin J., 46, 418, 427
Ashton, Wendell, 153, 156
Assistants to the Twelve, 256
Auxiliary organizations, 260
Avant, Gerry, 436

Balderas, Eduardo, 329
Ballard, M. Russell, 33, 253
Balles, John, 44
Ballif, Jae, 207

Bangerter, W. Grant, 8, 18, 358, 435
Barker, Dr. Allen, 387, 413, 420
Basic Unit Program, 266
Bateman, Marvin, 124
Bear Chief, Clem, 289
Begin, Menachem, 48
Belaunde-Terry, Fernando, 144
Bennion, Lowell, 203
Benson, Ezra Taft, 19, 113, 227; as
    experienced administrator, 12;
    ability to delegate, 36; on
    evolution, 96–97; political
    statements of, 159; on working
    mothers, 173; critical of scholars,
    187; as aged president, 250;
    speaker at SWK funeral, 415
Benson, Stephen, on evolution, 96
Bentine, Johan, 327
Biography, candor of, xvii, 27
Bishops' workload, 272
Bitton, Davis, 327
Blood atonement, 99
Bond, Christopher S., 155
Bonzer-Suarez, Hugo, 144, 331
Book of Mormon, subtitle of, 102
Bountiful tabernacle, 276
Bowman, Harold I., 86
Boy Scouts of America, 147
Bridgeforth, Helena, 233
Bridgeforth, Ruffin, 205, 233
Brigham, Janet, 436
Brigham Young University (BYU):

Kimball Tower, 150, 404, 412; equalizing women's status, 165; women on board of, 166; women's conferences at, 167; athletics, 202; and Indian program, 291; and Jerusalem Center, 350; SWK talks given at, 389; Indian choir at, 405
Brinkerhoff, Spencer (nephew of SWK), 66, 445
Britton, Theodore, 206
Brodie, Fawn M., 62
Brown, Hugh B., 202, 205
Brown, Thomas E., 434
Brown, Victor L., 96, 297, 345
Buchanan, Golden, 290
Buffalo Tiger, Chief, 289
Buildings, construction of, 275
Bureaucracy, 268
Burkhardt, J. Henry, 366–68
Burton, H. David, 428
Burton, Theodore M., 35
Busbee, George, 371
Busche, F. Enzio, 255, 257, 445
Bush, Lester E. Jr., 203, 220
Bybee, Don, 426

Cahill, Jerry, 19, 230, 315
Camargo, Antonio, 426
Camargo, Helio R., 255
Cannon, Elaine: on teen marriages, 32; concern for, shown by SWK, 40; on SWK's humility, 424; and gift of fudge, 444
Cannon, Frank J., 62
Cannon, George Q., 62
Cannon, Ted and Janath, 241
Capital punishment, 100
Cardall, Duane, 19, 30, 230, 312, 321, 322, 415
Carter, Jimmy, 14; inquires about missionary work, 121, 141; on MX missiles, 157
Chastity, 83
Cherry, Alan, 45
Child abuse, 83, 170
Choc, Daniel, 302
Christensen, C.C.A., 52

Christensen, James C., 421
Christensen, Mac, 54
Christensen, Steven F., 191
Christiansen, ElRay L., 315
Christus statue, 108, 327
Church discipline, 38, 182, 286
Church history, 186
Church Office Building, 267
Church, only true, 97
Civil rights, 202, 285
Claridge, Linton, 56
Clarke, J. Richard, 96
Clean up, SWK's plea for members to, 91
Coalville tabernacle, 277
Coltrin, Zebedee, 196
Communications network, 280
Communism, 132, 135, 137, 139, 158
Conferences, general and stake, 271
Connally, John, 14
Conscientious objection, 284
Consensus, 34
Consolidated meeting schedule, 262
Contraception, 170
Cook, Gene R., 144
Corporate directorships resigned, 279
Correlation, 249, 252, 260
Cullimore, James A. and Florence, 336
Cuthbert, Derek A., 255

Dahl, Harvey, 53, 58, 278
Darley, Gary S., 47
David, John A., 352
de Jager, Jacob, 255
Deseret Industries, 299
Didier, Charles A., 255, 440
"Do It" motto, 384
Doctrine and Covenants, additions to, 103
Doxey, Graham W., 280
Drury, Edward, 362
Dummar, Melvin, 156
Duncan, Bill, 436
Dunn, Paul H., 30, 31, 59, 107, 227, 256, 258, 358
Durham, G. Homer, 52, 220
Durham, Reed C. Jr., 189

Dyer, Alvin R., 279
Dyer, William G., 71

Earthquake, in Guatemala, 302
Eastern Arizona College, 150
Ellsworth, D. Delos, 140
Ellsworth, Dr. Homer S., 170, 443
Ellsworth, Randal, 302, 330
Emeritus status, 258
Endowments performed, 362, 373
England, Eugene, 203
Environmental protection, 285
Equal Rights Amendment, 68, 163, 176, 177, 179
Espenschied, Bryan, 242
Euthanasia, 282
Evergreen, 87
Evolution, organic, 96
Excommunication, 182
Expo '74, 22
Extermination order, 155
Eyring, Henry (brother-in-law of SWK), 56, 427
Eyring, Henry B. (nephew of SWK), 82
Eyring, Joseph C. (brother-in-law of SWK), 44, 66
Eyring, Mary (sister-in-law of SWK), 72, 73
Eyring, Winifred, 419

Faith Precedes the Miracle, 211
Family history, 185, 377
Family History Library, 378
Fast(s): for African relief, 302; offerings, 302
Faust, James E., 31, 127, 253, 334, 337, 363, 426
Fayette, New York, dedication of, 338
Featherstone, Vaughn J., 434
Federal, Joseph Lennox, 99
Feminism, 162
Fernandez, Angel, 127
Fetzer, Emil, 358, 359, 363, 365, 369, 425, 434
Fijians, 201
Financial burden, 271
Firmage, Edwin B., 157

First Presidency, 10, 11; David Kennedy reports to, 37; on evolution, 97; on religious leaders, 97; on MX missiles, 158; on ERA, 177; on civil rights, 202; on blacks and priesthood, 214, 217; on vaccination, 282
First Quorum of the Seventy, 254
Fischer, Mark F., 47
Fleming, Monroe, 210, 232
Food storage, 303
Ford, Betty, 360, 361
Ford, Gerald R., 14, 146, 147, 361
Francom, Erma, 72
Freeman, Joseph, Isapella, and Alex, 207, 232
Freemasonry, 284
Freiberg Temple, 367, 368, 370
Funerals, 283

Gardens, 93
Garden Tomb, 348
Gardner, R. Quinn, 445, 446
Gardner, Teryl and Paula (grand-daughter of SWK), 374, 395
Garris, Robert W., 22
Gathering. See Zion
Geisel, Ernesto, 143, 316
Genealogy, 377
Genesis branch, 204
Gibbons, Francis M.: as First Presidency secretary, 14; on delegation by SWK, 35; and priesthood revelation, 216, 218, 225, 228
Gilmore, Gary, 99
Glick, Harry, 125
Grant, Heber J., xiv
Gray, Darius A., 203, 205
Groll, Ferris, 435
Growth problems, 265
Gutierrez, Adan, 438

Hafen, Bruce C., 107
Hafen, Scott, 44
Haight, David B., 30, 36, 223, 253
Hales, Robert D., 108, 257, 328
Hamblin, Jacob, home of, 53

Han, In Sang, 317, 320
Hanks, Marion D., plans to evacuate missionaries, 128; and priesthood revelation, 203, 228–29; waiting for elevator, 256; and welfare service missions, 306
Harris, Alonzo, 207
Harris, Martin, 190
Haycock, D. Arthur, 333, 350, 352, 389; maintains SWK journal, xv; as aide and secretary, 5, 14, 93, 126, 312, 314; on teen marriages, 33; on persistence of SWK, 34; on delegation skills of SWK, 35; gives shoes to SWK, 54; rescued child, 317; blesses SWK, 323; reads SWK addresses, 388, 406; and enthusiasm for Hinckley as counselor, 398–99; speaks at funeral of SWK, 416; on work ethic of SWK, 424; on humor of SWK, 442–43
Haymond, J. Brent, 105
Health issues, 282, 383
Health missionaries, 303, 304
Heresy, 101
Herring, Barbara, 413
Heslop, J. Malan, 316
Hilton, Lynn M., 139
Hinckley, Gordon B., 19, 179, 336; shoulders burden, xvi, 407, 408; on importance of president, 27; travel of, 28; on delegation by SWK, 35; on child abuse, 83; on MX missiles, 157; on Hofmann forgeries, 190; organizes Genesis Branch, 205; and priesthood revelation, 215, 222; on revelation, 225, 235; on decentralization, 249; on aged president, 250–51; visits Philippines, 319; temple building, 372; called as counselor, 398; consults with SWK, 402; ordains apostles, 410
Hinckley, Marjorie, 268
Hinckley, Shane, 149
Historic preservation, 276

Historical Department, 186
Hofmann, Mark, 190
Holland, Jeffrey R., 31, 402
Home dedication, 283
Homosexual activities, 85
Hope, Len and Mary, 199
Howard, Richard P., 99
Howells, Grace (niece of SWK), 66
Hübener, Helmuth, 133
Hughes, Howard, 156
Hunter, Howard W., 180, 349, 350
Huxford, Gary, 80
Hymn book, 270

Idaho Constitution, amended, 155
Immunizations, 282
Incest, 170
Indian Student Placement Program, 290
Inouye, Yukus Yokiyoshi, 364
International Mission, 140

Jacobsen, Florence, 52, 53, 277
Jagger, Dean, 141
Jerusalem Center, 350
Jews, proselytizing program for, 124
Johnson, Edward A., 99
Johnson, James, 239, 242
Johnson, Joseph William "Billy," 208
Johnson, Sonia, 180
Johnson, Terry (grandson-in-law of SWK), 412
Jonassaint, Jacquez, 233
Jones, Earl, 316, 333
Jordan River Temple, 359
Joseph Fielding Smith Institute for Church History, 186
Joseph Smith Translation, 102
Journals, xiii, xvi, 92, 184

Kakol, Kazimier, 135
Kennedy, David M., 37, 130, 143, 240, 341, 365
Kennedy, Lenora, 329
Ketcher, James, 290
Kikuchi, Yoshihiko, 106, 255, 257, 318, 342, 364, 365, 446
Killebrew, Harmon, 124

Kimball, A. Gordon (brother of SWK), 65

Kimball, Andrew E. (son of SWK), 60, 119, 416

Kimball, Andrew E. Jr. (grandson of SWK), 67

Kimball, Camilla Eyring (wife of SWK): eases burden of SWK, 9; cooking skills of, 56; fishing trip, 57; correspondence of, 62; relations with son; 62; thrift of; 68–75; education of, 68; black experience, study of, 69; public speaking by; 70; ailments of, 70, 138, 386, 394, 408; BYU chair named for, 71; spirituality of, 73; canning skills of, 73, 387; gardening skills of, 93; and revelation, 231; refugees, meeting, 305; last years of, 419

Kimball, Delbert G. (brother of SWK), 65

Kimball, Donald E., 124

Kimball, Edward L. (son of SWK), 44, 46, 60, 67, 119, 346, 388, 402, 404, 416, 426, 432

Kimball, Elias (uncle of SWK), 353

Kimball, Evelyn Bee (daughter-in-law of SWK), 60, 444

Kimball, Heber C. (grandfather of SWK): portrait of, 64; family organization of, 65, 376; biography of, 67, 186, 377; death of, 389

Kimball, J. Golden (uncle of SWK), 62, 353

Kimball, Kathryn (daughter-in-law of SWK), 60

Kimball, Mary (granddaughter of SWK), 119

Kimball, Phyllis (daughter-in-law of SWK), 60

Kimball, Spencer (grandson of SWK), 119, 341

Kimball, Spencer L. (son of SWK), 50, 60; strained relations with father, 61; missionary service of, 119; photograph of, 395

Kimball, Spencer Woolley: heart surgery of, 3–4; succession to presidency, 5–6; first press conference as president, 7; experiences stress of new calling, 8; others have low expectations of, 8; delegates correspondence, 12; threats against, 15–17; focuses on missionary work, 18; sermons and talks of, 20–22, 88; sustained in conference, 21; emphasizes spirituality, 28–29; informal nature of, 29–32; reports to Lord, 29; resigns corporate directorships, 29; open to change, 32–33; politically astute nature of, 34; persistent nature of, 34; delegation skills of, 35–36; hard-working nature of, 36; able to balance reproof and compassion, 37–38; kind nature of, 38–41; loving nature of, 42; visits prison, 46–47; studies scriptures, 51; education of, 51–52; musical skills of, 53–54; simple clothing preferred by, 54–55; simple food preferred by, 56; frugal nature of, 56–57; generous nature of, 56–57; enjoys travel, 57; recreation habits of, 57–59; expresses anger, 59; has strained relationship with son, 61–63; extended family of, 64–65; ordains brother as elder, 65; biography of, 67; and *The Miracle of Forgiveness*, 79–80; on revelation, 81, 216–17, 234, 236; on chastity, 83; on child abuse, 83–84; on homosexuality, 85–86; speaking engagements of, 88–89, 384; on cleanliness and home repair, 91; on keeping journals, 92, 184; on distaste for hunting, 93; on gardening, 93–94; on Adam-God theory, 95–96; discusses heresy issues with Elder McConkie, 101; teaching moments of, 104–7, 109; emphasizes missionary work, 113–15; donates dollars to children to start personal mission funds,

116–17; and missionary quotas, 122–23; appoints David M. Kennedy as special assistant, 130–33; opens Portugal for missionary work, 133–34; opens Poland for missionary work, 135–38; meets national leaders, 143–44; meets with press, 145–47; receives honorary degrees, 150; and Kimball Tower, 150, 404, 412; and public relations, 153–55; and MX missile program, 156–58; counsels with Ezra Taft Benson about his political statements, 159–60; on Communism, 161; on Mother in Heaven, 164; and special women's conference, 167–68; on family roles, 167; on reproductive issues, 170–72; on abortion, 172–73; on Equal Rights Amendment, 176–83; promotes Church history, 186–90; and Hofmann forgeries, 190–91; and blacks and priesthood, 195–246; establishes Genesis branch, 205–6; searches for answers regarding question of blacks and priesthood, 209–17; receives answer regarding question of blacks and priesthood, 218; receives priesthood revelation, 220–24; and announcement of priesthood revelation, 229–31; and missionaries in Nigeria and Ghana, 240–44 ; reorganizes First Quorum of Seventy, 254–56; establishes emeritus status for General Authorities, 258–59; suspends office of Church patriarch, 259; initiates correlation, 260–61; and growth of Church membership, 265–66; and emphasis on historic preservation, 276–77; acquires land in Missouri for Church, 279–80; develops Church policies, 282–87; and Indian Student Placement Program, 290–92; and contracts for welfare farms,

298–99; and Teton Dam failure, 299–300; requests fasts for African relief, 302–3; and area conferences, 311–43; and solemn assemblies, 344–46; and Orson Hyde Garden, 348–50, 392; and BYU Jerusalem Center, 350–51; and efforts in temple building, 357–72; prays in Senate, 361; has pacemaker installed, 371, 395; increasing health problems of, 383–413; brain surgeries of, 389–92, 400–401; performs last wedding, 396; calls Gordon B. Hinckley as third counselor, 398; last public address of, 406; ninetieth birthday party of, 412; death of, 413–14; funeral of, 415–16

Kimball, Stanley B. (cousin of SWK), 66, 186, 445
Kimball Tower, 150, 404, 412
Kimball, Wilfred and Marylee, 362
Kinard, J. Spencer, 426
King, Doug, 337
Kite, Greg, 44
Kleason, Robert, 127
Kollek, Teddy, 348, 351
Komatsu, Adney Y., 210, 255

Lakey, Jimmie, 339
Lamanites, 288; progress of, 294; BYU Indian Choir, 405
Landau, Elliot, 125
Language units, 272
LaPaz altitude sickness, 328, 331
Laugerud-Garcia, Kjell Eugenio, 144, 329
Law, Vernon, 124
Leadership training, 268
LeBaron, E. Dale, 240, 337
LeBaron, Ervil, 15
LeBaron, Verlan, 15
Lee, Freda Joan, 396
Lee, George P., 210, 253, 255, 292
Lee, Harold B.: administration of, xii; counsels SWK on surgery, 3; becomes president of the Church,

4; death of, 5–6; funeral of, 7; dreamt of by SWK, 9; on blacks and priesthood, 197, 204, 206; correlation implemented by, 249; proposed area conferences, 311

LeFevre, Don, 182

Leifson, Thor, 427

Lind, Don, 124

Linkletter, Art, 141

Lopez, Danny, 141

Lopez-Portillo, José, 144, 365

Ludlow, Daniel H., 102, 348

Lyanov, Alexis, 141

Mabey, Rendell and Rachel, 241

Mack, Camilla (granddaughter of SWK), 174

Mack, Grant M. (son-in-law of SWK), 60

Mack, Olive Beth K. (daughter of SWK), 60; lived by parents, 63; gives mother gift of orange juice, 73; returns to work as teacher, 174; hears news of priesthood revelation, 231; in Korea, 319–20; photograph of, 387; cared for parents, 402, 410

Madsen, Frank, 439

Madsen, Louise W., 426

Madson, Arch, 147

Maori cultural program, 324

Marcos, Ferdinand, 133, 318, 341

Marren, Tony, 338

Marriage, interracial, 211, 237, 287

Martherus, Lou, 45

Martins, Helvécio, 206, 233, 245, 334

Martins, Marcus, 206, 233

Martins, Mirian, 233

Mason, James O., 282, 304

Matheson, Scott M., 47, 157, 158

Matthews, Robert J., 102

Mauss, Armand L., 27, 34, 80, 203, 236

Maxwell, Neal A.: on N. Eldon Tanner, 13; receives assignment from SWK, 31; on SWK's delegation skills, 35; on Church history building testimony, 190; on priesthood revelation, 227; called as apostle, 253, 399; on leadership training problems, 268; as Church Commissioner of Education, 274; attends conferences with family, 312; in South Africa, 336; on SWK's character, 424; on SWK's friendliness, 434

Mayfield, David, 378

McConkie, Bruce R., 179; on Adam-God theory, 96; on evolution, 96, 97, 101; on blood atonement, 100; on heresy, 97, 101; works on new edition of scriptures, 101; on blacks and priesthood, 216; on priesthood revelation, 221–22, 235, 238, 407; announcing the revelation, 225–26; prophesies in Chile, 330; shakes hands with Bolivian Saints, 333; teased by SWK on singing ability, 442

McConkie, Daniel, 207

McConkie, F. Briton, 207

McConkie, Oscar W. Jr., and Judy, 38

McFarland, Oscar L., 206

McKay, David O., xii, 28, 62, 187, 198, 200, 201, 202, 277, 361, 386

McKay, Thomas E., 62

McKinney, Joyce, 128

Microfilm, 377

Military, 284

Milne, Arvil, 212

Miracle of Forgiveness, The, 83, 86, 446

Missionary meetings, 126, 336

Missionary Training Center, 116

Missionary work: as main theme of SWK's administration, 113; and length of service, 119–20; by all members, 120; by women, 120; by couples, 120, 140; goals for, 122; through temple open houses, 125; by blacks, 244

Missouri Land Fund, 279

Mitch, Domingo, 320

Monson, Thomas S.: on improving stakes, 37; on SWK's old shoes, 54; on new edition of scriptures, 101;

at area conference in Copenhagen, 108; oversees work in German Democratic Republic, 139, 366; establishes Genesis branch, 205; and priesthood revelation, 226

Morgan, Lea Marie, 446

Morgan, Sharon, 446

Morgan, William B., 447

Mormon Experience, The, 187

Mormon Pioneer Memorial Bridge, 148

Morrill Act repealed, 155

Morrison, Alexander B., 230

Mortimer, William James, 102

Mother in Heaven, 164

Mothers, working, 173, 174

Mountain Meadows massacre, 155

Moyle, Henry D., 277, 278

Mt. Tabor, 347

Muldoon, Robert David, 323

MX missile system, 156

Name extraction, 378

National Organization for Women, 182

Native Americans. *See* Lamanites

Nauvoo, expulsion from, 155

Naylor, Jordan, 339

Nelson, Alice (sister of SWK), 65, 389

Nelson, Russell M.: performs heart surgery on SWK, 3–4; and SWK's concern for missionaries, 47; on Church history building testimony, 190; called to Twelve, 253, 410; blesses SWK, 323–24, 385; installs pacemaker for SWK, 371, 396; speaks at SWK's funeral, 415

Nihipali, Ben, 40, 346, 436

Noble, Brother, 440

Normandeau, Lorena, 338

Novaco, Oscar, 362

Oaks, Dallin H.: photograph of, 89; on inequities at BYU, 165–66; on Church history building testimony, 190; called to Twelve, 253, 410; reads SWK address, 389

Obinna, Anthony, 241

Orr, Eugene, 205

Orson Hyde Memorial Garden, xii, 346, 348, 349, 392

Ottley, Jerold D., 425

Packer, Boyd K.: on SWK's appointment as president, 8; on balancing church discipline with love, 38–39; and Church museum of art and history, 52; on homosexuality, 87; and new edition of scriptures, 101; attends area conference in Copenhagen, 108; on Church history, 187–88; establishes Genesis Branch, 205; and revelation on priesthood, 216, 221, 235, 421; and announcement of priesthood revelation, 225, 226; ordains Ruffin Bridgeforth, 233; on balancing family and church responsibilities, 271, and microfilm records in Israel, 378; on SWK's character, 425, 438

Palmer, Spencer J., 115

Parker, George "Sam," 55, 388, 441

Parker, Saundra, 444

Patch, Robert, 102

Patriarch to the Church, 259

Pea, John L., 214

Peale, Norman Vincent, 43

Periodicals, 189

Perpetual Education Fund, 275

Perry, L. Tom: and revelation on priesthood 222; called to Twelve, 253; and fireworks at Guatemalan conference, 329; on Elder McConkie's prophecy in Chile, 331; has picture taken with SWK, 442

Personal Ancestral File (PAF), 379

Petersen, Mark E.: exercises at Deseret Gymnasium with SWK, 57; counsels homosexuals, 85; on blacks and priesthood, 219–20; absent for priesthood revelation, 221, 226–27; and decision to remain single after wife's death,

254; on Tokyo temple dedication, 364; death of, 409

Peterson, Ann, 408

Peterson, H. Burke, 40, 96

Pinegar, Rex E., 108, 440

Pinochet-Ugarte, Augusto, 144

Poland, dedication of, 138

Policy changes, 286

Polve, James H., 212

Polynesian Cultural Center, 125

Pornography, 84

Power, Ted, 378

Prayer circles, 375

Preservation of historic buildings, 276

Press conferences, xi, 145

Priesthood, blacks and, 7, 146, 195–245, 407

Psychological counseling, 305

Public Communications Department, 153

Pusey, Merlo J., 187

Rainer, Howard, 44

Rampton, Calvin L., 14

Randall, Naomi, 424

Rape, 170

Rasmussen, Ellis G., 102

Reagan, Ronald W., 142, 143, 158, 182, 297, 376

Refugees, from South Vietnam, 305

Reid family, photograph of, 321

Relief Society, 165, 261–62

Rennett, Phillip, 125

Reorganized LDS Church (Community of Christ), 99

Reyes, Mexican government minister, 365

Richards, LeGrand: and missionary effort to Jews, 124, 125; sees vision of Wilford Woodruff, 219; briefcase carried by SWK, 345; head of Orson Hyde Foundation, 349

Ringger, Hans B., 255

Ripplinger, Donald, 439

Rodriguez, Michael, 429

Romney, George W., 124

Romney, Marion G.: and death of Harold B. Lee, 5; as counselor in First Presidency, 7; as assistant manager of Church Welfare Plan, 13; on SWK's efforts in missionary work, 113; answers questions from President Jimmy Carter, 121; and revelation on priesthood, 228; attends conference in Bolivia, 331–32; and Mexico City temple, 365; mistaken introduction of, 392; declining health of, 402; on SWK's willingness to greet visitors, 430

Romney, Mitt, 442

Rose, Pat, 353

Roueche, Earl J., 182

Sacrament, participation in, 22, 284

Sadat, Anwar, 48, 140

Sadat, Jirhan, 347

"Salamander" letter, 191

Salt Lake City, flood in, 301

São Paulo Temple, 314, 358, 363

Sapena-Pastor, Raul, 143

Satellite transmission, 280

Schein, Brother, 445

Schmidt, Duwayne, 413, 414

Schmitt, Charles, 326

Schools, 274

Schult, Hans, 440

Scriptures: new edition of, 101; translation of, 123

Security, 15–17, 48, 391, 402

Seminaries and institutes, 274

Sex, purposes of, 171

Sex-change operation, 85

Sheets, Kathleen, 191

Shepherd, Robert, 52

Sherman, Barbara Kimball (granddaughter of SWK), 64

Simmons, Roy, 440

Simonsen, John, 442

Sing, Jack Kong, 427

Single adults, 264

Smart, William B., 226

Smartt, Philander, 353

Smith, Barbara Bradshaw: called as general president of Relief Society, 30; on ERA, 177; transfers grain storage to Church, 261–62; speaks at SWK's funeral, 416; asks SWK about creating a world, 421; grandson of, and Articles of Faith, 430–31

Smith, Eldred Gee, 259, 338

Smith, George Albert, 187, 200, 288, 421

Smith, Hyrum, photograph of descendant of, 338

Smith, Joseph: and Mother in Heaven, 164; and Mark Hofmann frauds, 190–91; and priesthood restriction, 196, 197; photograph of descendent of, 338

Smith, Joseph F., 251

Smith, Joseph Fielding, 101, 202

Smith, Melvin, 338

Smith, Samuel, photograph of descendant of, 338

Smith, Wallace B., 99

Snow, Eliza R., 164

Soares, Mario, 134

Social services, 304

Solemn assembly, 21, 344–346

Sonne, Alma, 435

Sonnenberg, John, 255

Sonntag, Richard, 388

Sorensen, Bruce F., 389, 391, 392, 400

Spafford, Belle S., 177, 426

Special Affairs Committee, 177, 178

Stapley, Delbert L., 188, 221, 227

Stewart, Jimmy, 154

Story of the Latter-day Saints, The, 187

Sturlaugson, Mary Frances, 232, 233, 237

Tabernacle Choir, 122, 125, 142, 147, 154, 361, 425

Taggart, Stephen G., 203

Tanner, N. Eldon: and death of Harold B. Lee, 5; counselor in First Presidency, 7; and Church finances, 13; and calling special assistants, 130; visits Africa, 201; concerned for SWK, 219; and priesthood revelation, 221; announcement of priesthood revelation, 229–30; attends conference in Cape Town, 336; and BYU Jerusalem Center site, 350; carries SWK out of meeting, 385; gives blessing to SWK, 389; telephones SWK daily, 393; suffers from Parkinson's disease, 402; death of, 408

Tanumafil, Malietoa II, 371

Tax protest, 285

Taylor, John, 81

Taylor, Robert, 350

Teatairangikaau, Dame, Maori queen, 324

Teichert, Minerva, 52

Temple: and additional recommend questions, 169, 374; and Korean travel restrictions, 320; and attendance quotas, 374–75; prayer circles, 375; garment styles, 376

Temple(s), building: responsibility of First Presidency, 13; in São Paulo, 214; smaller sized, 275; increased pace of, 357; in Scandinavia, 313; in Samoa, 322–23

Temple(s), dedication of: of Washington D.C., xii, 360; of São Paulo, 314; of Tokyo, 342, 359, 363; of Jordan River, 359

Teens, marriage of pregnant, 23

Terry, Leona, 414

Teton Dam failure, 299

Thayne, Emma Lou Warner, 167

Thomas, Robert K., 350

Thompson, James R., 155

Tobongo-Pastillo, Rafael, 333, 423

Todd, Jay M., 171

Tuckett, Pamela, 429

Tu'ipelehake, Prince Fatafehi, 325

Tupou, Taufa'ahau IV, 371

Tuttle, A. Theodore, 315

Udall, J. Nicholas, 441

Udall, Jesse A., 150

Unanimity, 34
Urbino, Orlando, 143

Vaccination, 282
Vernon, Eric, 117

Wallace, Douglas, 213
Ward, Lyle, 80
Warnick, John, 390
Webb, L. Robert, 429
Weigand, William Keith, 99
Welfare: program, 243, 296, 306;
    assessments, 298; service
    missionaries, 306
Welfare Services Department, 297
Wells, Robert E., 19
Whitaker, Wetzel O. "Judge," 45
Whitmer cabin, 338
Whitney, Orson F., 53
Wilkinson, Ernest L. Jr., 3, 313, 318,
    333, 335, 347, 350, 385, 388, 389,
    393, 402, 421
Wilkinson, Marjorie, 329
Williams, LaMar, 201
Willis, Jeffrey H., 182
Wilson, Ted C., 47

Wirthlin, Joseph B., 352
Wolsey, Heber G.: suggested Book of
    Mormon subtitle, 102;
    recommends press conference for
    SWK, 145; develops television
    specials, 153; defuses
    demonstrations on college
    campuses, 202–3; and
    announcement of priesthood
    revelation, 226, 230
Women: and priesthood ordination,
    163; and praying in sacrament
    meeting, 166; violence against, 169
Woodruff, Wilford, xiv, 219
World Conference on Records, 378
Wright, L. Harold, 258, 443
Wright, Marsha, 414

Young, Brigham: on blood atonement,
    99; biography of, 187–88; on
    priesthood restriction, 196, 203
Young, S. Dilworth, 254, 396

Zeidner, Rod, 125
Zenha, Salgado, 134
Zion, 119, 312, 322